THE FINAL
EMPIRE

WM. H. KÖTKE

THE FINAL
EMPIRE

THE COLLAPSE OF CIVILIZATION

AND

THE SEED OF THE FUTURE

ARROW POINT
PRESS

Portland, Oregon

ARROW POINT PRESS
605 S.E. 15th Ave.
Portland, OR   97214
SAN 297-7842
©1993 by Wm.H. Kötke
All rights reserved
Printed in the United States of America
First Edition
First Printing

Library of Congress Cataloging in Publication Data:

    Kötke, Wm. H.
    The final empire ; the collapse of civilization and the
    seed of the future / by Wm.H. Kötke -- Portland, Or :
    Arrow Point Press, c1993.
         p. : ill. ; cm.
    Includes bibliographical references and index.
    ISBN: 0-9633784-5-7
    1. Human ecology. 2. Civilization. I. Title.
    GF75.K   304.2- dc20
                      92-73283

Text illustrations—Lisa Pucci
Portraits of Apache leaders—Jay Scott
Preliminary text design—Crystal Rae and Michael Perrone
Cover art and design—Rastovision Design and Animation,
                      Portland, Oregon
Final book design and production—Kirk La, DIMI PRESS,
                      Salem, Oregon
Printing by Gilliland Printing, Inc., Arkansas City, Kansas

THIS VISION OF THE FUTURE IS DEDICATED TO
THE GRANDCHILDREN

SHUANA LYNN
AARON MICHAEL
BRADY ALAN
LEIGH MICHAEL
JOHN POTTER

and to

Spartacus

Acknowledgments

One's perspective of life is formed by all of the experiences from birth and beyond. Though I am responsible for each word, much of the focus of this book comes from a wide variety of people and events. Certainly the ranching culture of Central Oregon should be acknowledged, where I gained an early experience as a ranch hand. The years as a sawmill worker in Oregon and California caused me to understand the point of view of those people. The Civil Rights Movement, the Vietnam War and the Summer of Love in Haight Ashbury woke all of us up to the realities of the planet. Years as a labor organizer and union business representative allowed me to understand why it is so difficult for the masses of us to make sudden beneficial changes. Living in the mountains of Northern New Mexico I came to understand how the four century old insular Spanish culture there, established before the pilgrims reached Plymouth Rock, had been able to endure as a self sufficient society. The years spent chopping wood and herding sheep for Katherine Smith, an elder of the relocation-threatened, Big Mountain Navajos, instructed me of the great strength of people who live with the earth. In residing with the Jicarilla Apache of New Mexico I came to understand the functioning of a tribe. In living in the Gila, in Catron County, New Mexico I personally experienced the problems and insecurities of rural U.S. people as they face the chaotic future over which they have little control.

A number of people assisted directly with the production of this document. Lisa Pucci created the beautiful illustrations and helped with early production. Jay Scott of Silver City, New Mexico created the portraits of the honored elders of the Gila who resisted empire. Ellen Gellert, former instructor of Women's Studies at the University of Buffalo and later resident of the Gila, provided valuable insights. Cecelia Ostrow, singer and noted earth philosopher provided valuable editorial work as did novelist Gary Stallings. As any starving artist knows, there are many more people who have done much. Some have provided shelter to a hungry hitch-hiker, others have imparted advice on where and how to catch freight trains and still others have given valuable direction concerning the plant and animal world. To all who have contributed, I thank you and hope that the effort meets your approval.

Wm. H. Kötke

BOOK I
THE COLLAPSE OF CIVILIZATION

BOOK II
THE SEED OF THE FUTURE

Introduction

The crisis of the planet Earth is so profound that all of our lives will be caught up in it. Our lives will change because of it. Our lives will change because of the apocalyptic events happening now and the even greater dislocations to come. We cannot avoid these great trends of history but we can exersize awareness and skill in action in dealing with them. The tumult will be environmental and it will also be within the social body of civilization.

Book I begins with a straight-forward examination of our ecological situation on the planet. This is not pleasant knowledge but it is imperative that we understand the full dimensions of the problem before we invest our lives in a solution. Book I also includes an explanation of how we humans have arrived at such a point of personal and planetary suicide. In this section the cultural dynamics, the psychology and the history of our culture is examined in order to gain insight for the future.

Book II is a plan of action for us to regain paradise. This section answers the question of how to live in balance with nature. This is not a theoretical answer. It involves an actual watershed, what its ecology is and what the food sources are. This section takes those much abused words, "sustainable" and "balance with nature," and puts them on the ground. We will be urged to immediately create a new ecologically sustainable land based culture that will take us through the future times. Those who can respond will be accepting an initiatory challenge such as has seldom happened to our kind. The challenge is to bring out of the greatest wave of death and destruction the earth has ever known, a new world of wholeness and relationship of all of the tribes that live in ecological sustainability. This era is the first time in two million years that all of the tribes can connect as a planetary whole in a geographical and material sense.

When our great, great, great grandchildren look back at the crisis that their ancestors had lived through they will understand why we changed ourselves, our culture, our relationship with our mother the earth and our relationship with the creative spirit of the cosmos.

BOOK ONE

THE COLLAPSE

OF

CIVILIZATION

CHAPTER 1

PATTERN OF THE CRISIS

Collapse on the Periphery

Individual empires have suffered cyclical collapse since civilization began. The Babylonian, Greek and Roman empires are classical examples. These civilized empires initially expanded, funded by their base of arable land, grazing areas and forests. As they reached out, conquering new lands and peoples, their growth was fueled by slave labor and appropriated resources. Growth continued until the ecological base of the empire was exhausted. At that point, the empires imploded. Sumeria and Babylonia stripped their lands through overgrazing and deforestation. This brought down huge amounts of eroded material that threatened the irrigation works. They inexorably salinized their soil by irrigation. Early on, in the history of the Greek empire, Plato complained of the ecological devastation in the area of Attica. By the end of that empire the ecology of that land mass of Greece was severely injured. Both Greek and Roman empires used North Africa as a "breadbasket" and by the close of the Roman empire it was ecologically destroyed along with much of the rest of the Roman territories.

Though the standard political and social histories of these empires do not stress an ecological view, there is certainly no question that at the end of their cycles these empires had little ecological energy remaining.

Anywhere the culture of empire (a.k.a., civilization) has spread one finds devastated ecologies. The life is literally "rubbed out," the original life is gone. Much of the living flesh of the planet does not now exist in those places. But, we know that it did exist. The life in those areas has suffered a die-back. The forests are gone, the topsoil is depleted and the land is eroded. The richness of the land has been used up. The wealth of the earth's life has been spent by the extortion of empire.

Empires implode, they collapse from within. This is beginning now on the edges of world civilization where the ecology has been stripped, the population is exploding and the resultant social turmoil insures further decline. These implosions of the colonies will eventually become general throughout the cultural system.

Islands such as Madagascar, the Canaries, the islands of the Caribbean, many south sea islands and others have been ecologically stripped. In areas like Peru, whole mountainsides fall off because of the ecological devastation caused by deforestation and hillside farming. In Brazil's Northeast, the coastal rain forest and the fertile areas further inland have been replaced by desert. In some areas of the former fertile southern interior of Brazil, coffee plantations have reduced the land to such eroded conditions that cows cannot even graze it for fear that they will fall into the canyons created by soil erosion. In the U.S.S.R. many bodies of water such as the Azov, Caspian, Black Sea and Baikal are severely injured. The supply of caviar in Russia has almost ceased because the waters are so polluted that the fish die. In Tibet where the Chinese empire has invaded, devastation is spreading as trees are cut, steep areas are plowed and mines are begun.

The story of the brief empire of Venice is instructive as to how the ecological base of empire injures the earth and how the culture of empire uses up the life of the earth to generate its ephemeral power. By the end of the fifteenth century the City of Venice was emerging as a sea-power. Venice traded all the way from the eastern Mediterranean to England. Galley ships were the power behind the merchant fleet. The oar-powered galleys ultimately depended upon slave labor. They were fast and could navigate where sailing ships could not. The whole arrangement was based on wood for ships, and in turn depended upon forests, which in the beginning were abundant near Venice. As the power of Venice was coming to an end, the City was obtaining ships in Barcelona built with lumber from the forests of northern Spain and finally from the Baltic region of northern Europe, which had not yet been stripped. By this time there were no forests anywhere in the Mediterranean that could fund a sea-faring empire.

This phenomenon of implosion is occurring now in the present world empire. The country of Bangladesh shows us one type of implosion. In the distant past the whole of the area was populated by forager/hunters such as those threatened tribes who live now in the Bangladeshi hills. As the waves of empire culture came, first with the Indo-Aryans thousands of years ago, the life of the area was progressively degraded. Bengal as it was formerly called, was conquered by the English early in the colonial period. Prior to the conquest it had been a fertile and self-sufficient area. When the English moved in they began to put heavy pressure on the organic fertility. They established the plantation system and mined the agricultural land to ship valuables to the "mother country." Later in the Twentieth Century when England was severed from its colonies on the Indian subcontinent the region became part of Pakistan and finally an independent country. In the later years, Bangladesh has suffered flooding, a constant population explosion and periodic drought.

Bangladesh is located on the delta of the Ganges River which drains the Himalayan range. With the Chinese now stripping Tibet, floods and erosion material race down out of central Tibet borne by the Bramaputra River which joins the Ganges and comes through countries that are being stripped along the southern tier of the range: Bhutan, India and in particular Nepal. Because the forests are being stripped, the land no longer can absorb water and the floods grow larger. *The State of India's Environment: 1982*, a report by non-governmental groups, states: "From Kashmir (far west) to Assam (far east) the story is the same. Below 2,000 meters (6,500 feet) there are literally no forests left. In the middle Himalayan belt, which rises to an average height of 3,000 meters (9,800 feet), the forest area, originally estimated at being a third of the total area, has reduced to a mere 6-8 per cent."[1]

A global environmental study, <u>Gaia: An Atlas Of Planet Management</u> says that the erosion is so bad that an island of five million hectares (12,355,000 acres) of erosion material is beginning to surface in the Bay of Bengal. "Around one-quarter of a million tonnes (255,325 U.S. tons) of topsoil are washed off the deforested mountain slopes of Nepal each year, and a further sizable amount from the Himalayan foothills in India's sector of the Ganges catchment zone." The study notes that the countries of India and Bangladesh are geared up to contest possession of the island when it surfaces.[2]

Due to the periodic catastrophes of flood and drought the society of Bangladesh is beginning to disintegrate into a low-level warlord society where even the central government cannot exert control much distance from the capital city. One effort that the government is making to alleviate its population crush is an attempt to settle a relatively small "hill country" area of the country with lowlanders. These hill areas contain remnant tribes of non-civilized people. The Bangladesh government has warred against these people for some years, attacking them with modern armies and rounding up the survivors into concentration camps. As the lowlanders invade into the vacuum, they level the forest and attempt to raise crops.

On the lowlands, a large share of the population lives in the delta. Here the impoverished people fight each other for small plots of land. As the floods come and go, the islands and marshes change continually. As the above-water areas dry out following a flood, the people rush in to claim small plots on which they attempt to grow food before the next flood or drought.

The combination of exploding population and ecologically based disasters is causing the society to disintegrate. This process which began years back in Bangladesh is one of the effects that we can expect to see in the years ahead in other parts of civilization.

Writer Mohiuddin Alamgir, researching his report, *Famine in South Asia; Political Economy of Mass Starvation*, asked villagers in Bangladesh during a famine in 1974, about the reasons why people were dying around them. He found that the villagers had only a vague notion about the true cause. The villagers could see that people were dying of disease and that they had various symptoms but few villagers could see or admit that people were starving. The villagers were in a weakened condition, which allowed them to die of the first disease that came around. Death was the end result of the steady social deterioration that they had experienced. "Once people ran out of resources to buy food grains, they sold or mortgaged land, sold cattle and agricultural implements, sold household utensils and other valuables (such as ornaments), and, finally their homesteads," says Alamgir.[3]

When there is nothing left and people are starving, they leave and wander aimlessly about the country of Bangladesh. Many of the uprooted households that Alamgir studied had begun to disintegrate, with members of the same household wandering off in different directions toward separate areas of the country. Deserted children, deserted wives, deserted husbands and deserted elders are becoming commonplace. Bangladesh society has gone over the brink. The centralized control by the wealthy elite and the military has broken down. The population is destined to continue as a wandering, increasingly hungry mass until, sometime in the future, all coherent human society and culture dies and human cooperation and optimistic effort disintegrates. It is this condition, as shown by Bangladesh, that is the ultimate end of a culture that eats up its survival systems.

We need keep in mind that forager/hunter populations lived stably in this area for hundreds of thousands and perhaps millions of years because they did not destroy that which sustained them.

Alamgir states that after previous famines in Bangladesh, the society returned to near normal social relationships, but, he reports:

"Both separation of families and desertion represent a breakdown of the system of security provided by family and kinship ties under traditional social bonds. This is, of course, not unique in the 1974 Bangladesh famine, as reference to erosion of social ties can be found in almost all preceding famines. However, two points should be noted: First, a slow process of disintegration of traditional ties had already set in Bangladesh rural society and famine only accelerated it. Second, manifestation of breakdown of kinship and family bonds were reversible in the past in the sense that old relationships were restored through the normal process of post famine societal adjustment. This is no longer true in the Bangladesh scenario today where such processes seem to be irreversible, which is reflected in the rate of permanent destitution."[4]

The horn of Africa region where the country of Ethiopia is located represents another example of implosion. Set upon the top of the dwindling ecology of Ethiopia is tribal warfare and contests between the capitalist and Marxist empires manipulated through their "allies" in that area. Ethiopia is hit with periodic drought. If the region were in its climax ecological condition the droughts would likely have minimal impact but like Bangladesh, the region's ecology is so ravaged that any perturbation of climate becomes a disaster and the human created situation is called an "act of God."

Ethiopia originally had a stable population of forager/hunter people but it became one of the "cradles of civilization." The life of Ethiopia is now almost gone. Almost all of Ethiopia is high, mountainous country with good rainfall, but there is little vegetative life left. The ancient empires were nourished on it and the vitality has evaporated. It is estimated that three quarters of the country was originally forested yet at present only four percent of the country has forest.

One study estimates that the volume of live trees now, is 800 million cubic meters and then goes on to say that the annual fuel wood consumption is 20 million cubic meters and rising rapidly.[5] Even if the remaining forests were only used to heat houses and cook food they would not last long.

Despite having one of the highest death rates in the world, the country's population continues to rise. One would think it would decline but unlike our former forager/hunter culture which sought to keep their population within the carrying capacity of the environment, people of the culture of empire do not. The people of civilization have many motives other than simply lack of awareness, that propels population growth. One important reason is that civilized people work at exploiting the land and the more hands the more production. Agrarians traditionally have large families to help with farm work for example and hard times call for more hands to force the land to produce more. There is also motive for large families so that one will be cared for in old age. There is the motive of the pride of the patriarch in large families. Though there are a number of basic motives, there is a functional reason also why population is not responsive immediately to food supply. This reason is that even if there is a famine or drought, the children already born will have children. Demographers say that population responsiveness has a time lag of seventy years to social/environmental events and even this responsiveness is only a momentary blip on the over-all graph line of exponential growth.

One researcher highlights the continued drama of destruction in Ethiopia partially attributed to population growth:

A dramatic alteration in environmental quality has been visible within a single lifetime in the hills surrounding Addis Ababa. When the capital was founded in 1883 by the Emperor Memelik II, it was still surrounded by remnants of rich cedar forests and reasonably clear streams. Deforestation and erosion were immediately spurred by the influx of humans. In the ensuing nine decades, virtually all the available land in the region has been cultivated, while charcoal producers cut trees within a 160-kilometer radius for sale in the city. Now the waters of the nearby Awash River and its tributaries are thick with mud, and waterways are shifting their courses more markedly and frequently than in the past.[6]

Addis Ababa sits in the high mountains of central Ethiopia. It is near the headwaters of the Awash river. From Addis Ababa, the river courses northeast into a rapidly widening valley that eventually reaches the coast at Djibouti on the Red Sea. U.N. researchers expect the whole Awash Basin to soon become rocky desert; but the eye of civilization sees only war, ideology and revolution. The problem is ecological but the cultural attention and media focus emphasize war. As civilization fixates on war and violence in Eritrea, Somalia and Ethiopia, in the Horn of Africa, the life of the earth dwindles in that area and starvation spreads. Although the destruction of the life of the earth is caused by civilization, civilized society is unable to see its own problem because the organic life of the earth is below its threshold of consciousness.

El Salvador, in Central America, is another country that is imploding on the periphery of the empire of civilization. The Spanish empire invaded the area that is now El Salvador early in the sixteenth century. They immediately began to enslave the stable and sustainable cultures of the region as factors of imperial production. At that time the western two-thirds of the country was inhabited by a Nahuatl speaking culture. The Nahuatl language group includes Aztec, Hopi and Ute. In the eastern one-third of the country, across the Lenca river, lived the tribes named Lenca, Jinca, Pokomám, Chortí and Matagalpa. There are now some half-million "invisible" Indians in El Salvador, in a country of five million. They are invisible because they have been forced to abandon their native dress and language. The first census from the years 1769-1798 listed 83,010 Indians in a population of 161,035. Initially, the native people of the lowlands were enslaved into the Spanish estates. These original estates exported cacao and balsam. By the end of that century, indigo plantations were spreading out further into the last Indian communal lands in the higher elevations. Soon cattle ranching moved into the northern tier of the country and masses of Indian people who were not among the indentured workers, were wandering through the area in a detribalized condition. The native people's habitat had been destroyed. Inasmuch as their cultural knowledge and skills were related to the living world, the native people became powerless and dependent upon the invading culture. By the middle of the Nineteenth Century, coffee began to be the major export crop and this agriculture with its need for the last available, higher elevation land, began to finish the remaining communal Indian lands as well as their forest habitat. By 1930, coffee was more than ninety percent of El Salvador's exports.[7]

In 1932, in the midst of the world depression, Indians in the highlands around Sonsonate revolted against both the imperial conquerors and their latino subjects, the mestizos. The army of the oligarchy was unleashed against the unarmed Indians. The virulent anti-Indian racism of "latinos" was also unleashed as they, also, began to participate. By the time the massacres were over, somewhere variously estimated at between 15,000 and 50,000 children, women and men had been murdered and the native land base was occupied by the aliens.[8]

The story of El Salvador is of native tribes who lived stably with their habitat, the forests and other ecosystems of the isthmus. The events since that time have been created by the far different culture of empire which invaded, to extort valuables from the area. The pattern displayed has been consistent since empire culture began. A few new wrinkles have been added by the industrial revolution and markets. The pattern is that of a small powerful elite taking land and labor from the colony for free or at very low price. The extorted valuables are then exported in exchange for currency that supports the elite of the colony who, in return, keep the native populations in control. This is the classic picture of third world colonies and is the picture of El Salvador. This pattern has persisted in El Salvador and is largely the reason for its environmental destruction. The oligarchy runs the country on a feudal basis little changed from the days of the conquistadors. This means that in the pursuit of their profits they need observe no environmental laws. They may take any land they need, they may use any type and amount of agricultural chemicals on their crops and they may dump toxins in any manner that they please. One group that researches Central America's environmental problems says that as of 1990, "75 per cent of pesticides exported to Central America from the U.S. are either banned or severely restricted for use in the U.S.."[9] This elimination of the cost of environmental protection controls makes El Salvador a high-profit enclave for its rulers and for the transnational corporations located there. They are provided with an impoverished and cheap labor pool which is unable to organize effectively because of military repression and death squads. They do not have the expense of meeting environmental standards so this gives them a decided competitive advantage over other countries.

Since the arrival of civilized culture, 95 per cent of the country's original tropical, deciduous forest has disappeared. Twenty mammal species and eighteen bird species are gone. Serious soil erosion affects 77 per cent of the country. Following deforestation, groundwater is disappearing, sediments are beginning to fill the dams and stop the hydroelectric supply and the United Nations Food and Agriculture Organization says the country is undergoing a process of desertification.[10]

In the familiar pattern, particularly since World War II, the alliance between the domestic oligarchy, U.S. aid agencies and transnational corporations have increased exports which has led to the clearing of the last viable stands of old-growth ebony, cedar, mahogany and granadilla trees. Where the country was once food self-sufficient it now exports cash crops of food items and even flowers to the industrial countries (for the profit of the oligarchy) and imports food.

The Environmental Project On Central America (EPOCA) says that: "Today unequal control of resources remains at the root of poverty and environmental destruction in El Salvador. A small elite, referred to as the 'Fourteen Families,' comprises less than 2 per cent of the population yet enriches itself from ownership of more than 60 per cent of the country's arable land. The poorest 20 per cent of the Salvadoran people own no land and receive only 2 per cent of the national income." In the countryside, the report says that: "two-fifths of the population cannot afford a basic diet of corn and beans."[11]

The EPOCA report says that one in ten have access to safe drinking water. "Look at a body of water in El Salvador and you will see a reflection of almost every major environmental problem in the country: pesticide and fertilizer contamination; industrial pollution; municipal waste and sewage; sedimentation from deforestation and soil erosion; and waterborne diseases. All the major waterways in El Salvador are contaminated by raw sewage and variety of toxic chemicals, according to a 1982 report by the U.S. Agency for International Development."[12]

With the oligarchy occupying the land that an agriculturalist would call "arable," the poor are forced up onto the mountainsides where they use slash and burn agriculture. Because the people are overcrowded and there is not enough land, the fallow periods on the slash and burn plots are too short. This quickly erodes the topsoil and leaves the mountains denuded of all vegetation except for hardy brush. In 1974 there were 400 people for each square mile of El Salvador. The population doubling time in El Salvador is now twenty-two years.[13]

These three countries with their varying histories and varying types of impact from civilization, characterize the periphery of what we may term the industrial empire. These are the conquered and colonized resource and labor areas and their societies are collapsing under the pressure of environmental degradation, population explosion, militarism and export economies. If the oligarchy of El Salvador were to suddenly depart for Miami, the country would still be in a state of disintegration. The soil, water and air are poisoned. There are few natural resources left and importantly for our analysis, the civilized culture of the people of El Salvador would not be disposed to restore the land mass to the climax ecosystem, even if that were possible.

This is the beginning of the end for the Final Empire of civilization. Here we see in these examples that there is little remaining to take out and the populations are exploding. When two people have five children and then fifteen years later those five children have five children, the stage is being set for disintegration. As these factors of soil and ecosystems work themselves out into social turmoil and breakdown, the reports of the media, refer to revolution, economics and politics. The life of the earth is not within their consciousness.

As the regions on the periphery of the empire implode, the center is also imploding, though in a qualitatively different way. The most general statement to make on the system-wide implosion of the industrial empire has to do also with the cultural consciousness. Because of the nature of the culture, it lives and profits by exhausting the life of the earth. Within the cultural bubble we tend to measure our progress by our wealth. The more pressure that the farmer puts on the soil, the more the farmer and the banker profit. The more forests that are cut, the more the timber company and the employees benefit. What this means is that as the life of the earth is eradicated, the information feed-back system (bank accounts) report that things are getting better and better. Progress is being made. This is another major example of how the reality of life is below the threshold of consciousness and also helps to explain why civilization cannot extricate itself from the fall toward apocalypse.

As we approach the end of the Final Empire, societies become paralyzed and disintegrate. There is nothing left with which the society can regenerate itself. In El Salvador, even the "arable" soils are exhausted and poisoned because they have been subjected to years of industrial agriculture with its poisons and artificial fertilizers. The other side of this grim equation is the population explosion. This is compounded by the fact that a majority of the population now is youthful and just beginning to come into their child bearing years. This means that the already overbearing population has reached a take-off point and will climb ever more steeply.

The life of the earth dies out at varying speeds. So that we do not lose contact with reality we must look at this. These examples show swift destruction. It is possible to see the huge erosion canyons in Ethiopia. It is possible to see the floods of Bangladesh and it is possible to count the children in hospitals in El Salvador who have been poisoned with agricultural chemicals. Although not as dramatic, we must realize that our own backyard is degraded and poisoned. If any of us walk out of our back door and look, we will see gross injury to the life of the earth. We may view a lawn that has been subjected to poisons and artificial fertilizers. At some point in the history of that small area, toxins may have been introduced such as motor oil, household cleansers or maybe air drift or subsoil moisture seepage of some industrial dump. The point is that if the climax ecosystem is not there then the earth is losing its life. This is a difficult concept for modern people to deal with mentally. The statement is that the life of the earth, the climax ecosystem, must regain balance or the earth will become substantially dead. The natural state of health and balance of the earth is to be covered with climax ecosystems or ecosystems closely approximating them.

There are examples in the Mid-East of reg pavements (rock-hard soil) where forests once stood. The reg pavement is a hard, virtually impermeable, layer of clays and other dirt that covers wide areas. We have the example of El Salvador proceeding toward desert status (and there are other examples in other parts of the world of tropical forests becoming deserts). With both of these examples we can trace the historical devolution of these ecosystems and soils, which usually begin with the cutting of the forest. When we travel about the earth we don't always realize that where we are seeing a desert now, there may have been a thriving semi-arid ecosystem. Where there is a brushwood hillside, there was once a magnificent forest. In those areas where we now see forest we will soon see deserts.

The life of civilization is only an eye-blink in the eons of time of the life of the earth. We can see the killing of the life of the earth in the rapid dramas as well as the long range spirals of descent. As we continue to examine the condition of our earth we must maintain contact with reality and realize that everywhere civilization has spread the earth is hurting, injured and dying. Even if an area is green with vegetation, it may only be the first aid crew of weeds struggling to heal the earth and the chances are good that soon the bulldozers will come to destroy even that, so that the "real estate" can be "developed."

Collapse From the Center

Our generation is on the verge of the most profound catastrophe the human species has ever faced. Death threats to the living earth are coming from all sides. Water, sunlight, air and soil are all threatened. When eskimos of the far north begin to experience leukemia from atomic radiation and eskimo mothers' milk contains crisis levels of PCB's, we must recognize that every organism on the planet is threatened.

Compounding this crisis is the fact that the prime force in this affair, the civilized humans, are unable to completely understand the problem. The problem is beneath the threshold of consciousness because humans within civilization (civilization comes from the latin, civis, referring to those who live in cities, towns and villages) no longer have relationship with the living earth. Civilized people's lives are focused within the social system itself. They do not perceive the eroding soils and the vanishing forests. These matters do not have the immediate interest of paychecks. The impulse of civilization in crisis is to do what it has been doing, but do it more energetically in order to extricate itself. If soaring population and starvation threaten, often the impulse is to put more pressure on the agricultural soils and cut the forests faster.

We face planetary disaster. The destruction of the planetary life system has been ongoing for thousands of years and is now approaching the final apocalypse which some of us will see in our own lifetimes. Far from being a difficult and complex situation it is actually very simple, if one can understand and accept a few simple and fundamental propositions.

The planetary disaster is traced to one simple fact. Civilization is out of balance with the flow of planetary energy.

The consensus assumption of civilization is that an exponentially expanding human population with exponentially expanding consumption of material resources can continue, based on dwindling resources and a dying ecosystem. This is simply absurd. Nonetheless, civilization continues on with no memory of its history and no vision of its future.

Possibly the most important source of life on this planet is the thin film of topsoil. The life of the planet is essentially a closed, balanced system with the elements of sun, water, soil and air as the basic elements. These elements work in concert to produce life and they function according to patterns that are based in the laws of physics, which we refer to as Natural Law.

The soil depth and its richness is a basic standard of health of the living planet. As a general statement we may say that when soil is lost, imbalance and injury to the planet's life occurs. In the geologic time-span of the planet's life, this is a swift progression toward death. Even if only one per cent of the soil is lost per thousand years, eventually the planet dies. If one per cent is gained, then the living wealth, the richness, of the planet increases. The central fact must be held in mind of how slowly soil builds up. Soil scientists estimate that three hundred to one thousand years are required for the build up of each inch of topsoil.

The nourishment of the soil depends upon the photosynthetic production of the vegetative cover that it carries. There are wide differences in the Net Photosynthetic Production of many possible vegetative covers. As a rule it is the climax ecosystem of any particular region of the earth that is the most productive in translating the energy of the sun into the growth of plants and in turn into organic debris which revitalizes the soil.

A climax ecosystem is the equilibrium state of the "flesh" of the earth. After a severe forest fire, or to recover from the injury of clearcut logging, the forest organism slowly heals the wound by inhabiting the area with a succession of plant communities. Each succeeding community prepares the area for the next community. In general terms, an evergreen forest wound will be covered by tough small plants, popularly called "weeds" and the grasses which hold down the topsoil and prepare the way for other grasses and woody shrubs to grow up on the wound. ("Weeds" are the "first aid crew" on open ground.) As a general rule, the "first aid crew" - the first community of plants to get in and cover the bare soil and hold it down - is the more simple plant community with the smallest number of species of plants, animals, insects, micro-organisms and so forth. As the succession proceeds, the diversity, the number of species, increases as does the NPP, until the climax system is reached again, and equilibrium is established. The system drives toward complexity of form, maximum ability to translate incoming energy (NPP) and diversity of energy pathways (food chains and other services that plants and animals perform for one another). The plants will hold the soil so that it may be built back up. They will shade the soil to prevent its oxidation (the heating and drying of soil promotes chemical changes that cause sterility) and conserve moisture. Each plant takes up different combinations of nutrients from the soil so that specific succession communities prepare specific soil nutrients for specific plant communities that will succeed them. Following the preparation of the site by these plants, larger plants, alders and other broadleaf trees will come in and their lives and deaths will further prepare the micro-climate and soil for the evergreens. These trees function as "nurse" trees for the final climax community, which will be conifers. Seedling Douglas Fir for example, cannot grow in sunlight and must have shade provided by these forerunner communities.

The ecosystems of this earth receive injury from tornado, fire, or other events and then cycle back to the balanced state, the climax system. This is similar to the wound on a human arm that first bleeds, scabs over and then begins to build new replacement skin to reach its equilibrium state. The climax system then is a basic standard of health of the living earth, its dynamic equilibrium state. The climax system is the system that produces the greatest photosynthetic production. Anything that detracts from this detracts from the health of the ecosystem.

Climax ecosystems are the most productive because they are the most diverse. Each organism feeds back some portion of energy to producers of energy that supports it (as well as providing energy to other pathways) and as these support systems grow, the mass and variety of green plants and animals increases, taking advantage of every possible niche. What might be looked at as a whole, unitary organ of the planet's living body, a forest or grassland, experiences increased health because of its diversity within.

On a large scale, the bioregions and continental soils, substantially support sea life by the wash-off (natural and unnatural) of organic fertility into aquatic and ocean environments. This is a further service that these whole ecosystems perform for other whole ecosystems.

A few basic principles of the earth's life in the cosmos have now been established. Balance is cosmic law. The earth revolves around the sun in a finely tuned balance. The heat budget of the planet is a finely tuned balance. If the incoming heat declined, we would freeze or if the planet did not dissipate heat properly we would burn up. The climax ecosystem maintains a balance and stability century after century as the diverse flows of energies constantly move and cycle within it. In the same manner the human body maintains balance (homeostasis) while motion of blood, digestion and cell creation, flow within it.

The life of the earth is fundamentally predicated upon the soil. If there is no soil, there is no life as we know it. (Some micro-organisms and some other forms might still exist). The soil is maintained by its vegetative cover and in optimal, balanced health, this cover is the natural climax ecosystem.

If one can accept these few simple principles then we have established a basis of communication upon which we may proceed. Anyone who cannot accept these principles must demonstrate that the world works in some other way. This must be done quickly because the life of the planet earth hangs in the balance.

We speak to our basic condition of life on earth. We have heard of many roads to salvation. We have heard that economic development will save us, solar heating will save us, technology, the return of Jesus Christ who will restore the heaven and the earth, the promulgation of land reform, the recycling of materials, the establishment of capitalism, communism, socialism, fascism, Muslimism, vegetarianism, trilateralism, and even the birth of new Aquarian Age, we have been told, will save us. But the principle of soil says that if the humans cannot maintain the soil of the planet, they cannot live here. In 1988, the annual soil loss due to erosion was twenty-five billion tons and rising rapidly. Erosion means that soil moves off the land. An equally serious injury is that the soil's fertility is exhausted in place. Soil exhaustion is happening in almost all places where civilization has spread. This is a literal killing of the planet by exhausting its fund of organic fertility that supports other biological life. Fact: since civilization invaded the Great Plains of North America one-half of the topsoil of that area has disappeared.

The Record of Empire

The eight thousand year record of crimes against nature committed by civilization include assaults on the topsoils of all continents.

Forests, the greatest generators of topsoil, covered roughly one-third of the earth prior to civilization. By 1975 the forest cover was one-fourth and by 1980 the forest had shrunk to one-fifth and the rapidity of forest elimination continues to increase. If the present trends continue without interruption eighty percent of the vegetation of the planet will be gone by 2040.

The simple fact is that civilization cannot maintain the soil. Eight thousand years of its history demonstrate this. Civilization is murdering the earth. The topsoil is the energy bank that has been laboriously accumulated over millennia. Much of it is gone and the remainder is going rapidly.

When civilized "development" of land occurs the climax system is stripped, vegetation is greatly simplified or cleared completely and the net photosynthetic production plummets. In the tropics, when pasture land is created by clearing forest, two-thirds of the original net photosynthetic production is eliminated. In the mid-latitudes one-half the net photosynthetic production is lost when cropland is created from previously forested land. The next step is that humans take much of even that impaired production off the land in the form of agricultural products so that not even the full amount of that impaired production returns to feed the soil.

This points out a simple principle: Human society must have as its central value, a responsibility to maintain the soil. If we can create culture that can maintain the soil then there is the possibility of human culture regaining balance with the life of the earth.

The central problem is that civilization is out of balance with the life of the earth.

The solution to that problem is for human society to regain balance with the earth.

We are now back to everyone's personal answer concerning how to respond to the planetary crisis. Most proposals for salvation have little to do with maintaining the soil. All of these seek to alleviate the situation without making any uncomfortable change in the core values or structure of existing society. They only try to "fix" the symptoms. If we had a society whose core values were to preserve and aid the earth, then all of the other values of society would flow consistently from that.

In many important ways civilization functions in an addictive fashion. The culture of civilization functions so that it is self destructive, suicidal; as if it were a person addicted to alcohol, white sugar, drugs or tobacco. The addict denies that there is a problem. The addict engages in the denial of reality. Civilization is addicted in the same way.

The civilized people believe they have an obligation to bring primitive and underdeveloped people up to their level. Civilization, which is about to self-destruct, thinks of itself as the superior culture that has answers for all the world's people.

An addict, truly, is a person who is emotionally dependent on things: television, substances, personality routines, other people, mental ideologies, total immersion in some cause or work. If the object of dependency is removed, addicts will experience insecurity, discomfort, distress, the symptoms of withdrawal.

Civilization, is a cultural/mental view that believes security is based in instruments of coercion. The size of this delusion is such that the combined military expenditure of all the world's governments in 1987 were so large that all of the social programmes of the United Nations could be financed for three hundred years by this expenditure.

Looking back at the simple principle which says that humans cannot live on this planet unless they can maintain the topsoil, demonstrates the delusion. The delusion of military power does not lead to security, it leads to death. The civilized denial of the imperative of maintaining topsoil, and the addictive grasping to the delusion that security can be provided by weapons of death, is akin to the hallucination of a alcoholic suffering delirium tremens! The first step in the recovery of any addict is the recognition that what they have believed is a delusion. The alcoholic must come to see that "just one more drink" is not the answer, the workaholic must come to see that "just a little more effort" will not provide feelings of self worth and a rounded life. The bulimic must come to see that "just one more plate of food" will not provide emotional wholeness. Civilization must come to see that its picture of reality is leading it to suicide.

If the addict can admit that his existence is in fact out of control and that all that he has been doing is in fact leading to self injury and self destruction- then, and only then, can restoration begin. It is often difficult for complex minds to understand simple things, so this must be emphasized. The addict lives on topsoil and is destroying that topsoil. This is ultimately a self destructive act. The road to restoration for the addict must first begin with the recognition that they are destroying the topsoil and that without topsoil, they will die. The addict must accept responsibility and abandon the beliefs which result in destruction of topsoil, beliefs such as that wealth and militarism are mechanisms of security. Unless the addict can change, self destructive behavior will reach its logical end.

Here we have the whole of it. The problem is imbalance and the solution is to regain balance. Here we have the simple principle: if human actions help to regain balance as judged by the condition of the soil, then we are on the path of healing the earth. If the theory, plan, project, or whatever, cannot be justified by this standard, then we are back in the delusional system.

All of us are addicts. We of civilization have lost our way. We are now functioning in a world of confusion and chaos. We must recognize that the delusional system of civilization, the mass institutions and our personal lives, function on a self destructive basis. We live in a culture that is bleeding the earth to death, and we have been making long range personal plans and developing careers within it. We strive toward something that is not to be.

We must try to wake up and regain a vision of reality. We must begin taking responsibility for our lives and for the soil. This is a tall order. This will require study and forethought. That is what this book is about. Humans have never dealt with anything like this before. This generation is presented with a challenge that in its dimensions is cosmic. A cosmic question: will tens of millions of years of the proliferation of life on earth die back to the microbes? This challenge presents us with the possibility of supreme tragedy or the supreme success.

Creating a utopian paradise, a new Garden of Eden is our only hope. Nothing less will extricate us. We must create the positive, cooperative culture dedicated to life restoration and then accomplish that in perpetuity, or we as a species cannot be on earth.

NOTES

1   Natural Disasters: Acts of God or Acts of Man?. Anders Wijkman &
     Lloyd Timberlake. New Society pub. Santa Cruz, Ca. 1988. p.58.

2   Gaia: An Atlas Of Planet Management. Dr. Norman Meyers, General
     Editor. Anchor Books. Garden City, New York. 1984. p. 41.

3   Famine In South Asia : Political Economy of Mass Starvation.
     Mohiuddin Alamgir. Oelgeschlager, Gunn and Hain Pub. Sweden.
     1980. P. 135.

4   ibid. p. 135.

5   Physical Environment & Its Significance For Economic Development
     With Special Reference to Ethiopia. Sven Beltrens. C. W. R. Gleerup.
     Lund. Sweden. 1971. p. 110.

6   Losing Ground: Environmental Stress and World Food Prospects. Erik
     P. Eckholm. W.W. Norton & Co. New York. 1976. p. 94.

7   "The 500,000 Invisible Indians of El Salvador." by Mac Chapin.
     Cultural Survival Quarterly. Vol. 13. #3. 1989. pp. 11-14.

8   ibid, p. 14.

9   "EPOCA UPDATE." "Pressure Mounts To Halt Pesticide Exports."
     Summer 1990. The Environmental Project on Central America. Earth
     Island Institute, 300 Broadway suite 28, San Francisco, CA. 94133. p. 13.

10   El Salvador: Ecology of Conflict. Green Paper #4. The Environmental
     Project On Central America. Earth Island Institute, 300 Broadway #28,
     San Francisco, Ca. 94133. p. 2.

11   ibid. p.3.

12   ibid. p.3.

13   Margin of Life: Population and Poverty in the Americas. J. Mayone
     Stycos. Grossman Pub. New York. 1974.
     See also:
     Losing Ground: Environmental Stress and World Food Prospects. Erik
     P. Eckholm. W. W. Norton Co. New York. 1976.

CHAPTER 2

THE END OF CIVILIZATION

If the planet and the human species are to survive we must create paradise. We must restore the life of the earth. The only way that the planet can heal itself is for the soils of the earth to be restored along with the ecosystems that will maintain those soils. To do this, human culture must undergo transformation from a culture of suicide and immediate gratification of immature impulses for material goods into a culture of wisdom and life centeredness, in a word, paradisiacal culture.

We must get below the threshold of consciousness of civilization and examine the real basis of the life of the earth- the soil. All of us have to struggle to throw off the mind conditioning that we have received in civilization. Our reality molding would have us believe that there are environmental problems such as toxic chemicals, radiation and acid rain. The fact is that our life crisis began with empire/civilization. The environmental crisis began thousands of years ago, when the Han Chinese began to destroy the vast forests of China and when the Indo-Europeans began to overgraze the vegetation and exhaust the soils of central Asia. For two to three million years humans lived on the planet in a stable condition then suddenly with the cultural inversion to civilization, the earth began to die. Civilization is the environmental crisis and the loss of topsoil is our measure of the etiology of the disease.

The materialistic values of civilization teach us that the accumulation of wealth is progress. The material wealth of civilization is derived from the death of the earth, the soils, the forests, the fish stocks, the "free resources" of flora and fauna. The ultimate end of this is for all of the human species to live in giant parasitical cities of cement and metal while surrounded by deserts of exhausted soils. The simple polar opposites are: the richness and wealth of the natural life of earth versus the material wealth of people living out their lives in artificial environments.

The ecological survey that follows will first focus on the basic reality, the soil. It will then examine the health of the planetary forests. Then will follow an examination of the greatest ecological disaster, agriculture. We will focus on these matters because these are the basic and enduring damages and unless these are set right, there can be no recovery. Then the focus will turn to the last phase of civilization, the destruction caused by industrial culture such as poisons and planet-wide imbalances such as the greenhouse effect. Here we will see in detail how the options are rapidly narrowing for the human family as soil erosion, overgrazing and deforestation continue their inexorable spread throughout civilization. Industrial society has provided a swift push toward the climax. The seminal study, *The Limits to Growth: Report For The Club Of Rome's Project On The Predicament of Mankind*, shows how the dynamics of industrial society point us toward the final paroxysm.[1]

The *Limits to Growth* study was done in the early 1970's by an international team of scholars at Massachusetts Institute of Technology (MIT). The team, which came from many diverse disciplines, isolated the dynamic and interactive movements of the five basic factors of industrial society: resources, food per capita, population, industrial output per person and pollution.

The standard model computer run of all of these factors shows that industrial society will begin its swift collapse sometime in the 2020's. Here we quote the authors statement concerning the "World Model Standard Run:"

> "The 'standard' world model run assumes no major change in the physical, economic, or social relationships that have historically governed the development of the world system. All variables plotted here follow historical values from 1900 to 1970. Food, industrial output, and population grow exponentially until the rapidly diminishing resource base forces a slowdown in industrial growth. Because of natural delays in the system, both population and pollution continue to increase for some time after the peak of industrialization. Population growth is finally halted by a rise in the death rate due to decreased food and medical services."[2]

The standard extrapolation of the growth curves since the 1900's can easily be drawn out to the end, though chances are very good that war, depression, nuclear disaster, or eco-catastrophe will occur sometime before then. We live in a material civilization. We can count the barrels of oil, we can count the acres of wheat fields, and we can count the number of people. All the scholars who created the MIT study did, was to put all of the numbers from all of the scholarly fields on computers and extrapolate. The thing the computer cannot do is anticipate unpredictable breakdowns in the world system.

The scholars did examine the possibilities of averting disaster (which assumes a very unlikely world society, nimble enough to coordinate a survival strategy). The scholars programmed the computers so as to double the estimated resource base, they created a model that assumed "unlimited" resources, pollution controls, increased agricultural productivity and "perfect" birth control. None of these or other aversion strategies could take the world system past 2100.

The reason that the world system cannot go on with unlimited growth is because each of the five factors is interactive. If we assume unlimited fuels such as a simple fusion process, this simply drives the growth curves faster. There is more cheap fuel so the wheels of industry churn faster and resource exhaustion comes more quickly, population continues to climb and pollution climbs. If there is more food production, then population climbs and resources are exhausted more rapidly. If population is stabilized, resources still continue to decline and pollution increases because of increased consumption. If the factors of resources, food, and industrial output grow then population grows but the resulting pollution creates the negative feedbacks of having to maintain cancer hospitals and institutions for the birth defected and the mutations caused by pollution as well as pollution damage to factors such as farm crops.

Growth had been the fundamental pattern of the culture of civilization long before Alexander conquered the "known world." The difference now is that the growth is approaching its outer limits and soon will have nothing left to feed on. We have come to the final cycle in which civilization will fall into entropy because it cannot any longer be sustained. There are no more virgin continents to exploit. There are no more forests to cut down so that new soils can be exploited and exhausted. In addition to this the world population is now counted in the billions. The world has never before known this kind of exponentially increasing volume of flow and consumption of food, resources and industrial poisons.

Because of these interactive forces world society is trapped within a system of cultural assumptions and patterns of behavior from which it cannot extricate itself. There is no way out. There will be a collapse of civilization. There is no question that there will be future famines in the ecologically devastated and desertified region of Ethiopia with its exploding human population, just as there is no question that civilization which eats up its resources and poisons the earth, will collapse. We are examining the process now in order to gain knowledge, because we are the people who will be attempting to live through the climax.

An Inheritance Of Destruction

Life on earth has a long history. Bacterial microfossils have been discovered associated with some of the oldest unmetamorphosed rocks which are 3.8 billion years old. We know that at least twice in this history, life has faced ecological catastrophe roughly equal to the one that we now are in. The first massive die-off was when cyanobacteria evolved oxygen and poisoned vast numbers of creatures. The second die-off, 65 million years ago, was the well known period when dinosaurs became extinct.[3] After immense periods of time in which life proliferated, the human form appeared on earth. The fossil record, as unearthed in the Oldavi Gorge in Africa by the archeologist family, the Leakeys, goes back three million years. According to anthropologists, for that period of time, 99 per cent of human existence, we have been forager/hunters. Suddenly, and only an eyeblink in time of approximately ten thousand years, a different social form irrupted among the humans. This form is the monolithic social form known as empire. We are now assembling information on a third cataclysm to face life on earth, the age of human empire and its final apocalypse. The culture of empire, which also travels under the euphemism, civilization, is the cause of the third event. The culture of empire is characterized by ecological imbalance caused by cities, centralization, hierarchy, patriarchy, militarism and materialism. We find aspects of this cultural form among the Aztecs and Mayans of Meso-America, the Incas of Peru, Certain African kingdoms, the Egyptian dynasties and a few other locations but the most virulent strains of this cultural pathology developed in China, the Indus river valley and in Central Asia among the Indo-Europeans. It is the inheritance of this cultural form that is destroying the earth.

China

J. Russell Smith, author of a classic text of Permaculture, *Tree Crops: A Permanent Agriculture*, gives a characteristic picture of the land occupied by the old Asian empires:

"I stood on the Great Wall of China high on a hill near the borders of Mongolia. Below me in the valley, standing up square and high, was a wall that had once surrounded a city. Of the city, only a few mud houses remained, scarcely enough to lead one's mind back to the time when people and household industry teemed within the protecting wall.

"The slope below the Great Wall was cut with gullies, some of which were fifty feet deep. As far as the eye could see were gullies, gullies, gullies-a gashed and gutted countryside. The little stream that once ran past the city was now a wide waste of coarse sand and gravel which the hillside gullies were bringing down faster than the little stream had been able to carry them away. Hence, the whole valley, once good farm land, had become a desert of sand and gravel, alternately wet and dry, always fruitless. It was even more worthless than the hills. Its sole harvest now is dust, picked up by the bitter winds of winter that rip across its dry surface in this land of rainy summers and dry winters.

"Beside me was a tree, one lone tree. That tree was locally famous because it was the only tree anywhere in that vicinity; yet its presence proved that once there had been a forest over most of that land- now treeless and waste."[4]

At one time nearly half of China was forested. The famous agricultural scholar, Georg Borgstrom estimates that 670 million acres of China were once covered.[5] This forest with its complex ecosystem was gone almost before written history. There is no doubt that it contained many species that became extinct and of which we will never know. One major consequence of the denudation of the vegetation of China is that its major rivers now carry more silt than any other river system in the world and the stories of the floods in China are as old as the Chinese empire.

Indus River Valley

The Indus River valley of western India once hosted an empire. Some one thousand years before the Chinese began the ecological destruction of China an empire existed in this area that is dated between 2,500 B.C. and 1,500 B.C. Evidence suggests that this was a forested region with an ecology that among other things contained elephant, rhinoceros, water buffalo, tiger, crocodile, bear, goose, lizard and tortoise.

Edward Hyams, in his study, *Soil and Civilization*, indicates that the forest was cleared for agriculture, the fuel needed for the firing of mud bricks and the smelting of metals. This plus soil exhaustion created the destruction of the ecology and the implosion of the empire. This means that much of the area of the former empire of the Indus River valley was forest and it is now semi-arid desert. While this seems at first like an unlikely change, Hyams points to examples from Australia where that change has happened in the past hundred years. He says:

"The present vegetation of Sind is tamarisk and scrub. In not dissimilar climatic conditions in Australia in our own times, such a vegetation has sprung up upon soils rendered semi-arid by forest clearance, by overstocking with cattle, or by soil-fertility 'mining' with wheat."[6]

The Indo-Europeans Of Central Asia

Some seven thousand years before the present, the origin culture of what we now call the Indo-European language group, domesticated wheat and barley which were wild plants of the region of the Caucasus Mountains. They also domesticated sheep and goats. This was the beginning of the culture of empire in Central Asia. The history of this culture along with the culture of the Han Chinese, leads right down to the present day.

From Afghanistan, through northern Persia to central Turkey the mountain areas have been deforested and eroded to the point that they are now simply bare, arid ranges.[7] Grazing, deforestation for smelting, heating and cooking, and trees removed for the plow are the chief culprits that have destroyed the soils and the ecology. The soils of Central Asia and the Mid-East have gone to the ocean. Massive erosion of soils on the watersheds of the Tigris-Euphrates river system have been created by at least five thousand years of

imperial abuse. Scholars calculate that the erosion material from this watershed
has filled in the Persian Gulf for one hundred and eighty miles in the last forty-
five hundred years. An area of more than 2,000 square miles has been filled.
Prior to the empires, the Tigris and Euphrates had separate mouths that
emptied into the Persian Gulf.[8] Throughout this region we can see what will be
the final stages of the whole of civilization.

After the forests are cut and the grasslands overgrazed, plant regimes from
drier environments move in. Spiny and thorny brush move in along with the
hardier, tougher grasses. As the region continues to be razed for firewood and
goat fodder, the harder layers of subsoil are exposed. Finally, the hard surface
of desert pavements form. As bedrock and hard subsoils are reached a moon-
scape is created from which no recovery is possible.

The Empires Of Greece And Rome

As we follow the denudation of the Mediterranean, we see that Greece was
well advanced toward ecological destruction early in that country's imperial
career. Many of the wars of conquest were simply to gain new forests for use in
building warships. Author David Attenborough describes the type of effects
caused by the denudation of the Greek mainland:

"Thermopylae, on the Greek coast, was the site in 480 BC of one of the
most heroic battles in ancient history. A tiny detachment of Greek soldiers,
commanded by the king of Sparta, held a narrow pass between the sea for
three days against a huge Persian army. Today, that pass no longer exists.
The soil from the hills above has been washed down by the rivers and
deposited at the edge of the sea in such quantities that the pass has been
transformed into a wide plain."[9]

One of the colonies that was used to gain shipbuilding lumber was Ephesus
on the western coast of Turkey. By the fourth century, B.C. the harbor was so
silted because of deforestation and soil abuse in the uplands that the harbor had
to be moved farther along the coast. The new harbor quickly filled in and the
location now is three miles from the Mediterranean.[10] In Italy and Sicily soil
destruction has been epidemic. "The Italian coast from south of Ravenna; north
and eastward almost to Trieste has been extending itself into the Adriatic Sea
for at least twenty centuries," one scholar reports. The city of Ravenna, once on
the coastline is now six miles inland.[11]

The impact of the successive empires on the "breadbasket" of North Africa
has been to destroy it. Both Greece and Rome used the luxuriant North Africa
as a mainstay of empire. Finally the Arab, Ottoman Turks and other minor
empires destroyed the last shreds of the ecology. At one time six hundred
colonial cities stretched from Egypt to Morocco and the area provided Rome
with two-thirds of its wheat budget. Now much of the area is barren, eroded
and can hardly support goats.[12]

It is no accident that now the diet of these former empires is based on goats, grapes and olives. This is ecological poverty food. As these cultures have destroyed their lands, the plants and animals that remain such as goats, grapes and olives are ones that can subsist on denuded and dry soils.

This brief review of the original areas of civilization can help us visualize what the earth will eventually look like in most areas where it has spread. But because of our massive modern population and technology, the destruction that took place over thousands of years is now being accomplished in very brief time spans. The ecological destruction has not stopped even now, but in the present continues on, headed for bedrock.

NOTES

1   The Limits to Growth: A Report For The Club Of Rome's Project On
    The Predicament Of Mankind. Donella H. Meadows, Dennis L.
    Meadows, Jørgen Randers & William W. Behrens III. New American
    Library. New York. 1974.
2   ibid. p. 129.
3   1990 Catalog of Seeds. A.M.Kapuler,PhD. Peace Seeds, A Planetary
    Gene Pool Resource and Service. 2385 SE Thompson St., Corvallis,
    Oregon 97333. p. 1.
4   Tree Crops: A Permanent Agriculture. J. Russell Smith. Devin-Adair
    Co. Old Greenwich. 1977. p. 3.
5   The Hungry Planet: The Modern World at the Edge of Famine. Georg
    Borgstrom. Collier Books. New York. 1972. p. 106.
6   Soil and Civilization. Edward Hyams. Harper & Row. New York.
    1976. p. 69.
7   ibid. pp. 55-64
    see also:
    Man and the Meditterranean Forest: A History of Resource Depletion.
    J.V. Thirgood. Academic Press. New York. 1981. p.62.
    And
    Losing Ground: Environmental Stress and World Food Prospects. Erik
    P. Eckholm. W.W. Norton & Co. New York. 1976. p.94
8   Man's Role In Changing The Face Of The Earth. William L. Thomas,
    Jr., Ed. U of Chicago Press. Chicago, Ill. Vol. 2. p. 510.
9   The First Eden: The Mediterranean World and Man. David
    Attenborough. Little, Brown & Co. Boston. 1987. p. 169.
10 ibid. p. 118.
11 Thomas, op. cit. p. 511.
12 Attenborough, op. cit. p. 116.

CHAPTER 3

SOIL: THE BASIS OF LIFE

The Organic Rights

All beings of the earth, from microbes to elephants exist in a web of organic energy flows. Everything in the material world is food and everything is excrement. When the flow of energy comes from the sun to be consumed by the plant, this begins a succession of energy transformation called the food chain. Beings eat each other. This flow of solar energy undergoes many transformations. In addition to these connections in the food chain there are many more energy connections that are of a cooperative and contributory nature. Beings provide many services for one another that have nothing to do with eating each other. Bees pollinate flowers, birds transport and deposit seeds. Fungi combine with the root hairs of plants and the ensemble generates food for both plants and fungi that otherwise neither would be able to absorb. Each being, because it lives according to its nature, contributes to the smooth functioning of the whole.

There are beings such as elephants, tigers, humans and others whose consciousness is such that the intellectual function is well developed but the organic memory is not highly developed such as it is in animals like the earthworm or frog. Earthworms and frogs do not need to be taught what they are, their identity, they simply know what their nature is. The elephant, tiger or human on the other hand have to be taught their culture by their parents or clan. This is shown by the fact that these animals, if raised in captivity and turned loose in their natural habitat, will starve, because they have not learned their culture from their parents or clan. Many civilized people have starved in the midst of abundant food that native people utilize with ease. These beings, deprived of knowledge, do not know their organic identity.

For two to three million years humans lived in clans and tribes as forager/hunters. In that culture we learned our personal identity within the clan and we learned that we had an organic identity as one among many beings of the earth.

We learned of the other beings and their habits of life. We learned of life and the conditions for the growth of life.

This organic right, to know who and what we are and that we are located within a web of living energies must be a birthright of all humans. The earthworm conducts its life and contributes its excrement to help create the valuable humus of the soil. The bird visits one oasis in the desert and then transports seeds from there to another oasis. All beings must act responsibly and do their part for the world to function. For life to persist they must act according to their natures. For a being such as the human who can be so constructive or destructive this is important, important for the continuance of the human species so that they do not ignorantly destroy that which feeds them. All beings of earth have a vital interest in humans knowing their organic place in nature, because when humans do not know, they become organic psychotics and wantonly destroy other beings.

If the human species intends to exist in perpetuity, children must be provided with these organic rights. Most people in civilization grow up in boxes. Artificial environments and designer landscapes are most childrens' formative, environmental experience. Even farm children do not have a sense of the beauty and complexity of a completely natural and unaltered environment. In order to give the human species a chance of survival, all children should have a right to the organic knowledge that they are an integral part of the life of earth. They need this knowledge in order to make rudimentary ethical and survival decisions. Children should at least be taught fully what soil is. Soil is the foundation of life of the planet, only the uninformed think of it as dirt. They pave it over, they dump poisons on it and they strip the vegetation so that the soil runs away without even realizing what they are doing.

Children should be told that soil must receive sustenance. This factor, the decline of the soil's food, applies to all of the land mass where civilization exists, not just farm fields but ballparks, golf courses, wetlands that are drained, houses, yards, pastures and any other place that has had the climax ecosystem removed. Anytime biomass is removed from the land in the form of cattle, logs, corn, vegetables or even grass clippings, the soil is deprived of that amount of feed.

Because civilized people do not know what they are, they talk politics, religion, science and pursue material wealth while the basis of their life on earth, the soil, slips away beneath their feet.

The Soil

Soil is the gut of the earth, the principal digestive organ of planetary life. Soil is partially composed of rock chips, clay, sand, minerals and organic detritus, but it is also an interdependent living community of micro-organisms, insects, worms, small animals, reptiles and other organisms (even some birds) which live in, contribute to and feed on components of the soil. Like the bacterial community in the human gut that predigests the human food, the soil is a living community of organisms which produces the necessary conditions for the plant communities to exist. The excrement of the gut community feeds the human, and the excrement of the soil community feeds the vegetative community which lives on the soil. Plants do not absorb earth. Plants absorb nutrients that are in solution in the soil moisture. These nutrient solutions are the result of many energy transformations as they pass through a number of organisms.

The creation of soil, begins with an inert and infertile subsoil of clay, sand, rock chips and rocks. When the first pioneer or "first aid" plant germinates it begins to thrust its roots down into the hard compacted earth. It pumps moisture and minerals up from the earth to its stems and leaves. It drops its leaves and stems on the surface. The decomposers, small insects and microbes which live in the soil, eat the organic material that the plant has dropped.

The organic material, by covering the raw earth begins to shade it from the evaporative and oxidizing effect of direct sunlight. Moisture retention improves the habitat for small creatures who burrow, opening up the earth to more moisture and to oxygen which will allow more micro-organisms to exist.

Porousness and organic build-up on and in the soil, help increase the soil's fertility. The organic material on the surface feeds the soil community and other beings eat primary soil ingredients such as rock chips, roots and other micro beings, both dead and alive. As roots die and leave micro tunnels and as earthworms and others create tunnels, passageways are created for the infiltration of water and oxygen, two vital needs of the soil community. As the soil increases its fertility it becomes more porous, it retains more moisture and the temperature extremes are moderated.

As the soil builds, the richness and diversity of the habitat increases. More varieties of beings can find niches in the web of life. As the soil is opened up a succession of plants follow the pioneer species and find it easier to get their roots down into the soil. Bill Mollison, in his definitive work on Permaculture, *Permaculture: A Designers' Manual,* says of the living component in a typical soil: "50 per cent is fungi, 20 per cent is bacteria, 20 per cent yeasts, algae, and protozoans, and only 10 per cent the larger fauna such as earthworms, nematodes, arthropods and mollusc fauna (the micro-and macro-fauna), and their larvae." He adds that, "Such classes of organisms are found in soils everywhere, in different proportions."[1]

The activities of the fungi are especially interesting. The body of the fungus stretches itself through the soil like a giant spiderweb. When the time comes for sexual reproduction most varieties of these fungi thrust up out of the soil, and produce what we call a mushroom. This is the sexual organ of the underground body. The web strands underground grow toward the root hairs of plants. As the threads of the fungi touch the root hair, the cells of the fungi invade the cells of the plant root. The fungus does not have the ability to translate solar energy into biomass (photosynthesis) but it can receive foods from the tree. The tree itself begins to absorb the cells of the fungi. Sir Albert Howard who wrote the historic treatise on organic agriculture, *The Soil and Health: A Study of Organic Agriculture,* explains that:

"Here we have a simple arrangement on the part of Nature by which the soil material on which these fungi feed can be joined up, as it were, with the sap of the tree. These fungous threads are very rich in protein and may contain as much as 10 per cent of organic nitrogen; this protein is easily digested by the ferments (enzymes) in the cells of the root; the resulting nitrogen complexes, which are readily soluble, are then passed into the sap current and so into the green leaf. An easy passage, as it were, has been provided for food material to move from soil to plant in the form of proteins and their digestion products, which latter in due course reach the green leaf. The marriage of a fertile soil and the tree it nourishes is thus arranged. Science calls these fungous threads mycelium..., the whole process is known as the mycorrhizal association. This partnership is universal in the forest and is general throughout the vegetable kingdom."[2]

The soil breathes through the sponge-like passages in it. One cause of air movement is the lunar gravitational attraction. Just as the moon causes tides, it also pulls on aquifers and soil water. This water movement exhales and inhales air in the soil. Differentials of high and low pressure zones in the atmosphere passing overhead also effect the earth's breathing and even such things as noted by Mollison, of the bodies of worms pushing through the tubes, effect earth respiration.

As the soil becomes what we might call "mature" or climax, it is porous, it holds more water and air. As its diversity and richness increase, the vegetative cover grows richer and more diverse, thus feeding the soil more. Trees move in. They put out their feeder roots horizontally in the soil and the tap roots deep into the subsoil. From the subsoil they bring up water which is transpired, improving the local microclimate. Minerals are also brought up from the deep, which go into leaf structure and finally end up on the soil surface. When the trees die, their decaying root systems leave deeper cavities. Within this enriching soil, the burrowing animals are working, churning the soil/subsoil, as other plants are growing and dying to deposit their dead bodies on the surface as food for the community. In this way the soil circulates toward increased fertility.

Mollison points out the high value of soils by reminding us that the only place that soils are conserved or increased are: in uncut forests, in the muck under quiet ponds or lakes, in prairies and meadows of permanent plants and where we grow plants with mulched or non-tillage systems.[3]

The general rule of thumb used by ecologists is that three hundred to one thousand years are required to build one inch of topsoil. This means that thousands of years of production can easily be wiped out in a season.

The Process of Soil Collapse

Soil injury and death is a severe health problem for the earth. Natural processes that severely injure or destroy soil over large areas are rare. They occur in geologic time spans such as the ice ages, vast climatic changes, earthquakes, volcanic eruptions and the movement of tectonic plates. On a smaller scale, intense fires, landslides, or floods can damage local soils. The history of "rapid" and large scale soil injury is actually the history of the activities of civilization.

The process of soil collapse and destruction is essentially the reverse of soil build-up. When soil builds it opens up, breathes and accumulates moisture. More and more niches are provided to expand the diversity of the soil community. As soil deteriorates these factors decline and soil degenerates toward a solid clay-like impervious mass that inhibits life activities.

Soil Exhaustion

The soil is in a continuous cycle that must be fed organic detritus continually. If this cycle is stopped the primary food of the community ceases. If the food ceases and the plants continue to feed on the soil, as in a corn field, the soil will become exhausted. When cattle graze, they remove essential elements from the cycle. A ton of beef has depleted the soil of approximately 26 pounds of calcium, 54 pounds of nitrogen, 3 pounds of potassium, 15 pounds of phosphorus and many other trace elements.

This same situation obtains in a forest where the biomass is hauled away in the form of logs. Anything that detracts from the circulation of essential elements, injures the soil. Any decline in the climax vegetation will cause a decline in the health of the soil community because of the decline of flow in the nutrient cycles.

When a forest is cleared or a prairie is plowed, soil health is impaired. The first growing season on this land may be highly productive, but after several years even with manuring and fallow periods, the soil can function only at a level considerably below its optimum. Agricultural soils that can be maintained over centuries, are generally heavy clay soils but even these erode, lose humus and become compacted. Even these soils must be maintained with great care to maintain sustainability at their greatly lowered level of health.

Unless large amounts of organic material are added each year, the soil will decline, because the soil community continues to feed, consuming the available organic and the biological nutrients until there is no more. At this point we have what farmers call "farmed out" land.

On a small piece of land near Willits, California a group of experimental gardeners called Ecology Action began to build soil on a hillside that was considered of "intermediate" value for grazing. They report that it was difficult to get a shovel into the original soil. After seventeen years of intense work, they have created a soil that will support luxurious plant growth through a method that they call "biointensive gardening." To increase soil fertility, they leave three-quarters of the soil in fallow crops of sunflowers, vetch, fava beans, wheat and rye. This experiment is deliberately a closed system, with no organic material being imported for compost (which would deprive other soils). This experiment gives us a rough standard to judge how much must be done to keep a soil sustainable and increasing in fertility. It means that three-quarters of the soil must be planted with plants that build up the soil while one-quarter are used by plants that feed on the soil and are then removed.[4]

A test conducted for 41 years, between 1894 and 1935 by the Ohio Agricultural Experiment Station at Wooster, Ohio, demonstrates the soil loss and yield on three sets of experimental plots devoted to continuous corn cultivation. This test shows the effect on the soil of "normal" farming methods.

crop every year	Soil Treatment	Soil loss in inches 1894-1935	% of original organic matter remaining in soil	Average annual yield measured in bushels per acre 1894-5	1931-5
CORN	NONE	10.3	37%	26.3	6.5
CORN	ARTIFICIAL FERTILIZER 500 Lbs. of 10-5-10 per Acre	11.1	35%	44.4	28.9
CORN	MANURE 5 tons per Acre	9.5	53%	43.1	30.0

(The table is taken from the *Yearbook of Agriculture, 1938*, USDA, p.102)

(10-5-10 is 10 nitrogen, 5 phosphate and 10 lbs. potassium per 100 lbs. total ingredients)

This study demonstrates that even with manuring, the soil suffers. In order to fully complement the nutrient cycle so that the soil does not become depleted, even larger amounts of organic matter need to be applied. This is part of the problem of civilized agriculture. Where does the organic matter come from? In pre-industrial days, fallow periods were used. Plants were grown on the fields and then plowed into the soil. Manure from draft animals, cattle, pigs and chickens was also applied to the soil. This slowed the depletion of the soil. Then came the tractor. The draft animal manure was lost. The land that was used to grow feed for the draft animals was turned to other crops. Vast fields of corn, wheat, soybeans or other monocrops were put in and fertilized artificially.

In the above table, the greatest loss of organic matter occurred with the use of artificial fertilizers. The artificially fertilized soil lost even more than the plot with no treatment. This happens because the artificial fertilizers do spur plant growth and this in turn draws more energy out, thus causing the soil to lose even more organic matter.

This study points out a crucial, but seldom noticed, fact. Everywhere in the world where the industrial agricultural system and the "green revolution" has spread, this process is happening to the soil. Farmers physically take biomass off the soil and this short circuits the nutrient cycle. But even though the soil health is declining, crops continue to be raised because artificial fertilizer is injected into the soil. To industrial agriculture the soil itself is irrelevant. In fact, many modern farmers say that all they need the soil for is to "prop up" the plants while they artificially inject the nutrients. While this is true, it is equally true that this process is masking the actual biological deterioration of the planet's soils. The short term gain might be large, but if artificial fertilizers become too costly to purchase, or if easily extracted petroleum energy from which artificial fertilizers and agricultural poisons are generated, becomes exhausted, the world will face starvation because the soils are dead. The final yield on the top line of the chart where no help was given to the soil shows about where the world population will be when the petroleum fueled fertilizer plants shut down. A billion and a half people in the world are now fed simply because of the added increase made possible with chemical fertilizers. If chemical fertilizers were eliminated, world agricultural production would drop by at least one-third.[5]

Soil Compaction

Compaction of soils is another common injury that occurs on and off the farm. Anytime weight is put on soil, the pores tend to be crushed. This causes the moisture holding ability to decline and decreases soil breathing. This also inhibits plant growth because plants must expend more effort in order to get their roots down into the soil. As compaction increases, less water infiltrates and more water runs off, which increases the erosion of the topsoil. Plowing, is a cause of much compaction because it requires heavy equipment. Trampling by confined livestock also compacts soil.

The plow is probably the cause of more soil death than any other factor. When the iron bottom plow was invented, a great change occurred in agriculture. Light soils had earlier been worked with wooden plows, but when the iron bottom plow was created, deep, heavy, clay soils could be worked and this greatly expanded the area of civilized agriculture. Finally the moldboard plow was created which completely overturns the soil because of its increased curvature.

The plow historically has been associated with Indo-European field agriculture. It is associated with the Indo-European cultural value of increasing production and as such was used by the Roman Empire in their vast agricultural enterprises. Prior planting had been done by digging stick and hoe, often in slash and burn plots in forests. This method had minimal interference with the soil and usually the cover vegetation of small plants was not eliminated. With the plow it is possible to completely clear the land and in this way much more land can be worked. Plowing also has the result of burying the cover vegetation. When the open fields are disced or harrowed after plowing, which break up clods and level the soil, the planting can be much more "efficient" and therefore much more land can be farmed.

Plowing breaks up and collapses the soil pores and water/air passageways. When the soil is overturned the entire soil community and their relationships are overturned. After a forest is cleared and the land is first plowed, the soil still maintains its crumbly, granular nature. It is soft and friable. After a few seasons the crumb structure has broken down and the clay aspect of the soil begins to predominate. The plowing, which creates chunks and clods, impairs the soil's ability to receive soil moisture which "wicks" upward by capillary action.

Edward H. Faulkner who wrote the classic treatise, *Plowman's Folly,* has shown how plowing disturbs the capillary action and how the moldboard plow by completely overturning the soil, reinforces this disturbance.

After plowing, the layer of surface vegetation comes to lie upside down in the soil. Thus, a layer of loosely pressed organic matter is compressed under the soil surface. This breaks the capillary action. The capillary action occurs when moisture evaporates from the surface and draws moisture upward. The ability of the water to move either up or downward is decreased.[6]

Plowing many soils results in the creation of a hardpan just below the bottom of the plow. As the plow goes through the soil year after year the layer created just below the foot of the plow becomes more and more compacted until it becomes an impervious layer. This allows water to accumulate and build-up to the level of the plant roots where it can drown the plants and kill the soil by salinization. The layer of hardpan traps minerals held in the water so that they concentrate as the water slowly evaporates. Eventually this creates a dead soil that can only be reclaimed with great difficulty.

When the soil is plowed, the deeper layer that contains soil moisture is overturned and exposed to wind and sun. This dries out the soil. The effect of direct sunlight on raw soil is very destructive. The sunlight oxidizes the soil. When the soil oxidizes, chemicals combine with oxygen and decreases their use to the soil community. The effect is to dry it out and lessen its fertility. All of this prepares the soil to be carried away by the wind and water.

As the plowed soil deteriorates, its clayey nature begins to predominate. The surface becomes more and more impermeable. Less moisture infiltrates to the ailing soil community. Water running off soil is the beginning of the end. As water runs off, it begins to carry soil with it. As the more friable top layers go, lower layers with less water absorbency are exposed so that the water runs off faster. As this occurs even more soil is carried away. Even in an undisturbed environment there is some erosion of soil off the land but it is much less than the volume of soil build-up. The following figures show the comparisons of erosion in the same area that have different types of soil cover:

"In Ohio it was reckoned that 174,000 years would be required to remove from 7 to 8 inches of top-soil by runoff in a forested area, 29,000 years in a meadow, 100 years if the soil is wisely planted with crop rotation and 15 years if corn alone is planted " (Bennett, 1939).[7]

The phenomenon of leaching is a pivotal factor in soil conditioning. Rainforest soils are leached constantly by the heavy rains. The large volume of water carries minerals from the topsoil down into the subsoil, but in desert environments, soil moisture evaporates more rapidly than it can be leached downward. This results in a higher level of nutrient/mineral buildup which can be exploited by irrigators. They can utilize the sandy soils, which have a relatively low concentration of humus but nonetheless are nutrient rich and grow substantial crops if water can be obtained. But buildup of nutrients in desert soils happens over a long period of time and soil can be exhausted quickly unless artificial fertilizers are applied. Organic feed for the soil could be applied, but in a desert environment the production of organic material is limited. In the formerly forested areas of Lebanon, now degraded to a semi-arid desert environment, people collect manure from the goats that graze the sparse brush in the mountains and transport it to Beirut and the coastal city, Tripoli, to the north, to fertilize orange and banana plantations.[8]

Soil Erosion

Soil can become exhausted in place and soil can be removed by erosion. Plow agriculture leads to soil erosion but there are also other civilized practices that create soil erosion. Grazing by livestock, deforestation, mining, and many other human activities all lead to erosion.

There are three basic types of erosion, these are gully, sheet and wind erosion. Gully erosion results in the familiar "erosion canyons" that we see on hillsides. Sheet erosion is a more camouflaged type in which large areas of a hillside slowly creep downhill to a "slump" at the foot of the slope. This type of erosion is sometimes only apparent when closely examined or when a "slump" can be seen at the bottom of an hill. Sheet erosion is generally found on inclined, plowed fields and steeper grazed pastures. Wind erosion occurs when the soil simply blows away. In some areas, especially flatlands, this type of erosion can become the predominate source of deterioration.

Soil impermeability, the failure of rain water to be absorbed and seep into the soil is the beginning of erosion. Deforestation, overgrazing, plowing, or other stripping of the vegetative cover lessens the possibility that rain will be slowed down and stopped by the absorption and containment by vegetation so that it may seep into the soil, subsoil and the underground waterways. As more soil is carried away, the more impermeable subsoil layers are exposed which causes more volume of water to run off faster. Because the less fertile subsoil is exposed, the vegetation that is adapted to the topsoil has less chance to re-establish itself. This contributes to the self-perpetuating downward spiral. This is the reason that the downward spiral, once triggered, is self-perpetuating. The rains continue to come, and continue to erode, but once the plants can no longer get a foothold the process will simply continue until it reaches bedrock or other impervious layer.

The failure of water to infiltrate to the groundwaters effects the hydrology of the entire region. Even in a semi-arid region, if the topsoil is intact and the vegetative cover exists to absorb a large percentage of the rainfall, the water will seep in to collect in the subsoil. There it will be held away from the heat and evaporative effects of the sun for the deeper plant roots. The water that drains further into the earth will come to reside in underground aquifers. In many cases these aquifers will drain out in springs in lower elevations, providing a slow dependable flow that energizes local ecosystems and creates a slow dependable year around stream flow in the area.

When soils are abused and the spiral of deterioration is triggered, the familiar flood/drought cycle begins. When the water runs off rapidly rather than infiltrating, this creates the flood. In the other half of the cycle, because the water is not retained by absorbent topsoil and as subsoil water, the springs dry up, the streams dry up and there is less vegetation to transpire moisture. Transpiration of moisture creates a more salubrious micro-climate for small micro-ecosystems under trees and in thicker patches of vegetation.

As the unnatural floods begin, and increase in severity, erosion canyons are torn out of the earth. Narrow stream beds with well vegetated banks are torn out and stream courses are widened. Anywhere that wide, primarily dry streambeds exist that are filled with boulders, gravel and large, dry sandbars, severe erosion is taking place. This is the image of a stream that has suffered flooding because of upland abuse.

As the flood waters rush down carrying sterile sand and gravel from an abused watershed, the erosion material begins to bury fertile lower elevation floodplains with this debris. The aquatic ecology of the stream is impaired or destroyed along with the fertile riparian (stream side, or canyon bottom) habitat. This is the history of civilization from China, to India, to the Caucuses of Central Asia, to Europe and now to the whole world. Civilization equals aridity.

The stark reality of this spiral of deterioration can be seen now in areas of India and in Southern Mexico where areas that were formerly rainforests are now desert in spite of occasional, heavy rains.

Researchers Anders Wijkman and Lloyd Timberlake in their study, *Natural Disasters: Acts of God or Acts of Man?*, find that drought and floods are the "natural" disasters that effect by far the largest number of people around the planet. As the planet deteriorates, the numbers rapidly increase. In the 1960's 18,500,000 people were effected by drought: in the 1970's 24,400,000 were effected. In the 1960's, 5,200,000 people were effected by floods and in the 1970's floods effected 15,400,000. [9]

Soil erosion is not an esoteric matter. Anywhere one is, it can be seen. It is possible to view any area and roughly conclude the erosion rate. In an uninjured climax condition, most waterways of the earth are, or were, clear. The discoloration of any stream or river means that the watershed is being abused. If the color of a body of water is green, it indicates that nutrients are eroding into the water causing a population explosion of plant organisms. If the color of the water tends toward brown, it is simply from gross movement of the soil and subsoil into the water.

Soil erosion is not a "glamour" issue with the world media but it is one of the most life threatening problems on the planet. Erosion hot spots are U.S. grain lands, Eastern Mexico, Northeast Brazil, North Africa, Sahel, Botswana-Namibia, Middle East, Central Asia, Mongolia, Yangtze River watershed of northern China, Himalayan foothills, Baluchistan, Rajasthan and Australia. This listing is of regions with present erosion emergencies, it does not list for example, regions already lost to erosion such as the southeastern U.S. or most regions which are experiencing, not emergency depletion, but serious and steady erosion. In addition to exhaustion of the soil, half of all arable land on the planet is experiencing erosion over and above any build-up of soil.[10]

Erosion is a contributory mechanism in the loss of arable land on the earth. Erosion, desertification, toxification, and non-agricultural uses will eat up one fifth of the world's arable land between 1975 and 2000. Another one fifth will go by 2025. These figures are for arable land and do not include the general erosion and degradation of lands all over the earth from human activities such as deforestation, overgrazing, fire, and other injudicious human occupancy of the land.

Soil Abuse by Grazing: Herding The Hooved Locusts

The herding of animals is the lowest possible productive use of the land, yet it is done over much of the planet. If the purpose were to feed people, rather than to pay off bank loans or make profits in the money economy- or in the pastoral, nomadic cultures, to inflate herd size and patriarchal egos- much better use of most lands could be instituted immediately.

The authors of *Forest Farming*, a permaculture textbook, report that herders can get an average of 200 pounds of meat from an acre of optimum grazing land. That same area of land could produce one and one-half tons of cereal grain, seven tons of apples, or 15-20 tons of flour from the pods of honey locust trees. Although there is no commercial market for it, honey locust flour is superior in nutritional value to any cereal grain.[11]

Much of the grassland, savanna, steppe-type area of the earth has evolved with wild grazing animals. The vegetation and the grazers perform many services for each other. The grazing animals act as seed transport and manuring agencies. When a herd of herbivores occasionally comes over an area their hooves churn up the topsoil, aerate it and press seeds into the soil so they can germinate. The hooves create small pockmarks in the soil where organic debris and water can collect- this is especially helpful in semi-arid areas. Given this moisture and the water or wind-borne mulch in the pockmark to retain water and to retard desiccation, the grass seed will have a good chance of germination. It is said that one could follow the bison herds of the Great Plains on their migration routes by tracking the kinds of grasses that they preferred. As the bison would travel these "highways of grass" each year they would also replant their preferred grasses.

Natural herbivores migrate, following the abundance of vegetation. With free-roaming animals in a natural setting there is no danger of overgrazing because when the vegetation is sparse in one area they simply move to another. Though this migration might appear to be casual, the life of the herbivore/vegetation association, evolving through tens of thousands of years, is a natural, potentiative system where all of the beings contribute to their collective survival.

The original herbivores in the Western U.S. were bison, elk, pronghorn, bighorn sheep, mule deer, blacktail deer, some small animals and some insects. Nancy and Denzel Ferguson, in their exposé of overgrazing, *Sacred Cows At The Public Trough*, write:

"Originally, between 5 and 10 million bison roamed the plains of Montana, Wyoming, Colorado, and the intermountain valleys and mountains of the West. Today the 11 western states (excluding Montana) support 495 bison—less than one ten-thousandth of the original number. Original pronghorn populations in the 11 western states numbered between 10 and 15 million compared with about 271,000 today, which is about 2 or 3 percent of the original number. Bighorn sheep have dropped from an estimated 1 to 2 million to 20,400 (perhaps 1 percent of the original number). Original populations of mule deer and blacktail deer are estimated at about 5 million (which may be high) as compared to about 3.6 million today. Finally, pristine populations of elk, which probably numbered about 2 million, have dwindled to about 455,000, a decline of about 75 percent."[12]

Each of these herbivores ate different varieties of plants. As they roamed, they cropped the land evenly. In the undisturbed natural world overgrazing is not a common problem. When these animals were replaced with domesticated cows (and sheep), the ecosystem began to go downhill, and the topsoil began to go down the river.

In Africa, it has been shown that when cows are inserted in grasslands and the multiplicity of herbivores occurring naturally, is eradicated, the production of meat goes down. According to a recent study, "... an untouched savanna is capable of an annual production of 24 to 37 tons of meat per square kilometer in the form of wild animals, while the best pasture-cattle systems in Africa can yield only eight tons of beef per square kilometer per year. Yet in the name of agricultural progress and the imperative of control, many ungulates are being threatened with extinction, and other herd sizes are being substantially reduced."[13]

The above comparison underlines a basic point. This point is, that always the insertion of civilized agriculture into natural systems lowers the net photosynthetic production, simplifies the environment and in many cases the amount of food civilized systems realize is much lower than could be realized by forager/hunters from the very same area.

The reason that the natural system is so much more productive in terms of grazing animals is that the natural animals can migrate, sometimes long distances, to crop the most abundant growths. They also crop different types of plants in the same area. That is, the elk with its wide mouth is primarily a grass grazer, the deer with it narrower mouth pokes about in the brush and trees for food, the pronghorn is a grass grazer though its preferred grasses are different than the elk's. The mountain sheep prefers a different set of plants, as do the rabbits, rodents and other herbivores. In the natural setting the entire range of vegetation is grazed and in the cow-sheep operation, a few species of annual grasses are the predominate target, and the natural animals are killed off or driven away.

Livestock have species of plants that they prefer. These confined animals will graze their preferred grasses until they are all gone, after which they will then start on their second preference, and so forth. As the annual and perennial grasses are grazed out, pioneer plants, tough grasses, forbs and brush that are acclimated to more arid conditions, move in to rescue the situation as soil erosion increases.

The damaging characteristic of the cow, to graze its preferred grass until it is gone, is one of the reasons that the natural mix of grasses in an ecosystem is so severely altered by grazing of domesticated animals. Even where there is an abundant stand of grass it may be grass that has succeeded because it is not favored by the cow. This is damaging to the ecosystem because this alters the food availability of the natural herbivores (if any have survived) and alters the ecology of the entire area.

The confined cattle alter the mix of native vegetation and eliminate species. They trample vegetation and compact soil. Historically, the cow and sheep have been used to graze land that has some ecological health. Later when the land is driven to more arid conditions with little grass and a predominance of woody forbs and brush, the goat will be brought in to crop that vegetation. Finally the land can be driven to the point that the goat can no longer benefit from it. There are millions of acres of the planet that began as forests or grasslands and are now in this condition of being so poor that they cannot even support goats.

The United States government, which controls most of the rangeland in the western United States, is standing by while the ranchers overgraze and destroy the lands of the American west. Because of overgrazing, millions of acres of the U.S. west have been invaded by exotic plants which colonize the bare ground where native grasses formerly grew. One of these grasses is "cheat grass," also known as feathery brome.

Cheat grass is an annual that has invaded from Asia, possibly transported in the gut of an imported animal or brought in by some misguided herder. It has a peculiar strategy for preparing its habitat. It is a fire adapted plant; that is, it uses fire to spread itself. With its fine lacy leaves and stems, it is considered to be 500 times more flammable than native grasses. The plant greens up early in the spring for about six weeks, sets seed and dies, covering the ranges with highly flammable material. Once it ignites, it burns rapidly, eliminating any other grass and vegetation that is not fire adapted. In this way other plants are burned off and new areas are opened for the spread of cheat grass. As with the exotic grasses planted by range management people such as crested wheat grass, few natural beings in the ecosystem are able to utilize cheat grass. Cows and domestic sheep can eat cheat grass for only about six weeks in the spring, when the plants are green. The bristlelike, spear-pointed covering of the seed of the cheat grass plant, called the awn, is designed to stick to animals and birds for transportation. If an animal grazes on the dried grass, there is danger of the seedheads of this grass imbedding themselves in the jowls of the animals and even in their ears and eyes. This causes infections and sometimes death.

Some of the damage caused by overgrazing in the U.S. west is readily apparent. One can observe the differences in grasses between the road-side right of ways and the grazed pastures. It is hard to miss the huge erosion canyons throughout the west. It takes considerable study, however, to realize how many of the native and proper plants which fit the natural array of the ecosystem have disappeared. Many of the plants now covering western range-lands are either part of the pioneer "first aid team" of native plants which has come in to save the area or are exotics from other continents invading the greatly degraded ecology.

As overgrazing triggers erosion the familiar syndrome of drought/flood begins as the entire hydrology of the area changes for the worse.

Today, 70 per cent of the land mass of the 11 U.S. western states is being grazed by domesticated animals. Only 17 per cent of land that the U.S. Bureau of Land Management manages in the west is described as being in good to excellent condition- by the BLM's own "in house" study. [14] Given the predilection of government agencies to inflate estimates of their own good works, there is no doubt that the land is in even worse shape that this dismal assessment indicates. Nonetheless, we may take this as an indication of the condition of private lands and of other public lands in the western U.S., including wildlife refuges, military bases, wilderness areas, and national forests, all of which are grazed.

In Australia large herbivores never existed until they were imported by Europeans. Recently, when aborigines decided to get away from populated areas and back to their lands in the outback near Ernabella and Papunya in the semi-arid area of the continent, they found that 60 per cent of the food plants for which they traditionally had foraged were extinct, and the rest were greatly diminished in numbers. This destruction has been caused by overgrazing by unnatural herbivores that have gone wild. Feral cattle, brumbies (wild horses), donkeys, camels, goats and rabbits are destroying Australia's interior.[15] Because these animals and the domesticated herbivores such as sheep and cattle are exotic, there are few pre-existing ecological relationships that they fit. For example, in areas that naturally host large grazing animals there are insects and microbes which inhabit and eat herbivore dung, break it down, bringing it into the food chain and into the soil as nutrient. In Australia none of this network has developed because there have never been large grazing animals. Every year, the nitrogen and other nutrients contained in many millions of tons of manure evaporate into the Australian air instead of enriching the soil, due to this lack, even though the introduction of these insects and micro lives has been attempted a number of times.[16]

In the semi-arid region of the Middle East, the stock population, consisting primarily of goats and camels, continues to eat up the remaining life. In their study of desertification, *Spreading Deserts - The Hand of Man*, Eric Eckholm and Lester Brown observe:

"The rangelands of northern Iraq, forage specialists figure, can safely sustain only 250,000 sheep without degradation — a far cry from the million or so that are currently eating away this resource base. Likewise, Syria's ranges currently feed triple the number of grazing animals they can safely support. In the initial stage of such degradation, inferior plant species replace more useful varieties. Then, sheep pastures become suitable only for the hardiest goats and camels. Finally, in the words of Ibrahim Nahal, 'In the advanced stage of deterioration the plant cover disappears as it is apparent in many of the steppe zones in Syria, Jordan, Iraq and the United Arab Emirates, etc., where the rangelands have turned into semi-arid deserts covered with a layer of gravel or into semi-sand deserts.'"[17]

Eckholm, in *Losing Ground*, documents land deterioration in the Rajastan, a semi-arid area of northwestern India which has experienced the severe pressure of the human population explosion familiar throughout the world:

"The practical consequence of this pressure has been the extension of cropping to sub-marginal lands fit only for forestry or range management, helping to make this perhaps the world's dustiest area. Meanwhile, as the land available for grazing shrinks, the number of grazing animals swells— a sure fire formula for overgrazing, wind erosion, and desertification. The area available exclusively for grazing in western Rajasthan dropped from thirteen million to eleven million hectares between 1951 and 1961, while the population of goats, sheep and cattle jumped from 9.4 million to 14.4 million. The livestock population has since continued to grow, while during the decade of the sixties the cropped area in western Rajasthan expanded further from 26 per cent to 38 per cent of the total area, squeezing the grazing even more."[18]

The experience of the Rajastan follows the basic pattern occurring on the grazed lands of the Earth. Despite all of the ballyhoo in the United States and other First World industrial nations about professional range management, technical expertise and technical solutions, grazed land everywhere is suffering. The overgrazing of the earth has nothing to do with range management, but has everything to do with money, political power and the values of empire culture.

Desertification

Deforestation and overgrazing eventually produce desertification. While the natural undisturbed deserts of the Earth are healthy, thriving, diverse ecosystems with many types of plants and animals, deserts created by poor land use are much more devoid of life. This is because the ecosystem has been shredded, unlike a natural desert where the organisms have mutually proliferated over tens of thousands of years.

The desertification of the planet is proceeding rapidly. Each year millions of new acres fall within the definition of "desert" to add to those already created. Deserts are usually created by destroying the vegetation of formerly semi-arid lands but deserts are sometimes the result of deforestation.

The total drylands of the world are 3.2 billion hectares (7.9 billion acres). Of this area 61 per cent are desertified. This is defined as a loss of more than 25 per cent soil nutrient and the consequent decline of the productivity of biomass. In 1980 the percentage of some dryland areas that had become desertified were; Mediterranean Europe-30 per cent, N. America-40 per cent, S. America & Mexico-71 per cent, Southern Africa-80 per cent, Mediterranean Africa-83 per cent, West Asia-82 per cent, South Asia-70 per cent, U.S.S.R.-Asia-55 per cent, China and Mongolia-69 per cent. The U.N. Environment Programme estimates that desertification threatens one-third of the earth's land surface. [19]

While deforestation and devegetation caused by clearing land for the plow contribute to desertification, as does firewood gathering, the chief culprit is overgrazing. In every area of the world where herding is a significant industry, desertification is spreading. One thinks of the goats of the Middle East and the devegetation of the Sahel in Africa but in all semi-arid ecosystems on the planet, deserts are spreading.

A Council on Environmental Quality report, published by the U. S. government in 1981 states:

"Desertification in the arid United States is flagrant. Groundwater supplies beneath vast stretches of land are dropping precipitously. Whole river systems have dried up; others are choked with sediment washed from denuded land. Hundreds of thousands of acres of previously irrigated cropland have been abandoned to wind or weeds. Salts are building up steadily in some of the nation's most productive irrigated soils. Several million acres of natural grassland are, as a result of cultivation or overgrazing, eroding at unnaturally high rates. Soils from the Great Plains are ending up in the Atlantic Ocean.

"All total, about 225 million acres of land in the United States are undergoing severe desertification-an area roughly the size of the 13 original states." [20]

In many areas of the world, firewood gathering is contributing greatly to deforestation, devegetation and desertification. In many Third World nations, most of the people must rely on wood as the source of their heat and cooking.

As the population explodes and urbanization rises, huge bare spots spread out for many dozens of miles from the cities as the country is gleaned of any combustibles. In many countries now the purchase of firewood takes a large share of the family income, in both rural and urban areas.

As a consequence of firewood shortage, people begin to use animal dung for fires. In the Andes, llama dung is used and in other areas sheep and cattle manure. As this dung is not returned to the soil, it represents another deprivation of the soil's fertility. "Between three hundred and four hundred million tons of wet dung—which shrink to sixty to eighty million tons when dried—are annually burned for fuel in India alone, robbing farmland of badly needed nutrients and organic matter. The plant nutrients wasted annually in this fashion in India equal more than a third of the country's chemical fertilizer use."[21]

Evapotranspiration is the phenomenon of moisture evaporation off the land. This moisture evaporates from soil and it is also transpired by plants. Bill Mollison in his *Permaculture: A Designers' Manual*, says that soil moisture varies from 2 per cent to 40 per cent of soil volume.[22] It should be noted also that the tons-per-acre of micro-organisms in soil, contain water in their bodies and this contributes to soil water retention- if the soil is healthy and has a high level of micro-organisms. As the natural cycles proceed, this moisture rising up from the land helps charge rain clouds by providing minute droplets of water which atmospheric moisture can condense around in the colder, higher altitudes. All of the fertile topsoil, world-wide, is a tremendous reservoir of water. The loss of topsoil and the progress of desertification lessens rainfall. As topsoil loss and desertification proceed the land itself becomes drier and a more desert type of plant regime becomes established. Civilization equals aridity.

Irrigation Projects: Green Today, Gone Tomorrow

Farmers, government bureaucrats and bankers love irrigation projects. They usually appear to give everybody something for nothing except the taxpayer who finances them and who often pays the subsidy to grow the food on the irrigated land. Large dams, irrigation projects and the modern industrial farming methods that have come with them have swept the world.

Water loss caused by evaporation from dams in semi-arid regions averages 50 per cent. As the water is impounded in a dam and then runs for sometimes many miles through canals, the salts and minerals in the water are continually being concentrated. More evaporation takes place when the water is spread across the earth. As irrigation water is spread over the fields, the water that is not taken up by the plants sinks toward the subsoil. In many cases this excess water fills the subsoil aquifers under the fields and the groundwater begins to rise toward the plant roots. Once this saline water hits the plant roots, they die. The rising water table evaporates through the surface of the soil by capillary action in a kind of "wick effect," leaving the characteristic snowy salt covering of the "alkali flats."

Another contributing factor in creating waterlogged, salinized soils is the buildup of fine silt which is brought into the fields by the irrigation water. This claylike material often collects into an impervious layer well below the surface. When this "hard pan" effect occurs water will build up on top of it and begin to drown the plant roots.

Irrigators manage to keep the concentrated salts and minerals from killing their cultivated plants by running enough water through the system to "flush" the fields, draining the runoff into some lower-elevation area. In modern irrigation projects this often involves digging deep under the field to place perforated pipes that drain the subsoil water out of the area. This expensive solution can only be used in selected high-profit areas that can justify the cost, or in areas where taxpayer subsidy is available. Where funds are not available for drainage and the land is subject to waterlogging, the land is eventually ruined. These problems effect tens of millions of acres of the planet.

Irrigation runoff water from modern systems contains all of the chemicals used in industrial agriculture including nitrates from fertilizers as well as concentrations of heavy metals, in addition to the salts and minerals concentrated from the soil. These poisoned waters have been responsible for the epidemic deaths of many animals and birds in wetlands where it collects. As irrigation water runoff goes back into the streams and rivers it adds to the destruction of the ecology of these bodies of water and also adds to the problems of other irrigators downstream who must try to irrigate with water that is more saline than normal and contains unknown quantities of fertilizer and poison. Runoff water from irrigated fields is often drained into natural wetlands and into low-lying "waste" areas. In these areas, the former life of the land tries to survive amid the whole inventory of life-killing effluent of industrial agriculture. The fish, frogs, birds and other life develop cancers, open sores, mutations, and other deadly afflictions. A recently-publicized case in point is the Kesterson Wildlife Refuge in the San Joaquin valley of California where wildlife, especially waterfowl, have been dying from concentrations of selenium and other poisons in the agricultural runoff that drains into the adjoining wetland refuge. Game officials have now closed the refuge and are trying to drive migrating waterfowl away from the area.

The San Joaquin valley in central California produces a large share of U.S. farm produce. A 1981 U.S. government publication states, "Today about 400,000 acres of irrigated farmland in the San Joaquin are affected by high, brackish water tables. Ultimately, by the year 2080, 1.1 million acres of San Joaquin farmland will become unproductive unless subsurface drainage systems are installed."[23] Many areas in the U.S. are losing land to salinization. As salinization increases, the land produces smaller and smaller crop yields over time. Eventually, when the soil community is completely destroyed, all farming will cease in these areas.

Irrigation projects are very expensive. In order to justify irrigating a new area, the entire mass production, mass marketing system must be brought in. In Third World countries, especially, this means eliminating subsistence farmers and indigenous tribal people. The industrial agriculture methods of the Green Revolution are inherently centralizing. They need large areas of land to which machines and industrial methods can be applied. This has the effect of strengthening the national elites and the hold of the transnationals in the countries where these methods are used.

The modern industrial practice of using wells for irrigation, which is now spreading world-wide with the Green Revolution, is fraught with problems. In the first place, most of these systems require motors that use fossil fuel which is in short supply and due to run out. Modern well irrigation salinizes the soil just as do other methods. But the most serious problem is that in many cases the irrigation well system is pumping the underlying aquifers dry. In some of these cases the land is subsiding, that is, it is cracking open in huge chasm rifts, or suddenly sinking a number of feet.

In the U.S., one fifth of the irrigated cropland is above the Ogallala aquifer which runs down the east side of the Rocky Mountains from South Dakota to Northwest Texas. The Ogallala contains water that was accumulated during Pleistocene times, fossil water. Since that time little additional accumulation has taken place. This aquifer is one half gone under 2,223,900 acres. It is calculated that it will be substantially gone sometime early in the next century.

European countries currently use three times more water than returns to natural sources. In North America the groundwater outtake is twice the replenishment rate.[24] In areas of Northern China, Tamil Nadu, India, Israel, Arabian Gulf, Mexico City, Southwestern Soviet Union, Europe, and in North America on the Great Plains, southern Arizona, and California, the ground waters are dropping precipitously.[25]

While the underground waters decline, the soil on the surface suffers from salinity and waterlogging.

In Pakistan, according to Georg Bergstrom:

"An estimated area of over two million hectares, a fifth of the annually cultivated area of the Indus Plain was severely affected; either yields were significantly cut by waterlogging and/or salinity, or production had ceased altogether. As many as forty-thousand additional hectares were falling into that category each year, a good share of them lost to cultivation altogether. And the productivity of many more millions of hectares was well below its potential level due to saline soils. Pakistan was losing a hectare of good agricultural land every twenty minutes, but gaining a new claimant on that land by birth every twenty-four seconds."[26]

Like the one-third of the arable land in Iraq that is still salinized and unusable from the Sumerian empire, many currently-irrigated acres will be permanently destroyed. Roughly one-third of the world's irrigated land is presently in danger.[27] Eckholm, quotes Soviet soil scientist V. Kovda, who estimates:

"60 to 80 percent of all irrigated lands are, due to inadequate drainage or canal lining, becoming gradually more saline and, hence, infertile. By (Kovda's) calculations, twenty to twenty-five million hectares of land have been laid waste over the centuries after the introduction of improperly managed irrigation, and two hundred thousand to three hundred thousand additional hectares—out of a total worldwide irrigated area of nearly two hundred million hectares—pass from cultivation each year due to waterlogging and salinity."[28]

Although touted as a "solution" to world food problems, irrigation has only short term benefits and many long term problems. Some major problems are already being caused by the large-scale dams central to many irrigation projects.

The Damn Dams

No dam will last indefinitely. Sooner or later, they will all silt up. This fact is never mentioned by the industrialists who profit by building them. Some dams in eroding watersheds in Latin America have an expected life of ten to fifteen years; others built in more ecologically stable areas may be expected to last as long as several hundred years. Silted up dams become wetlands or simply large banks of earth. Since the present dams are now constructed in the most optimum places on each river, there is little chance their benefit can be replaced by building more dams in less desirable sites. As the dams fill up with erosion material their use for hydroelectric generators is lessened because the flow of water cannot be maintained.

Large dams are such a bonanza, such a massive physical (if temporary) answer to immediate problems that everybody recommends them even though the dams of the planet will eventually choke much of the aquatic life flow system. Not only do dams feed the industrialist, the banker, the politician and the temporary laborer, but they are also an instrument of cultural transformation because the whole mass production regime of industrial agriculture with its fuels, fertilizers, and machines must be inserted with them. This means markets, profits, the realization of political strategies, centralization of power, and the continued marginalization of the poor. With enough money and guns, industrialists can ignore any consideration of the people, earth or cosmos —for awhile.

The water in freshwater lakes above the Panama Canal is used to regulate the level of the locks in the canal. Deforestation and destruction of the rainforest watershed above these lakes is causing them to silt up so that there is not enough volume to even out the wet/dry cycles. Eventually there will only be water during the rains. Ultimately, there will not be enough water to fill the locks of the canal during the dry season. This is an example of the types of problems that develop with large scale waterworks when large scale ecological destruction is occurring.

Other problems with large-scale waterworks are shown by the Aswan Dam in Egypt. For millennia the annual flooding of the Nile has refertilized the fields of the Egyptians. Its biological circulation is so rich that even after the ancient Egyptians destroyed the watershed's incredibly rich natural wetland ecology, an empire has been able to exist in this area for thousands of years. The huge Aswan dam, built in modern times by U.S.S.R. engineers, is finally succeeding in depleting and destroying what remains of Egypt's survival systems. The $1.3 billion dam which halted the flooding of the Nile was planned by the engineers to have two effects; irrigation and hydroelectric generation. Though the dam project is hailed for producing half of the country's electrical "needs," the authors of *Gaia: An Atlas of Planet Management* report on some of the problems it has created:

"Over one hundred tons of silt, clay, and sand, which once fertilized downstream fields during periods of flooding, are now silting up Lake Nasser, forcing increased imports of fertilizers. This lock-up of silt also hit downstream industries, starving Cairo brickmakers of a vital raw material, while the offshore sardine fisheries, which depended on the flow of nutrients from the Nile, were early casualties. The Nile Delta itself is in retreat....Simultaneously, problems of soil salinity and waterlogging have been accentuated. An FAO (Food and Agricultural Organization) study concluded that 35 per cent of Egypt's cultivated surface is afflicted by salinity and nearly 90 per cent by waterlogging. To crown all this, the water-based parasitic disease schistosomiasis has exploded among people living around Lake Nasser."[29]

An investigation revealed that the sandstone bottom of Lake Nasser, the artificial lake created behind the dam, did not seal but allowed considerable seepage through the lake floor. Evaporation from the surface of the 200-mile long Lake Nasser, and from the extensive system of irrigation ditches is high and there is less total water available for use than before the dam was built.

Worldwide, an estimated 250 million people are infected by schistosomiasis. The parasite which causes the disease, a blood/liver fluke, lives in snails part of its life cycle but lays its eggs in humans. The mature parasite, a forktailed worm, affixes itself to humans when the people enter the water of irrigation ditches or the river. The worm bores into the human and seeks out the liver where it lays its eggs. The eggs pass from the person by excretion. As they enter the waterways, they are ingested by the snails in the form of larvae. The parasites drain their human hosts' physical energy. Persons infected in these agricultural countries are able to work only a few hours each day.

The alternate flooding and drying of the land near the Nile formerly controlled snail populations who host part of the worms' life cycle. The flooding washed them out to sea. Since the building of the dam, the snails have multiplied. It is estimated that 70 per cent of the population of Egypt is now infected with schistosomiasis.

Sharp declines in agricultural production among a population with one of the worlds' low ranking, average annual incomes, already close to starvation levels, forced the Egyptian government to use a part of the electrical power produced by the new dam to operate fertilizer plants. The application of chemical fertilizers has, to some extent, temporarily offset the losses, but yield is still 20 per cent less than in pre-Aswan days.

A result of the new industrial agricultural techniques has been to inject herbicides, insecticides and chemical fertilizers into the now nutrient-poor Nile, through irrigation runoff. This effluent plus the lack of nutrient flow once provided by the river has damaged the five shallow lakes in the Nile Delta. One of these lakes alone formerly yielded 15,000 tons of fish annually for this protein-starved nation. The lakes themselves were created when sediments carried by the flooding river created sandbars in the delta, which in turn caused the large shallow lakes behind them. Now that the annual deposition is filling up Lake Nasser rather than flowing downstream, the ocean is eroding the sandbars and soon there will be no lakes. Nineteen thousand people live in this area and are dependent upon the fishing industry in those lakes.

For many years, a sizable fishing industry had existed off the Mediterranean coast of Egypt. Nearly half of the 18,000-ton annual catch consisted of sardines. When the nutrients of the Nile ceased to be injected into the marine ecology, the Egyptian fish exportation dropped by one-half and the sardine catch went down 500 tons.

Now that the waters of the Nile are either evaporating from Lake Nasser or seeping into its sandstone floor, the Mediterranean is deprived of an important fresh water supply. Because of this, the salinity of the entire Mediterranean is rising and threatening all fishing industries of the area.[30]

In this review of irrigation we see that in many areas it is only a short-term gain. The long term deficits will arrive in the next decades for us to deal with just as the exploding human population is overwhelming food supplies.

NOTES

1   Permaculture: A Designers' Manual. Bill Mollison. Tagari Pub.
    Tyalgum, Australia. 1988. p. 205.
2   The Soil and Health; A Study of Organic Agriculture. Sir Albert
    Howard. Schocken Books. New York. 1975. p. 24.
3   Mollison, op. cit. p. 183.
4   Mother Earth News. "John Jeavons:Digging Up The Future." Pat Stone.
    Jan/Feb. 1990. #121. pp.45-51.
    Seed Catalogues and books on Biointensive methods may be ordered
    from: Bountiful Gardens, 19550 Ridgewood Road, Willits, California
    95490.
5   State of the World 1985. Lester R. Brown, et. al. W.W. Norton & Co.
    New York. 1985. p. 29.
6   Plowman's Folly. Edward H. Faulkner. U. of Oklahoma Press.
    Norman, Oklahoma. 1943.
7   Before Nature Dies. Jean Dorst. Houghton Mifflin Co. Boston. 1970.
    p.134.
8   Man and the Mediterranean Forest; A History of Resource Depletion.
    J.V. Thirgood. Academic Press. New York. 1981. p. 102. (sourced as
    Rollet, 1948).
9   Natural Disasters; Acts of God or Acts of Man?. Anders Wijkman &
    Lloyd Timberlake. New Society pub. Santa Cruz, CA. 1988. p.24.
10 Gaia: An Atlas Of Planet Management. Norman Myers, General Editor.
    Anchor Books. Garden City, New York. 1984. p.40.
11 Forest Farming: Toward A Solution To Problems of World Hunger and
    Conservation. J. Sholto Douglas & Robert A. de J. Hart. Rodale Press.
    Emmaus, Pa. 1978. p. 5 (nutrition- p.37).
12 Sacred Cows at the Public Trough. Denzel & Nancy Ferguson. Maver-
    ick Pub., Drawer 5007, Bend, Oregon 97708. p. 116.
13 Ecosytems, Energy, Population. Jonathan Turk, Janet T. Wittes, Robert
    Wittes, Amos Turk. W.B. Saunders Co. pub. Toronto. 1975. p. 123.
14 Free Our Public Lands. Lynn Jacobs, P.O. Box 2203, Cottonwood,
    Arizona 86326. pp.3,4.
15 Arid-Land Permaculture: Special reference to central Australian
    Aboriginal Outstations. Bill Mollison. Tagari Community, P.O. Box 96,
    Stanley, Australia. 7331. November, 1978. pp.2,18.
16 The Hungry Planet; The Modern World at the Edge of Famine. Georg
    Borgstrom. Collier Books. New York. 1972. p.196.
17 Worldwatch Paper #13. Worldwatch Institute. Washington, D.C. p.12.

18   Losing Ground: Environmental Stress and World Food Prospects. Erik
      P. Eckholm. W.W. Norton & Co. New York. 1976. pp.63,64.
19   World Resources 1987: An Assessment of the Resource Base that
      Supports the Global Economy. A Report by The International Institute
      for Environment and Development and The World Resources Institute.
      Basic Books. New York. 1987. p.289.
20   Desertification of the United States. David Sheridan. Council on
      Environmental Quality. U.S. Government Printing Office. #334-983/
      8306. 1981. p.121.
21   Eckholm. Losing Ground. op. cit. p.105.
22   Permaculture:A Designers' Manual. Bill Mollison. Tagari pub.
      Tyalgum, Australia. p. 203.
23   Sheridan. Desertification of The United States. op. cit. p.31.
24   Too Many: An Ecological Overview Of Earth's Limitations. Georg
      Borgstrom. Collier Books. New York. 1969. p.144.
25   Brown. State of the World 1985. p.53.
26   Eckholm. Losing Ground. op. cit. p. 120.
27   ibid. p.124.
28   ibid. pp. 124,125.
29   Myers. Gaia. op. cit. p. 132.
30   The Last Days of Mankind: Ecological Survival or Extinction. Samuel
      Mines. Simon & Schuster. New York. 1971. pp. 10-12.
      The Hungry Planet: The Modern World at the Edge of Famine. Georg
      Borgstrom. Macmillan. New York. 1972. pp. 499-501.
      Ecology and Field Biology. 2nd. ed. Robert Leo Smith. Harper & Row.
      New York. 1974. p. 81.

CHAPTER 4

THE FOREST

The forests are the "lungs of the earth. "They respire oxygen and inhale carbon dioxide; they also build soil, absorb moisture and translate sunlight into biomass more efficiently than any other ecosystem on earth.

In the view of Rudolf Steiner, the German mystic and creator of Biodynamic Gardening, the forest organism itself has organs. These include the soil, the plant stalks and the wind. The soil is the digestive organ of the forest.

The wind is the breath of the forest.

The tree bodies are the vascular system. From their roots deep in the ground trees bring up both water and minerals. Transpiration humidifies the air, moderates extremes of temperature, and create complex micro-climates, rich habitat for many diverse life forms. The minerals come to rest in the tree's body, which will one day become topsoil.

One of the great benefits of forests is to moderate hard rains so that the water soaks into the soil and subsoil. Rain soaks into the forest and feeds the streams and aquifers. Because a native old growth forest recycles nutrients so efficiently, the water running from it is very pure, with little mineral content and few suspended solids.

In this way a forest supports the adjacent aquatic ecology. It is the quality of water that drains from the forest which is important. In the temperate zone forests whole fisheries have been destroyed when logging, especially clear-cut logging, takes place. Without the trees, erosion soon begins to change the chemical and particulate composition of the water. Migrating salmon for example require small gravel in the stream bed for their spawning. The gravel must be just the right size relative to their eggs so the eggs will be protected from predators. It must be porous enough so that the fry, when they hatch, can escape. When silt covers the gravel, the fish eggs die, fisheries are destroyed, the habitat of the aquatic plants is impaired and culinary water supplies are degraded.

Forests have a great effect on rainfall. They actually create rain. Trees send a huge volume of moisture into the atmosphere. One medium sized, ordinary elm tree for example, will transpire 15,000 pounds of water on a clear, hot, dry, day. As a storm front moves through from the ocean, the moisture that has evaporated upward from the land helps to recharge rain clouds in a continuous cycle. The moisture from the earth surface is in micro-droplets that atmospheric moisture condenses around, then falls back to earth. Vast amounts of water vapor rise to the clouds, then fall again as rain.

In both temperate and tropical rainforests there is also the phenomena of fog drip. As fog rolls through, water droplets are caught on the vegetation and drip down to moisturize the lower zones. The capture of water by this action of fog drip adds significantly to the moisture levels of these forests.

Another significant effect of forests is the creation of electrically charged, negative ions. Negative ionization occurs heavily near waterfalls, on ocean beaches and in moist forests. A concentration of ionization creates an electrical field. The work of pumping water up out of the subsoil and transpiring it tends to moisturize the area and contributes to the negative ionization. Laboratory experiments show that plants will grow significantly larger in a negative ion-rich environment than in neutral or positively-charged environments such as cities or hot, windy deserts.

The forest is not simply a random group of trees. It is a vast complex of organisms which have lived together and differentiated their forms and relationships over millions of years. Their circulation of energies creates a giant metabolism. Native forest provides habitat for the largest number of species per acre of any ecosystem, except possibly a coral reef. Because of this, reforestation cannot repair damage. When industrialists replant forests they do not replant with the intention of returning a native forest ecosystem. Usually the land is replanted with some designer tree species that has economic importance and other species are left out. Tremendous amounts of money are now being spent to create genetically engineered trees for replanting cutover or damaged sites. In fir forests for example, after the clear cut, the industry spends millions of dollars, mostly on poisons, trying to defeat the healing succession of the forest in order to immediately replant fir trees. If the previous forest was a mix of cedar, alder and other trees with the fir, only the commercially valuable fir will be replanted. All of these replanting efforts are essentially "tree plantations" and were never meant to recreate a native forest. The true native forest with all of its complex web of life is gone and replaced by a tree farm, more like a corn field but with a longer life-span. Far from being a perpetual forest, as the ballyhoo of corporate public relations offices would like to picture it, these tree farms function in permanently damaged soils and reduced nutrient condition.

The human family has done very well as forest dwellers for several million years. Native people of the great forests of China, Europe, and the mixed forest of the eastern North American continent lived in one of the richest habitats possible. The few native agriculturists remaining in tropical rainforests can today easily grow more food per unit of energy input than the modern industrial system. Some continue to practice <u>swidden</u> agriculture, one of the most energy-efficient systems known. The ancient system rotates small clearings in the forest. The dozens of domesticated and semi-domesticated garden plants feather off into the mature forest so that there is no real break in the ecosystem. These complex gardens are products of the natives' deep knowledge of living things. The gardens flow with the tendency of natural life toward diversity and mutual benefit.

Later, as a part of our analysis of solutions we will present a modern version of this sophisticated food system.

How the Forests Went Down

It is estimated that more than one third of the earth was forested prior to the culture of empire. This is roughly 30 billion hectares (nearly 94 billion acres).[1] The most recent estimates show that only about a tenth of the forests remain, some 4 billion hectares (about 9.9 billion acres).[2] It is important to note here that these figures refer to any assemblage of trees, not just the climax ecosystems. The amount of uninjured old growth forest remaining has never been calculated; indeed, this minuscule, high-value remainder is so much in demand by the timber industries of the world that any calculation would be immediately outdated because the trees are disappearing so fast.

When forests are cut, the rainfall which the trees had moderated, rushes over the bare surface of the Earth, carrying off the loose soil. The silt-laden runoff swells and overflows the riverbanks, flooding the lowlands, scouring out and widening the riverbeds. When the living system of roots which held the soil on the hillsides is gone, landslides become increasingly frequent. When the dry season returns, no reserves of moisture remain in the ravaged soil. A worsening cycle of flooding and drought begins. Without the moderating effect of the transpiration of the trees, and without the forests' tendency to attract rainfall, drought increases.

Throughout the world this process of depletion is occurring. If it were not for all of the other crises on the planet, the disappearance of the world's forests alone would be considered a planetary emergency, so important are the services of forests to the planetary ecosystem.

All of the major forest ecosystems of the planet are under severe attack. The forests of all continents are suffering severely.

Throughout the foothills of the Himalaya Mountains forest destruction is proceeding rapidly. Goat herders work their way up the slopes felling trees, selling the firewood, burning it for their own use and feeding the twigs and leaves to the animals. These goat people are often followed by people who then try to farm the steep slopes. The demand for firewood in the denuded lowlands and the attempts to farm even the steep, high mountainsides, is stripping the land. Floods, erosion and drought are the result.

Nepal is headed toward desert status. Firewood shortages in Nepal force the people to use dung and crop residues for fuel to heat their habitations and cook their food. Authorities calculate that depriving the soil of this dung and residue reduces the annual grain yield of the country by 15 per cent.[3]

Through the ages of empire, forests have receded before the goats of the herders and the people with the plow. Because forest soils are rich, civilized people always seek to clear them and plow the fertile soil. This destruction is rivaled by that of the charcoal burners who have gone out like locusts and stripped the forests for the metal smelters, for limekilning, for the ceramics industry, and to provide fuel for cooking and heating of houses. The areas of the ancient empires were deforested early. For example, the plateau east of the Turkish mountains, where the present city of Ankara is located, was once a forested region. Its fate was similar to that of the Armenian highlands. Authorities believe that the original forest covered 70% of the land area of the plateau; forest cover is now reduced to 13%. The remainder of the plateau has now irreversibly regressed to steppe conditions.[4]

Author Thor Heyerdhal has made many journeys in reed rafts since his book Kon Tiki was published. In a recent journey he sailed his reed raft along the southern coast of Arabia. He and his crew hauled ashore in a desolate area of Oman. In a short expedition inland they discovered a huge open pit copper mine from the Sumerian era five thousand years in the past. It is difficult, now, to imagine that this desert once harbored forests which could support smelting on such a scale. But the evidence is there.

Even the Sinai and the Negev which are located to the East and Southeast of the present state of Israel, bear evidence of past, perhaps abundant forests. The 1960 investigations of Sir William Flinders Petrie into mining operations in the Wadi Nash area of the western Sinai desert, believed to date from the third millennium, B.C., yielded unmistakable clues:

"(Petrie) found a bed of wood ashes 100 feet long, 50 feet wide and 18 inches deep, and also a slag dump from copper smelting, 6-8 feet deep, 500 feet long and 300 feet wide. It seems that the adjacent area, now desert, must have borne combustibles during the period when the mines were operating. Similarly, in the Negev, copper smelting kilns of a highly developed kind dating from 1000 B.C. have been found in the now quite desert-like Wadhi Araba."[5]

The forests of the Mediterranean region all figured centrally in the strategies of the empires through the ages. Besides being burned at the smelters, forests were the raw material for the shipbuilding industry. As nearby forests disappeared, a major thrust of imperial strategies was to conquer the forests of other areas to be used to build more ships for war and for trade. Whole empires rose and fell based on the availability of forests.

The wars of the empires also caused much deforestation because of deliberate burning of whole forests in order to debilitate the enemy. Many of the instruments of war required forests. Wood was used for chariots, battering rams, fortifications, scaffolding and other instruments of the siege against walled cities. Forests were used in the siege of Lachish, in 588 B.C. by the Babylonian, Nebuchadnezzar. "After 2500 years, layers of ash several metres thick still remain, higher than the remains of the fortress walls. The hills for miles around were cleared of trees. The wood was piled outside the walls and fired. Day and night sheets of flame beat against the walls until eventually the white-hot stones burst and the walls caved in."[6]

Archeology corroborates Biblical reports that much of what is presently Lebanon had closed canopy forests and Israel was once forested or at least had considerable natural tree cover. The cedar forests of Lebanon were logged early by the Egyptian empires to be used for building materials and ships, and by all the following empires until they were gone. Today, the only remaining remnant groves of the Cedars of Lebanon are located in some of the monastery yards which exist in the former forest habitat. A few years ago, when a small amount of forest still stood outside of the monasteries, a U.N. Food and Agriculture report recorded a scene that is ages old but still continues in remnant forests throughout the world:

> "In the Lebanon mountains...the scene had to be witnessed to be believed for there one can see the most incredible scenes of wanton destruction of the last remnants of these beautiful trees. Not only are the last trees being sought out and hacked down for timber and fuel, but one sees mature trees being lopped and actually felled in order to provide goat fodder. So heavy is goat grazing...that the flocks have already consumed nearly all forms of vegetation within their reach. The shepherds, unperturbed, have therefore resorted to felling the last remnants of high forest in order to satisfy the empty bellies of their ravenous flocks. It is an astonishing sight to see a fine cedar or silver fir tree felled for this purpose and then to see hundreds of hungry goats literally pounce upon it the moment it falls to earth and devour every vestige of foliage from the branches. It does not take many minutes for such a flock to strip a tree of its foliage. The felled tree has then served the shepherd's purpose and is left to rot where it fell, he then turns his attention to the next tree and so on. (FAO,1961)"[7]

The practice of destroying forests as a war strategy continues today. Defoliation of the tropical forests of Vietnam stands out as an egregious example. As of this writing [1989], U.S. "humanitarian" aid to the Nicaraguan Contras is being used to purchase chainsaws so that they can destroy and incidentally make some money from the sales of irreplaceable tropical forest along Nicaragua's southern border. Contra attacks have also targeted ecological restoration efforts. In Guatemala, the Drug Enforcement Administration of the United States government has sprayed many thousands of acres of tropical rainforest. Because of the secretive nature of the project it is not known what is being sprayed but it is known that many unnatural fires have been occurring in the Guatemalan forests recently and this indicates that the forest has been debilitated.

Deforestation Follows the March of Empire

The bulk of what was left of the North African forests was burned by the Moors in the early Middle Ages on their way to Spain. The forests of Spain and Italy dwindled over the time of the empires and then their destruction was given a sudden spurt by the Moors who brought sheepherding. The deforestation of Spain and Italy became severe at that time.

The great forests of Europe and the British Isles began to go down for Celtic bronze smelters. Destruction stepped up with the Romans, who cleared the land for agriculture and shipbuilding. European forest destruction continues to the present day.

As colonists invaded North America, they simply burned huge tracts of forest in order to open it up to European-style agriculture. In 1756 John Adams spoke for the perception of the empire. Referring to the area of the continent now covered by cities, industrial wastelands, toxic waste dumps, poisoned air, poisoned waters and forests dying from acid rain, he observed:

"The whole continent was one continued dismal wilderness, the haunt of wolves and bears and more savage men. Now the forests are removed, the land covered with fields of corn, orchards bending with fruit and the magnificent habitations of rational and civilized people."

In Canada the southern agricultural regions have lost two-thirds of their forests. In the United States, deforestation has had a longer history. "In the United States 900 million acres were originally wooded with more than 1,100 species of trees, a hundred of which had great economic value. Only 647 [species] remain and only 44 million acres have preserved their original forest."[8]

Farther south on the American continent, Mexico, which was originally 50 per cent forested[9] has lost one-fourth of its forest lands each century since the conquest.[10] Much of the forest of Mexico went to fire the smelters to melt the ores of Mexico's mines. In some areas whole forests have disappeared for this purpose. Today, there are no forests in Mexico that are in their original condition.

The Poison Air, The Poison Rain

Not only are chainsaws, roadbuilding and land clearing threatening forests, now, the airborne poisons that float up off of civilized areas are killing the forests of the earth. Notice first began to be taken when lakes began to die. After the biological death of hundreds of lakes in Scandinavia and North America, scientists concluded that it was something in the air that was causing it. Then it was realized that forests were also dying. There is controversy as to which combination of chemicals is doing the most harm, but there is no doubt that the airborne poisons floating off industrial areas is the cause. These contaminants are changing the chemistry of whole regions. The acidity is changing the pH (acid/alkaline) balance of the soils. Plants are specifically adapted to this balance. Different species can tolerate different levels of acidity. The plants that grow in any ecosystem, grow there because they are adapted to exactly that soil. As acid rain changes this balance over time, not only forests but whole ecosystems will die out.

There are many areas in Russia, Scandinavia, Europe and North America near industrial zones where forests are already dead. Even areas where there are green and apparently healthy forests there is also damage. Close study has shown that the rate of growth of trees slows down when they are impacted by the poisoned air. Investigation has shown also that regeneration rates slow down or stop. That is, there are fewer or no infant trees growing up from the forest floor.

In Central Europe, the Worldwatch Institute says that: "Trees covering more than 5 million hectares-an area nearly half the size of East Germany- now show signs of injury linked to air pollutants." In North America, forest death is beginning in some areas of the northeastern U.S., southern Canada and with trees in and around Mexico City. In southern California, the Southeast and Appalachia studies have shown impact. It is safe to say that anywhere indus- trial poisons reach, ecological damage occurs.

Acid rain not only effects the natural ecology, but people and agricultural crops as well. The Worldwatch Institute states that: "In the United States, [ground level] ozone is lowering the productivity of corn, wheat, soybeans, and peanuts, with losses valued at $1.9-4.5 billion each year."[11] Poison industrial air causes human allergies, contributes to emphysema, heart disease and other medical conditions.

The Vanishing Tropical Rainforest

Tropical rainforests are the womb of life on this planet. Some of the older tropical forest areas have been standing for 70 to 160 million years. Norman Myers points out that, "Following the glaciations of the Ice Ages, when much of the temperate zones became barren, tropical forests supplied a reservoir of life forms by which the sterilized areas recovered much of their biological health."[12] As we slide into the depths of the crisis of the Final Empire much disruption will be due to the destruction of tropical rainforest. One of the immediate effects is the greenhouse effect. The destruction of tropical forests contributes a large portion to the carbon dioxide buildup because tropical forests are the major reservoirs of carbon on the planet. As tropical forests are burned and decomposed, the carbon dioxide goes into the atmosphere along with that from burning fossil fuel to produce the greenhouse effect.

Forests in general and tropical forests in particular are stabilizers of climate for the planet. The green mat absorbs heat and generates rain. These factors have led to the climatic patterns that we now have. When these factors are gone, we can expect wild fluctuations in all meteorological systems. Civilization equals aridity. As we reach the depths of the crisis we can expect heat and aridity, interspersed with torrential rain. There will be unusual winds, tornadoes and cyclones as weather systems at different elevations of the atmosphere mix.

The destruction of the bulk of the tropical forests has happened in the last half of the Twentieth Century. It is a phenomenon of excess human population, extortion by the transnational corporate elite and clearance for temporary cattle grazing by colonial elites. In 1950, 15 per cent of the earth's surface remained covered by tropical forest. By 1975 this was down to 12 per cent and, given the general exponential increase of civilization, it will be gone by 2000.[13] The rate of destruction is so large and increasing so fast that in the eighteen years between 1966 and 1984 the area of tropical forest in Ivory Coast was down 56 per cent; in Gambia, 35 per cent; in Costa Rica, 45 per cent; in El Salvador, 37 per cent; in Nicaragua, 33 per cent; in Ecuador, 17.5 per cent; in Thailand, 40 per cent; in the Philippines, 28 per cent; and in Australia, 23 per cent.[14]

The earth's islands have been devastated by the expansion of the European empire. Islands, because of their isolation usually develop delicate and unique life systems. They are easily approached and easy to ship "resources" from, so they are easily extorted. Because islands are usually small and easily controlled, colonial elites have been able to remove their raw materials quickly. Haiti was once a tropically forested island. Now, less than 2 per cent of its original forest remains. After the Native American population was worked to death, the colonial elite used African slaves to work the soils of the bottom lands with plantations. After the elite was dispatched by a slave revolt, population began to climb and even the mountainsides were stripped. The denudation of the remaining forest has reduced the rainfall by nearly half in the last ten years. The country now imports 70 per cent of its food.[15]

The Planetary Greenhouse

Among the swift planetary changes about to occur within the next several decades is the warming of the earth caused by the "Greenhouse effect."The warming of the atmosphere is caused in part by the increase in carbon dioxide created by human activities. The burning of fossil fuels and deforestation are the primary producers of the carbon dioxide abundance. The other sources of warming are methane, the chlorofluorocarbons, oxides of nitrogen and low elevation ozone. The effect of these substances in the high atmosphere is to reflect heat back to the surface of the earth rather than allow it to refract off into space. Beginning with the industrial revolution, the level of carbon dioxide in the atmosphere began to rise. In the past one hundred years the level of carbon dioxide has risen twenty five per cent and the level of atmospheric methane has doubled.[16]

There is little scientific dispute that a planetary warming will occur because of the Greenhouse phenomenon, although there is considerable dispute concerning the intricacies of all of its effects, especially in local regions. This change that the planet is about to undergo will be extremely swift on a geological time scale. It will shred ecosystems. We know that some plant and animal species are more resilient when impacted with temperature and climactic changes than others. The most susceptible will be the first to go and as the web of the ecosystem begins to develop "blank spaces," the natural flows of biological energy will be disrupted.

The effects of empire are to shift planetary energy flows out of cycle. The Greenhouse effect is one of the major influences in this disruption. As the cycles of life are deformed on earth we can expect to see wild fluctuations in temperature, moisture, winds, ocean currents and other macro-flows of planetary energies.

One aspect of our prescription for balanced living will be to create large inventories of seed. We do not know what the climates will bring specifically, but the wider range of seed that we have and the wider diversity of our food growing system will add to our survival.

The Failing Ozone Layer

An important role of the high atmospheric ozone layer is to filter out ultra-violet light. A hole in the ozone layer has been opening over the Antarctic each year and growing larger. The breakdown of the chemical makeup of the ozone layer is caused by chlorofluorocarbons, particularly, cfc-11, and cfc-12. These are produced by refrigerants, aerosol propellants, solvents and blowing agents for plastic foam production.([17]) The immediate effect of increased ultra-violet light on humans will be increased incidence of skin cancer. The effects on the ecology are less well understood. Different species of plants and animals will react in different ways to the increase in ultra- violet light. As these impacts deepen the ecological system will be damaged in ways similar to the changes being created by the Greenhouse effect. The species most susceptible to the changes will be the first to go and as they go the ecosystems will progressively deteriorate. The changes from the thinning ozone layer and the Greenhouse effect will be so swift that ecosystems will not have time to adjust to the changes such as they did when the ice age retreated over many hundreds of years.

NOTES

1   1988 International Green Front Report. Michael Pilarski. Friends of the
     Trees pub. P.O. Box 1064, Tonasket, WA 98855. p.11.
2   World Resources 1987: An Assessment of the Resource Base that
     Supports the Global Economy. International Institute for Environment
     and Development and the World Resources Institute. Basic Books. New
     York. 1987. pp. 58,59. (This study gives a figure of 4.1 billion hectares
     of forest remaining).
     State of the World 1988. Lester Brown, et. al., Worldwatch Institute.
     W.W. Norton. New York. 1988. p.83. (This study gives a figure of 4.2
     billion hectares of forest remaining).
3   Brown. op. cit. p.88.
4   Man and the Mediterranean Forest: A history of resource depletion. J.
     V. Thirgood. Academic Press. 1961. p. 52.
5   ibid., p. 57.
6   ibid., p. 58–59.
7   ibid., p.73.
8   Before Nature Dies. Jean Dorst. Houghton Mifflin Co. Boston. 1970.
     p.136.
9   Losing Ground: Environmental Stress And World Food Prospects. Erik
     P. Eckholm. W.W. Norton & Co. New York. 1976. p.35.
10   The Hungry Planet: The Modern World at the Edge of Famine. Georg
     Borgstrom. Collier Books. New York. Second Edition. p. 309.
11   State of the World 1985. Lester R. Brown, et. al. W.W. Norton & Co.
     1985. p.121.
12   The Primary Source: Tropical Forests And Our Future. Norman Myers.
     W.W. Norton & Co. 1984. p. 12.
13   Gaia: An Atlas of Planet Management. Norman Myers, General Editor.
     Anchor Books. Garden City, New York. 1984. p. 42.
14   World Resources 1987. op. cit. pp. 268-269.
15   The Oregonian. (newspaper) Portland, Oregon. 7/21/88. p. B-3.
16   Scientific American. September, 1989. Vol. 261, #3. "The Changing
     Climate," by Stephen H. Schneider. P. 73.
17   Scientific American. op. cit. "The Changing Atmosphere," Thomas E.
     Graedel & Paul J. Crutzen. p. 63.

CHAPTER 5

THE PHANTOM AGRICULTURE

The spread of civilized agriculture is undoubtedly the greatest catastrophe ever to strike the planet. Previous disasters such as the die-off of the dinosaurs are measured by the number of species lost. Since the advent of agriculture we are beginning to count the number of ecosystems destroyed. Each major food gaining method of the imperial system —herding, irrigation, plow agriculture, and industrial agricultural— progressively depletes the ability of the earth to sustain life. Civilized agriculture cannot endure.

The incredible growth of food supply which has supported the huge populations of past and present empire cultures has been funded by extorting fertility from the planetary life. Use of fossil fuels has exponentially increased the damage. These very food production systems have ravaged much of the earth where empires have historically been based. Empire food systems short-circuit the natural energy flow systems of the earth, first by eliminating the natural vegetation, then by draining the fertility of the soil with alien crops. The natural climax ecosystem's fundamental contribution to life on Earth is to build soil. The exhaustion of the solar gain deposited in the planetary soil bank for our future life is ultimately the most devastating effect of empire. If any climax ecosystem remains it can spread again in hundreds or thousands of years but soil build up occurs in longer time frames.

The most complex natural systems generate the largest amount of energy and provide maximum stability. One reason for this is because a complex system includes a large number of sub-systems which can be used as alternatives in case of crisis. Complex ecosystems generate specialized plants and animals uniquely suited to maximize the energy of the system. Diversity creates stability.

Russell E. Anderson, a student of biological energy flows and energy pathways explains the energetic potential of the climax ecosystem in his book, *Biological Paths To Self-Reliance*:

"An undisturbed ecosystem, ...will develop or mature to a level of complexity in which energy-use efficiency is maximized and a steady or 'climax' state is achieved in which no <u>net</u> production occurs, i.e., the total bio(logical)-mass does not change. This climax status, characterized by great complexity, redundancy and diversity in the food chain, represents the ecosystem with the greatest energy capture and use efficiency."[1]

While the thrust of the life of the planet is to increase complexity (diversity) and maximize energy circulation (sharing), the thrust of Empire is to simplify. Even if the agriculturalist did nothing but clear away the climax ecosystem, the planet's life would eventually run down. Because the soil is a perpetual flow system itself, it must be fed so that it can continue to maintain. If deprived of feed it will decline. Civilized development of all types interferes with the creation of soil. The climax ecosystem is the real planetary life. The whole living system we call the "natural world" functions together as a unified whole. Every piece of vegetation removed from the planet's surface by freeways, housing developments, logging, dams, airports, cities, estuary destruction, and clearing for agriculture, represents a decline in the planet's life, a deficit in the solar budget.

The following chart gives a general illustration of what occurs in the drive of life toward maximum diversity and energy flow. This is seen as a forest ecosystem matures, by monitoring the increase of population and number of species of one kind of life form through the succeeding phases of development. Each living thing contributes a number of different benefits to the system. We see in the chart that the diversity of species and also the general bird population increases as the system moves toward climax. This increase is necessarily supported by rising populations of plants and other animals in the system.

STAGES IN ECOSYSTEM DEVELOPMENT AND ASSOCIATED INCREASE IN BIRD POPULATIONS

ECOSYSTEM DEVELOPMENT	Grass land	Shrubs	Low trees	High trees
Years	1-10	10-25	25-100	100+
Number of different species of birds	2	8	15	16
Density (pairs/40 ha.)	27	123	113	233

(from *Human Impact On The Ecosystem*, Joy Tivy and Grag O'Hare.)[2]

Increased complexity potentiates life and life's energy pathways. Different species of birds disperse different types of seeds, control various insect populations, and become food for various predators who can then live in the developing forest. The activities of each species can be looked upon as a specialized organ functioning within the life of the earth. As each organ is added, the life of the whole is multiplied because each organ creates new paths for energy circulation, connecting individual parts of the system in new ways. Each factor performs more than one function.

Honey bees are an excellent example of this multiplier effect. The energy which they expend pollinating the flowering plants is far less than the energy expended in their other activities. If a human helps the population of honey bees, the multiplier effect goes up even more. As the pollinated plants increase, the bees increase and as both increase, the honey and plants available to humans increase as well as other benefits to the surrounding life.

The now extinct dodo bird of the Mauritius Islands in the Indian Ocean had a unique relationship with the Calvaria tree. The tree fed the dodo and the dodo transported seeds for the tree. The heavily coated seeds of the Calvaria tree had to pass through the abrasive digestive system of the Dodo in order to germinate. Now that the dodo is gone the Calvaria trees are dying out. None have germinated for three hundred years since the last dodo died.[3] It is probable that this tree has vegetation, insects or other animals that lived in association with it or the micro-climate that it created. Those connections are being severed also.

Howard T. Odum is perhaps the foremost student of ecosystem energy flows. Odum points out that "loop rewards" or "positive feedback loops" are necessary in any energy flow system. Odum explains how this energy sharing principle works:

"In ecological studies there is the positive feedback loop through which a downstream recipient of potential energy rewards its source by passing necessary materials back to it. For example, the animals in a balanced system feed back to the plants in reward loops the phosphates, nitrates, and other compounds required for their growth. A plant that has a food chain which regenerates nutrients in the form it needs is therefore reinforced, and both plant and animal continue to survive. Species whose work efforts are not reinforced are shortly eliminated, for they run out of either raw materials or energy. They must be connected to input and output flows to survive."[4]

Odum propounds the rule that states; "That system survives which maximizes the availability and uses efficiency of power from all sources." This the organs of life do by establishing themselves in a way that they potentiate the whole system and so that other organs can grow upon them to further continue the purposes of life.

In order to further clarify this by contrast, we can look at the way in which the culture of empire has replicated itself upon the Great Plains of North America. When the invading Europeans broke up the land mass with fences and private property, the net photosynthetic production of the Great Plains was degraded tremendously. Sixty million buffalo and millions of individuals of other species were eradicated because the European diet and system of mass production could not utilize this ecosystem in the way that the forager/hunters had for centuries. As the buffalo were slaughtered, there was no adequate market for all the buffalo meat or even all the hides. The "sod busters" who plowed the prairie sod had less usable product in terms of protein than the previous tribes of "buffalo hunters" who utilized the buffalo, deer, pronghorn, elk and other species. The present industrial agricultural system cannot produce the Net Photosynthetic Production or the variety of life of the original climax system. It is designed to interlock with a greatly simplified, but massive, food system based on bread, milk and meat eating, which lends itself to mass production and sale to markets. To the industrial agriculturalist, biological energy efficiency is irrelevant. The industrialists' purpose is to provide production and profit, not to be biologically efficient.

Industrial Agriculture

Pundits and propagandists of the Chamber of Commerce and the "boomers" of the industrial system are fond of claiming the great productivity of industrial agriculture by pointing out how few farmers there are in ratio to the population. In reality, the most efficient systems are the most "primitive." Industrial agriculture is by far the most energy inefficient system of food production.

Hundreds of industrial workers participate with each industrial farmer. There are the oil field workers, oil refinery workers, the truck drivers, the plastics plant workers, the workers who create the packaging of farm produce, the packagers, distributors, wholesalers, delivery people and retail clerks. An enormous amount of machinery is required for this process. All machinery is produced by factories somewhere by people who must be counted in the food production network. All the seed is dependent upon years of development by cadres of technical workers. The drying, freezing, canning, distribution and other processes rely upon an infrastructure of transportation and industry. If the food is from irrigated fields the input of effort stretches back through the digging of canals, the building of dams, laying out of the electrical systems to run the pumps, the planning of these systems and often the disruption of many lives that formerly occupied the space where the dam and its accouterments now exist. The industrial agriculturist does not simply go out to the swidden plot by his village and eat a fruit from the tree. Industrial agriculture is not just a planting of seed, it is a vast complex, expensive, energy intensive, destructive system that will ultimately collapse without possibility of recovery.

Like the imbalanced systems of grazing and irrigation, the industrial agricultural system is simply an extrapolation of the imbalance of the basic, time honored agriculture. The great difference is that with so much energy invested in it the destructive results are apparent much sooner. Industrial agriculture is tremendously destructive of soils, of the nutritional content of the food and of the environment. The water borne runoff of manure, fertilizer and agricultural poisons are unbalancing life on a continental scale. The cost of this must be added to the already huge cost of producing industrial food. Every deformed baby in farming regions and every poisoned farm worker must be added into the cost.

As humankind has deviated from the natural balance, the energy cost and labor cost of feeding populations has gone up. The tribal Tsembaga people of the highlands in New Guinea, raise sweet potatoes at an expenditure of approximately one kilocalorie of energy for each 16 kilocalories of food produced. Studies of the industrial system indicate that approximately 20 kilocalories of energy are required to produce <u>one</u> kilocalorie of food. The industrial system is obviously a high-cost, energy intensive system when all production factors are counted.[5]

The following table shows the true energy cost of selected agricultural methods and foods. In this table, rice grown in Indonesia is the most energy efficient crop/method while feedlot mutton has the highest energy input cost per unit of protein formed. For example to raise peanuts in Florida required 1,000 kilocalories of energy for each pound of peanut protein grown while it cost 10,000 kilocalories of energy to gain a pound of egg protein in the factory egg raising system of the U.S.A.

Energy Input Per Unit Protein Formed (Kcal/lb.Protein)	
Rice, Indonesia, 1964	
Rice, Burma, 1964	
Rice, Thailand, 1964	
Peanuts, Florida	1,000
Potatoes, England	
Processed leaf protein	
Wheat, Illinois	
Inshore fishing, Scotland	
Rice, Japan, 1969	
Beef, Venezuelan Llanos	
Soya flour, USA	
Fish protein concentrate	
Milk--Grass feed Peru	
Eggs--USA	10,000
Distant Water Trawling Fish protein concentrate.-USA	
Intensive beef raising-USA	
Feed-lot mutton-USA	100,000

This chart from the British magazine Ecologist shows relative inputs of energy per pound of protein output for selected food producing systems.[6]

The largest part of the industrial farming system is the industrial infrastructure itself. If that infrastructure falters and machines are not produced, the food production system will not function. Within this general support of agriculture by the industrial infrastructure there are a few basic systems that support it directly. Each of these is a nonsustainable, disintegrating system.

The first of these factors is the enormous energy investment. The industrial infrastructure relies upon it for transportation, research and all of the other things that go into it and it comes directly to the field in terms of trucks, tractors, irrigation water, fertilizer and poisons. Through the techniques of industry, trade-offs have been made that replace the organic cycles of soil and climate. No longer do soils need to be replenished by organic feed. Now the fertilizer trade-off is injected into the soil that is directly translated from fossil fuel energy or fertilizer created from ocean fish- itself a part of the factory (fishing) system that is basically dependent for fuel upon petroleum. Petroleum is the base of artificial fertilizer. This is shown by Nitrogen which is one of the components of artificial fertilizer. It is industrially synthesized out of the atmosphere and requires five tons of coal equivalent energy for one ton prepared nitrogen.

With a system of food production that is so energy intensive, and is being spread to the Third World so rapidly, we must ask about the energy to sustain this. The myth in the imperial centers is that the First World is assisting the "Under-developed" countries to reach the same standard of living as exists in the First World. This notion which is generally held, does not involve the reality of the petroleum resource base. The research team that produced the study *Limits To Growth*, found that if the whole world population had the standard of consumption that exists in the USA, the basic reserve of resources on the planet would be gone within ten years.[7] Similarly, "If every nation expended as much oil per head in agriculture as the U.S., current world oil reserves would be emptied in a dozen years."[8] But, as this non-sustainable survival system develops it becomes more energy intensive each year. There is a definite law of diminishing returns in the industrial agricultural system:

> "The best and most sobering example of that law comes from an assessment of the cost of past agricultural gains. To achieve a 34 percent increase in world food production from 1951 to 1966, agriculturalists increased yearly expenditures on tractors by 63 percent, annual investment in nitrate fertilizers by 146 percent, and annual use of pesticides by 300 percent. The next 34 percent increase will require even greater inputs of capital and resources."[9]

The agricultural poisons that are a necessary part of the system translate from petroleum. During World War I, it was the oil industry that began to create the poison gases for the war. After the war their market began to wither until they realized a new market for the nerve gases as bug killers on the farm.

Although not all farm poisons are now nerve gas related, the origins of the pesticide industry lay in WWI and are still based in the chemical-petroleum industry.

Many millions of people in the world today are fed by the increased food production produced by petroleum based agriculture. Georg Borgstrom said in 1969, "Close to 600 million people depend for their survival upon artificial fertilizers. Without this annually repeated supplementation of the soil with man-extracted minerals, approximately that number of humans would lack food."[10] Even by 1980 we see that this system, even with added petroleum input, cannot keep up with population increase and when the petroleum runs out, the millions will be sitting perched on a branch with no trunk. There is no going back to the farmed out fields. We have already seen what these artificial fertilizer fed soils will be- exhausted. At that point, monstrous disasters will take place.

In addition to the petroleum base of the pesticide industry becoming exhausted, there is another nonsustainable aspect of the pesticide industry and that is that insects develop immunities to the poison so that more is needed in greater strength, more often. The number of insect, tick and mite species that are now immune to agricultural poison is set at 428. As the pests develop resistance the industry turns out new and more deadly poisons but the industry is now hard pressed to keep up with insect resistance.

In its war with nature the industrial system literally kills the soil community with poisons and the beneficial work of that ecological community stops. Dead also are the predatory insects that would eat the pests that the agriculturalist seek to eradicate. Dead also are birds, animals, and people. "In 1981, OXFAM stated that there were 750,000 cases of accidental pesticide poisonings a year. Third World countries, accounting for less than 15% of world pesticide consumption, suffered 50% of poisonings and 75% of the resulting deaths."[11]

Agriculturalists sell food by weight- not nutritional content. Taxpayer financed research that is pointed toward increasing yields and profits has nothing to do with taxpayer nutrition. As yields have increased by weight, nutritional content has declined. The authority, Georg Borgstrom states: "In modern high-yielding rice strains the protein content is down to between 5 and 7 percent, in high-yielding wheat strains to 10 percent, in hybrid corn to 7 percent. A piece of cheese or ham has to be added to the sandwich to become equivalent in terms of nutritive value to the same sandwich without any additions around the turn of the century." As a comparison, Borgstrom mentions Russian wheat strains with 22% protein content.[12] Even as modern yields increase it has less meaning because the nutritional content declines. This is another failing subsystem of industrial agriculture.

Living on Oil—The Green Revolution

The Green Revolution is simply the insertion of petroleum based industrial agriculture into Third World societies. Necessary factors of industrial agriculture are; large acreage, specialized seed, adequate water- on demand, artificial fertilizer in large amounts, agricultural poisons, agricultural machinery, fuel, and shipment of product. Industrial agriculture is the most highly developed in the First World industrial nations. It is simply the application of industrial technique to agricultural mass production.

Given this intense focus, it is the most productive system in gross terms. With the industrial system, huge energy inputs, relatively good soils and a temperate climate, the U.S. produces so much food that more than half of the food on international markets originates there. "American farmers produce 15 percent of the world's wheat, 21 percent of oats, 36 percent of sorghum, and 46 percent of maize on only 11 percent of the world's croplands."[13]

Empire culture and the industrial system are inherently centralizing forces. When the Green Revolution moves into a country it must have large acreages so that it can achieve "economies of scale," meaning simply that within the mass production system it is cheaper, on a per unit basis, to produce a large amount of one item, than it is to produce only one of those items. This means that self supporting, subsistence agriculture families in the area must move to the periphery, attempt to farm the hillsides and gain occasional labor on the new industrial farm. This means that the hold of the colonial elite grows stronger on the population. This means also that the hold of the international political/financial system grows on the colonial elite. Either large loans or opening the country up to the transnational corporations are necessary to start the industrial agricultural system because the factors of production must be shipped in, the trucks, the seed, the irrigation works, the fertilizers and the other components. Because of the huge capital investments needed for industrial agriculture, the chances are good that the country will ultimately be forced into the hands of the international bankers for loans. When the system is well established and the indigenous population is heavily in debt, (in the tradition of the more advanced First World farmers), then the international banking system will send in teams of bankers to administer the government's economic planning and will promote austerity measures that milk the population for interest money to send to the imperial capitals. As the farm system centralizes and the profit making industrial farmer takes more land, homelessness increases. The phenomena of cities exploding as people are forced out of the countryside is a familiar one in industrial societies. This trend is now particularly serious in the Third World where there is a low level of industrial infrastructure in urban areas. As the "labor saving" machinery is brought in, unemployment increases and people are forced to work at a lower wage under worse conditions. As the production of food increases with the industrial system, the people grow more hungry because much of the food is now in the international system. The food is grown for export to bring in hard currencies to repay loans, purchase manufacturing equipment for the industrial centers and consumer items for the colonial elite- not to buy food for the poor. A major point must be emphasized, the calculation of how much food a country grows has nothing to do with how well fed the people of that country are. The important question in the industrial system is how much money people have to buy food. The international flow of protein goes to the First World countries, they have the money to bid for the food.

The Monocultural Instability

There are at least 5,000 plants that have been used for human consumption on the planet yet the civilized diet is made up from less than ten types of plants. The reason for this is the cultural style of using agriculture itself, dietary habit, mass production and profits (or quotas in the socialist industrial variant).

There are basically ten food plants grown in the world today when looked at on a volume basis. Wheat, rice and corn alone make up one half of the food consumed on the planet, with barley, oats, sorghum, and millet making up the next one quarter. "Ninety five per cent of our global nutritional requirements are derived from a mere 30 plant kinds and a full three quarters of our diet is based upon only eight crops."[14] If we add beans and potatoes to the above eight plants, these ten species of plants are the essential basis of world agriculture. These varieties of plants are adapted to mass production. Much more protein per acre could be grown by harvesting the tubers of cattails or many other plants, but the harvesting is difficult by mass machine methods. The few plant varieties that are used are given extraordinary chances of producing. The plant is grown on vast acreages that are completely controlled. The plant receives as much artificial fertilizer as its roots can take up, it is given adequate water at all times that it needs it and the area is sterilized by agricultural poisons because the plants often have little natural resistance. It is this optimum and energy/ capital intensive conditioning that allows the tremendous production.

In the U.S. where we have the example of the most advanced state of industrial agriculture, we also have the example of its tremendous destruction. "An astonishing 80 million hectares [193.36 million acres] of U.S. croplands, an area almost twice the size of California, have been rendered unproductive, if not ruined outright. The nation has lost at least one-third of its best topsoils, and erosion rates are now worse than ever, as much as five billion tons [4.45140 billion tons] per year."[15] Organic materials are carbon compounds, and the level of carbon compounds in the soil is the measure of soil health. Soil scientists calculate that, "On a global basis, we have squandered more soil carbon than the fossil fuel variety. Roughly a third of our [world] soil carbon was lost with the opening up of the North American continent."[16]

Because we stand on top of the ground and look at plants, it slips from our consciousness that by far the largest volume of organic material normally lays in the soil and the largest volume of living things, are the lives in the soil community-spread all over the whole planet. This measure of carbon loss (most ultimately translated to gases in the atmosphere) shows the profound loss that has occurred.

The nitrates from fertilizers and agricultural poisons now pollute many underground aquifers in agricultural regions. Where it does not kill them, the runoff of poisons makes the fish and shellfish in inland and coastal waters dangerous to eat.

The industrial agricultural system is contrary to "family farming" in many ways. Contrary to the image most of us have of the family farm, modern industrial agriculture is a complex technical pursuit that requires many exotic inputs. Many of these inputs are highly dangerous such as hormones, antibiotics, and poisons. One might say that these factors are also part of the failure of industrial agriculture in that they maim and kill the customers from whom they seek to make a profit. There are cases such as in Puerto Rico where the use of hormones, apparently in excess of the levels used on the mainland, have created the maturation of sexual organs, breasts and the growth of pubic hair in babies. The hormones in dairy and meat products spread over the civilized population certainly have some effect on the sexual health of the population, just as in selected cases it can be shown that these "agricultural" hormones cause the development of sexual organs in babies one and two years old and create female sexual development in boys.[17]

Because of the crowded and unsanitary conditions in which chicken, pigs and cattle are raised, the animals are subject to many diseases. Because of this the animals and their feed must be subjected to many drugs. Antibiotics are one class that are used in large volume. These are passed on in the tissues of the animals to the top of the food chain- the consumers- and alter micro-organic communities within the human body.[18]

As of 1989, one in three U.S. citizens will have cancer in their lifetime (but not necessarily die). "In 1900, cancer was the tenth leading cause of death in the United States, and was responsible for only three percent of all deaths. Today it ranks second, and causes about twenty percent of all deaths."[19] Many agricultural chemicals are proven carcinogens. These toxins come to the animal through their feed. Fish, poultry, dairy and meat products contain high levels of toxics. Even a Reagan era Environmental Protection Agency publication reports that: "Foods of animal origin [are] the major source of...pesticide residues in the diet."[20]

With 99% of the mother's milk from every part of the country containing significant concentrations of DDT and PCB's, we know that the entire ecosystem is also saturated with it. Human mother's milk we know from tests also contains dieldrin, heptachlor, dioxin and many other toxic substances ingested from food, air and water.[21]

The Seeds of Monoculture

One other serious matter for the human family is the seed system of industrial agriculture. (It will become serious indeed when civilization collapses and we try to grow our own food). The plant varieties of each species of the "ten plants" of industrial agriculture developed with empire culture. They are basically the grains that were originally developed when agriculture started and have been spread by various empires to conquered territories. The origins of the ten plants are primarily the temperate regions where empire developed, though a few items have come from tropical rainforest cultures (tomatoes, chocolate, coffee). These regions are called Vavilov centers after the Russian botanist N.I. Vavilov. They are: Chile, the Amazon, the Andes, Central America, the Mediterranean, Ethiopia, Anatolia-Caucasus, Central Asia, India, Northern China and Southeast Asia. At least until recently, these regions contained many strains of primary plants. These strains were held and selected over thousands of years by native and peasant cultures that lived an agrarian lifestyle. In older times there were hundreds of varieties of each of these plants in each region. For example, in each small valley in Afghanistan, farmers might develop their own strains by selection over long periods of time. These selections would be appropriate to that specific soil, the specific pests that are in the area, the specific amount of rainfall and the climatic temperature variations. From this inventory, modern agriculture has selected the best producers and after manipulations in research stations, spread these world-wide. Because of the techniques of the industrial agricultural system (ordinarily, only the most productive variety will be used) only a handful of varieties of each species is spread worldwide. The following table gives some examples of crops, the number of dominant varieties and the percentage of the whole crop that those mass production varieties represent, in the U.S. [22]

CROP	VARIETIES	%
millet	3	100
cotton	3	53
soybeans	6	56
dry beans	2	60
snap beans	3	76
peas	2	96
corn	6	71
potatoes	4	72
sweet potatoes	1	69

Any large acreage of any single variety is extremely vulnerable to pests because any particular pest successful in feeding off the variety will have a population explosion of many descendants that will do the same. When only a few varieties are spread world-wide, the vulnerability is spread accordingly.

"The genetic uniformity of a crop amounts to an invitation for an epidemic to destroy that crop. The uniformity itself may result from the inherent pressures of the market place (machine harvesting, processing, etc.) as well as the absence of genetic variety in the crop breeding program. As 'erosion' spreads in the Vavilov Centres, the danger of crop epidemics in the industrialized world will increase. Southern corn leaf blight is only the most recent of a long history of epidemics common to every continent. "Historically, the most dramatic example in the western world was the Irish Potato Famine of the late 1840's. At a European symposium on plant breeding held in the summer of '78, Dr. J. G. Hawkes traced the disastrous potato blight back to its root causes in South America. English explorers returned from the Caribbean coast in the Sixteenth Century with only one variety of potato. Planted everywhere in northern Europe, it was only a matter of time until this genetically-uniform crop was struck by blight. In a remarkably short space of time, the Irish lost their primary food source, leaving at least two million dead and two million more searching for a new life in other countries. Although significant efforts have since been made to diversify potato varieties, Europe still remains vulnerable and in need of additional genetic material."[23]

Amazingly, the First World potato crop is still based essentially on the same variety of potato that was involved with the Irish potato famine. The native communities of the Andes where the potato originated grow some 40 varieties of potatoes. They have not yet been reached by the Green Revolution.

Each of the props of the industrial agricultural system, petroleum, water, air (acid rain), sun (climate-greenhouse effect-ozone layer depletion), soil and seed are degenerating, non-sustainable systems and each of these props have degenerative subsystems. The elimination of gene banks (the ecosystems where target seed is produced) is one of the degenerative aspects of the seed prop, along with the elimination of seed varieties themselves by the transnational seed companies.

The seed system of modern agriculture works by creating a facsimile of the natural change in plant genetics. Selected varieties are grown by researchers who strictly control pollenization as they genetically mix varieties for particular results (usually increased volume, almost never for increased nutrition). As modern varieties and hybrids are bred, ancient and wild strains which have productivities and resistances of various kinds are bred with the modern varieties to create new strains. The ancient and wild strains that are used are generally taken from the Vavilov Centres, those areas where that species developed historically. A point of crisis now in the seed business is that these regions are being wiped out by destruction of habitat of the wild plants and by the new seed of the Green Revolution replacing old family varieties. For example, a researcher who had seen "Virtually thousands of flax varieties growing on the Cilician plain [in Turkey] returned after twenty years to find only one variety- imported from Argentina."[24]

As the Green Revolution invades, the people eat up the old seed and become dependent upon the new seed and thus the strains that have been selected for thousands of years for their strength and productivity are lost. This has special significance for regions outside of the Vavilov Centres, because there are no wild or selected varieties outside the Vavilov centers to use to continue to develop the plant strains. The seeds for industrial agriculture come from the Third World, are shipped to the First World, manipulated and then go to the whole system, as "miracle seeds" Even for the biotechnologist this is significant because they do not create genes, they manipulate existing genes and they must get these genes from a wide variety of plants.

The Starvation that is Called Progress

To think that food is grown by the imperial agricultural system in order to feed hungry people is ridiculously naive. The industrial society and its agricultural system was not established as a charity enterprise, it is part of the power and profit organization of elite international groups. As Georg Borgstrom so effectively points out, high-grade protein flows to the rich and whatever low grade protein is left over after the First World livestock have been fed, flows to the poor of the Second World and Third World. It requires money to buy food and if hungry people do not have money they will get no food, no matter how much food their own country grows. Once subsistence culture is destroyed and markets are created, food flows to those who have money in the money economy. In Costa Rica, as the rainforests are destroyed to create pasture for cattle, the percentage of meat in the diet of Costa Ricans declines because the beef is sold to the U.S. fast food hamburger chains. There are few people in Costa Rica who can bid against the U.S. consumer for the meat. Empire culture is arranged to percolate value to the elite at the top of the pyramid. This percolation in the case of agriculture occurs through the concentration of protein by animals. We have seen that one-third of the ocean fish catch is used as fertilizer and fed to live stock to produce ham and eggs rather than fish cakes for the poor. In Peru where the industrial system sucked up the huge Peruvian anchovy stock in just a few years, Peruvians sat starving on the docks watching millions of tons of protein flow through, headed for the chickens and pigs of the First World. It is said that 90 per cent of the grain fed to livestock in the U.S. could eliminate human starvation. The shrimp, lobster, crab, pork chops and prime rib that flow to the elite of First World societies graphically represent the basis of the whole imperial system. Power, money, land ownership and life security also flow in the same direction as the food. The establishment of colonies, either by migration of masses from the mother country, domination by military power or domination by economic power, is done so that valuables may be derived from the colony for the mother country. Colonies are not established as acts of charity toward the colonized.

If everyone in the world suddenly began eating only grain that now goes to livestock and if the colonial elites of the world suddenly disbanded and distributed land to the landless, there would be a sudden flow of food to the hungry. These actions would momentarily halt world starvation. These actions would not solve the ecologically destructive basis of agriculture itself, only prolong the time in which the soil was destroyed. It would not answer the ten thousand year history of empire culture either (the culture would not be disbanded along with the colonial elite). Neither would it answer the population explosion. In some Third World societies the population doubling time is only twenty-five years! The exploding mass, based on dwindling survival systems would still be in motion. A demonstration that there are many factors other than land reform is given by Vietnam.

Although land reform is an obvious and just need, the rulers of the empires have demonstrated that they will attempt to destroy a colony rather than see their puppets, the colonial elite, dissolve. Professor Vo Quy, Faculty of Biology, University of Hanoi calculates that the U.S. military destroyed over two million hectares [4.834 million acres] of tropical rainforest (not including other areas in SE Asia) during the Vietnam War. These areas were destroyed by bombs, shells, napalm, bulldozers, and agricultural poisons (especially "agent orange"). They are now wastelands. He states that there are 25 million bomb craters, an area of 125,000 hectares [302,125 acres] which have the topsoil completely blown away. A direct result of the poisons dumped on the country is the destruction of over half of the biologically rich mangrove swamps on the coasts of Vietnam.

Professor Vo Quy says that in 1943, 44 per cent of the country was still covered by forests, even with the French colonialists stripping it. By 1975 it was down to 29 per cent and by 1983, 23.6 per cent. Because of deforestation the country is now experiencing the familiar "drought/flood syndrome." After the victory by the anti-colonialist forces, land reform was instituted, and the population continued to climb along with the deforestation. Farmland erosion is now rated at 100-200 tons topsoil per acre [per annum] and the forest is now shrinking at a rate of 200,000 hectares [483,400 acres] a year. The population doubled in the last forty years and the country now has 200 people per square mile. Professor Vo Quy says that by 2000, there will be one-half hectare of land per person- not all of it arable. One hundred thousand acres of tropical forest go down each year now for simple cooking and fuel needs and this need increases as industrial developments are attempted. The forests put on 10 million metres of new growth per year but the present annual demand for wood is 30 million cubic metres.

Professor Vo Quy recounts the story similar to the recent history of all industrial societies:

"Looming big as a major concern is water pollution. Waste water from industries is discharged into containers and used for agriculture or for daily use. ...In Hanoi, tens of thousands of cubic metres of dirty, untreated water containing inorganic and organic toxins, bacteria and parasites are drained into lakes, ponds and canals within the city and its outskirts. Population increase will accelerate industrial growth and result in 6 billion cubic metres of waste water per year by AD 2000.

" 'To clear the waste water, 6,000 cubic meters of water per second would be needed. This is more than the combined flow rate of all major rivers in Vietnam during the dry season. The dangerous effects of pesticides are becoming widespread, in 1959 only 100 tons were used. Twenty years later the figures rose to an astonishing 22,000 tons, applied to 50% of the farmland.' "[25]

The centralizing tendencies and the mass production techniques of industrial agriculture are the same wherever they are applied. Stalin allegedly murdered 20,000 Kulaks in order to install industrial mass production agriculture on the Kulaks' former land in Russia. The U.S. historically murdered millions of native people to make way for agriculture and the imperial system in the U.S. Its agricultural system still continues to concentrate into fewer elite hands. The system must have large areas of land on which some one is now living. As the remaining natural tribes are being murdered, the cry is that the land is "unused" and "undeveloped" therefore the imperialist is justified in stealing it and either enslaving or murdering the people that live there. Now, there are more Chinese in Tibet than there are Tibetans, as the imperial surge comes into that country to colonize and "develop" Tibet. As the tens of millions invade out of China into Tibet, the Mongolias and Sinkiang; the wheat, vegetables and meat flow to the imperial center of China. As the Chinese empire has invaded their neighbors they have instituted all of the mass industrial agriculture techniques that they could afford. These lands are going the same route as the former soils of China itself.

In the "Western Countries," agriculture is dominated by the elite who control the transnational corporations which produce the inputs of financing, fertilizer, machinery, technical assistance, seed, marketing and agricultural poisons. The flow of grain in the western world is controlled essentially by five corporations, the majority of them privately held family companies. The petroleum supply is controlled by five giant world-wide companies and they in turn dominate the pesticide, fertilizer and designer seed industries, as well as provide the fuel to ship all of the factors of production. It requires a large share of the industrial production of an industrial society to raise food. When the Green Revolution invades a Third World society it means that huge new markets are created for the factors of industrial agricultural production, such as tractors, seed, and etc. It means that the colonial elite will need access to credit. It becomes a bonanza for the international financial system.

As the international financiers have come to control world agriculture, they, as a group, are also continually centralizing. The oil companies control the energy supply (oil, uranium, coal), they are heavily invested in fertilizer production and in pesticides. Now, with the Green Revolution the matter of plant seeds has become a high profit item and one of the non-sustainable aspects of the system. As has been discussed, the flow of new seed must be constant in order to outmaneuver the pests. Recently, hybrid seeds have entered the system. These seeds cannot even be kept by the farmer for the next year's planting because they do not breed true. This requires the farmer to return to the seed company year after year.

As the "New Seed" has become important in the Green Revolution, the financiers began to move toward control of the seed system and its profits. In the past fifteen years "mergers" in the seed industry have become notorious as the transnational elite moves to control the international food supply. The Royal Dutch Shell oil company for example, now owns over 30 seed companies. The large oil companies, pharmaceutical companies and chemical companies have moved to solidify their control of the world's seeds.

Because of the large variety of people that came to colonize North America and because many of these people, being subsistence/peasant stock, brought the seed of their native lands, the U.S. had one of the largest and most varied inventories of "heirloom" seed in the world. Because people saved seed from their gardens and because there were many regional seed companies, this condition continued until the financiers moved in. As the seed companies have disappeared into the elite class, the human family is now losing its seed heritage.

The needs of the mass production system are to have a few seeds of each species that are appropriate to many climates and conditions because their emphasis is on mass marketing. Because of this, seeds that are regionally adapted and hardy are dropped. Seeds of unusual plants are also dropped in favor of the standard supermarket items. For ten thousand years the peasants and planters have selected and husbanded the seed that now exists. This human family heritage is destined to be wiped out in one generation by the transnational elite and by politburos who create centralized industrial agriculture in socialist countries.

As the seed banks in the Vavilov centers are eliminated and the heirloom seeds eliminated from seed companies' inventories world-wide, the control of the seeds remaining is centralized with the elite. Plant patenting legislation is being instituted throughout the non-socialist world, at the direction of the elite. This means the elite will own the seed variety and will get royalties from its use. In some cases now, a person can be arrested for planting the seed of any plant whose original patented seed they have purchased. The elite have not yet achieved their full plan. They also own the biotechnology firms that are working on producing "miracle" plants. When these patented plants are created they will then be in full control of the western world energy and food system. Kent Whealy of the backyard gardeners group, Seed Savers Exchange[26] states that already by the early nineteen eighties:

> "Seed company takeovers in the United States have reached epidemic proportions: ARCO took over Desert Seed Co; ITT now owns the W. Atlee Burpee Co.; Sandoz (of Switzerland) purchased Northrup King Co.; Upjohn bought out Asgrow Seed Co.; and Monsanto purchased DeKalb Hybrid Wheat. These are just a few of the more than 60 recent North American seed company takeovers.
>
> "Multinational agrichemical conglomerates... are already manufacturing pesticides, fungicides and chemical fertilizers. With their newly purchased seed companies, they are now able to give commercial growers a package deal —seeds which will grow well with their chemicals. Some agrichemical firms have even started selling pelleted seeds, which wrap each individual seed in a small capsule of pesticides and fertilizers. It is doubtful that such corporations whose very existence depends on selling pesticides and chemical fertilizers, will spend any time or money to develop disease- or pest-resistant crops."[27]

Just as it takes more energy to smelt a lower concentrate ore body in a mine, energy use will actually increase as the society disintegrates. The energy intensive industrial societies will last about as long as the agricultural system that feeds them. As we have seen, the characteristics of the agricultural system, like all the other systems of the empire, make no real provision for their continuance beyond the short term profit. There are no positive feed-back loops, nothing to feed the system itself- the soil, the seed production system; the social body of empire is simply a drain, an extortion system that is unravelling into incoherence. Soon the world supply of petroleum will be exhausted and the world population will be out on the proverbial limb. By that point they will have little seed that can grow without its industrial aids. By that point much of the world's irrigated acreage will be salinized, many of the dams silted up and the underground aquifers drained. As these pressures are in motion, acid rain will be increasing because of the inevitable increase in energy use and the climates will be beginning to change from the Greenhouse Effect, completely altering or eliminating the existing agricultural system. In the ten to twenty years that it will take for the world to reach that point, many hundreds of millions of people will be added to the world's population.

This is the reason that people who are capable of making a commitment must move swiftly to establish "seed" communities that can thrust a viable human culture into a future time beyond the inevitable crash of empire. These must be communities that have viable seed harboring strategies.

The Inventory

There is the persistent and socially encouraged tradition of viewing the "ecological crisis" as something that has to do with toxic chemicals, an oil spill or maybe acid rain. What our review demonstrates is that the fundamental basis of the culture of empire is an ecological crisis. History is written by the conquerors and the reality view of empire culture is generated from elites with a culture bound view. For the soils, for the forests, and for the native people world-wide, the ecological crisis began thousands of years ago with the growth of empire culture.

What we see is that this culture could not continue indefinitely even without the additional problems of population and pollution that we will review shortly. The import of this is to realize that it is the culture itself which is suicidal and that what is called the "ecological crisis" is only the final and gross symptom of a social/organic life form that is out of balance with the earth and cosmos.

The conclusion is inescapable. Civilization is a culture of suicide. It cannot be sustained indefinitely and its growth is only fueled by running a net deficit of the fertility of the earth. We look now to the conditions created by the industrial society which are presently serious. We are going to live through these conditions, so it is important that we understand the minefield through which we negotiate.

NOTES

1 Biological Paths To Self Reliance: A Guide to Biological Solar Energy Conversion. Russell E. Anderson. Van Nostrand Reinhold Co. pub. New York. 1971. p.36.

2 Human Impact on the Ecosystem. Joy Tivy & Grag O'Hare. Oliver & Boyd pub. New York. 1981. p. 16.

3 The New Biology: Discovering The Wisdom In Nature. Robert Augros & George Stanciu. New Science Library, Shambala pub. Boston. 1988. p.109.

4 Environment, Power and Society. Howard T. Odum. Wiley-Interscience. New York. 1971. pp.150,151.

5 Anthropology And Contemporary Human Problems. John H. Bodley. Second Edition. Mayfield pub. Palo Alto, Ca. pp. 126,128.

6 The Ecologist. February, 1982. Cornwall, England. p.8.

7 The Limits To Growth. Meadows, Meadows, et. al. Second Edition. New American Library. New York. 1974.

8 Gaia: An Atlas Of Planet Management. Norman Myers, General Editor. Anchor Books. Garden City, New York. 1984. p.65.

9 The Limits To Growth: A Report For The Club Of Rome's Project On The Predicament Of Mankind. Donella H. Meadows, Dennis L. Meadows, Jorgen Randers & William W. Behrens III. New American Library. New York. 1974. p.62..

10 Too Many: An Ecological Overview Of Earth's Limitations. Georg Borgstrom. Collier Books. New York. 1971. p.26.

11 Myers. Gaia. op. cit. p. 123.

12 Borgstrom. Too Many. op. cit. p. 51.

13 Myers. Gaia. op. cit. p. 64.

14 Development Dialogue. Dag Hammarskjold Foundation, Ovre Slottsgatan 2, S-752 20 Uppsala, Sweden. 1983:1-2. "The Law of the Seed" Pat Roy Mooney. p.7.

15 ibid. p. 64.

16 Soil and Survival: Land Stewardship and The Future of American Agriculture. Joe Paddock, Nancy Paddock & Carol Bly. Sierra Club Books. San Francisco. 1986. (from the introduction by Wes Jackson) p. ix.

17 Diet For A New America. John Robbins. Stillpoint Pub. 1987. pp. 309,310.

18 ibid. p. 335.

19 ibid. p. 326.

20   ibid. p.315.

21   ibid. p. 345.

22   Seeds Of The Earth: A Public or Private Resource? Pat Ray Mooney.
      Food First, Institute for Food and Development Policy. 1885 Mission
      Street, San Francisco, Ca. 94103. 1979. p. 14.

23   ibid. pp. 12,13.

24   ibid. p. 12.

25   Overthrow. "Vietnam: Trying to Reconstruct A Tattered Economy And
      An Ecological Mess," (from a paper presented by Professor Vo Quy to
      the International Conference On Ecology In Vietnam, May 28-30, 1987).
      (newspaper). vol.10, no.1. Spring 1988. p.5.

26   Information can be obtained from, Seed Savers Exchange, P.O. Box 70,
      Decorah, Iowa 52101.

27   The Alliance. (newspaper). 2807 SE Stark, Portland,Ore. 97214. vol. 6,
      no. 3, March, 1986. p.7. (quoted from, The Garden Seed Inventory. by
      Kent Whealy. Seed Savers Exchange. Decorah, Iowa.)

CHAPTER 6

THE DYING OCEANS

During the first part of the twentieth century, as ocean fishing increased in intensity, stocks of in-demand fish began to be "fished out." Their populations were driven so low that they were unable to repopulate. Other species occupied their food chain niches. Recent historical crashes of fish stocks include: 1935, the Antarctic Blue Whale; 1945, the East Asian Sardines; 1946, the California Sardines that fed John Steinbeck's Cannery Row; 1950, the Northwest Pacific Salmon which is one of the many species of migrating salmon on the West Coast of North America; 1961, the Atlantic-Scandian Herring; 1962, the Barents Sea Cod; 1962, the Antarctic Fin Whales; and in 1972, the Peruvian Anchovy stocks. The annual world fish catch rose from 2 million tons in 1900 to 18 million tons in 1950.[1] From 1950 to 1970 the catch rose an average of 6 per cent per year to 66 million tons. In 1970 it leveled off to a 1 per cent per year increase, an average rate of growth which continued until 1982 when it levelled off at 76.8 million tons. Since 1984, the world fish catch has begun to shrink, even though investment in fishing equipment has risen substantially.[2] In the northwest Atlantic, catches of cod, haddock, halibut, herring and other major human food species peaked in the late sixties. The catch of these species has dropped sharply since then, with declines ranging from 40 per cent for herring to over 90 per cent for halibut.[3] Today massive factory fishing fleets of the industrial nations scour the world looking for protein, yet investment in fishing brings a smaller and smaller return. The catch continues to fall, especially for choice table fish. Still investment continues because the exploding populations will pay higher prices for food and the bankers who continually finance new equipment must be paid off.

Thirty-two percent of the world fish catch is now "trash" fish that are processed into fishmeal, fertilizer, livestock food and fish oil.[4] This means that even though humans are finding ways to use more kinds of fish, the total catch, now including "trash fish," does not increase. As humans destroy the upper links of the ocean food chain, we will focus more heavily on plankton and krill, the tiny organisms that are the base of much of the ocean life. Japanese and Russian factory fleets are already taking 100 tons per day of krill from Antarctic waters, destroying the food chain for the entire ecology of beings dependent upon krill in that area.[5] The phytoplankton of the oceans produce some 70 per cent of the earth's oxygen. As these populations of phytoplankton decline because of pollution and ozone layer weakening, the oxygen available for life on Earth will be impaired. The ocean food chain will weaken further as well. As the ocean fish stock declines more pressure will be put on the decreasing amount of arable land. This is because one-third of the ocean fish catch goes into agriculture as livestock food and fertilizer. The energy pathways of fish protein, to agricultural fertilizer and livestock food, will wither, adding further pressure on the soil and oil-based, artificial fertilizer supplies. Meanwhile population increases.

Ocean Pollution

The waters of the oceans continually flow. Jacques Cousteau notes, for example, that all of the water of the Mediterranean will be exchanged with the surrounding bodies of water within 90 years. Cousteau points out that there is already DDT in the livers of the penguins of Antarctica; and that while rivers and semi-enclosed seas are in worse shape than the oceans today, that will not long remain the case.[6]

The open oceans are considered, "biological deserts." It is the continental shelves that produce the basic populations of life in the sea and it is the bays, wetlands, estuaries, mangrove swamps, coral reefs and other coastline sanctuaries that incubate that life. As garbage, sewage, chemical poisons and oil spills flow with the currents, they concentrate near coastlines and eliminate the basis of ocean life. What is being done by New York City and surrounding municipalities is similar to stories of ocean ecology injury world-wide. Since 1987, barges carrying all of the sewage sludge from New York City, two adjoining New York counties and six New Jersey counties have dumped about 24,250 tons of wastes every day —that's eight million tons a year— into the last place in the U.S. where ocean dumping is still allowed, a 100-square-mile area of ocean located 106 miles offshore of Cape May, New Jersey, called the 106 Deepwater Municipal Sludge Site. The wastes include substantial amounts of industrial and household toxic chemicals. A 1983 report by the U.S. National Oceanic and Atmospheric Administration estimates the "area of influence" of toxic wastes deposited at this dumpsite at 46,000 square miles. The area is a spawning ground for about 200 species of fish, and is frequented by dolphins, whales and turtles, some species of which are already considered to be endangered.[7]

Fishermen off the New England coast report that the 1988 lobster catch was down between 70 and 90 per cent, while the lobsters that are caught often have black holes burned into their shells from contamination. That year, Debbie Wynn, a Rhode Island fisherman's wife, told *In These Times* newspaper:

"My husband has been lobstering 17 years and we've never seen anything like this. A year ago, fishermen were returning more short lobsters than they'd seen for years. Not a single one has been seen since the fall. We're fishing with 20 per cent more gear and catching 70 per cent less lobsters. And the red crabs look like somebody's taken a blowtorch to them.

"There's a yellow scum floating on the surface 150 to 175 miles away from the dumpsite itself, and all the shellfish have burn spots from exposure to heavy metals. I'm so scared. The meat isn't contaminated [sic?] but these creatures can't survive without their shells. And the pollution affects crabs and lobsters first, then clams and scallops, then goes into the fish. That's when consumers will have cause to worry, and we may all be out of business."[8]

Tilefish caught off New Jersey in 1988 were suffering epidemics of fin rot and lesions. In the summer of 1987, an unexplained virus killed over 1,000 (a conservative estimate) of the 6,000 to 8,000 dolphins believed to inhabit the waters north of Cape Hatteras, North Carolina. In November and December of that year, about two dozen whales were found beached, mostly near Cape Cod, Massachusetts.[9] Eighty-five percent of ocean pollution originates on land. The run-off of heavy metals from the continents into the oceans now averages two and one half times the natural background level for mercury, 4x for manganese, 12x for zinc, 12x for copper, 12x for lead, 30x for antinomy, and 80 times the background level for phosphorus.[10] Toxic wastes have been found in the deepest part of the ocean and in most ocean habitats.[11]

The United States has the largest industrial production and one of the worst ocean polluting records in the world. By the 1970's the U.S. alone was discharging over 100 million tons of waste per year into the oceans. The U.S. as well as European countries, Japan, and others have dumped radioactive waste into the ocean.

It has recently been discovered that acid rain is also significantly impacting the life of the coastlines. In a 1988 study done for the Environmental Defense Fund, investigators found that atmospheric sources account for 25 per cent of the nitrogen pouring into Chesapeake Bay. (The additional nitrogen came from water run-off. Thirty-four per cent was from farm fertilizers, 23 per cent was from sewage and industrial discharges, and 18 per cent was from animal manure runoff, according to the study.)[12]

Petroleum spills such as the huge spills of 1989 will continue to increase as oil is extracted from increasingly remote, difficult-to-reach areas of the planet. An estimated 6.61-7.71 million tons of petroleum now reach the ocean each year from sources such as leaks in refineries, runoff from land, dumping from ships, leaks from drilling platforms, blowouts and the actual breaking up of tankers.[13] The spills destroy huge numbers of birds, mammals, and marine organisms. The oil is toxic when spilled into the sea and may become more toxic over time through processes of chemical breakdown. Oil residues can remain in sea sediments for as long as a century.[14]

In the United States it is predicted that, given present migration rates, 75 per cent of the human population will live within 50 miles of the coast by the year 2000. Already 8 billion gallons of municipal sewage is dumped into coastal waters per day off the U.S. coast.[15] One-third of the shellfishing areas of the U.S. are closed because of toxic contamination.[16]

Coastal and island "development" often includes the draining of wetlands and filling in of beach areas. The building of dams, diversion of river flows, irrigation, all destroy the life-generating ability of coastlines. In California's San Francisco Bay, for example, 65 per cent of the inflow of fresh water has been stopped.[17] In Louisiana, one acre of coastal wetlands is lost to development every 14 minutes.[18] More than one million hectares [2,417,000 acres] of mangrove swamp has been cleared in the Indo-Pacific region for fish farming.(19) Diego Garcia Island, in the Indian Ocean, an example of the wide-spread coral reef destruction, was once the fertile tropical home of large coral reefs and 2,000 native people. It is now covered with the concrete of a U.S. military base, its biology destroyed.[20]

The massive topsoil runoff that the land masses are now experiencing would normally fertilize the ecosystems of the coasts, lending some kind of saving grace. (An example of where this does happen is the relative fish abundance in the South China Sea, which benefits from the eroding topsoil of China.) The elimination of estuaries by development and the direct kill of coastal life by pollution have obviated the possibility of topsoil erosion increasing the fertility of continental shelves.

The National Academy of Science estimates that commercial fishing fleets dump 52 million pounds of plastic packing material and 298 million pounds of plastic fishing gear, nets, lines and buoys into the ocean every year. An estimated 270-640 miles of monofilament netting is lost each year by the huge Japanese fishing fleet alone. Shoreline garbage accounts for more millions of pounds of plastic. (A plastic six-pack holder ring will last 450 years.) One hundred thousand marine mammals die each year from entanglement and ingestion of plastics. It is estimated that 15 per cent of sea birds eat plastic, confusing it with their natural food. Sea turtles often eat plastic bags which they think are jellyfish. This plastic causes havoc with digestive systems and often plugs the intestines, killing sea creatures and birds.[21]

Ecological Sinks are the Sores of the Earth

Ecological sinks are areas where the life function has broken down completely. In these dead areas, the interlocking energy flows, the food chains and the chemistry of life, are so disrupted or destroyed that they fail to function even in a rudimentary fashion. Some continental examples of ecological sinks include extremely desertified areas, bodies of water where eutrophication has used up the oxygen, and lakes killed by acid rain. Ecological sinks are now being created within the oceans, particularly along coastlines and in enclosed seas. Huge algae blooms and the dead fish, seals and dolphins washing ashore in many areas signal the approaching death of the oceans. The Golden Horn estuary of Turkey, areas all through the Mediterranean, and portions of the coast of Europe and North America are already "dead." A band of oxygen-starved, dead water which can support neither shrimp nor fish life, now extends from the Mississippi River delta off the Louisiana coast across the Gulf of Mexico nearly to Texas, a "dead zone" 300 miles long and ten miles wide.[22]

The largest die-off of seals to occur to date (as of Spring, 1989) took place in Europe's North Sea during the summer months of 1988. Some 12,000 of the region's 18,000 seals were killed by a mysterious virus. Scientists believe that the reason why the seals succumbed in such great numbers is because their immune systems were weakened by exposure to pollutants in North Sea waters. Up to 30 per cent of the waters of Europe's Baltic Sea are permanently deprived of oxygen. Some reports state that 80 per cent of female grey seals in that body of water are known to be sterile, while approximately three-fourths of Baltic Seals that have been examined show pathological changes in some organs and in their skins. The species is not expected to outlast this century.[23]

The toxic pollution of ocean waters is heaviest in the most heavily industrialized countries but this does not mean that other areas are not ecologically damaged. The mangrove swamps of coastal areas for example are being decimated world-wide. When we learn that eskimos are poisoned with PCB's and that penguins in Antarctica contain DDT, we know that the problem of ocean death is planet-wide.

NOTES

1   The Hungry Planet: The Modern World at the Edge of Famine. Georg
     Borgstrom. Collier Books. New York. 2nd. Revised Ed. 1972. p.438.
2   State of the World 1985. Lester Brown, et. al. W. W. Norton Co. New
     York. 1985. p.74.
3   Building A Sustainable Society. Lester R. Brown. W.W. Norton Co.
     New York. 1981. pp.36,37.
4   Gaia: An Atlas Of Planet Management. Norman Myers, editor. Anchor
     Books. Garden City, New York. 1984. p.82.
5   ibid. p.81.
6   U. S. News & World Report. January 23, 1985. p. 68.
7   In These Times. "They're Killing Our Oceans." Dick Russell. April 27-
     May 3, 1988. p. 12.
8   ibid. p. 22.
9   ibid. pp. 12,22.
10   Myers. Gaia. (atlas). op. cit. p.85.
11   ibid. p.79.
12   Associated Press. 250790 New York. 3:36 am. 4/25/88.
13   Myers. Gaia. (atlas). op. cit. pp.84,85.
     Neptune's Revenge: The Ocean of Tomorrow. Anne W. Simon.
     Franklin Watts, pub. New York. 1984. p.63.
14   Simon. Neptune's Revenge. op. cit. p.57.
15   ibid. p.87.
16   ibid. p.87.
17   "In Order to Save the Fisheries We Must Rescue Our Estuaries." M. L.
     Edwards, Field Editor. National Fisherman. January, 1988. p.22.
18   ibid. p.21.
19   Myers. Gaia. (atlas) op. cit. p.87.
20   ibid. p.87.
21   "We're Choking the Ocean With Plastics." Kris Freeman. National
     Fisherman. January, 1987. pp.4,5,32.
22   Time. "The Dirty Seas." August 1, 1988 p.46.
     and M.L. Edwards. National Fisherman. op. cit. p.20.
23   ibid. pp. 6-7.

CHAPTER 7

EXTINCTION OF LIFE BY
SPECIES INCREMENT

"Many scientists believe that a larger share of the earth's plant and animal life will disappear in our lifetime than was lost in the mass extinction that included the disappearance of the dinosaurs 65 million years ago. It is likely to be the first time in evolution's stately course that plant communities, which anchor ecosystems and maintain the habitabiity of the earth, will also be devastated."[1]
—State of the World 1988—

"In its scale and compressed time span, this process of extinction will represent a greater biological debacle than anything experienced since life began."[2]
—Gaia: An Atlas of Planet Management—

The destruction of the living world, the destruction of habitat by farms and cities is the unravelling of the web of life. Because of the complex food chains and the even more complex web of services of all kinds that each living thing performs for others, the elimination of any species and especially key species, eliminates others also. Peter H. Raven, Director of the Missouri Botanical Garden, estimates that because of the specialized feeding mechanisms of most organisms feeding on plants, every plant species that goes extinct takes an average of 10-30 other species with it.[3]

The destruction of the life of the earth is happening so rapidly that no one knows what the cumulative effects will be. The natural human family always assumed that the earth was one living organism and now scientists with modern technology find evidence for this same assumption. (The term "natural" is used to describe the aboriginal, forager/hunter culture of the human family that has existed for 99 per cent of human history and continues to exist as remnant groups in remote parts of the world. The term natural is used because this culture existed in full integration with the natural world.) The earth is a living entity, a self-regulating organism. Each of the various species play a part in this regulation especially of the atmospheric gases that are the Gaian breathing mechanism and the collective breath of many species.[4] As these species and their habitats such as the rainforest are wiped out there is simply no way of knowing specifically what will occur, other than the surety that the macro cycles of metabolism of the earth will go into wild fluctuation. The whole matter is so poorly understood that humans are not even sure of how many species there are on the earth. Edward O. Wilson of Harvard University says: "We do not know the true number of species on Earth even to the nearest order of magnitude."[5]

Because of the deepening planetary crisis, scientific research has focused on the question of species extinction. The current range of estimates is that we are losing one species somewhere between one per day and one per hour. By the year 2000 this may be down to one per minute or if there is a nuclear war it may become ten million in one millisecond.

Any alteration of the life of the earth that causes a decline in the Net Photosynthetic Production is an injury to the earth. That is the standard that we should focus upon. When we approach the stage of extinction of species we are near the death throes of the earth. Civilization responds, perfunctorily, to the threat of extinction of individual species, especially large mammals, but there is no basic understanding of the wiping out of whole ecosystems by airfields, agriculture, housing projects, urbanization, Agent Orange or wanton "resource extraction." There is concern about the larger life forms, many of whose remnants are saved in zoos, but there is yet little understanding that micro-organisms, insects, and microscopic plant species are going also. Mammals are only one percent and vertebrates only three percent of all species. And they all are totally dependent on micro-organisms. Such absurd spectacles as the "saving of the California Condor" are symptomatic of the empire culture perspective. The condor is only one organism in a web of life. It is the destruction of the web of life that has caused the condor to be on the edge of extinction. Even if the condor can be "saved" in a zoo, the habitat that the condor requires for its life will be destroyed. The reality view of empire culture is no preparation to allow it to understand that as habitat is destroyed the basic life of the earth dwindles. As habitat goes, species dwindle in numbers, vegetation lessens and topsoil disappears. The view of urbanized society is that the question of species extinction can be solved by preserving a few representative living things in parks and zoos. The next question, "Preserved for what?," never seems to be asked.

Even if fragments of ecosystems are called "parks" or "preserves," they are still not large enough to prevent the loss of species. *State of the World 1988* reports that:

> "Many parks are simply too small to maintain populations sufficient to ensure species survival. As ecological theory predicts, the smallest parks have lost the greatest share of their original mammal species, but even very large parks such as Rocky Mountain and Yosemite have lost between a quarter and a third of their native mammals."[6]

Rather than attempting to preserve a few remnant species in zoos or in small guarded habitats, we must begin restoring the earth to its former health.

The simple and hard answer is that the human population must be brought down to the level that is in balance with the Net Photosynthetic Production, the Solar Budget. The damage to the earth must be stopped and the life of the earth must be restored. There is no other way that life can continue to exist on this planet.

It is difficult for us in this era to realize how rich and abundant the life of this planet was. Our natural human family lived in a world of affluence. Skies would be dark for days with the flights of migratory birds. Barry Lopez in his book *Of Wolves and Men*, says there was a population of animals numbering 500 million on the Great Plains, with 60 million bison migrating north to south. Millions of pronghorns occupied the plains and plateaus of the U.S. west. The salmon runs on both coasts were truly massive and supported the people for tens of thousands of years without change.

Farley Mowat, in *Sea of Slaughter*, his important work on the natural history of the North Atlantic says:

> "I look out over the unquiet waters of the bay, south to the convergence of sea and sky beyond which the North Atlantic heaves against the eastern seaboard of the continent. And in my mind's eye, I see it as it was. "Pod after spouting pod of whales, the great ones together with the lesser kinds, surge through waters everywhere a-ripple with living tides of fishes. Wheeling multitudes of gannets, kittiwakes, and other such becloud the sky. The stony finger marking the end of the long beach below me is clustered with resting seals. The beach itself flickers with a restless drift of shorebirds. In the bight of the bay, whose bottom is a metropolis of clams, mussels, and lobsters, a concourse of massive heads emerges amongst floating islands of eider ducks. Scimitar tusks gleam like a lambent flame...the vision fails.
> "And behold the world as it is now.
> "In all that vast expanse of sky and sea and fringing land, one gull soars in lonely flight-one drifting mote of life upon an enormous, almost empty stage."[7]

Great dangers are involved with destruction of the rainforest habitat and other remaining unsettled regions but the decimation of species also goes on in settled regions. Europe, which has hosted the industrial society the longest, is losing the final remnants of its life at an astonishing rate. In France for example, 57 per cent of the- remaining- mammal species are threatened with extinction as are 58 per cent of the bird species, 39 per cent of the reptile species, 53 per cent of the amphibian species and 27 per cent of the fish species.[8] Much of the land in Europe was drained and logged off, the life system was eliminated. The auroch, the european wild ox is extinct, the last one died in 1627. The european bison exists only in a relict population and the caucasian subspecies of bison is gone. Relict populations of bex, chamois, bear and wolf exist but simply because a few exist has nothing to do with the reality that a huge living continental ecosystem is now gone. The large mammals are simply symbol species of the vanished habitat in which they once lived.

In Europe we see the final extrapolation of the imperial culture. We see that human beings are capable (with sufficient conditioning) of living in crowded artificial environments, breathing poisonous air and drinking equally poisonous water. The sheltering, heating and feeding of the social complex in artificial environments, is maintained by exponentially growing injections of petroleum energy to run the system and to inject into the soil in place of natural fertility. We can place our bets on whether in a few years, when the petroleum and the biological life are exhausted, the collapse of civilization results in saving some species or whether all will go as a by-product of its death throes.

NOTES

1   State Of The World 1988: A Worldwatch Institute Report on Progress Toward a Sustainable Society. Lester Brown, et. al. W.W. Norton & Co. New York. 1988. p. 102.

2   Gaia. An Atlas of Planet Management. Norman Myers, Editor. Anchor Books. Garden City, NY. 1984. p. 154.

3   Extinction: The Causes and Consequences of the Disappearance of Species. Paul Ehrlich & Anne Ehrlich. Random House. New York. 1981. p. 139.

4   Gaia: A new look at life on Earth. J.E. Lovelock. Oxford U. Press. 1979.

5   State of the World: 1988. op. cit. p. 104.

6   State of the World 1988. op. cit. p. 104.

7   Sea Of Slaughter. Farley Mowat. Bantam Books. New York. 1986. p. 404.

8   World Resources 1987: An Assessment of the Resource Base that Supports the Global Economy. A Report by The International Institute for Environment and Development and The World Resources Institute. Basic Books Inc. New York. 1987. p. 295.

CHAPTER 8

POPULATION, POISONS AND RESOURCES

The Human Population Disaster

There is no such thing as unlimited growth of numbers in the natural world. The populations of organic beings in the web of the natural world do not press constantly against their food supply. For several million years humans maintained a stable population with respect to their environment. The idea that there is something inevitable about human population expansion is wrong. Historically, population explosions have only happened within the human culture that we know as civilization. The idea of linear increase of population was popularized by Thomas R. Malthus and picked up by Charles Darwin in his theory of evolution. Population increase was the basis of the biological dynamics of Darwin's model. Darwin says that, "A struggle for existence inevitably follows from the high rate at which all organic beings tend to increase." Here is one of the grim assumptions that are typical of Darwin's era.

Darwin's concept of population increase fits with the reality perspective of empire culture. In Darwin's scheme organic life is a grim struggle of competition, violence and "survival of the fittest."

The reading of the social values of empire culture into biology is not accurate:

"No species strives to increase without limit, any more than an individual tends to grow to infinity. And animal populations are limited not by struggle, starvation, and death, but by restricting the number of breeders in various ways and by varying the number of offspring produced at a time by each female. Biologist V. C. Wynne-Edward's comments on Darwin's assumption that every living thing strives to increase its numbers geometrically.

" This intuitive assumption of a universal resurgent pressure from within held down by hostile forces from without has dominated the thinking of biologists on matters of population regulation, and on the nature of the struggle for existence, right down to the present day.

" 'Setting all preconceptions aside, however, and returning to a detached assessment of the facts revealed by modern observation and experiment, it becomes almost immediately evident that a very large part of the regulation of numbers depends not on Darwin's hostile forces but on the initiative taken by the animals themselves; that is to say, to an important extent it is an intrinsic phenomenon.' "[1]

Self regulation of populations occurs in natural, undisturbed ecosystems but once those ecosystems are disturbed, populations fluctuate wildly. The apologists of empire will attempt to say that there has been a "social" evolution (linear increase) and that this has progressed since "man the toolmaker" first chipped a rock for use as a tool. This is social ideology, not reality. The human family remained stable for millions of years until the recent inversion to empire. It was only at that point that the "linear increase" of population began. Anthropologist, John H. Bodley states that; "In practice, various cultural controls helped maintain population well below any theoretical maximum carrying capacity based on the ultimate limits of food production."[2] It appears that with the human and other species, population levels are quite elastic. Much evidence in the field of biology suggests that; "A wide range of animals vary their litter size and clutch size according to the amount of food available."[3] This means that in years when the traditional foodstuffs of a species is not abundant, they limit reproduction or do not breed at all.[4] This picture of self-regulation of population by species is contrary to cultural ideology (which is why it took researchers so long to focus on the question) but it agrees with what we know of ecology. The life of the earth is not some mindless, random event. The more modern society learns of the natural world and its ecology, the more we see that life is an extremely complex, balanced, cooperative, intelligent and self regulating organism.

Once the natural culture of the human family was destroyed by conquest and forced acculturation, the natural wisdom was gone and the lid came off human population. With natural culture, which lived in conscious balance with the surrounding life, the cultural motive was to limit human population. When culture inverted with empire, the cultural motive of linear increase resulted in increased population as the patriarchs had conscious motive to increase family size for economic reasons as well as patriarchal pride. With empire agriculture more human labor was needed because they did not gather, they "worked" the land and needed the labor of more sons and daughters. More people were needed for agriculture and more people were needed for militaries. As this increase in the number of people occurred, further pressure existed to then increase food production.

When the balance was exceeded, the compounding effect of the exponential increase began. If two people have three children and those three have three and this occurs among millions, the compounding of numbers becomes a rush. Now, in present day reality we have the unnatural Malthusian spectacle of population increase in exponential amounts- just like the rabbits that were turned loose in Australia where there were no adequate predators.

As imperial culture's development of techniques to extort fertility from the earth progressed, there were surges in population that correlated with surges in food supply. Fritz M. Heichelheim, Professor of Greek and Roman History at the University of Toronto, describes the change that occurred when the Romans invented the steel bottom plow:

"When the heavy soils, the most fertile of our globe, were taken under the plow for the first time in human history, enormous population increases outside of Egypt, Babylonia, and other territories of 'hydraulic' civilizations were the consequence." [5]

When the mercantilist-industrialist elite of the industrial revolution succeeded in finally breaking the last vestiges of culture inherited from tribal Europe, which existed then in the form of self-supporting, subsistence-agriculture peasantry, population, which had been creeping upward, began another compounding surge that we now see world-wide. The relatively stable, landed peasant culture was broken, their lands confiscated and the peasants were forced into the cities to become a growing labor pool."

The European Population Explosion

By 1650, the explosion of population in Europe fueled major colonization efforts. By improved technical ability to extort fertility and materials from the earth, plus the increased efficiency of the newly invented weapons allowing conquest of colonies, a massive increase was financed. Scholarship reveals that the increase in the population of European settlements <u>outside</u> of Europe went from 113 million in 1650, to 935 million in 1950. In that same period of time the population of Europe itself (Europe and Asiatic U.S.S.R.) went from 103 million to 594 million.

The population of Europeans increased much more rapidly than other peoples at the time. Armed with extractive technologies, the Europeans spilled into "rich" ecosystems still undamaged by the march of empire. Experts estimate that world population stood at approximately 545 million in 1650. By 1950 the world population had increased to 2,406 million, an almost 2 billion increase in 300 years.[6] The doubling time of world population from 1 A.D. to 1800 A.D. was somewhere between five and seven hundred years. As the exponential increase began to gain momentum the doubling time had shortened to one hundred and twenty years in 1800. In 1988 the world population doubling time stood at 40 years. Since 1900, most of the increase, <u>of the increase</u>, of world population has happened in the Third World nations.

The projected future increase in human population appears very grim, according to the World Resources Institute:

"Africa's projected growth rate is the highest of all regions, increasing from 555 million in 1985 to almost 2.6 billion in 2100. Latin America and the Caribbean are expected to grow from 405 million in 1985 to 1.2 billion in 2100. Asia is projected to add the largest number of people, growing from 2.7 billion to 4.9 billion. Developed regions are expected to follow a low-growth pattern; by 2100 they are expected to account for only 14.1 percent of the total population, compared to 24.4 percent today."

World population will never reach those projected numbers. At some point the population begins to completely eliminate their survival systems and major die-offs will begin. The world rate of death from starvation now stands at 40 million per year, but this is not yet because of massive die-offs of whole regions.[7] Lester Brown of Worldwatch Institute describes a three-stage decline to disaster. In the first stage the population of a region is well within its ecological support systems. In the second stage it begins to eat up its survival systems (by such things as burning up fuel wood faster than it grows or destroying the soils). In the third stage the biological support systems collapse and a population die-off follows.[8] Many Third World countries have now passed the threshold of increased food per person and are now sliding backward, as population outpaces food supply. Brown states that there are now some 40 countries where per capita grain production is going down.[9] At the same time as these preconditions of starvation develop, the age structure of the populations of dozens of Third World countries grows younger. Now, in the early 1990's, 40-50 percent of the population of many Third World countries is under the age of 15. This means that the age of child bearing is just beginning and that another surge is on its way.

The Industrial Poisons

There was never a poison problem with the natural human family. Pollution, garbage, poisons, are specific to empire culture. Any refuse or debris of natural culture would simply biodegrade, but with a culture that is out of balance with the cosmos, there is no integrated flow and the garbage simply backs up into giant mountains or is dumped in the backyard of others. No one really knows what to do with it.

The question of industrial poisons must be considered in the context of the whole of civilization, which itself is out of balance with planetary life. It is not just the matter of industrial poisons which do not fit with the web of life, they are simply a more recent manifestation of a cultural system that has been fundamentally injurious to life since it began.

Industrial poisons now pervade the planet Earth. Many of the chemical poisons produced by industrial processes have never existed in any quantity or for any duration on the earth before. The count stands now at 70,000 different, artificially produced chemicals, with at least 1,000 new ones produced each year. The industry dominated Environmental Protection Agency of the U. S. government classifies 35,000 of these as harmful or potentially harmful; the actual count is no doubt much larger.

The poisoning of the planet by toxic chemicals is not a static problem. It is a problem that is exploding. Recent statistics from the U.S. shows the trend world-wide. According to a current report: "U.S. production of organic chemicals grew from 4.75 million tons [5.3 million tons] in 1967 to 7.9 million tons [8.48 million tons] in 1977- an increase of 67 per cent."[10] Only a handful of the more popularly known toxins have been thoroughly tested for their carcinogenic, tetragenic (producing deformities of the fetus) or mutagenic properties (producing physical mutations that travel down the generations). The process of testing toxins is long and expensive. The testing process itself can also be corrupt as seen with the case of International Biotest Laboratories in the U.S. whose actual faking of tests called into question approximately 500 compounds that had been approved based on their work. Several of those company executives were sent to federal prison but the system that produced them was not changed nor were the chemicals in question pulled off the market.

Most toxins that have been approved for use by the U.S. Environmental Protection Agency have not been tested for their cancer causing or birth defect causing properties. Years ago the U.S. congress ordered the agency to begin testing already approved compounds for these additional dangers but by 1990, only six of those chemicals had been thoroughly tested.

The U.S. National Academy of Sciences, National Research Council states that enough studies and tests have been done to make complete health hazard assessments possible on 10 per cent of the pesticides produced, 2 per cent of cosmetics, 18 per cent of drugs and drug excipients (binders) and 5 per cent of food additives. In all, we can get this complete information on only between 10 - 12 per cent of the chemicals used by commerce.[11]

Even if the impossible could be achieved and all seventy thousand plus the one thousand new compounds per year could be thoroughly tested, there is the matter of what compounds are created when these substances are indiscriminately mixed together. Agricultural poisons are often mixed before they are applied. The substances are mixed in waste dumps. The substances mix in the industrial production process itself. The substances also mix when they escape into the environment. Even non-toxic chemicals when mixed, can become toxic at times. If we have 70,000 substances and we calculate the number of possible mixtures, we then see the absurdity of <u>guaranteeing</u> any safety.

The production of many of the furnishings of the industrial lifestyle produce toxins. 70 per cent of hazardous waste comes from the chemical and petrochemical industries. Production of such necessities of the industrial lifestyle as plastics, soap, synthetic rubber, fertilizers, synthetic fibres, medicines, detergents, cosmetics, paints, pigments, adhesives, explosives, pesticides, and herbicides produce toxic byproducts, are toxic themselves, or both.

The U.S. leads the world in production of heavy metals and toxic chemicals. In 1981 the estimate was that the U.S. alone was producing 320.7 million tons of hazardous waste.[12] World totals are not precisely known but informed estimates for that year run between 363.73 and 551.15 million tons.

There is no compelling motive for industry to devote much money or attention to the determination of the exact volume or the effects of the poisons they are producing. The motive for obvious reasons, is to hide the numbers. Industrial society gropes in the dark when this entire question of heavy metals, industrial chemicals or radiation poisoning is raised. The public has no way of knowing the facts unless they are given by industry or government. It is in the interest of industry not to do studies, as it only furnishes ammunition for their opposition and often government is in complicity with industry, directly or indirectly. In actual fact the humans and the environment are the guinea pigs. Historically it usually has not been until human cancers, birth defects or die-offs occur, that the discovery of poisoning has been made and any legislative action taken.

As we saw with the case of Agent Orange and the Vietnam veterans, establishing absolute proof of the connection between toxic chemical or radiation and resulting health effects is very difficult. Cancers from radiation exposure appear typically twenty to thirty years after exposure and effects from toxic chemicals often have a similar time lag. In addition, these poisons trigger malfunctions in the body (such as damage to the auto-immune system) and it is difficult to prove in a court of law, the direct link- that one caused the other- especially when there are a number of possibilities.

In one particularly clear and unique case, that of the Navajo Uranium miners, on the Navajo Reservation in the Southwestern U.S., the connection was obvious. A large number of miners lived in the same area under similar conditions-and a preponderance of them developed lung and other cancers while the surrounding people did not. Most of these cancers did not begin to develop for twenty to twenty-five years.

With the transience of modern society, it would be difficult to say what toxic field, ingested substance, or water borne chemical one may have been exposed to twenty years ago! Because the absolute proof is so difficult, killers —mass murderers— go right on killing life (people included), wreaking damage upon the earth and her forms. It is only because of the heavy mental conditioning that the public does not react to their own poisoning. When the government approves a substance that causes only one cancer death per one million people, this is hundreds of people who will die out of a population of several hundred million people. Without the twisting of words and reality the public would ordinarily call this mass murder. The industrialists find it more profitable to dump their poisonous excrement on the public than to figure out what to do with it themselves. In one recent "toxic incident" during the summer of 1988, 730,000 gallons of diesel fuel were accidentally allowed to enter the Ohio river near Pittsburgh, Pennsylvania. Several days after the crisis began, workers found that quantities of other unrelated chemicals were appearing in the water. They found high concentrations of chloroform, methylene chloride, and 1,1,1-trichloromethane, all proven cancer causing substances. The consideration for the environment and other people is so low that other industries were using the crisis as a cover to dump their own poisons in the river!

Poisoning of the planetary waters is extremely serious. Underground aquifers, where it is permanent, are being poisoned by industrial toxins. This is done by deliberate injection of waste into wells, a common industrial practice; by percolation down from the surface; seepage from common municipal landfills; from hazardous waste landfills and from nuclear installations. Agriculture also poisons underground aquifers. In the U.S., at least 30 states have been found to have more than 50 different pesticides in their underground waters. One quarter of the people of Iowa drink pesticide contaminated water.[13] So far, 200 substances have been identified in U.S. underground aquifers, this includes 175 organic chemicals, many already known to cause cancer or birth defects. A vague estimate of the U.S. EPA is that 2 per cent of the underground aquifers of the U.S. are contaminated.[14] Nearly 20 per cent of the wells surveyed in the U.S. by the U.S. Geological Survey in 1985 were found to be contaminated with nitrates used in industrial agriculture.[15] The world's rivers suffer the fate of being the dumping ground of many industries. The Rhine of Europe, for example, drains 150,000 square miles of the most industrialized and populated region on earth. The Rhine discharges into the North Sea each year, 10,000 tons of toxic chemicals and heavy metals. Its waters are fifty times above normal background levels for cadmium and twenty times the normal background level for lead and mercury.[16] "The Rhine, Elbe and Weser carry more than 450,000 tons of phosphates and nitrates into the sea. The concentrations of these nutrients, which contribute to the lethal algal blooms, have increased four-fold over the last 20-30 years adding five to ten times the nutrients that derive from natural sources. Coupled with the industrial inputs of the Ems and Scheldt, these rivers annually channel some 50 tons of cadmium, 20 tons of mercury, 12 tons of copper, 10 tons of lead, 7,000 tons of zinc, 300 tons of arsenic, and 22.5 million tons of sewage and other human detritus into the sea."[17] The Thames River, on Britain's east coast, contributes an annual load of 150 pounds of the pesticide Lindane, 225 pounds of DDT, plus about five million tons of partially treated sewage. On the coasts of Norway and Sweden, mines, mining dumps, logging operations and paper mills, dump and leach a host of pollutants into the sea. Emissions from cars, power plants and factories contribute up to 50 per cent of the heavy metals absorbed by the North Sea, plus tons of sulfur and nitrogen.[18] This is only a partial accounting of the total toxic load dumped into the North and Baltic seas annually from Europe and the British Isles. As these poisons constantly grow in volume and accumulate, we are seeing the actual death of the whole ecology in the North Sea and Baltic sea areas. The die-off of seals and fish populations in these two areas, many scientists are calling late symptoms of eco-death. The North and the Baltic seas are in the advanced stages of where many other ocean areas are rapidly headed. It must be kept in mind that these chemicals are tested on animals to determine their cancer causing properties. These poisons are not just a threat to humans, they are a threat to every organism in the ecosystem.

There are four considerations in the subject of industrial poisons (toxic chemicals, heavy metals and radiation). The first issue is the low-level dispersion throughout the planetary environment. The second issue is the contact with these substances from simply being in the normal artificially created environments of civilization and eating the commercial food. The third issue is the waste produced by industry. The fourth and by far the most important issue is that there is now no known method, that scientific opinion agrees upon, of disposing of this waste and until this disposal is created, the material continues to contaminate the planet.

Researchers say that the body of every person in the world contains some DDT and some PCB's. The contamination by chemical toxins is so great that in some areas of the U.S., nursing mothers are advised to cease breast-feeding. The amounts of toxic chemicals in some mothers are so high that mini-seizures are caused in the infants from the poisonous milk. In the Netherlands, contamination is so heavy that human mothers milk contains even polychlorinated dibenzodioxin and polychlorinated dibenzofurans which are produced and spewed out into the environment by the incineration of waste.[19]

Toxins come to us in the water, the air and in our food. During the period 1982-1985, several studies detected 110 different pesticides in fruits and vegetables commercially sold in the U.S. "Of the twenty-five pesticides detected most frequently, nine have been identified by EPA to cause cancer (captan, chlorothalonil, permethrin, acephate, DDT, parathion, dieldrin, methomyl, and folpet)."[20] Many toxins are airborne and researchers have found that water droplets of fog concentrate poisons. In a study released in 1987, U.S. Department of Agriculture researchers Louis A. Liljedahl and Dwight E. Glotfelty and James N. Seiber of the University of California at Davis report that they found 16 pesticide compounds in fog. These substances came up off of agricultural areas. The poisons occasionally reach very high concentrations relative to reported rainwater concentrations of these same poisons.[21]

It is one thing to examine particular poisons such as radiation, many chemicals and heavy metals that can't be seen, tasted or smelled. It is another to view the gross contamination of industrial societies. A good example of what the outlines of the future are for the whole of industrial culture is shown by Poland.

The Case of Poland

Poland is a mid-range European industrial country. There the citizens were finally prompted by industrial pollution to organize into the Polish Ecological Club (and this caused the government to create a tame, government controlled environmental group). The PEC has been successful in bringing the problems to the attention of the government. The government has made some plans for clean-up but it is very expensive and it remains to be seen if it can be accomplished.

Airborne poisons are so strong in the Polish industrial area of Krakow that they corrode the railway tracks, forcing a speed limit of forty miles per hour for railway trains in the summertime. Don Hinrichsen, an environmental writer says: "Strolling around Krakow on a windless day is like walking through a coal yard. The 'Pearl of Poland' is under siege from an unusually virulent mixture of pollutants ranging from coal dust and carbon monoxide to airborne lead, hydrocarbons, and corrosive acid rain."[22] He says that in the town of Zabrze, near Krakow, there is a "15 percent higher incidence of circulatory illness, a 47 percent higher rate of respiratory ailments, and 30 percent more cancers than the rest of the Polish population."[23] The rise in mental retardation among Polish children is related to lead poisoning. A survey in the Katowice area found 35 percent of the children had lead poisoning. In that same city, the soil was found to be contaminated with lead, cadmium, copper and zinc. Garden vegetables had lead and cadmium 30-70 per cent higher than World Health Organization standards.[24] The Vistula, the river that drains most of Poland is so poisoned that in most areas it cannot be used even for industrial purposes. Yearly, the Vistula pours 90,000 tons of nitrogen, 5,000 tons of phosphorus and 80 tons of mercury, cadmium, zinc, lead, copper, phenol, and chlorinated hydrocarbons into the bay at Gdansk, where the beaches have been closed for years.[25] One-fourth of the agricultural land of Poland is so contaminated that it is unfit to grow human food and only one percent of the water is safe to drink. The industrial elites make no provision for the people, the forests or the rest of the life of the area. Like all empire cultures, the population of Poland exists simply as a productive mechanism to increase the power of the elite. Because of this, the land, water and people continue to be abused. Twenty percent of the food products from one poisoned area were classified as hazardous to public health by the corrupt government's own inadequate standards. Vegetables contained 220 times the limit for cadmium, 165 for zinc, 134 for lead, 34 for fluorine and 2.5 times for uranium.[26] In Poland's worst ecological disaster areas, even Polish law says the people should be evacuated, but there are 11 million of them (30 per cent of the population) and there is no where for them to go.[27] "...Life expectancy for men between 40 and 60 years old has fallen back to the level of 1952. Thirteen million of the country's 40 million residents are expected to acquire at least one environmentally induced illness- respiratory disease, cancer, skin disease, or afflictions of the central nervous system."[28]

The direct annual cost of environmental deterioration in Poland may now equal half of the government's annual budget. The government has created some ambitious plans to clean up the country, which it uses as propaganda to placate and confuse the people, but like other industrial countries little has been done. The Polish economy has been in a state of depression for years. It is mortgaged to the hilt to the International Bankers and there is little money left over for such "frills" as environmental clean up. The U.S. also has said that it will clean up its toxic waste dumps and nuclear leakages but they say too, that it will cost billions of dollars- hundreds of billions-and so far little has been done.

In the World War II era in the U.S., one in thirty people died of cancer. Now, between one in four and one in five die of cancer. The rate of birth defects has doubled since 1950. Cancer is a problem of the auto-immune system as are many other maladies such as asthma, AIDS, candida albicans and allergies. It is known that toxins shock and affect the auto-immune system.

The medical establishment may replace war as the central industry and source of profits for the elite of civilization- and toxins alone could put an end to civilization if somehow it continued indefinitely. Now, in the U.S., the medical establishment is the third largest industry. How can it be that the scientist/technologists surge ahead with their creations, oblivious to any harm to others or the environment? In his profound work, *The Technological Society*, Jacques Ellul points out that technique and technology have their own internal logic. What is most efficient and profitable will be done and this has little to do with side effects or long term effects. Ellul makes the point that instead of technology serving people, technology has now taken over and is conditioning the industrial culture itself as people learn to accommodate it.[29] After Oppenheimer and the gang at the nuclear bomb factory in Los Alamos, New Mexico had developed the first nuclear device, they still did not know if it would set off a nuclear chain reaction that would blow up the entire planet or if it would be a limited reaction and just explode the bomb. In fact the scientists facetiously placed bets on the outcome of the first test. Here we have the culture of empire. After a huge social effort by thousands of people and hundreds of millions of dollars spent, finally a device is created, but there is danger involved. A choice exists between extinction and power, glory and promotions for the makers. The well known choice was made and fortunately the test was only a limited chain reaction. But, now we have nuclear energy with all of its dangers. This choice between individual and institutional gain versus the life of the earth is made throughout civilization every day.

Modern Living Environments are Toxic

This is the reason that we live in toxic environments. The social consider-ations of power and profit for the emperors of the corporate mini-empires are stronger than consideration for living things. Because of this, even the average house in civilization is an ecological sink of poisons. Aerosol sprays, asbestos, fiber glass, building materials of various types, dry cleaning fluids, spot removers, rug and upholstery cleaners, fabric finishes and cements, antistatic agents and fabric softeners, shoe-care products, spray starch, flame retardants, furniture and floor products, detergent soaps, lead soldered pipes, gasoline, oven cleaners, drain cleaners, bleaches, toilet bowl cleaners, window cleaners, scouring powders, plastics of various types and many more common house-hold products may injure or kill.[30]

A typical example is polyvinyl chloride (PVC), a plastic used in many products including food packaging and water pipes. Vinyl chloride is used in its formulation and during manufacture. This substance often leaches out into the environment. Vinyl chloride is a proven cancer causing substance. After tremendous energy and effort, citizens groups have forced the government to pay attention to vinyl chloride (with a limit of one part per million). But even so, the plastic product PVC, from which vinyl chloride leaches, is not controlled. It exists in building construction materials, household furnishings, consumer goods, electrical uses, packaging, vehicle parts and even in some commercial mouthwashes.[31] There is so much PVC in the interiors of modern aircraft for example, that if one is not killed by a plane crash, one will certainly die from the poisons as the interior burns.

If there is any doubt about the morality of the industrial elite, one need only look at the fact that one-quarter of the pesticides exported from the U.S. each year are either severely restricted or banned for use in the U.S. DDT was banned for use in the U.S. in 1972 but 18 million kg is still produced in the U.S. each year for export to the Third World.[32] Actually a whole range of dangerous products are dumped on the Third World. Massive citizen lawsuits finally stopped the sale of the birth control device, the Dalkon shield in the U.S. but it is still sold throughout the Third World with impunity.

The link between one specific poison and a specific cancer in a specific person may not always be demonstrable but we can certainly discover the connection of pollution rates and illness rates. New Orleans for example, exists at the final outflow of the Mississippi river which drains the poisons from much of the east-central U.S. In a test concluded in 1969, the over-all cancer rate there was found to be 32 per cent higher than the national rate. For specific cancers, the New Orlean's rate was three times higher than Atlanta or Birmingham which do not drink Mississippi river water.[33]

Municipal Waste

Eutrophication occurs when an excess of nutrients enters a waterway, the life activities of plants are speeded up and the oxygen suddenly is used up, creating a dead area. While nutrients are good for plants, nutrients in unnatural amounts are harmful. Eutrophication does not normally happen in the natural world, it is a function of the culture that is not resonant with the order of the cosmos. Municipal landfills create a similar situation-even if it were just biodegradable household garbage put all in one place. If we add the poisonous articles of household garbage and the other poisonous items produced in municipalities we have a toxic waste dump of considerable proportions. Even if only moderately toxic, there are so many of them and the volume is so large that municipal landfills themselves pose a serious threat to the water tables and waterways of industrial countries. Municipal landfills leach carbon dioxide, hydrogen sulfide, chrome, zinc, lead, iron and other poisons into water tables.

Poisonous garbage is dumped into municipal landfills by small businesses and industry with little or no monitoring and dumpers often slip extremely toxic waste into municipal landfills.

Toxic Industrial Waste

As if the matter of slowly leaking municipal landfills that are spread ubiquitously over the industrial countries were not enough, there are the dumps that society defines as "hazardous waste sites." One indication of how serious this exploding problem of poisons in the environment is, can be seen by the fact that so little is known about them other than that they exist. Because of the control of information and its deliberate falsification, we can only see the broad outlines of the problem, but what we do know indicates disaster. The disaster is compounded by the fact that the profits and power of the elites are seriously hindered by the proper disposal of industrial poisons. Proper disposal is extremely expensive and the motives on the part of the industrial elites to continue "free dumping" are compelling. The estimate of annual world production of 551.15 million tons is only an educated guess. There are few countries where it is known who is producing it, in what quantities and exactly what chemical or metal it is. The Federal Republic of Germany, for example, has a cradle to grave tracking system but this only functions within the country. Shipments of toxic waste that cross borders, are becoming commonplace, and these shipments disappear from the system. It is estimated that Europe exports 500,000 tons of toxic waste each year (usually to Third World countries). Exactly where this waste goes and under what conditions it is disposed of no one knows.

What we do know is that there is not now any competent method of disposal of toxic waste. Toxic waste is dumped on the ground, injected into wells, dumped into municipal sewage systems, loaded into "approved" toxic waste dumps, dumped into rivers, dumped into oceans and incinerated by low technology and high technology methods which themselves produce toxic waste. Much toxic waste is clandestinely dumped on backroads, back lots and in various bodies of water. Industrialists will pay substantial but still cut-rate amounts for shadowy figures to come to their plants and make their problems disappear. It is well established that Organized Crime (in the U.S. at least) is now well entrenched in this, yet another, super-profit business.[34]

In the U.S., government agencies have begun to estimate the number of toxic waste sites. So far the estimates of the number of sites seem to correlate with the exposure of each agency to industry influence. The Government Accounting Office which is possibly the most independent, estimates the number of priority sites at more than 4,000, with the clean-up cost estimated to be $40 billion. Other sites, which are not classed as "priority," the Environmental Protection Agency says numbers 20,000 and they are not scheduled for clean-up at this time. The U.S. congress set up a Superfund for clean-up of especially hazardous sites, but after five years, only 13 sites have been "cleaned up" and there remains disagreement whether these sites themselves were adequately sanitized.[35] The joke is that they simply scoop up the poison along with the contaminated dirt and move it to another landfill that will eventually leak or incinerate it, spewing or leaching poisons out into the atmosphere.

Just as the medical industry generates huge profits from environmentally induced cancers, a large, powerful and profitable industry has grown up around garbage and toxic waste. Like the medical industry that does not point the finger at the actual source of the profitable cancers, the waste industry generates public relations propaganda about recycling but resists source reduction of waste. The most recent "technological fix" that has been waved in front of the public and the politicians is the very expensive (and profitable) practice of incineration. It is yet to be conclusively demonstrated that any of these plants can be operated without emitting poisons- especially the deadly dioxins-into the atmosphere. There is also no answer to the question of where to put the toxic ash from the plants. In March of 1987 a Norwegian freighter docked in Guinea on the west coast of Africa. It was hauling incinerator ash from a garbage incinerator (not a toxic waste incinerator) in Philadelphia. Bulkhandling, the name of the Norwegian company, had contracted to haul away 250,000 tons of ash laced with heavy metals and dioxin. Some of the waste had fraudulently been sold to a Guinean cement company to use as a brickmaking material. Fortunately the environmental organization Greenpeace blew the whistle on the deal and the Guinean government ordered the shipment out of the country. Greenpeace earlier had notified Panama that a deal had been made to dump the same ash in a pristine Panamanian wetlands area inhabited by the endangered manatee and other rare wildlife. When Panama refused to accept the poisoned waste, the contract with Philadelphia fell through but Bulkhandling was stuck with 30,000 tons of ash. An Ohio landfill was used to dump 15,000 tons and the rest had been sent to Guinea.[36] This is only a small example of the mysterious ways in which much toxic waste disappears.

Radioactive Waste

In the period 1970-1985 alone, commercial, electricity generating, atomic reactors in the non-communist countries generated 65,697 tons of radioactive waste. This does not count shutdown reactors or military reactors in those countries.[37] This is an inconceivably large amount of bulk material and it does not include low level waste, medical or military generated waste. It also does not include the statistics from the socialist world. The figures on total world radioactive waste are not available but the above figure indicates the enormity of the problem. In the almost fifty years since radioactive substances began to be produced there is still no acceptable method for the disposal of the waste. It sits in landfills, ponds and other makeshift sites, often leaking into the ground or air with no solution in site.

The human family has never before dealt with anything as dangerous as nuclear radiation. It can cause immediate death, burns, cancers, birth defects, mutations and many other maladies. A study done by the U.S. Council on Economic Priorities of 50 commercial reactors and 175 nearby counties indicates that the nuclear power plants are causing 8957 extra premature deaths per year. 2113 of these were infant deaths and 6532 of these were cancer deaths.[38] The radiation already produced must be isolated from the life of the earth for the duration of its toxicity. In releasing this monster, the elites of imperial society are assuming that organized society will endure for an unimaginable length of time and that the society will have the means and the will to guard the deposits of poison. Uranium 238 has a half-life of 4.5 million years. Plutonium 239 has a half-life of 240,000 years.[39] Other radioactive elements have shorter lives but they are nonetheless toxic until they expire. Researchers state that little more than one curie of radiation can cause genetic abnormalities. By 1984, the U.S. alone had accumulated 16,200,000,000 curies of radioactive waste. Projections are that the U.S. will accumulate 42,000,000,000 by the year 2000.

Although the elites blithely continue to increase their production of this waste year after year, there is not yet any satisfactory method to deal with it. The only underground depository created so far, the Waste Isolation Pilot Project, a deep cavern dug in a salt formation near Carlsbad, New Mexico has already been found to be leaking water. The Project was created, "for the express purpose of providing a research and development facility to demonstrate the safe disposal of radioactive wastes resulting from the defense activities and programs of the United States."[40] In 1987, a group of scientists from the University of New Mexico found, after a study of the site, that the salt formation contained much more water than the builders had anticipated and they concluded that, "over time, a liquid mixture of brine and nuclear waste could form and eventually reach the environment through unintentional human intrusion or fractures in repository shaft and tunnel plugs and seals." The scientists then explained a factor that would make any underground or undersea depository problematical. Concentrated nuclear waste is not moribund, but continues to, "bubble and boil." The scientists stated that migration would occur, "because of pressurization of waste rooms resulting from gases generated within TRU [transuranic] waste drums and the gradual closing of the waste emplacement rooms due to the creeping action of the surrounding salt.[41] There is not now a solution at the end of the nuclear cycle and the beginning of the nuclear cycle is marked by similar industrial incompetence. On the Navajo Reservation alone there are roughly 80 million tons of uranium mine tailings exposed to the atmosphere. On that reservation..."At Shiprock, New Mexico, uranium mine tailings are within one mile of the public school, a housing development, the business center, and a daycare center." Lora Mangum Shields and Alan Goodman, using a March of Dimes grant, investigated the outcome of 13,300 Navajo Births from 1964 to 1974 born at the Shiprock Indian Health Service hospital:

"Birth defect rates two to eight times higher than averages of the nation or other Indian tribes was found in this high radiation exposure period at Shiprock. In 1975, coincident with a number of reductions in the [atmospheric] radiation exposure, birth defect rates fell decisively towards normal."[42]

On that same reservation, another example of the dangers of the mining portion of the nuclear fuel cycle occurred. On July 16, 1979, ninety-four million gallons of effluent from a uranium mine tailings pond near Churchrock, New Mexico, owned by United Nuclear Corporation, spilled into a local stream, the Rio Puerco. The Rio Puerco is on the watershed of the Colorado River. This spill spread more radiation than did the accident at Three Mile Island. In 1985, the Rio Puerco, at Chambers, Arizona, from which Navajos drink and water their sheep, still tested over the EPA limit by a factor of 50, for gross alpha and beta radiation.

Further along the fuel cycle we have the example of Rocky Flats Nuclear Arsenal, near Denver. This installation, which produces parts for nuclear bombs has spread plutonium and other isotopes into the surrounding suburbs and into the water supply causing a rise in the cancer rates.

Covered by the characteristic secrecy, little had been known about the military reactors that are spread around the U.S. until the incompetence of the operators became so great that radiation began leaking off site. Investigations were begun, some military nuclear plants were shut down and the controversy is whether to spend the tens of billions of dollars to clean up the areas or simply to close them up and leave them set... slowly leaking out onto the earth.

An example of the dangerous irresponsibility of the bureaucratic hierarchies that control radioactive waste is that of the inactive, temporary, waste sites under the control of the U.S. Department of Energy (military only), the contamination that has been allowed will require $60 billion to clean up. This figure is for old inactive sites alone and does not include any other sites.[43]

Managers of the military weapons plants have been criminally irresponsible. Investigators state that: "Billions of gallons of radioactive wastes from making bomb-grade material have been dumped directly into soil and groundwater. Millions more gallons of concentrated waste have been stored in tanks, many of which have leaked. These wastes are now beginning to contaminate public water supplies. The wastes also form explosive gases that could rip the tanks open and spew the material over a large area, creating a Chernobyl-scale accident." This statement is from investigators, Robert Alvarez and Arjun Makhijani, writing in Technology Review.[44] DOE estimates now, before the cost-over-runs have begun, that $100 billion will be required to clean up all its weapons plants.

Although there is now no answer to where the final resting place would be of radioactive materials from a decommissioned reactor, "expert" opinion is that the cost of decommissioning will be between tens of millions of dollars and a billion dollars per reactor.[45] DOE is presently decommissioning the Shippingport plant at an estimated cost of $98.3 million before cost over-runs. There were in 1981, more than 250, electricity generating reactors alone, existing in 22 countries.[46] The irresponsibility of going ahead with this energy system without considering or revealing these huge costs to the public and of going ahead without even knowing where the waste could be safely placed demonstrates the dire danger the planet is in, simply because of the immaturity and corruption of the people in control of these dangerous substances.

The Profits and Losses of Empire

The costs to society of the killing, maiming and deforming humans by industrial poisoning is tremendous and as this cost grows it will be an important factor in the final implosion of civilization. The negative feedbacks of industrial poisons could themselves, ultimately drag it down. Other sources of radiation are medical x-rays. "Probably most cancers of childhood and even some of those during the puberty period are contracted during pregnancy," because of x-rays of the mother. X-rays have been implicated in causing cancer in adults and they have been shown to increase the rates of heart disease in adult males.[47] Public health researchers calculate that cutting the exposure of the U.S. population to radiation by 50 per cent would save $53.2 billion at current prices. The social costs of learning disabilities and birth defects they set at $4.3 billion and added that diseases of the aging process cost $48.9 billion. This cost is calculated for the exposure to x-rays during pregnancy, x-ray exposure to the general population, and fallout from nuclear plants and bomb testing.

The same sources calculate that heavy metals pollution results in $9.6 billion costs in birth defects and learning disabilities and more than $10.2 billion in auto-immune system damage, cancers and early senility in the general population. Chlorinated chemicals and dioxin are calculated to cost the society $1.5 billion in birth defects and learning disabilities and there is no estimate yet available for the general population. Simply halting the use of prescription therapeutic drugs during pregnancy could save the society $3.4 billion in the cost of special programs, medical attention, and etc. for the birth defected and the learning disabled.[48]

A 1984 study in Australia further points out the negative feedback problem of the "quick fix." Rather than feed the soil and nurture the health of the soil community to help it produce human food, the industrial society uses artificial fertilizers which are more profitable to industry and agriculture. This practice pollutes underground waters with nitrate compounds (among other things) wherever industrial agriculture has spread. The Australian study found that drinking well water contaminated with nitrate compounds, rather than rainwater, increased the occurrence of neural tube, oral-alimentary tract, and muscle-skeleton birth defects 2.8 times. (The same effects were found in laboratory animals.) A complete inventory of all poisonings and costs in industrial society would fill volumes but the above examples illustrate the trend. The quick fix, the rapid extortion of energy from the system, can temporarily finance higher population and more "wealth" but ultimately there comes the time of the balancing of the account books, the period the Hopis call "The Great Purification." The actual heavy metals behind these numbers, many chemicals and many atomic isotopes do not go away, they continue to accumulate.

Poison and the Morality of Empire

Certainly, if we could strip away the Public Information Officers, the media consultants and the psychological-operations groups and question one of the handful of human beings of the elite, they would respond that they are seeing the "big picture." The response would be that it is they who are making the "hard decisions" for the whole people, not just for the "special interests," such as the consumers who eat poisoned food, the workers who are poisoned on the job, the farmers suffering pesticide poisoning, the urbanites breathing poison air, the parents complaining of deformed babies or the youth who ask for a future. Like the villages that were bombed in Vietnam to save them, we must industrially produce our way out of our problems, even if it kills us.

The industrial poisoners now pose a grave threat to the entire earth. It is their strategy to confuse, obfuscate and lie to conceal their criminality. A long-haired hippie with a protest sign or an aggrieved black man with a gun gets a lot of attention from the elite controlled media but elite groups who kill, maim and deform millions with their poisons are seldom exposed. In the few cases that have been exposed, we find that the asbestos manufacturers knew of the danger of their products long before the citizens exposed and stopped them. The manufacturers of Agent Orange, which was dumped on Vietnam, knew that it contained dioxin long before it was stopped. The U.S. military also knew long before they banned it. The examples are profuse of industrialists who will dump injurious articles, pharmaceutical drugs and poisons on their earth and their fellow human beings in order to increase their financial power.

The automatic response of the elite when exposed is to deny, lie and cover-up. The first response of the elite after the accident at Three Mile Island was to issue a press release stating that there had been no accident. The British nuclear disaster at Windscale in 1957 was simply covered up and the facts leaked out slowly over the years. In the Soviet nuclear disaster at Chernobyl, the elite was silent for three days until the Scandinavians began to monitor the severity of the crisis and expose it. Other governments, heavily invested in nuclear technology, began damage control of the Chernobyl crisis by putting out the line, "Yes, but it couldn't happen here because...." Over 20 countries received doses of airborne poisons from Chernobyl. The response of many of these countries that are nuclear invested, was to minimize the danger so as not to alarm the people about the nuclear question. Elites in Italy, United Kingdom and France especially, maneuvered to downplay the threat. The French government even falsified a weather map shown on national TV to show that the toxic cloud that in fact came over France, went somewhere else. The childish irresponsibility and deficient morality of the bureaucratic hierarchies puts the whole earth in danger when substances such as toxic poisons, heavy metals, nuclear radiation, the genetic tinkering of biotechnology, and radiological, chemical and biological warfare are involved. Just having these substances under the control of irresponsible bureaucracies is dangerous. It has been demonstrated time and again in the construction of nuclear plants for example, that it simply is not possible to construct a plant without massive cheating on material quality and safety standards by contractors. When the plants are built, it has been amply demonstrated that it is not possible to operate such dangerous devices without massive cheating on the safety of the workers in the plants or the public outside. Civilization as presently constituted simply does not have the moral necessities to avoid it's own suicide because the social institutions set up to guard against these dangers such as toxins and radiation are so morally corrupt that they can't function so as to guard the public safety.

The Fuels of Empire

Imperial culture finds it more profitable and easier to dismantle an ecosystem or suck the fluids from the earth and profit from the brief burst of energy rather than to add to the Net Photosynthetic Production and live from the increase.

Since the beginnings of empire, fuels have been the fountain of its growth. Early, the fuels to heat buildings, cook food and smelter metal were taken from the forests. Forests were also the source of materials for building construction and ships. The course of empire can easily be charted by tracing the exhausted forests of Asia and Europe. As the forests of Europe were becoming exhausted, particularly near smelters and ports, civilization began to depend upon coal. The utilization of coal energy spurred the development of iron and steel refining. From the energy base of coal and the material base of iron, a phase of civilization developed in which iron and steel were used as materials for many applications in society.

As the petroleum age developed, that substance also became the base of plastics, which have replaced wood and metals for many uses. Now society is as dependent upon petroleum for materials as for fuel. Since the "oil crisis" of the early 1970's many citizens have looked to other, small scale sources of energy such as solar, wind, water and ocean power. As the threat of this development became real, the oil cartel moved to buy out the research on these new technologies and to usurp the field. Citizen action in these areas has essentially been stopped and the only plans in the field are for huge centralized technologies such as solar collectors in space. With the immense profits from the oil price rise in the early 1970's the oil cartel has moved into dominant positions in coal, uranium and now the "alternate energies" of solar, wind, etc.

The Transnational corporate elite no doubt feel that they have now positioned themselves so that they will profit by each of the shortages and exhaustions in the coming years. As petroleum runs out they will profit by the coal that they control; as coal runs out it will be discovered that they control the remaining reserves of uranium ore and if that ultimately fails, they will hold the patents and the technology of wind and solar energy.

There is no question that these fuels of civilization will become exhausted and there is no question that this will bring a massive restructuring of that same civilization. The strategy of the elites is simply to stay on top of it as it shifts, and of course it remains to be seen whether they will be successful. Capitalism and socialism are simply window dressing for the basic fact of industrialism. Neither capitalism or socialism works if there is no industry or "resources." In the last two centuries we have seen the pristine living earth devoured by industrialism and much breast beating about the myths of efficiency and ideology. The truth is that machines and abundant primary materials, not ideology, are what have allowed the industrial revolution and it is cheap energy that has fueled its one act production. Energy will now become more and more expensive until it is finally gone.

We can expect massive catastrophe in the next several decades as the supply of petroleum runs out. As the whole of industrial society is predicated on cheap petroleum energy and we are running out of that energy with no replacement in sight, there can only be one result. Although the Transnationals have control of the coal and other energy sources, those sources are not a substitute for petroleum. They are a different energy regime and the switch cannot occur without tremendous dislocation.

The industrial society which now exists, is a product of truly gargantuan injections of petroleum energy. The huge quantity of petroleum and the constantly growing volume of its use means that if a switch were made to coal on an equal basis, simply the smoke from the coal plants all over the earth would asphyxiate us in a short time.

M. King Hubbert, in his book *Energy Resources of The Earth*, points out how swift the growth in the use of fossil fuel has been. Hubbert explains: "It is difficult for people living now who have become accustomed to steady exponential growth in the consumption of energy from fossil fuels to realize how transitory the fossil fuel epoch will prove to be when viewed over the longer span of human history ... The period that encompasses most of the production is notably brief. The 102 years from 1857 to 1959 were required to produce the first half of the cumulative production: Only the ten year period from 1959 to 1969 was required for the second half." The volume of energy to keep the industrial society going is so great that now the discovery of large oil fields only provides a few years supply. The decline of discovery rates (barrels of oil per foot of well drilled) in the U.S., began in 1970 and continues today. Phillips Owen in his *Last Chance Energy Book* says: "The flow from Alaska will not reverse the decline, we can anticipate arresting it for a year or two, but after that, it will resume its dismal course. The fact is that between the time the Alaskan oil fields were discovered and put into production, the other oil reserves declined by more than the total amount that had been found. We're not ahead-we're behind, because we're using oil at much faster rates now."[49] The North Sea oil field of Europe is similar in size to the Alaska field. Here we see within context what these two, much publicized oil fields actually represent- only a few years of use. As a general view of the petroleum energy situation it can be said that we are extracting oil twice as fast as we are discovering it.[50]

In a mid-summer, 1988, interview with journalist Thomas A. Petrie, William L. Randol who heads the Oil Analyst Team of the U.S. based Transnational bank, First Boston, said that oil consumption was up 3 per cent that year. He said that gasoline was the main component of that rising demand. Further, the declining U.S. domestic output means that oil imports will rise to over 50 per cent in several years, from the 41-42 per cent in 1988. Already, Randol sees that the decline in the Alaskan, Prudhoe bay oil field is not far off.[51]

In 1987, the Worldwatch Institute calculated that the U.S. energy reserves within the U.S. were 36 million barrels which was enough to propel U.S. society for 8 years at the 1987 rate of consumption- if it used only U.S. supplies.[52] The supply of natural gas is also declining swiftly. According to the Transnational corporation, Exxon: "U.S. natural gas production peaked in 1972 and has been declining ever since. Production is not expected to recover to 1972 levels, even with production from new offshore leases and from the Alaska north slope.[53]

The supply of uranium ore was never abundant anywhere on the planet. The U.S. is calculated to have had the equivalent of 630,000 tons of which 270,000 tons have already been used and the rate of discovery is declining precipitously.[54]

World energy consumption increased 38 per cent between 1970 and 1984 even with the huge price increases of the early 1970's. If somehow the world population were able to halt the <u>increase</u> of usage and maintain energy use at the 1984 rate, the known global reserves of petroleum would last only 31 years, natural gas 52 years and bituminous coal 175 years.[55]

The increase of energy use in Third World countries has been enormous just to stay abreast of population increase. The following table describes why there is much less than 31 years worth of petroleum remaining:

INCREASE IN ENERGY CONSUMPTION 1970 - 1984 [56]

	TOTAL	PER CAPITA
WORLD	+38%	+6%
AFRICA	+112%	+41%
N. & CENTRAL AMERICA	+7%	+13%
S. AMERICA	+78%	+29%
ASIA	+106%	+55%
EUROPE	+21%	+13%
USSR	+65%	+45%
OCEANIA	+58%	+25%

Caution needs to be exercised in viewing the figures that relate to petroleum and its reserves. The only people who really know how much oil there is are the companies who explore and drill. We can none the less use these numbers as a broad gauge of trends in the field. The number of barrels recovered per foot of exploratory well drilled gives us a good gauge and the reports of experts like M. King Hubbert who have worked inside the industry are helpful.

Another aspect of the amount of reserves is that some of the reserves in old fields are not now economical to recover. Here, as with minerals, we have the situation in which there may be oil but its recovery may be prohibitive. Thus the calculation of reserves is a function of how much energy and money we are prepared to spend to recover the oil. At the point that it requires more energy to extract a gallon of crude oil than exists in that gallon of crude oil, it won't matter what the reserves of it are.

Given the massive exponential expansion of oil consumption which must keep growing to avoid industrial collapse, a few years in the calculation of reserves is of minor importance. The compounding of an exponential growth curve is so swift, from 1 to 2 to 4 to 16 to 1056 to 1,115,136, that only if the oceans were filled with petroleum could the supply continue. Another aspect that becomes important in these later days is the external effects of using the substance. If by chance some new reserves were found it would only increase acid rain, the greenhouse effect, smog, the churning of the wheels of industry which spew out poisons and which would use up remaining resources faster.

The Minerals of Empire

"... Since 1950 human beings have managed to consume more minerals than were mined in all previous history..." says Richard J. Barnet. Of the eight most important metals in world industry in the past twenty years (aluminum, copper, lead, nickel, tin, zinc, iron, steel), the U.S., U.S.S.R. and Japan are the largest consumers. As a gauge of the exponential increase of consumption of minerals and specifically these eight metals, *World Resources 1987* states that the increase in <u>world</u> consumption of the eight has been from 416.67 thousand tons in the year 1965, to 648.61 thousand tons in 1985. [57]

There are plenty of minerals remaining for world society. If we pulverize the crust of the earth and extract all of the minerals from the waters of the ocean there will be plenty. The problem of computing how much remains, is, that even in a handful of dirt there is some percentage of minerals. The question <u>is</u>, how concentrated the ore and how much capital and energy it will take to extract it. Barnet says for example:

"In 1700, typical copper ores contained 13 percent copper. By 1900 the super rich deposits had been exhausted but technology had improved to the point where deposits from 2.5 percent to 5 percent copper were profitable to exploit. Today copper is frequently extracted from 0.5 percent deposits."[58]

Just as the energy intensiveness of the agricultural system is increasing, Barnet points out also that the energy cost of producing minerals is high. "To produce a ton of copper requires 112 million BTU's or the equivalent of 17.8 barrels of oil. The energy cost component of aluminum is twenty times higher."[59]

Critical shortages and steeply rising prices are the obvious future for world minerals. When more energy, more technology, more water and more capital are required to process increasingly lower grades of ore, the future can only go in one direction.

Elite Control of the Industrial Process

The elites control the sources of information concerning energy and mineral resources. It is the elites that decide on the technologies that will utilize different fuels or different metals. It is the elites also who control the supplies and prices. In the past twenty-five years the oil cartel has been able to spread its ownership and control into all energy industries except hydro. They have even usurped the fields of solar and wind generation of energy. The decisions concerning the industrial configuration of society and the social conditions of the individual citizens of society are made by these small elites when they make broad industrial/military decisions. The decision to scuttle non-centralized energy production (solar, wind, small private hydro, wood) was made by elites who control centralized systems (oil, nuclear, electric grid, coal). These decisions will have much to do with the fate of the earth as the primary resources become exhausted. As these finite resources become increasingly scarce, military, industrial and technical attention and conflict will focus on the locations of the remaining resources, such as the Middle East.

One of the basic reasons that empire can generate "surpluses" from the earth is that industrial technique and the "productive masses" can be mobilized under the control of small elites. To give the general picture on a global scale, at the beginning of the last decade of the Twentieth Century, 20 per cent of the world's population were consuming 80 per cent of the world resources.[60] In the capitalist countries in particular, there is a further severe imbalance where a minority owns the majority of resources. The control of world industrial society has come to rest in fewer hands and its control begins with energy and minerals, the backbone of industry. In the socialist countries control rests in the politburos and heads of the giant bureaucracies. In the Capitalist world, control rests with the international financial elite, people who are members of the Bilderberg group and the Trilateral Commission. Coal energy, because of the heavy investments in mining and distribution, have traditionally been under centralized control. Petroleum began to be utilized in the era of the great trusts at the beginning of the 19th. Century. Until recently, what were called the Seven Sisters, (five U.S. corporations and two British and Dutch) controlled the capitalist world oil supply. Due to mergers, there are now even fewer Transnationals that are dominant in the world oil business. It is this elite who plan the volume of production and from which area it will be produced. The minerals industry is very centralized. "The marriage of high finance—Morgans, Rothschilds, Schiffs, Bernard Baruch—and the most successful mining entrepreneurs, principally the Guggenheims, in the early years of the century laid the foundation for the minerals oligopolies that control the world market today."[61]

As the collapse of civilization begins to accelerate in the coming years it is these small elites who will continue to make the planning decisions. The well known diplomat and author George F. Kennan, who was known as a liberal, stated the groundwork for this contemporary era in a State Department Policy-Planning Staff paper (#23), in February 1948, when he was head of this group. He wrote:

> "We have about 50 percent of the world's wealth, but only 6.3 percent of its population....In this situation, we cannot fail to be the object of envy and resentment. Our real task in the coming period is to devise a pattern of relationships which will permit us to maintain this position of disparity.... We need not deceive ourselves that we can afford today the luxury of altruism and world-benefaction ... We should cease to talk about vague and ... unreal objectives such as human rights, the raising of the living standards, and democratization. The day is not far off when we are going to have to deal in straight power concepts. The less we are then hampered by idealistic slogans, the better."[62]

It is from this perspective of muted desperation that the present structure of world society has developed. Since that time a centralized military-industrial complex has developed in the First World and the Third World has become thoroughly militarized. In 1979, $35 billion and one-half million scientists and engineers were engaged in military research.[63] The military weapons industry is now the second in size in the world after the oil industry. Military spending in the Third World doubled between 1974 and 1984.[64]

The profits and production of the armaments industry is so huge that all the U.N., programmes for health, children, food and such could run for two centuries for the amount of money spent in one year on planetary armaments (1982 figures).[65]

The concentration of power in the Transnational corporation-government-military complex group has created a foreign policy of industrialism. This strategy is to maintain control of the Third World and its markets and resources by feeding and controlling its militaries and preventing any "nationalist" movement that might attempt to use these resources for the benefit of the indigenous population.

The United States produces the largest volume of military hardware and it is followed by the Soviet Union who is a remote second (in 1980 the U.S. accounted for 50 per cent of the military hardware in world trade and the U.S.S.R., 30 per cent).[66] Now, the world imperial system of militarism has reached into the Third World countries with the U.S. weapons industries there. "The Department of Defense has more than forty coproduction projects under which it assists other nations to become weapons producers in their own right. Private U.S. firms have another seventy-five such projects."[67] When we look at the world perspective from this angle we see how readily the official policy of the U.S. government- Low Intensity Conflict- fits into the overall scheme. LIC simply means controlling the geography of resources and markets as long as possible.

The internal logic of empire is toward elitism, centralization, separatism, and militarism. As the world empire disintegrates, we will see the elite continue to draw off more energy and materials for their own purposes while strengthening their control over the increasingly impoverished masses. This will continue until the final shoot-out around the gas pump when the hegemony of the internationalist corporate-government-military elite itself begins to disintegrate.

NOTES

1   The New Biology: Discovering the Wisdom in Nature. Robert Augros & George Stanciu. New Science Library. Boston & London. 1988. p. 128.

2   ibid. p. 166.

3   ibid. pp. 126,127.

4   ibid. pp. 126,127.

5   Man's Role In Changing The Face Of The Earth. (International Symposium - Wenner-Gren Foundation for Anthropological Research). William L. Thomas, Jr. Editor. with collaboration of Carl O. Sauer, Marston Bates & Lewis Mumford. Wenner-Gren Foundation For Anthropological Research & the National Science Foundation, pub. U. of Chicago Press. Chicago. 1956. vol. 1. p.166.

6   Man's Role In Changing The Face Of The Earth. William L. Thomas, Jr., ed. U. of Chicago pub. Chicago. 1956. vol. 2. p. 972.

7   Gaia: An Atlas of Planet Management. Norman Myers, ed. Anchor Books. Garden City, NY. 1984. p. 48.

8   State of the World: 1987. Lester Brown, et. al. W.W. Norton pub. New York. 1987. p. 27.

9   ibid. p. 36.

10   Myers. Gaia. (atlas). op. cit. p. 123.

11   World Resources 1987: An Assessment of the Resource Base that Supports the Global Economy. Basic Books Inc. New York. 1987. p.204.

12   ibid p.202.

13   State of the World 1988: A Worldwatch Institute Report on Progress Toward a Sustainable Society. Lester Brown, et. al. W.W. Norton & Co. New York. 1988. p.122.

14   World Resources 1987. op. cit. p. 203.

15   The Amicus Journal. (a publication of the Natural Resources Defense Council) Spring 1988, vol.10, no.2. p.28.

16   Environment. December 1986. vol.28, no.10. "Editorial" by William C. Clark.

17   Greenpeace. "The Seal Plague: Pollution and the Collapse of the North Sea." Andre Carothers. vol. 13, no. 6. November/December, 1988. p. 7.

18   ibid. pp. 6-7.

19   Birth Defect Prevention News. November 1986, Fifth Edition. National Network To Prevent Birth Defects, pub. Box 15309, Southeast Station, Washington, D.C. 20003. p. 7.

20   ibid. p.7.

21   Nature. February 12, 1987. vol. 325. "Pesticides In Fog." D. E. Glotfelty, J. N. Seiber & L. A. Liljedahl. p.602.

22   The Amicus Journal. op. cit. p. 4.

23   ibid. p. 6.

24   ibid. pp.6,7.

25   Greenpeace. Nov/Dec, 1988. op. cit. p.14.

26   ibid. p. 19.

27   ibid. p. 15.

28   Brown. State of the World 1988. op. cit. p. 7.

29   The Technological Society. Jacques Ellul. Vintage Books. New York. 1964.

30   The Household Pollutants Guide. Center for Science in the Public Interest. Albert J. Fritsch, Gen. Ed. Anchor Books. Garden City, New York. 1978.

31   ibid. pp. 197-203.

32   Myers. Gaia. (atlas). op. cit. p.123.

33   Laying Waste: The Poisoning Of America By Toxic Chemicals. Michael H. Brown. Pantheon Books. New York. 1980. p. 103.

34   Poisoning For Profit: The Mafia and Toxic Waste In America. A.A. Block & Frank R. Scarpitti. Morrow pub. New York. 1985.

35   World Resources 1987. op. cit. p. 207.

36   Greenpeace. November/December 1988. vol. 13, no. 6. "Return To Sender: Clamping Down On The International Waste Trade," by Judy Christrup. p.8.

37   World Resources 1987. op. cit. p. 306.

38   Birth Defect Prevention News. March 1987. op. cit. p. 6.

39   Myers. Gaia. (atlas). op. cit. p. 125.

40   Department of Energy National Security and Military Application of Nuclear Energy Authorization Act of 1980 (P.L. 96-164).

41   Status of the Department of Energy's Waste Isolation Pilot Plant. statement of Keith O. Fultz, Senior Associate Director Resources, Community, and Economic Development Division Before the Subcommittee on Environment, Energy and Natural Resources Committee on Government Operations, House of Representatives. September 13, 1988. GAO/T-RCED-88-63.

42   Birth Defect Prevention News. March, 1987. op. cit. p. 7.

43   Nuclear Waste: Problems Associated With DOE's Inactive Waste Sites. United States General Accounting Office. August, 1988. GAO/RCED-88-169. p. 5.

44   Utne Reader. #31, January/February 1989. "Cleaning up after the Pentagon: The dangers of nuclear weapons waste." Robert Alvarez & Arjun Makhijani. reprinted from Technology Review. August/September 1988. p. 50.

45   Nuclear Regulation: NRC's Decommissioning Cost Estimates Appear
     Low. Report to the Chairman, Environment, Energy, and Natural
     Resources Subcommittee, Committee on Government Operations,
     House of Representatives. July 1988. GAO/RCED-88-184. p. 4.
46   Myers. Gaia. (atlas). op. cit. p. 124.
47   Birth Defect Prevention News. March, 1987. op. cit. pp. 5,6.
48   Birth Defect Prevention News. November, 1986. Fifth edition. op. cit.
     p. 3.
49   The Last Chance Energy Book. Phillips Owen. Johns Hopkins U. Press.
     Baltimore, MD. 1979. p. 38.
50   ibid. p. 39.
51   "Poison Peace: What The End of the Iran-Iraq War Means for Oil." by
     Thomas A. Petrie. Barrons Business & Financial Weekly, July 25, 1988.
     p. 6.
52   State Of The World: 1987. op. cit. p. 11.
53   Owen. The Last Chance Energy Book. op. cit. p. 48.
54   ibid. p. 50.
55   World Resources 1987. op. cit. p. 299.
56   ibid. pp. 300-301.
57   ibid. p. 299,307.
58   The Lean Years: Politics In The Age Of Scarcity. Richard J. Barnet.
     Simon & Schuster. New York. 1980. p.117.
59   ibid. p. 118.
60   EPOCA UPDATE. Summer 1990. The Environmental Project On
     Central America. Earth Island Institute, 300 Broadway suite 28, San
     Francisco, CA. 94133. p.2.
61   ibid. p. 138.
62   The Chomsky Reader. Noam Chomsky. James Peck, ed. Pantheon
     Books. New York. 1987. p. 318.
63   Myers. Gaia. (atlas). op. cit. p. 204.
64   ibid. p. 246.
65   Myers. Gaia. (atlas). op. cit. p. 248.
66   Barnet. The Lean Years. op. cit. p. 223.
67   ibid. p. 223.

CHAPTER 9

THE CULTURAL DYNAMICS OF EMPIRE

Human cultures obey rules of metabolism. They are an energy code. A large part of human culture deals with food and eating. The life forms of the planet fit into niches within the flow of solar energy (NPP). Each species of organism fits into a niche so that it receives food energy and also makes a contribution to help support the system. Birds transport the seeds of trees, bees pollinate the flowers that they rely upon for food and all bodies eventually die and feed the soil.

All beings in the flow system of life energy adapt in some manner to the whole. Human societies have been guided by cultures, adapted to certain ecosystems. On both coasts of North America, Europe and the British Isles there were massive migrations of fish at one time. This flow of protein in turn created niches for many life forms. Eagles, bears and humans were prominent in utilizing this food source. The young humans learned to fish. Fish were the subject of tribal art. Fish were the focus of spiritual attention through ceremony and ritual. Fish were food and their parts, such as bones, became useful tools and functional articles. All of these things were learned as part of the culture. The culture is an energy code instructing the young how to derive energy from their niche in the living world.

Our ancestors, the forager/hunters, had adaptations to reindeer migrations, bison migrations, salmon migrations and in the far north, whale, walrus and other migrations. There were many cultures also that had no one primary dependence but were adapted to the whole diversified ecosystem. We functioned according to the metabolism of the larger life flows. We followed the seasons nomadically, we knew each harvest of each watershed as it became available. The metabolism of the earth set the pattern of dynamics for the forager/hunter cultures. The success of our endurance for three million years as a human family was our adaptation, our congruence with the larger cycles of energy. Our ancient culture was diametrically opposed to the form of civilized culture. Civilized culture is not a linear and qualitative improvement, it is simply an inversion of our previous culture. In our ancient culture we functioned in what anthropologists call a "domestic mode of production." That is, we produced what we needed within the clan and tribe. We were nomadic, we did not attempt to accumulate surpluses or create markets. Bartering was a peripheral and minor activity. Food and goods were distributed through familial systems of sharing that were conditioned by each culture. Marshal Sahlins, a noted anthropologist and author of the widely circulated book, *Stone Age Economics,* reports that after studying many tribal economies, he finds that none of them come near the maximum yield of their environment. That made them stable and sustainable.

One of the myths of civilization is that our ancestors were hungry, lived short lives, and only by a high birth rate, could sustain their populations. Just the opposite is true. Tribal people consciously kept their populations under control by herbal contraception, abortion, abstinence, long nursing periods and infanticide.

Anthropologist Robert Allen in examining the !Kung Bushmen who live in the Kalahari desert of southern Africa finds that, "The proportion of men and women over 60 is 10 per cent—smaller than in the industrial countries of Europe and North America, but significantly greater than in the nonindustrial countries of the tropics."[1] We see here a tribal group living in an exceptionally harsh environment whose life expectancy exceeds most third world countries. Other tribal peoples, now gone, who lived in richer ecosystems must have been better off. The Kalahari is similar to the conditions of the Mojave desert of California in the U.S. or the Negev in the Mid-East.

Robert Allen says that, "The Dobe !Kung...eat more protein than the British. Indeed, each person's daily protein intake, 93.1 grams, is exceeded by only 10 countries today."[2] A time-and-motion study pointed to by Allen shows that the Bushmen were not desperate for food or they would have devoted more time to food gathering and hunting. Allen says that, "It was found that they never spent more than 32 hours a week searching for food, and that the average was half that—or just over two hours a day for a seven-day week!"[3] We must keep in mind that most tribal peoples conducted a full and rich human culture with voluminous oral literature that was continuously spoken and they conducted many ceremonials and tribal rituals. Their time was not all taken up with subsistence matters.

John H. Bodley in his, *Anthropology And Contemporary Human Problems,* [4] reports:

In 1965, 75 anthropologists assembled in Chicago to examine the latest research findings on the world's last remaining tribal hunting peoples, who were expected soon to become extinct. The result was a new description of life in these simplest of ethnographically known societies, showing their existence to be stable, satisfying, and ecologically sound, and not at all 'solitary, poore, nasty, brutish, and short,' as Thomas Hobbes had proclaimed in Leviathan in 1651. It was learned, for example, that even remnant hunters such as the Bushmen, who survived in extreme and marginal environments, were not eking out a precarious existence, constantly on the edge of famine, as was thought. Indeed, they devoted only a few hours a week to subsistence and suffered no seasonal scarcity. When uncontaminated by outsiders, tribal hunters seemed to enjoy good health and long lives, while they had the good sense to maintain their wants at levels that could be fully and continuously satisfied without jeopardizing their environment. One researcher even suggested that this was, after all, the original 'affluent society.'

"Most significantly, when the discussions ended, it was concluded that the hunting way of life, which had dominated perhaps 99 per cent of humanity's cultural life span, had been 'the most successful and persistent adaptation man has ever achieved....'"[5]

In viewing the cultural change that has occurred since we were all forager/hunters, we confront the myth of "man's evolution." There is the linear concept of biological, "genetic," evolution and a corollary concept of "social evolution." The picture is that "man the toolmaker" has laboriously evolved, socially, by his inventions. First the rocks were chipped for tools, then the bow and arrow, then agriculture and now computers. In order to logically justify this linear concept, those farthest back on the linear path must be understood to have been in much worse condition than we are today. In this myth, we, today, in the richest industrial countries are at the forefront of social evolution. We are the most "evolved." The emphasis is that we laboriously "invented" agriculture as an escape from the previous, less satisfactory condition. This is the standard myth. Others seek to use other functional reasons in addition, to explain why humans became civilized. Other theories to explain what influenced this cultural change are a rising population of forager/hunters which may have forced farming intensification or that the die-off of large mammals after the last ice age forced forager/hunters into agricultural intensification and a sedentary way of life.

The standard measure in the field of anthropology is that forager/hunters today, as in the past, spend an average of 500 hours per year per adult person in subsistence activities, the sedentary villager spends 1,000 hours and of course the modern 40 hour week amounts to 2,000 hours per year. As anthropologist John Bodley so ably points out, this presents a problem for the linear concept, namely why would the forager/hunters opt for a system in which twice as much time would be taken up with subsistence? He points out that there are examples where village agriculturalists have actually returned to forager/hunter life styles when the opportunity presented itself.[6] The linear concept would argue also that humans "discovered" agriculture somehow, as if foragers with their intimate knowledge of the natural world did not know that plants grow from seeds!

The big myth which we are confronting in this essay is the myth that says that there has been a qualitative advancement with the change from forager/hunter culture to civilization. We have already seen that only ten of the countries in the world exceed the protein intake of the !Kung Bushmen. This means that most of the civilized people of the world can't even feed themselves to the level of the forager/hunters and this is no doubt true for most of the people in history who have lived in "civilization." Civilization actually represents a lowering of living standards, using the values of longevity, food, labor and health for most people outside of the elite class. Only by restricting our view to "inventions," could we say that there has been a linear progression. We live in a world where starvation is increasing. It is a world of myth where millions and soon hundreds of millions, die of starvation and we still say we are making "progress" by counting the number of devices created. This may be the ultimate of materialism (the belief that material objects are the ultimate value), that as billions die on a dying planet, we say that we have made great progress because we invented airplanes, computers, satellites and we went to the moon in a rocket ship.

Many have theorized about the cause of the change from forager/hunter to civilization. We simply do not know for sure. None of us were there and little hard evidence exists. Though we don't have hard evidence for the why of the change we have abundant information about what the change was. We can easily understand the meaning and impact of these functional patterns in human society.

The functional change was the domestication of plant species for agriculture both in China and in the original Indo-European area of the Caucasus Mountains of Central Asia. The Indo-Europeans also domesticated sheep and goats. This was accompanied by the creation of villages. Early villages in what is now Turkey have been dated at 8,000 years in the past. Smelting and copper working in the area have been dated at approximately 5,000 years in the past.

The Cultural Inversion

The large question that we seek to answer is, "What is it about the culture of empire that has produced the prospect of planetary suicide for us?" To understand this we must look at how this culture functions, its functional basis, its dynamics. When this change to empire occurred, human culture in effect inverted. In forager/hunter societies we were ecologically balanced. The archeological evidence from one area, southern Africa, is that humans lived stably for 130,000 years without overwhelming the ecosystem that they depended upon.[7]

In the inversion, human culture changed from one of sharing and cooperation in clan society to one of deliberate inequality of goods.

The culture changed from one of social equality to one of hierarchies of authority and despotism ruled by the Emperor and associated elites.

The culture changed from emphasis on fecundity, mother nature and the female to patriarchy- control and ownership by males.

The culture changed from emphasis on cooperation in clan society to an emphasis on the cult of the warrior and violence. This is a change from cooperation to coercion.

The emphasis in tribal society was on sharing. In most tribal societies the chief spokesperson for the group was generally the poorest in material terms. This is because that person had shared the most and was therefore held in esteem by the group. This changed to an emphasis on materialism symbolized by the emperor who possessed riches amongst his peasant subjects who had little.

The inversion represented a severance from the consciousness of the living world, what some call a change from pantheism to deism. Natural culture has a continuing contact with the spiritual consciousness of the living world. Each person in Natural culture had the cultural understanding that each living thing was a spiritually conscious entity as well as the understanding that everything in material reality was spiritually vivified. When the inversion caused the severance from this, human spiritual sensibility became abstracted into "religion." No longer was the entire world spiritually animated but the focus was on a pantheon of abstract deities or on one deity. These entities were not part of the corporeal world but were abstracted somewhere in mental space. This was the first alienation and separation from life. This radically changed human perception. In the former world of the forager/hunter, the cultural experience was a continuing and direct spiritual contact with the cosmos. When the culture inverted this was severed and the narrow focus was placed on abstracted "Gods," priestly hierarchies and material goods. Natural culture, the forager/hunter culture that lived in integration with the natural world, viewed reality as a composite life where all beings worked together to produce the whole in a natural manner. With the advent of empire the reality view changed to centralized power concepts such as the abstracted gods and goddesses and the centralized authority of the emperor who in most cases claimed to be ruling by divine right granted by a male god. This tendency toward abstraction demonstrated itself in money as an abstraction of biological energy and in writing as an abstraction of human speech. We can also say that now, empire culture is abstracted- removed- from the earth and only retains a "resource" relationship with the living world.

Wisdom and human maturity were casualties of the inversion. Generally in Natural culture, humans managed their numbers and had great awareness of their cooperative relationship with the living world and great respect for it. All species are self-regulating with respect to their environments. This on the human level we could call maturity. Later, we will show that tribal society went to considerable lengths to be self-regulating. The examples of population control are equalled by the care not to overburden the environment with hunting or other use. There was respect for the living world as well as a concern about future generations. With inversion, group responsibility and responsibility to the young, so that they could endure, has been lost. This has been replaced by a focus on individual accumulation with disregard of responsibility to the group, the living world or concern about the future survival of the young. Animals all seek to protect their young and provide them with optimum survival but the culture of empire does not. A popular example of the wisdom of Natural culture is the rule of the Six Nations Iroquois Confederacy, that all decisions in council be viewed with respect to their effects upon the seventh generation. These values of Natural culture were centered around one fundamental- respect. People had respect for themselves-valued themselves- respect for others and respect for the cosmos that had given life to all. The effect of the inversion has been to elevate the negative social values of violence, selfishness, lying, stealing (conquest) and irresponsibility to the level of cultural standards.

The Dynamic Cultural Factors

Our ancestors lived by adaptation to the life of the earth. When the pathology of empire broke out in the human family this adaptation and unity with the cosmos faded, and rather than adapt to the cosmos, humans became "God," as it were. Humans sought control rather than adaptation. This is the pivotal fact of the culture of empire. Humans in empire culture began this control with domesticated "biological slaves": wheat, barley, sheep, goats, water buffalo and rice. When this change occurred, human culture changed from ecological balance to ecological imbalance. The biological slaves have historically been used along with human slavery to extort energy from the earth's metabolism in a parasitic relationship. This led to the idea that humans have no need to unify and act responsibly and cooperatively with the cosmos but instead it was the cosmic role of humans to control the cosmos. Thus, the suicide pact of empire began. This need to control, so characteristic, truly, of a position of weakness, is the pivotal fact from which the coercive dynamics of empire culture flow.

The attitude of control rather than cooperation with a greater power is a quantum shift in human perception. From a position that all perceived reality is manifest from unseen spiritual dynamics with which tribal people were in contact, humans in empire began to see the world as a source of gratification for culturally defined needs-the accumulation of material wealth and power over the earth and other people. Meaning was taken from the spiritual forces of the cosmos and placed on material accumulation. In this respect the cosmos became meaningless. Unfortunately this left humans unconnected so that their lives were meaningless also. The fundamental dynamic of the Culture of Empire is linear increase. The massing of human population into the early towns meant that people had gone above the natural, sustainable level. It meant that the humans would exhaust the foraging area and so must turn to some other method of obtaining food- that was agriculture and domestication of animals. Once this inversion had occurred, rather than the previous balance, it became to the advantage of the humans to spur further growth. Further growth in human numbers added to the human energy applied to agriculture, stock raising and the production of material goods. Further growth also increased the security of the sedentary population. Because the increasing, sedentary population needed military conquest to expand their food base, patriarchy, militarism and hierarchy were strengthened.

Once the human population exceeds that of balanced forager/ hunters, the ecology of the area inevitably becomes denuded. This is the trigger mechanism. When one eats up what is in one's own backyard- when one exceeds the natural productivity-it is necessary to go to other areas to get more to sustain the massed group. This requires militarism and the social ideology of conquest. The idea of accumulation of material goods and the idea of linear increase becomes ingrained into the social ideology.

A profound change takes place in the psyche of the culture when this change from gatherer/hunter to civilized, imperial energy systems occurs. Where natural human culture tended toward unities of person, tribe, and cosmos- in cooperative relationship, the culture of empire tends toward disintegration, separation and isolation on all levels. Conflict/competition, not cooperation, becomes the dynamic. The cooperative unities are supplanted by the coercion of the controlling elite with its military force, as in early empires, or with administrative-legal control in the later empires. Human culture, which had been passed down through generations, person to person, disintegrated, but the social body was still held in form by the power of the elites with their hierarchies of coercion. Order in imperial society ultimately rests upon the monopoly of violence. Within the imperial world view, the imperial cultural mind, power is the ability to compel another person or to force change in the material world. Power to compel and force is a central dynamic. This power is the dynamic by which the heathen are conquered, the aristocrat becomes emperor, material goods are produced or gold is accumulated. This coercion is the element of militarism in empire. The complete inversion of human society from Natural to Empire culture did not take place overnight but took thousands of years to become what it is today. What it is today, nonetheless, is a direct extrapolation of the original dynamics that were initiated when human population began to swell. When the inversion occurred, human attention shifted from relationship with the living world to extortion of the fertility of the living earth. The extortion factor of empire is in effect stealing. Though civilization fears to name it, conquest is piracy and as the anarchist theorist, Kropotkin, says, ownership is theft. Differential profits are theft. The First World sucking the Third World dry of their resources is theft. Male ownership of females and the use of their energy, which was sanctioned by common law until recently, is theft. Human slavery is theft. The using up of the earth's life by unbalanced culture is theft from one's children. Empire culture is based upon the theft of conquest and the socially sanctioned practice of theft runs throughout the society under many names. The deliberate inequality of hierarchy introduces competition and a struggle for power. Hierarchy is not a social form in which all share equally. It is a form in which the few in the elite are winners and the supporting masses are losers. Much of the conflict, covert and overt in the culture of empire concerns who gets the scarce goods. Any possible separation or difference such as race or gender is used to gain advantage. Hierarchy is a social context of coercion. Hierarchy creates a context of dominance/submission and a competition for power.

We see this lack of wise management, this immaturity of competition now in world society. Because the people of Empire culture are locked into an accumulative, competitive structure, there is no management of the whole. Each person, social institution or country simply struggles to maximize their power and wealth. There is only grasping for short-term gain at the expense of long-term survival. In a competitive market or a socialist collective farm, the farmer who incurs the long-term expense of preventing soil erosion- will go broke or will be replaced by another collective executive. In a hierarchal/ competitive environment, short-term gain must take place over long-term gain because the short-term gain will eliminate the possibility of long-term gain. No one in the empire advocates long term gain in soil fertility when the short-term gain of profit margins or production quotas are the whole point of the effort. This is the reason that nothing real will be done to avoid the final collapse of civilization. The structure of empire is to enrich the emperor/elite at the expense of the earth - not to manage affairs for the benefit of the whole life of the earth.

Agriculture and herding began the energy system of empire, rooting in the soil, extracting energy directly out of the planetary metabolism - and growing by the force of violence employed against the earth. The development of mass societies demands stasis, immobility rooted in the soil organ. As the hierarchy of human power relationships grows in the cult of empire, the energy of the soil community and the general life that finances it declines. Empires have historically run great net deficits of the fertility of the earth. The cultural ideology of the warrior cult of empire may have survived into our time, but the individual energy cycles of each empire such as the Indus Valley, Sumeria and Greece that have adhered themselves to the earth's metabolism, have each cycled into ecological exhaustion. Unfortunately, the cultural form had spread before they deflated.

Empire replicates itself in the mind of the young by means of the patriarchal family. The family itself is a mini-empire that provides the conditioning which prepares both the male and female children for their later roles in the larger social body. In the family the young females learn their submissive, dependent roles and the young males learn their roles as the favored "mini-emperors" of the hierarchal structure. The sexual imbalance of patriarchy and female ownership, or more accurately, female slavery, is inherently involved with militarism and with the inherent growth dynamic of empire. War, inherently brings the males to supremacy within a culture. Not only is empire forced to expand because of the exhaustion of "resources" in its central areas but there is a growth dynamic in the sociology of warrior cultism itself. It is simply that a general amounts to very little unless there is a war to fight. In a culture of militarism it is the role of the males of the culture to foment war. War is the raison d'etre of militaries. In ancient times, the country of Greece did not have to conquer the "known world" in order to feed and clothe itself. Nonetheless, Alexander laid down and cried when there were no peoples left to conquer. He cried not because Greece had any functional need to conquer the whole world but because he and his culture had internalized the values of empire.

Patriarchy, militarism and growth are defining characteristics of empire culture. The growth of a large family sired by the patriarch is a factor in the power of the patriarch's mini-empire (and in population explosions). In the whole empire, numbers mean power when the cultural destiny is to accumulate and conquer. Even now, with almost universal knowledge of the consequences of the population explosion, some empire culture governments still cannot help but worry about the slowdown of population growth. Some governments aid population growth through tax incentives and other subsidies not enjoyed by single people or childless couples. All the patriarchs of religions and governments of the various sectors of the final empire understand that even as poor as individual Chinese citizens are, the mass of them creates the fact of a world power (though the Chinese government has recognized limits and has instituted birth control programs). The present population explosion is not an inevitable or natural occurrence. It is clear that the human population explosion is the result of cultural and religious factors. For the millions of years of the human family there was no world population explosion until empires began.

It is these "values of imbalance" functioning in the human social body that are killing the life of the earth. These values are: materialism, militarism, patriarchy, hierarchy, linear increase and extortion. Superficial political reform of this culture is no answer, technological innovation is no answer, the answer is that all of these dynamics must end and new culture must be created. Any human group functioning according to these dynamics will ultimately destroy the earth. The planetary crisis now is a product of these dynamics. Whether one drains the ecosystem of its energy slowly or rapidly, the ultimate conclusion is nonetheless, death for all.

The Cosmology of Empire

Materialism is the end of the spiritual world. When humans began to believe that they could "own" part of a planet, when humans began to selfishly "possess" things, cutting themselves off from the reality of the beneficent cosmos and its flow of energy, spiritual contact fell away. When the empire erupted, when the focus of consciousness turned from the cosmos with all of its diversity of forces and beings, the focus narrowed, simplified. From the grand diversity of the cosmos, humans focused narrowly on the self and what the self identified with-its possessions- existing in a social context of the valuation of material objects. The value of humans became "wealth"- the objects that they possessed. One cannot live in holistic reciprocity with the forces and beings of the cosmos and be selfish. Generally, in the pattern of imperial culture the focus was turned inward, toward isolation, to concern with self rather than self/tribe/earth as was the focus of non-empire culture. Generally, in tribal society no one dies of starvation unless everyone dies. Food is shared. In present day empire culture the rich gaze out of the windows of fine restaurants at the poor starving on the streets. To them this is justified on a subconscious level by the linear increase-based, social- Darwinist programming of the cosmology of empire, with which they have been conditioned since birth. Social Darwinism says that there is only survival for the fittest, there are the weak and the strong, the evolved and the unevolved. That is why might makes right. In fact, it is said by some colonialists, that at times, the lesser should give up to the more fit, in order to aid "evolution." The mind conditioning of the societies of empire says that there is "evolution" measured now by technological invention. Those who are most progressed are leading the whole planet toward a utopian destiny for the human race. Inasmuch as these "most progressed" groups are carrying the burden for the whole, sacrifices of the other lesser peoples to help the more advanced are justified. Here, a biological theory has been inflated to become cosmology. Cosmologies are each culture's explanation of the plan and pattern of the universe as it works itself out on earth. The cosmology of a culture explains who we are, how we got here on this planet and what the purpose of life is.

The Darwinist myth of the "survival of the fittest" rests within a larger mental construct- the basic subconscious image of linear increase. Rather than the organic view of a cyclic pulsation of life maintained by our ancestors, the culture of empire rests upon the image of linear increase. For example, the religious perspectives of empire from China, India and the Mid-East are linear in the sense that they believe we are not now adequate (we are sinners or we are unenlightened) but we are progressing in a linear manner toward some distant point of perfection. In social and economic realms we are progressing toward the utopian goal of wealth by making economic progress. In the technological "man the toolmaker" realm, we are inventing utopia where mechanical slaves will do our bidding.

In the cosmology of empire, the earth, its life and material forms became simply objects for manipulation and accumulation. They have no inherent meaning. Empire culture began to invest meaning in material objects themselves, with no relation to the cosmos. One's identity became associated with one's material accumulation as it hopefully increased in a linear manner. Materialism became a basic factor in the cosmology of empire. In this world view, the earth is a "resource" to be used in service of empire.

The ideology of empire is fascism. From the belief in the centralized maintenance of "order" to the belief in the inherent racial, moral, physical, spiritual and intellectual superiority of the elites, the ideology has not changed since the first "son of heaven," Chinese emperor or first Sumerian tyrant. In our own era we had the exemplars of civilization, the Nazis. Just as with the "old boys" in English mens clubs, in private yankee boys schools in New England, among the inheritors of social priviledge in Italy, among the patrician class of Spain and in corporate board rooms throughout the industrial world, there is a bedrock belief in human inequality. All believe that the tribal people in the highlands of New Guinea are "less evolved" than they. They (as well as the social conditioning of all civilized people) state that they are on the forefront of linear increase, "advancement," "progress," "being civilized." The Nazis said that they were on the forefront of evolution. They were carrying the burden of human advancement, genetically and technologically. They said that this was demonstrated by their superior machines, their superior military power and their superior culture, things that were only said behind the doors of the private men's clubs of imperial England or now in transnational corporate board-rooms. Inasmuch as the Nazis believed they were carrying the evolutionary burden for the entire race and planet it seemed reasonable to them that other lesser breeds should step aside or be exterminated. Isn't this the basic belief of the colonists who landed at Plymouth Rock? Cortez in Mexico? the Chinese now in Tibet? Isn't this the social ideology of the last two hundred years of imperial conquest of the planet? Fascism is Empire, is Civilization!

In the natural human culture, life is adequate in and of itself. Life and its living is the point of it all. Life is a natural occurrence that is manifest as the intent of the cosmos. Life produces the needs of humans who live in balance. Life produces those needs as constantly as the tree grows and the rain falls. In the world of natural culture life survives by its successful adaptation to the larger whole, not by conflict and control.

In the empire culture, people struggle for materialist salvation. When the herder exhausts the grasses, more must be found. When the agriculturist exhausts the soil, more wilderness must be conquered. When the general conquers one country, there are always more. In the inadequate present, one must struggle, battle and compete in linearity toward salvation which is that point in which one has conquered and then owns and controls everything in the universe. This is linearity. This is mechanistic evolution in which repeated chance collision of chemicals rather than the intelligence of the cosmos pro-duced the world. The myth of linear evolution is laid as a template over reality. It allows academicians, politicians and personal egos to justify much of the destruction and death caused by the empire. It allows people who should know better to say that self-sufficient tribal people should be displaced by economic development so that "they can become educated and productive."

"Man the tool maker" is a correlate myth. In predicating that the cosmic role of humans is to make tools (to produce material goods), academicians find stone spear points, fit the many types of spear points into an evolutionary line and then declare that this is evidence for the role of "man the toolmaker." Of course humans have always made tools but this was not the basic purpose of the society. It is, though, the basic purpose of industrial society. By taking what the basic pattern of empire culture has been through history and looking at the world through that pattern, the leaders of empire have "discovered cosmic patterns" like, "the hidden hand of God in the 'free enterprise' market," "dialectical materialism," or "the survival of the fittest," and its derivative, social Darwinism- the theory that in the dog eat dog competitive social struggle the best always wins and that is what improves the human species. The linear growth myth justifies the contempt and racism directed toward Native people (who are not "evolved") and it justifies the contempt for the "lesser" in the hierarchy. As the empire races toward suicide it scorns the "less evolved" human ancestors that have lived sustainedly for a million years. As the materialism and markets of empire culture developed, humans began to increasingly focus human energy upon the production of material goods. Markets became the device that accelerated the extortion of the earth's fertility. Empire is a culture of violence, arranged according to coercive hierarchies of social power based on the extortion of the fertility of the planetary metabolism. An empire is a temporary, pathological human culture. It grows based upon declining resources and then collapses.

The general dynamic of empire culture assumes a life of doing on the part of humans. Humans work and produce goods and services. Humans invent new "tools." Prior to the inversion the emphasis of human life was on Being. There was nothing to do but gather and hunt the "fruits" of the earth and be in spiritual consonance with the cosmic pattern and will as demonstrated in the life of the earth. This is a clear inversion between being and doing.

The conditioning in empire, the "doing" culture, carries psychological consequences. Within the body of myth, that each of us play out each day in our personal lives, we assume subconsciously that life is not yet adequate but that we are moving toward utopia. This means that each of us see our lives as somehow wrong and as yet inadequate, none the less we are struggling toward completion. This is a bedrock psychological assumption. Life is not yet full, complete and adequate. It is in this manner that we live out the pathology of the imperial whole in each of our personal lives.

NOTES

1   <u>Natural Man</u>. Robert Allen. The Danbury Press. (no location given). printed in Madrid, Spain by Novograph S.A. & Roner S.A. 1975. p. 24.

2   ibid. p. 16.

3   ibid. p. 18.

4   <u>Anthropology And Contemporary Human Problems</u>. John H. Bodley. Second Edition. Mayfield pub. Palo Alto, CA. 1985.

5   ibid. p. 18,19.

6   ibid. p. 94.

7   ibid. p. 47.

CHAPTER 10

THE PSYCHOLOGY OF EMPIRE

Biological life on earth assembles and unifies energies. The tree sprouts from a seed and begins to draw the energies of air, water, soil and sun to it for assemblage into biological form. As the tree creates its unity of form it then integrates with the other systems around it, the soil community, the plants and animals. This interaction increases as energy pathways and new biological niches are created which support new life forms. It is the balanced integration and the proliferation of energy pathways that potentiates the living world and provides its power of endurance.

Wheat, barley and rice, the initial biological slaves of empire, were able to produce surpluses because they could drain the energy of the assembled unities of the soil community. It is this energy, gained by looting the laboriously assembled natural unities, that fuels empire. This has allowed the explosive growth of civilization. The ecologies of forests, grasslands, wetlands, continental shelves and so forth are dismantled and the energy is turned into the growth of civilization.

The life of the earth functions in its balanced way because each being lives according to its particular nature. The decentralized power of all life resides in each being. The pattern of empire culture in contrast, is to centralize power over life and consequently the natural patterns disintegrate. A golf course, for example, appears very neat and orderly. With its edged borders, well watered grass and trees, it represents the epitome of orderliness to the mind conditioned by empire. In the reality of earth life, created and conditioned by cosmic forces, it is a gross disorder. Where once stood a life potentiating, balanced and perpetual, climax ecosystem with its diverse circulating energies and manifold variety of beings, there are now a few varieties of designer plants kept alive by chemicals and artificial water supplies. A staff of maintenance people are kept busy battling the integrated life of the earth that attempts to rescue this wound by sending in the plants, animals and other life forms that are naturally adapted to live in the area.

This same disintegration occurs in human society when it is impacted by empire. When empire strikes the forager/hunter tribe, the fragile thought form of culture, all of the memories of the oral literature, the ways of making utensils, dwellings and tools and the natural modes of relationship begin to disintegrate.

The natural web of relationships disintegrate and the people become entrapped in a coercive relationship with the invader. In this pattern, the individual experiences physical and psychic disintegration. In empire culture the individual is alienated and thrust into conflict on all levels. Both the social structure of empire and its ideational contents shape the individual and it is not an integrative and healing system.

We live in a culture that conditions us toward psychological disintegration. It is a culture that confuses and masks our biological identity, encouraging us to believe that we are something other. The examination of these disintegrative factors will aid us in creating a new culture that is pointed toward healing and wholeness.

Human Life is Severed From its Source

The culture of empire has severed itself from its center in the life of the earth. Civilized people find their survival not in the life of the earth but in human society. They are dependent upon what human society produces. The empire feeds on the earth like a tumor, irrespective of natural patterns. The individual person in the culture of empire does not directly feed from the earth as do forager/hunters, it feeds from the tumor body. The social body sucks energy out of the earth by means of mass centrally directed organization and creates massive artificial environments conducive to this further extortion. The continual conflict of culture with the natural patterns of life creates insecurity which pervades the society. Natural culture is one of affluence. In empire scarcity and insecurity are created by unlimited demands and growth. The pattern of the culture itself also creates a context of competition and conflict for each individual. This leads to insecurity which follows most people throughout life.

Insecurity generates fear and defensiveness. Fear and defensiveness generate anger and negative emotional states. Anger and negative emotional states generate conflict. Individual fear, defensiveness, anger and conflict are entirely congruent with the career of empire itself. Empire is a culture of conflict internally and externally.

Disorder in the Society of Cells

The integrated nature of organic forms and the role of each life form is demonstrated by their place in the metabolism of the whole. But there is an example of a life form which like empire, does not follow the pattern. This example is cancer. The cancer cell breaks the cooperative and sharing relationship with its fellow cells and becomes "God," as it were, or from another point of view, ceases to be part of "God." Instead of remaining integrated and adapted to the body, the cancer cell creates a social body of its own design that feeds on its host.

Cell biologist L.L. Larison Cudmore examines the morality of cancer which opposes the natural pattern on the cellular level. She says:

"Cancer cells do not respect the territorial rights of other cells and refuse to obey the two rules obeyed by all other cells: they neither stop growing nor stop moving when they encounter another cell, and they do not stick to their own kind. Quite simply, they are cells that have decided on autonomy and independent growth, rather than cooperation. There would be little in this to criticize if they were discreet about it. But they are not. They run amok with as much violence and insensibility as any Malay caught in that terrifying frenzy. Cancer will not stop its hideous course of uncontrolled growth and invasion until it or its victim is dead. Cancer is illegal and dishonest. It secretes a substance that lures blood vessels to it once supplied with its own circulation network, it pirates nutrients from the body, in greedy and ever-increasing insatiability. It turns invasive, growing into other tissues, dissolving the connections between cells with Samson-like strength. It can bore holes in muscle and bones. As it divides, its daughter cells lose more and more of what were once the fine sensibilities of the cell. They do not stay with their parental mass they leave, and totally undismayed by the fact that they may not belong in a kidney, a liver, or a lung, they colonize these organs with as little regard for any of the right of the inhabitants as the worst of human imperialists. They grow and grow. Over cells, and around cells, stealing their food and space."[1]

The beginnings of individual psychology in empire start with the severance from the mother, the birth process. In the culture of empire, fear begins at birth. The birthing method of modern industrial medicine itself, causes deepset psychological fear and insecurity. Arthur Janov is the author of *The Primal Scream*, originator of Primal Therapy and a researcher for many years into the psychological complexities of the birthing process. He comments on the differences between contemporary and natural birthing methods:

"In one of society's great paradoxes, our supposedly most advanced methods have produced the most primitive consequences, and in the most primitive societies we find the most advanced (that is, natural and beneficent) birth practice: the simple stoop-squat-deliver method. Modern technology must not interfere with natural processes but should be used instead to aid those practices."[2]

Joseph Chilton Pearce in his study of childhood psychology, Magical Child, points out certain stage specific actions that are carried out during the birthing process. The periodic contractions of the vaginal canal massage and enliven the peripheral nerve endings in the skin of the baby who is emerging from a fluid environment of nearly 100 degree heat. The periodic contractions also begin compressing the chest, beginning the breathing action that is soon to come. As the baby emerges from the vaginal canal, it is grasped by the mother and put to her chest where it can again hear the heart beat that it has known for nine months. At this point the mother looks into the baby's eyes (Pearce says this is extremely important in the bonding process). As the mother looks into the eyes of the child she begins stroking the baby which further activates the nerve endings of the skin. At some safe point after this, the umbilical cord is cut and the mother presses the baby to her nipple. The chemistry of the mother's milk is stage specific and it changes as the baby grows through the biological stages until weaning.

Birthing is one of the great transformations of life and to help generate the vigor to survive this experience the common blood supply of the mother and child produce a stress hormone, cortisol. Pearce feels that drinking the mother's milk just after birth helps the body of the infant eliminate this substance so that it becomes calm.

The process of bonding of mother and child is exemplified by the old story of the baby duck that bonds to the first thing that it perceives after coming out of its shell. Humorous stories are told of how the baby duck bonds with the family dog, people and other animals. The process of bonding is as fundamental as the bonding of proton and electron. The process of bonding happens on many levels and in subtle ways. An important kind of bonding is for living things to be bonded with their home, the living earth and cosmos. Bonding is a positive psychological relationship that provides a sense of self and the security of being at "home."

Janov, Pearce and many others think that the brief sequence of bonding during birthing is one of the most important in an individual's life. It is this sequence that produces the proper bond between mother and child. It is at this initial point of the sequence of bondings, beginning with the mother and then radiating out to include the earth, that the subconscious tenor of the child is imprinted for the balance of its life. In the modern medical setting the infant may be subjected to the stress of a caesarean operation where there is no birthing sequence or alternatively the infant's first contact with the outside world may be the drugs carried to it from the mother through the placental wall. The chances are good that the infant will feel the metal of the forceps around its head, pulling it out of the mother. The infant will be held up, swatted to begin the breathing and then handed to a nurse for deposit on a cold metal scale. The baby is then deposited alone in the sterility of the maternity ward.

That the few moments in which all of this takes place can make such a substantial difference in one's whole life is shown by a discovery made in Uganda. Joseph Chilton Pearce relates that Marcelle Gerber who was doing research for the United Nations Children's Fund in Uganda discovered what the researchers considered "genius" babies:

"She found the most precocious, brilliant, and advanced infants and children ever observed anywhere. These infants had smiled, continuously and rapturously, from, at the latest, their fourth day of life. Blood analyses showed that all the adrenal steroids connected with birth stress were totally absent by that fourth day after birth. Sensorimotor learning and general development were phenomenal, indeed miraculous. These Ugandan infants were months ahead of American or European children."[3]

After causing a stir among child development specialists it was discovered that there were some babies in Uganda whose development resembled that of industrial medicine countries. These babies they found in the few hospitals in Uganda:

"Gerber found that they did not smile until some two and a half months after birth. Nor were they precocious in any sense. They showed no signs of sensorimotor learning, displayed no uncanny intelligence for some two and a half months, at which point some signs of intelligence were apparent. Blood analyses showed that high levels of adrenal steroids connected with birth stress were still prevalent at two and a half months. These infants slept massively, cried when awake, were irritable and colicky, frail and helpless. So the issue was not in some racial predisposition toward early intellectual growth. The issue lay solely with what happens to the newborn infant in hospitals."[4]

Birth trauma and the failure of bonding are serious matters to the future life of the baby. Such a simple thing as cutting the umbilical cord too quickly in the modern assembly-line hospital setting causes irreparable harm by causing brain lesions, minor strokes, which are referred to as anoxia. Newell Kephart, Director of the Achievement Center for Children at Purdue University, says that 15 to 20 percent of all children examined had learning and behavior problems resulting from minor undetected brain injury. Others say that 20 to 40 percent of the school population are handicapped by learning problems that may be related to neurological impairments at birth.[5]

Pearce in his study Magical Child, tells of the tests done by medical doctor William F. Windle. Windle became doubtful about the birthing methods of industrial medicine and created a test with monkeys, (who normally need no help giving birth). Windle took a number of pregnant monkeys and subjected them to the normal hospital birthing methods, including drugs, anesthesia, forceps and the cutting of the umbilical cord in the usual time he had seen it done in hospitals.

He found that because of the drugs and anesthesia the baby monkeys could not breath and needed the artificial resuscitation that hospitals customarily use. Instead of clinging to the mother shortly after emergence, Windle's monkey babies were helpless and could not perform this task. In fact they could not cling to their mothers for several weeks.

Later Windle autopsied the infants that had died during birth or who did not live full term. He found severe brain lesions in every case from the anoxia at birth. Later he autopsied the monkeys who lived to adulthood and found that they also had brain lesions. Windle later autopsied human babies that had died during birth or shortly after and found that they had brain lesions similar to the monkeys in his tests.

Brain lesions are not the only effect of modern birthing methods. The imprints of the birth trauma itself are often severe. The mass institution of modern industrially based medicine, with its vast array of expensive machinery and industrially produced drugs seems to produce results consonant with the quality of civilization itself- mechanicalness, unfeelingness and human alienation. Instead of the warm comfort of the mother, the infant is treated as an object, slapped by a stranger and taken away by another stranger into a nursery where it is put into a crib. It is at this point that civilized people often bond to material objects- namely, the security blanket. Pearce asks, "What is the great learning? What is being built into the very fibers of that mind-brain-body system as the initial experiences of life?" It is that, "Encounters with people are causes of severe, unbroken, unrelenting stress, and that stress finds its only reduction through contact with material objects."[6]

Even a satisfactory birth is one of the great traumatic experiences of any individual's life. The birth experience is in fact a fight for life. Fetal death is the fifth cause of death in the U.S. Arthur Janov as a psychiatrist had been early led to birth trauma as the origin of some of his patients' problems. After some years he created a method of therapy that involved conscious recall of the birth experience. He found that if the conscious adult could relive the birth experience and understand the experience within the adult context, the symptoms of fears, phobias, mental blocks and so forth would evaporate. He began to call this Primal Therapy.

After years of work with Primal Therapy, Janov concludes:

"I have seen every possible combination and permutation of mental illness. I have seen what bad families can do, what orphanages and rejection can do, what rape and incest can do and it is still my opinion that birth and pre-birth trauma are prepotent over almost any later kind of trauma. For in that birth process is stamped the way we are going to handle our lives thereafter. Personality traits are engraved, ways of looking at the world are imprinted, attitudes are shaped. What we will become is found in the birth matrix.

"The best testimony I know of to the importance of altered birth practices is the qualitative difference between children born naturally and non-traumatically and those born under conventional circumstances. The second best testimony I know of is the enormous change that takes place in Primal patients who have relived the traumas they underwent at birth."

The birth trauma, as Janov describes, is the first imprint upon the person, but is not the last. There is the important matter of the bonding sequence that Joseph Chilton Pearce and others describe.

The Failure of Bonding

The bonding of newborns, the integration and adaptation of natural culture to the living earth, food chains, and the web of ecology are all similar phenomena. These functions are how life integrates itself. As we proceed we will see that the violation of the bonding of infants is an important factor in the creation of the psychology of empire culture. In modern society we see the progressive violation of these patterns, especially with modern birthing methods. Marshall Klaus of Case Western Reserve Hospital, who is considered to be one of the top authorities on the functioning of the bonding process, feels that it is an instinctual response genetically built into mother and baby. It may be that hormones are involved in the process and it is obvious that breast feeding has much to do with it.

The innate phenomenon of bonding has long been observed in domesticated animals. In the case of domesticated sheep it has been found that if the mother sheep is prevented from licking the after-birth from the body of the baby sheep the chances are very high that the baby will die.

Some anthropologists have commented on the depth of bonding in Natural cultures. When observers were looking for that effect, they reported that bonding was so close that the children when carried (such as on the hip) were never messy because the mothers knew by conscious rapport when the child had to urinate or defecate.[7]

In civilization the process of bonding is often much distorted, creating stress in later life. Even before birth, if the baby is gestated by a neurotic, stress filled mother, the baby is already accustomed to stress through participation in the blood supply of the mother with its load of adrenal hormones. If the babies in utero are impacted by stress hormones from the mother they are already being imprinted with free floating, non-objective anxieties that may stay with them the rest of their lives.

Pearce says that the development of intelligence and the learning of identity happens as the child interacts with the environment that it is bonded to, its matrix. The child is filled with intent to explore and interact with its worlds. The worlds (matrices) are the content to be known. The process of bonding says Pearce, begins with the mind-brain structuring its knowledge of its first matrix, the womb. On emerging from the womb, the mother becomes the matrix. When the child emerges from the mother it is placed on her chest where it can hear the familiar heartbeat. In the developing series of bondings that Pearce describes a child going through, it is by its knowledge of the previous matrix that the child is able to relate to the new. In order to adjust to the new matrix the child must be able to relate it to something that it already knows, such as hearing the mothers heart-beat in utero and on the mother's chest.

"Biologically, we are supported at each matrix shift with enhanced physical ability, a spurt of new brain growth that prepares us for new learning, and specific shifts of the brain's ways of processing information," says Pearce.[8] The cycles of developmental bondings are timed essentially the same in the whole species, and in different cultures they may differ slightly in timing, but never in sequence. The physical changes accompanying these bonding sequences go on irrespective of the bonding or failure of bonding that takes place.

At birth the child emerges from the womb and learns, ideally, to bond to the mother. From its secure place near the heart-beat the child is focused on the mother's face and body. From this secure place the child begins to perceive the earth, the outer environment, its next matrix. At approximately the twenty-fourth month the brain of the child achieves a spurt of development and the next bonding, to that of the earth begins. The child, secure in its bonding to the mother begins to explore the world. The child touches and tastes the world and develops physical and personal power in dealing with it.

At age seven a bonding shift occurs and the child begins to become aware of self. "Autonomy—becoming physically independent of parental help and learning to physically survive the principles of the physical world—is the goal of the period," Pearce says.[9] At age seven the growth of the corpus callosum, a late-developing organ of the brain, has been completed and another brain growth spurt occurs. It is at this age that childhood art changes world-wide. Childhood art maintains an essential sameness up to this period when the art begins to change according to the new information of the culture that is being assimilated. It is at this stage that the child stands in the earth matrix and explores into the self. At this stage the child develops personal power and creative logic but this is power and logic based in the concreteness of the physical world. (Unfortunately it is at this point that civilized children are forced to deal with abstract word and idea systems that have no relationship with immediate physical reality.) At a point when the "left brain" system is attempting to develop, the child is put into the anxiety ridden, win/lose educational institution and forced to learn the abstract cultural logic and idea systems, rather than immediate cause and effect physical logic, such as arrow making or deer stalking. At around the age of eleven the child begins naturally to separate word from the object. Here the child begins to develop abstract thinking. After sexual maturity the person begins to bond to the mind, begins to understand that it is not its own thoughts and emotions, but is the observer of them.

An important point made in Pearce's work is that the trajectory of the series of bondings from child to adult is from matter toward abstraction. The series of bondings lead from the womb, to mother, to earth, to self, to mind and although not stressed by Pearce, one could consider the realization of spirit as the final outcome.

The design of the biological plan for individual human development is the growth of autonomy both as physical organism in the physical world and as an autonomous personality in the world of thought. In the intricate and complex pattern of nature, the final series of transformations bears the person out into the cosmos as an independent being.

Ideally, in a Natural culture surrounded by the living earth, this biological process should bear a human out onto the surface of the planet with full understanding of their identity as an authentic life form that will take its place in the natural world as do all other organisms. In the natural web of life, each organism has a purpose- to live, and to aid in the furtherance of biological life. Whether it is the bison spreading the grass seed and manuring the landscape or the tiny coral reef organisms creating rich habitat for many other organisms, all have a contributory role and each has an identity given by its nature and its place in the metabolism. There should be no identity crisis and there should be no anxiety with one psychically secure in the knowledge that they are doing what their nature dictates.

This does not necessarily mean that humans must be forager/hunters, but it does mean that humans need understand their grounding identity as organic beings and participants in the life of the earth and the necessity of living in balance with that life. As Pearce describes the experience of the child growing up in modern society, he finds violations of these natural bondings at every turn which reinforce the alienating effect of the original birth trauma. This is alienation from the body of the mother, the social body and the body of the earth.

Free Floating Anxiety: The Negative Psychological State of Civilization

From the point of the birth trauma and failure of proper bonding the young civilized human is beset by anxiety. Not being grounded in the reality of self and earth, the human tends to bond to and identify with material objects and to word-built ideological systems. The focus of attention is not the relationship between the humans and the living-earth- the focus of attention in industrial-empire culture is on the society and its products.

In this shifting field, the question of identity rages, but the underlying emotional state remains constant- anxiety. Fear and anxiety causes the decline of consciousness. Fear takes the mind off more expansive, intuitive questions of life in the universe and focuses the attention on immediate safety. Fear also creates the need to control. This urge to control, which is a fundamental factor of empire culture, comes about with the anxiety stricken child. The child (or adult in the same psychic situation) who is not centered within itself, experiences fear. The child attempts to reassure itself of its security by trying to control its environment, the things and people around it, usually in this case an adult. If the child can get the adults to respond on cue it becomes reassured of its security- momentarily. This is the civilized situation- suffering constant anxiety, attempting to control and manipulate a shifting social and ecological background. The culture as a whole in the larger realm relates to the planetary life in the same manner.

Both socially and individually, the culture of empire is devoted to the maximization of material wealth. Natural culture is devoted to the maximization of life. The culture of the empire is severed from its matrix in the life of the earth and becomes a reality solely of the intellect, furnished with symbols and meanings having little relationship to the earth. The child, having suffered rebuffs to the emotional body, having withdrawn emotionally because of birth trauma and the competitive psychic environment, is taught by the schooling system to seek rewards through the exercise of the intellect and restrict emotional empathy. The child begins to invest meaning in word-built worlds. The child begins to live abstractly, alienated by filtering its perception of reality through these intellectual images. Fear is the basic motor of the empire. It is a basic, fundamental, psychic fear convincing humans it is necessary to do something to achieve identity rather than to be something, inherently, as a source of one's identity. When this occurs people move out of balance with the natural world. The human of the empire no longer has a home, no longer has an identity in the balanced universe, so it is always seeking to create its emotional sustenance and security by accumulating material objects-inflating its identity- and by controlling its environment as much as possible. The subconscious mind, the vegetative mind, runs the body, just as the mind of the world runs its organic body on its level of being. Yogis, who have conscious control of their "involuntary" physical systems, or persons in hypnotic trance are able to control their heartbeat and circulation as well as direct their vegetative apparatus to do various things. This aspect of mind is the same mind as the consciousness of plants or that which empowers the bodies of all animals in a natural state. This organic mind is the whole mind of the world, our basic identity. In the psyche of empire this mind is submerged. People become cut off from the very basis of their existence. The focus of consciousness is forced up predominately into the intellect, the quick surface thinker needed when playing fast moving games of power and wealth. While the anxiety of not fundamentally knowing one's identity slips below the threshold of conscious attention, it still endures. The person becomes cut off from their dream life, cut from the hunches and intuition that formerly helped the human negotiate in the natural world.

Further disintegration develops when the socially conditioned mind begins to injure the body. A fundamental conflict develops between the conscious mind, its ideas and the vegetative mind with its realities of cellular cooperation and functioning. Negative emotion and negative thoughts immediately poison the body through the production of stress hormones that are loaded into the blood stream by the endocrine gland system. This injures the body just as do dietary habits- such as anorexia or bulimia-that have emotional motive rather than a feeding motive. A psychogenic illness is one in which the mind injures the body. In extreme cases of psychogenic illness, the ideas in the conscious mind have impacts on the vegetative mind resulting in organic damage and sometimes death. Bleeding ulcers, colitis, spastic bowel syndrome, asthma and migraine headaches are results of a conscious reaction to the environment that the consciousness exists in, which are communicated to the vegetative mind.

The organic aspect of the human body follows the pattern of the cosmos. It seeks to maintain balance internally among all its parts. Scientists refer to this balancing as homeostasis. This homeostasis results from the operation of the organic system adapting to the environment on its own level. As the body goes through its life, it makes internal changes in response to external stimuli of the environment seeking to keep the body on an "even keel" of blood pressure, temperature and so forth.

Though the biological organism maintains homeostasis, the mind can be the fly in the ointment. A human, living in the natural world responds to the physical reality of threat with the familiar fight or flight syndrome accompanied by shots of adrenalin and blood sugar into the system preparing them for the physical exertion necessary. In civilized culture there is a serious problem involved with this adaptive mechanism. The problem is that the physical operations of the flight or fight syndrome are connected with the emotions. If a saber tooth tiger is charging, the body responds to the threat by physically gearing up to meet it. The body responds in the same way when a person is sitting quietly in a chair watching television and sees something on the screen about the threat of Communism or Capitalism to which they have been programmed to respond, so that it makes them angry and emotionally upset. The stress hormones produced in the body are not used because there is no tiger and no physical exertion. Instead, the substance that would aid muscle activity lies in the physical system and slowly poisons it- because it has not been excreted in physical exertion. The culture of empire is a culture of insecurity, tension and competitive conflict. This generalized emotional tenor has profound effects. Most of the top ten causes of death for example are generally related to stress. Negative emotional states, interpersonal conflict or the bill collector may trigger the body's endocrine gland system to gear up for extreme physical effort when none is needed. Dr. Hans Selye who has done years of research on this, which he calls the General Adaptation Syndrome, describes what occurs in the body when this stress reaction is triggered:

"The stressor excites the hypothalamus (through pathways not yet fully identified) to produce a substance that stimulates the pituitary to discharge the hormone ACTH (for adrenocorticotrophic hormone) into the blood. ATCH in turn induces the external, cortical portion of the adrenal to secrete corticoid. These elicit thymus shrinkage, simultaneously with many other changes, such as atrophy of the lymph nodes, inhibition of inflammatory reactions, and production of sugar (a readily available source of energy). Their production is facilitated through an increased level of corticoid in the blood, but the autonomic nervous system also plays a role in eliciting ulcers."[10]

It is from the constant triggering of these physical systems that damage to the body occurs- caused by ideas in the mind-ideas conditioned into the mind by culture.

Heart disease, such as the stressed-based heart disease in the empire, is generally absent in Natural culture. Cancer is also unknown in Natural culture. Cancer is caused by a malfunction of the auto-immune system. Everyone's body produces malformed cancerous cells all of the time. In a properly functioning body these cells are eliminated by the body's auto-immune defense system. It is when the auto-immune system loses its sense of identity, loses its ability to tell self from other, that the cancer cell is able to multiply, create tumor bodies and establish colonies. This is doubly dangerous when the auto-immune system fails and toxic and other intrusions from the environment multiply.

Industrial medicine uses the words auto-immune system but this obscures the reality. The auto-immune system is the vegetative consciousness of the body. This function of telling self from other, knowing one's identity, is a function of consciousness itself and it is the malfunction of this that is causing serious medical problems in the culture of empire. Cancer, AIDS, allergies, candida albicans and other maladies are caused by "auto-immune system" failures. It is the failure of identity, the failure of the mind to know what it is, that is the base of the problem. Though this is the base of the problem it is known that events and substances such as toxics and antibiotics can "shock" the body consciousness into bewilderment about its identity.

The psycho-biological problem of identity exists with the individual as well as the body of empire which does not recognize itself as an organic entity of the earth.

The Crisis of Identity

The human identity crisis now threatens the earth. When one observes the activities of civilization, aside from all the talk, one sees that the dominant conception of human purpose on earth, is believed to be the creation and accumulation of material objects. People think of their possessions as part of their identity. Social status, positions and degrees are also accumulated but wealth is the base of the identity question.

The civilized baby that was, just after birth, symbolically and literally bonded to the material "security blanket," ultimately begins to identify with its accumulation. The child derives emotional gratification from material objects. No longer does the human have an organic identity but achieves identity by personal effort of accumulation within the context of a highly stratified and intellectualized society in which abstract mental symbology- ideology- has more perceived reality than the living forms of the earth. It is this cultural conditioning in the minds of billions that is driving the earth to destruction.

For several million years humans identified themselves as part of a living, spiritually vivified earth. One of the essential differences between nomadic, forager/hunter cultures and the culture of empire is that in a sharing culture, persons do not have the deeply imbedded impulse to hang on to things, especially when they have to carry them on their backs. Their existence and their identity is not predicated on what they have or the competitive heights that they may have struggled to. Although tribal people admire their members for innate talents and for personal achievements, these factors are not brought about by socially structured competition. Tribal people who are secure in the flow of life, secure in the knowledge that the mothering earth produces life and sustenance continually, do not allow material goods to divide them or to become an issue. In Natural culture it is people who share the most that are held in the most esteem. Jules Henry, who has lived with many natural cultures during his life as an anthropologist, summarizes his view of this issue in his book *Culture Against Man*. He observes that contemporary, civilized people place no limit on their desires for material goods. He says:

"Most, though by no means all, primitive societies are provided with intuitive limits on how much property may be accumulated by one person, and the variety of ways in which primitive society compels people to rid themselves of accumulated property is almost beyond belief. Distributing it to relatives, burning it at funerals, using it to finance ceremonies, making it impossible to collect debts in any systematic way—these and many other devices have been used by primitive culture, in veritable terror of property accumulation, to get rid of it. Rarely does primitive society permit the accumulation of vast quantities of wealth."[11]

In civilization, only by continual accumulation in the competitive field of object ownership can one continue to "furnish" one's identity. A study done by the Chicago Tribune shows that the urge to accumulate is not simply a motive of greed but is also an institutionalized behavior. It is a means of emotional sustenance. The study looks at shopping sprees of upper middle class housewives:

"Our excursions into specific stores—and particularly the excursions women take to fashionable clothing stores—indicate more than we realize about our status and our status aspirations. The clothing we buy says a great deal about our status. The Chicago Tribune's study of shoppers and their habits in three homogenous communities outside Chicago reveals that many women see the shopping trip to a prestige store (regardless of any purchase made) as a ritual which, if successful, reassures the woman of her own high status. The trip, the Tribune's investigators found, 'enables her to test her self conception status-wise against the conception others hold of her.'

"Such women dress up for the shopping trip. They strive to look their most chic and poised, and if the trip is a success they feel 'Pride, pleasure, prestige' in patronizing the store and in the satisfaction of 'looking down' on the customers of the lower status store (where women typically don't dress up to shop). Some women said it made them 'feel good' just to go into a high status store. The investigators concluded that 'shopping at a prestige store enhances the status of the shoppers and vice versa.' "[12]

The Anguish of Sexual Love in the Empire

Anguish, shame, guilt and automatic negative response to sexual love is so deep in the culture and in all of us that discussing it brings up fear and aversion. This is the reason that it must be discussed, because it is fundamental to understanding the social effects that radiate from this physical relationship. Here again is another force in personal psychology that tends to separate and fragment when the very functioning of sex and love is to unify. The eminent psychologist Wilhelm Reich became a martyr because of the anxiety concerning this act. In his clinics he looked at the condition of sexual love among thousands of people. He said that the culture causes people to be sexually dysfunctional and that this cripples their lives. The reaction of the culture and of the authorities to Reich displays the hysteria that tends to confirm what he was saying. When Wilhelm Reich began his work in Germany in the early 1930's he was ostracized from the Freudian circles of orthodox psychology. When he persisted in discussing the severe problem of sexual distortion among indus-trial youth, he was thrown out of the Communist Party of Germany. Still he persisted and had to flee Germany to Scandinavia when Hitler came to power. Still fleeing, he arrived in the U.S.A. where he was persecuted by the Food and Drug Administration, thrown in prison and because of complications died- in a U.S. jail. Reich was persecuted because he challenged what he called the "emotional plague," the "pleasure anxiety" (the fear of pleasure) that is gener-alized throughout civilized society, and particularly the Judeo-Christian heri-tage. With all organisms, the function of reproducing themselves is a central part of their life activities. Reproducing is as important a function as eating. In human society the sex and reproduction function is a central fact. In the patriarchal culture of empire, the control of sexual love and of women is a basic pattern. Women are culturally defined and socially controlled for the sexual use of men and for the reproduction of children and workers. The control of sex and the definition of women, as under the control of men, has been a pivotal fact in the history of empire. It is this pattern of sexual control mechanisms of the empire that Reich challenged. Reich states that:

"...All biological impulses and sensations can be reduced to the fundamen-tal functions of expansion (elongation, dilatation) and contraction (constric-tion)."[13] This elementary contraction/expansion function of organisms is ex-pressed in the human sympathetic and para-sympathetic nervous systems. Reich says that the para-sympathetic system is operative wherever there is "expansion, elongation, hyperemia, turgor and pleasure. The sympathetic is operative whenever there is contraction, withdrawal of blood from the periphery, anxiety and pain. In the state of being when the para-sympathetic nervous system is functioning, the body experiences pleasurable excitement, the peripheral blood vessels dilate, the heart itself expands (parasympathetic dilatation), the heart beat becomes slow and even and the skin reddens." This is a biological state akin to reaching out to the universe in acceptance and positive emotional states. In the contractive, sympathetic state characterized by fear and defense, "the heart contracts and beats rapidly and forcibly," it has to drive the blood through constricted blood vessels and its work is hard.[14]

In Reich's view, upbringing in a typical authoritarian and patriarchal, civilized family, promotes the contractive, damming-up of energies that lead to later emotional problems. It is the patriarchal family that instills the sex repression on a subconscious level. Toilet training at the same age is another culprit says Reich. Defecation is also a pleasurable act but because of authoritarian toilet training, becomes associated with negative emotion and anal retention. These childhood training practices plus the general experience of growing up in a sex-pleasure repressed culture create a generalized "pleasure anxiety" in the population. Just as they are taught by early conditioning, people react negatively and contractively to the experience of physical pleasure.

The natural sexual energy becomes dammed up and finds release in pathways other than natural sexuality. Release is found in expressions such as constant anxiety, muscular spasms, pathological sexual distortions, neurosis of various kinds and the internalization of the discipline practiced by society and family. In Reich's view, a fundamental of emotional health is orgiastic potency. "Orgiastic potency is the capacity for surrender to the flow of biological energy without any inhibition, the capacity for complete discharge of all dammed-up sexual excitation through involuntary pleasurable contractions of the body."[15] This is the positive emotional opening of oneself to the lover and the universe which is much different than "conquering" someone for a unilateral sexual act.

As the child is conditioned to avert itself from physical pleasure, says Reich, the emotional and sexual energy becomes contracted and accumulated in the body of the person. The person has become conditioned to be his own emotional censor. When this flow of energy is blocked it results in tension and spasms of the muscles that Reich describes as, "neurosis anchored in the musculature." From this he derives the concept of "body armor." Body armor is the peculiar contraction of the body and face that shows how people hold tension in the musculature.

Having stolen the individual's chance for psychic health and independence, civilization instills the authoritarian censor, dependence and conformity. Reich feels that the authoritarian, sex-repressed upbringing leads to a dependent person. This person has little personal power and being powerless-psychically and socially- yearns for, admires and focuses unnatural amounts of attention on questions of power. This is the key, says Reich, to the mystery of the working classes of industrial society who admire and vote for authoritarians like Hitler. They admire them because they represent power, which is the object of the yearnings of the financially, institutionally, and emotionally powerless laboring classes on the bottom rung of industrial society.

Characterizing the sex and pleasure repressed civilized person, Reich says, "He is helpless, incapable of freedom, and he craves authority, because he cannot react spontaneously he is armored and wants to be told what to do, for he is full of contradictions and cannot rely upon himself."[16]

The sex-repressed, armored and dependent person exists in a negative emotional state. This person is easy prey for philosophies of violence that tell him that he is the most "evolved." This is the emotional seed-bed from which spring violent mass movements. In joining the mass movement the individual identifies with it and becomes transformed into something of power and importance. In a more general way this is the same rationale as the justification for colonialism practiced by the more "evolved" imperial culture.

A Culture of Violence

Persons who are secure and centered with their place on the earth and within themselves do no feel a need to make gratuitous displays of power nor are they pre-occupied with questions of power. It is fear that generates the questions of insecurity, violence and power that rage within the culture of empire. It is fear that underlies the ubiquitous defensive responses in empire culture. Empire has always been a culture of violence. That is its basis. The historian Barbara Tuchman gives us a glimpse of earlier scenes from Fourteenth Century Europe- of the culture that we have inherited:

"Violence was official as well as individual. Torture was authorized by the Church and regularly used to uncover heresy by the Inquisition. The tortures and punishments of civil justice customarily cut off hands and ears, racked, burned, flayed, and pulled apart people's bodies. In everyday life passersby saw some criminal flogged with a knotted rope or chained upright in an iron collar. They passed corpses hanging on the gibbet and decapitated heads and quartered bodies impaled on stakes on the city walls. In every church they saw pictures of saints undergoing varieties of atrocious martyrdom—by arrows, spears, fire, cut-off breasts—usually dripping blood. The crucifixion with its nails, spears, thorns, whips, and more dripping blood was inescapable. Blood and cruelty were ubiquitous in Christian art, indeed essential to it, for Christ became Redeemer, and the saints sanctified, only through suffering violence at the hands of their fellow man.

"In village games, players with hands tied behind them competed to kill a cat nailed to a post by battering it to death with their heads, at the risk of cheeks ripped open or eyes scratched out by the frantic animal's claws. Trumpets enhanced the excitement. Or a pig enclosed in a wide pen was chased by men with clubs until, to the laughter of spectators, he ran squealing from the blows until beaten lifeless. Accustomed in their own lives to physical hardship and injury, medieval men and women were not necessarily repelled by the spectacle of pain, but rather enjoyed it. The citizens of Mons bought a condemned criminal from a neighboring town so that they should have the pleasure of seeing him quartered. It may be that the less than tender medieval infancy produced adults who valued others no more than they had been valued in their own formative years."[17]

Though everyday violence is not now as visible in the First World countries as it was in the Fourteenth Century, mass violence of modern warfare, mass starvation and poverty are ever-present. Violence also continues to pervade the culture on a more subtle level in such things as entertainment and war toys. The culture of empire is not a cooperative endeavor, it is a culture of competition, violence and coercion. Fear is used in the empire to condition the masses and maintain elites in power. The elites understand well that if the masses are powerless, fragmented and frightened they will assent to domination by a strong "protector." They will demand it. If societies in the culture of empire do not have enemies they will create them. If there is no current war, they will create one.

The Cold War is a classic example of the creation of fear in the populace so that the elite could consolidate power and get agreement to fund a vast militarization of society that gives huge profits to the elite and restricts the political rights of the masses.

The mass media which gives the point of view of the elite, focuses not on appealing to us to work peacefully, cooperatively and in a sharing way with each other for equal benefits for all, but on threats to the society and the individual's security. In this emotional climate, the most violent television programming attracts the widest audience. Violence, carnage and death are the themes of the mass media. When these impressions are created, the elites then appeal to the masses to give them more power and taxes so that everyone may be protected. If people are isolated, insecure and scared they will give up their self-determination and independence in return for protection.

Institutionalizing the Masses

The structure of hierarchal power in empire culture is holographically reflected in mass social institutions. Spontaneity and independent self-direction is conditioned out of the individual and in its place are put the values of empire. Obedience, "dependability" and mechanicalness are imposed. The patriarchal, authoritarian family is a mini-empire where the children are conditioned early for their later life in mass institutions. The lives of the people in industrial society are governed by these institutions (zoning departments, planning departments, investment councils, motor vehicle departments, educational institutions, huge industrial bureaucracies, government bureaucracies and all the others that govern mass society). The people have little or no control over these institutions and are dependent upon them. Their lives are controlled from birth.

The mass educational institutions controlled by political elites are the most important institutions for social conditioning. They teach empire culture. If Natural culture children are put in these institutions, they fail. The reason they fail is that the maturity of Natural culture teaches the young that it is unseemly to struggle to be superior to one's fellows. The immodesty and divisiveness of children frantically waving their hands to give the answer first and receive recognition in a modern classroom, is the epitome of the desperate win/lose competitive conditioning of empire culture. After we, in our youth, have sat in a classroom with our heads pointed toward the blackboard, nodding in an affirmative manner for eighteen years, we have been furnished with a world-view that exists on a subconscious as well as a conscious level. Acculturation-social conditioning- is the same phenomenon as a suggestion given in hypnotic trance. A suggestion given several times in deep hypnotic trance (a highly concentrated focus of attention) effects a change in the subconscious mind. But the same thing occurs in light trance (any focused state of attention) with repetition over a lengthy period of time, such as schooling (or television watching). In this way the culture creates images of reality that exist on subconscious levels. Though it has little relationship to the cosmically created reality of the life of the earth, it becomes real for the individual by the daily reinforcement in socially created situations. The personal daily life, the artificial environments and the images presented by the mass media, all combine into an internally consistent "picture" of the world, that to us is reality.

Mass institutions facilitate the control of societies by small elites. Control of society by a small elite insures inequality. Imperial culture has developed from the days when the emperor owned everything to the point now that a small elite own and control the important factors of society. They then delegate authority down the hierarchy. This pattern of ruling and owning other people is so thorough that patriarchy seems natural to the population. Paulo Freire, in his book, *Pedagogy of the Oppressed*, is concerned with empowering people in the urban slums of Brazil by teaching them to read. He writes of the difficulty of people on the bottom rung of the hierarchy, being able to realize their personal power and independence- their liberation. He writes, "...Almost always, during the initial stage of the struggle, the oppressed, instead of striving for liberation, tend themselves to become oppressors, or 'sub-oppressors.' The very structure of their thoughts has been conditioned by the contradictions of the concrete, existential situation by which they were shaped. Their ideal is to be men, but for them, to be men is to be oppressors. This is their model of humanity. This phenomenon derives from the fact that the oppressed, at a certain moment of their existential experience, adopt an attitude of 'adhesion' to the oppressor." In the social situation of powerlessness and dependency, Freire says, "The oppressed seek to ameliorate the conditions of their oppression by imitating the oppressor." (emphasis added)[18] The conditioning of social hierarchy is so deep that the people who colonized North America institutionalized political "freedom" but they could only conceive of white males as being included and then only the white male elite who owned property. Culturally, a hierarchy existed based on sex and race, with white males at the top. In early Babylonian hierarchies, brown males used huge, terrifying, blond, blue-eyed white tribal males of Northern Europe as palace guards. It is not race, it is the conditioning of empire culture that results in hierarchy. Hierarchy is distinction not inclusion. The culture highlights distinctions and differences because of the fundamental separative pattern. Everyone is not simply an equal member of a tribe, each person in empire has a different rank in the hierarchy of power that is demonstrated by wealth and privilege.

The dominance/submission syndromes conditioned into us by hierarchy are so deep that they cannot even be given up in the sexual embrace. In the empire, males are conditioned to "conquer" women and females are conditioned to "submit" to men. This is not an equal and real exchange of energies. This is a continuation of the psychic isolation. This alienation from our basic need for authentic human relationship is so deep that in the patriarchal, empire culture of the Arabs and some of the cultures in east Africa that have been contaminated by them, clitorectomy is practiced. Clitorectomy is the practice of cutting out the clitoris of young women. In some of these groups, most or all of the women have suffered this brutality. In all areas of empire, some degree of psychological clitorectomy is practiced.

In the culture of empire, most are suffering and they are conditioned to momentarily relieve the pain by sharing it with others. This shows the final spiritual destruction of the human family- to rob them of their humanity to the extent that they cannot even relate in terms of human relationship- spiritually, emotionally and physically. The exercise of the psychological pathology of empire is to coerce others and cause them pain as a demonstration of personal or institutional power.

It is the culture of empire that creates the ladders of power that in turn create anxiety stricken, dependent people who will ape the boss for survival. Everyone is robbed of authenticity. Dominance and coercion allow a person to control others without having a real and respectful relationship. It is also this cultural context that produces the dominance/submission syndromes wherein people become servile to superiors and abusive toward inferiors. People in industrial society are not like the forager/hunter. They do not have the power of providing their own food or shelter. They are dependent on others to provide their physical security. No matter how high the executive position, if the paycheck-dependency linkage to the mass institution is cut, they become totally powerless. The route of personal power by achievement within institutionalized society can be cut at any time by those who have the real power- the elite class, so people must conform.

The authors Stanton Peele and Archie Brodsky in their seminal work, *Love and Addiction*, broke through many stereotypes to view the phenomena of addiction/dependency in a context of a culture of dependency. They say:

"Addiction is not an abnormality in our society. It is not an aberration from the norm it is itself the norm. The dependency which is addiction is a mirror-image of more basic dependencies that we learn at home and in school. The addict's search for a superficial, external resolution of life (whether through drugs or so-called 'love') follows directly from the superficial, external relationships we are led to have with each other, with our own minds and bodies, with the physical world, with learning and work and play." [19]

The cosmos generates organic, self-regulating beings on the surface of the earth that function according to their own nature. The culture of empire enslaves the life of the planet and its beings and destroys this sense of identity for the aggrandizement of the elite.

The Social Isolate Becomes "Individualist"

Industrial society has seen a growth of mass institutions and an increase in the power of the elites. We have seen the clan disintegrate, we have seen the extended family disintegrate and the nuclear family has all but disintegrated. For millions of years the songs, oral literature, skills, wisdom and knowledge of the human family was passed down from generation to generation. This was human culture, decentralized and personally empowering to everyone. Now, the elites have usurped human culture and society is administratively and militarily controlled. No longer is human culture inherited familially. "Cultural" conditioning now comes from the institutions of schools, television and other forms of mass communications that are controlled by elites.

We are offered individual "success" by struggling up the hierarchal ladder of mass institutions. As power is consolidated by the industrial elites, the individual becomes more and more a social isolate. Contradictorily, the powerless, anxiety stricken individual is conditioned to believe that he is an individualist, a gunslinger or tycoon character amassing personal power. For several million years the clan has been our natural social reality. Now, not having a relationship to the natural world or the social reality of a clan, the individual human, who is already conditioned to be emotionally distant from others, becomes more of an emotional and social isolate depending on secondary relationships in the shadow world of glamorous illusions.

The ruse is total. Not knowing the security of life and the earth and not knowing the security of a natural clan providing the learning of human sociability, the industrial human becomes a victim of all the forces of society that tend to make the person powerless and dependent, the perfect subject of addictive dependencies. Rather than the satisfaction of physical pleasure and genuine social camaraderie, the person is conditioned to word-built realities—social and religious ideologies which are themselves separative from the living earth and cosmos.

The emotions are inclusive. When one is angry, one is angry all over. People experience emotion in a unitary way. The intellect, on the other hand is divisive and comparative. That is, its basic functioning is divisive in the way it works. The intellect divides and compares, measures each, decides this, not that. The intellect is by its nature divisive and this is what industrial people have been given- frozen emotional bodies, and over-exercised intellects.

Not only can ecological and social disintegration be traced to the structure of empire, but personal disintegration is caused as well. Psychologist Nathaniel Braden in his book *The Psychology of Self-Esteem*, says that:

> "It is generally recognized by clinical psychologists and psychiatrists that pathological anxiety is the central and basic problem with which they must deal in psychotherapy- the symptom underlying the patient's other symptoms. The neurotic's essential attribute, his chronic response to the universe, is uncertainty and fear."[20]

When we psycho-biological isolates are finally cut from all natural relationship, we end up living in the "whole world" of the ego, that construct of the intellectual mind that sucks energy (by material accumulation and constant ego-reinforcement and gratification) into itself to defend against the state of non-being. This contraction of energy is the pattern of the neurotic.

The cancer cell, that psycho-biological resonance of empire, is also neurotic in the sense that it follows the same pattern. It also sucks energy out of the system that supports it without having reciprocal relationship with the whole. To continue the wholistic, holographic analysis, the phenomenon of neuroticism that occurs to empire culture, as a whole, is reflected in militarism, conquest and acquisition- as its fear promotes it to suck energy into its contracted center.

The logical extrapolation of civilization is the mental institution. Because of the developmental failures that we have reviewed, we tend to fear authentic relationships with other people. We find our own personal world more comforting- the world of the ego/identity fortress. People who are so driven into themselves, who have become so self-centered that they can only focus on and talk about themselves (and their problems), we call neurotic. People who have retreated farther into the comfort of their own world and who begin to hear and sometimes answer voices, we call schizophrenic. People who retreat totally into their own satisfying world and who do not relate to the outside world we describe as catatonic. This, which is politically defined as insanity, is simply a logical extension of the already existing social isolation of the individual in the culture of empire. It is also the logical end of the culture itself in the cosmos, lost in space and surrounded by life but talking only to itself.

The culture of empire has stolen our natural power as human beings. By its cultural conditioning it has channelled the energy of emperor and slave alike into purposes that are anti-life and contrary to the welfare of the human family and the welfare of the earth. Significantly, we live in a culture of such limited psychological rewards that the children kill themselves rather than grow up in it. In the U.S. which is said to be "the richest country in the world," the youth are committing suicide in epidemic numbers. In the age group 15 to 25, suicide is the number one cause of death.

The End of Empire

Life is community. Community is biological. Our innate experience of natural morality is a biological feeling. It is not an intellectualization or romanticism. To be kind, helpful, sharing, and joyful is a natural state that comes right out of our cellular existence. That sense of unity and positivity is the way the universe works. No matter how damaged any of us have been by the culture of empire, almost everyone retains at least some shred of this positive sensibility. The personal experience of security, solidarity, sharing and love is the experience of beauty just as is a walk through an undamaged forest or sitting on a remote beach.

With the loss of our free roaming natural life and direct relationship with the life of the cosmos came an all enveloping attack upon the beauty of our lives and the earth. The beauty of our lives, the song, the dance, the direct participation in creation suffered, along with the beauty of the earth's body, the forest, the sparkling stream, the song of the bird and the call of the animals. The diseased human culture produced the ugliness of the injured and bleeding ecology, the eroding and withering life of the land and the visual ugliness of the modern city where the homeless huddle in cold doorways of architectural boxes and elites of the contracted social body grasp for absolute security behind heavily guarded barricades.

Separation, isolation, disintegration, and death is the process of empire that is suffered by the homeless, the executive of transnational corporations, social bodies of empire culture and the ecosystem alike. Eight thousand years ago we began to see death of ecosystems from over-grazing and agriculture in Central Asia, the Indus Valley and China. Five thousand years ago we began to see the death of the conquered, the slaves and the land, as the empires grew. Two thousands years ago, death was accelerating with the Mediterranean empires. Five hundred years ago death was spreading planet-wide. Now all of the corners of the world are filled up. The finale of disintegration is upon us.

The swelling mass that eats up its own sustenance has now reached the end. There is no more, but the mass continues to swell. It is not likely that the habits of empire, set subconsciously in the minds of billions, can be reformed in the decade or two decades that would be necessary to save the situation. Barring transcendental transformation of the whole culture of empire, we will see the trends of ten thousand years of imperial history culminate in our lifetime.

The power of the empire is the power to destroy. Our role is not to fight for the power of destruction but to unify with the creative power of the cosmos. Our role is not to isolate, extort and destroy but to love, live and create.

We are not fighting to reform a maladaptive and dying social body. There is no conflict with civilization, it is passing away. There is no battle for civilization's power, the power to kill. There is only the open, positive and sharing sustenance of the new life. The emergence of the new growth is our focus of attention. The emergence of our new babies, the emergence of our new culture and the emergence of the new earth. We have the standards of existence on this planet before us. They are simple and fundamental. We are simply righting the inversion.

As with a physical wound, the imperial tissue that has lost integration with the body, lost coherence with the complex flows of energy, falls away. One allows the diseased and injured portions to fall away, while resisting injury to that which is still healthy. One focuses on the new growth, the area of healing. One focuses on the smiling faces of that seventh generation of the future that will be created.

A crisis, according to Webster, is, "A stage in a sequence of events at which the trend of all future events is determined a turning point." In the case of civilization, it is now poised, tipping and beginning the slide into complete disintegration. We are at the cusp of the last cycle. Since World War II we have seen the acceleration of the disintegration. Human population and the consumption of the earth's life- "resources," has grown exponentially. Now the seepage of poisons is so great that everyone on earth is endangered. The seeping of poison is symbolic of the movement of the whole of industrial society. The popular parable of our situation is the boiling of the frog. If the frog is thrown in boiling water it will hop out. If the frog is put in cold water and the water is heated slowly the frog will not be able to recognize the rising of the heat. That is our situation. We are not consciously perceiving the increments of dissolution. We now are at the pivot point where we still have the ability to maneuver. We are not yet in a state of social collapse with most of our valid options closed off.

Our future is not a political problem or a technical problem, it is a cultural problem. We live in a diseased culture. It is our way of life that is destroying the earth. Look at the big, dead and poisoned spot on the planet that is called a city. Simply the poisons that run off of it in rain storms are killing life for miles around. Civilization is now so poisonous that if a city were blown up in a war the most severe danger would be from the spread of chemicals from factories as well as the nuclear power plants rather than simply from the bomb itself.

Humans easily could deal with the problem. Humans, individually have the innate abilities. If all humans on the planet could center their attention on the whole picture at the same moment, see the problem and then take action, the solution could be at hand. They would then reduce the birth rate to one child per woman and begin to live in balance and to restore the life of the earth. As the birth rate radically declined the "wealth" would increase proportionately.

Rather than wait for this to occur, we need take action now. We must overcome our paralysis of fear and confusion and take control of our lives. We must cease investing our emotional energy and condition in the events of civilization. It is diseased to the core. We must realize the "dear thing" cannot be saved, even with major surgery. Anytime change is presented to us we suffer a wave of reaction, a "security crisis." We begin to grasp for rationales. We begin to find reasons why we cannot change. "If we prepare to survive, 'they' will just come get what we have," is a customary response, which rests on some unexamined assumption that presents future masses of hungry refugees wandering about while "survivalists" sit on a pile of goodies. The image of the "survivalist" is the final extrapolation of the social isolate. The reality is, that if we cannot reach out to community, to cooperative self-organization, we cannot survive. It is the movement toward a positive and adaptive new culture that is needed.

The path leads back to the source. The standard to guide us is the "solar budget." We must allow the planet's life its net photosynthetic production, aid it, and live from the increase. The fullblown climax ecosystem is the standard of health for our earth. This means drastic reduction of human population density. We must return to what our human family has known for two million years, a life that produces life and encourages full participation by every member. This reality is our basic grounding. Our task is to create the healing of self, community and planet. There is no other way.

NOTES

1   The Center Of Life. L.L. Larison Cudmore. New York Times pub. 1978. pp. 127-128.
2   Imprints: The Life Long Effects of the Birth Experience. Arthur Janov. Coward-McCann, Inc. pub. New York. 1983. p. 249.
3   Magical Child: Rediscovering Nature's Plan For Our Children. Joseph Chilton Pearce. Bantam pub. New York. 1980. pp. 42,43.
4   ibid. pp. 43,44.
5   ibid. pp. 56,57.
6   ibid. p. 70.
7   ibid. pp. 58,59.
8   ibid. pp. 19,20.
9   ibid. p. 25.
10 Stress Without Distress. Hans Selye, M.D. N.A.L. New York. 1974. p. 30.
11 Culture Against Man. Jules Henry. Random House. New York. 1963. P. 42.
12 The Status Seekers. Vance Packard. Cardinal. New York. 1965. pp. 112,113.
13 Function of the Orgasm. Wilhelm Reich. World Pub. New York. 1971. p. 257.
14 ibid. p. 258.
15 ibid. pp.77,78.
16 ibid. pp. 209,210.
17 A Distant Mirror: The Calamitous 14th. Century. Barbara W. Tuchman. Ballantine Books. New York. 1979. p. 135.
18 Pedagogy of the Oppressed. Paulo Freire. Seabury Press. New York. 1970. pp. 29,30.
19 Love and Addiction. Stanton Peele & Archie Brodsky. Signet, NAL pub. New York. 1975. p. 6.
20 The Psychology of Self Esteem. Nathaniel Branden. Bantam Books. New York. 1981. p. 157.

CHAPTER 11

THE HISTORY OF MODERN COLONIALISM

If we imagine a hive of honey bees, working cooperatively, gathering nectar in the rhythm of the seasons, all working together, fanning their wings to cool the hive, working together to raise the brood and if we saw them adopt the social ethics of civilization we would see immediate social breakdown.

We would no doubt see warlordism break out. Factions would develop, fighting for the control of the hive. Other groups may develop to attempt to steal the honey for themselves. Hierarchies would develop and each war group would struggle against the other to enslave the workers for their own benefit. Cooperative efficiency would plummet. The hive itself would begin to deteriorate without the constant repair, but certain strong warlord groups would corner the large shares of the honey and live royally. Workers would be told that if they are loyal and if they compete, they may someday have a large horde of honey such as controlled by their warlord. The history of empire culture is not much more complex than this, other than the dates and names. It is a history of conquest, of thievery and killing.

The basis of this dynamic is the conflict/competition value imbedded in the cultural mind with material wealth and control as the objects of the struggle. The struggle for power goes on among family members, in the "office politics" of all mass institutions, between mass institutions and between governments. This struggle for power is at the base of modern colonialism. Much of modern colonialism has been a competitive struggle between the various empire culture governments of Europe in a race to loot the planet. We have examined the extortion basis of the culture of empire. The system of extortion began with the biological slaves and went on to female slavery and general plantation slavery of humans as a production mechanism within society. In examining the recent history of what has become the world industrial empire, we will see that the techniques of coercion have only grown more efficient since Babylonian, Greek and Roman armies went out on slave hunting expeditions. The development of mechanical technique (science) in important ways has been to facilitate and make more efficient the coercive extortion of fertility from the earth. We will see that those ruling the empires have never shrunk away from the most atrocious methods by which to obtain power. The quest for super-profits (economic power) has used slavery, drugs, munitions, the fomenting of war, sugar, rum and any other addictive, corrupting substance or product by which to gain control of the part of the world that they desired.

The morality of honesty, truthfulness, cooperation and sharing of the former forager/hunter culture existed on a functional basis. There was little hierarchal power to struggle for. The group hunts and the running of the camp needed truthfulness to benefit all and there was no reason to lie to gain advantage. The carrying out of cooperative enterprise requires that everyone be truthful in order for it to succeed. In our former culture there was a real functional basis for that morality. After the inversion, lies, thievery, murder, selfishness, and slavery became the path of power for individuals and emperor/elites. As we review the history of colonialism we see that the espoused social morality is only a facade to quiet the masses while those who are really serious about the strategy of power practice the opposite.

The Invasion of The Americas

"Like monkeys they seized upon the gold. They thirsted mightily for gold they stuffed themselves with it, and hungered and lusted for it like pigs." —from the Florentine Codex of the Mayas, a Sixteenth Century Mayan account of the Spanish invasion of the Americas.

In the islands of the Caribbean, Christopher Columbus and his Spanish crew were met with hospitality. The indigenous people came out to the ships with flowers, food and friendship. Great feasts were celebrated in the travellers' honor. Columbus and his colleagues came to hold these people in awe. The Europeans had never encountered a culture which gave such welcome to newcomers. Columbus called these people indios, from the Italian in dio (in God). This is the likely origin of the name, "Indian," rather than confusion on the part of the explorers about where they were. American Indian Movement leader Russell Means in a speech in 1980 pointed out that in 1492 the country now called India was then called Hindustan on maps. A careful reading of the first weeks of Columbus' encounters in the Caribbean suggests strongly that he in fact looked at this new world as a kind of paradise, much like the world biblical humans inhabited "before the fall."

The Spanish led the assault on the cultures of the Americas, pursuing gold. Nothing highlights the materialism of the cultures of Europe better than the "gold fever" that grips minds conditioned by ideas of power and wealth. In 1519, Cortez and his followers stormed into the Aztec capital of Tenochtitlán lusting for the yellow metal. Historical records state that human blood ran through the streets of the capital for days. The records maintain that the

Europeans and their native allies tired of the drudgery of butchering people day after day. The invasion of Mexico proceeded and after the invasion of Mexico, the Spanish invaded the Mayan regions in Central America. Had the Spanish been a different people, had they not been fanatics of the collective ego of European culture who could not see the value of any other culture, they would have been able to understand the value of the cultures they destroyed. The vast knowledge of the people of these groups and the productive capacity of their societies would have been worth far more to Europe than all of the gold they carried away. The art, the collective creativity of several cultures, was melted down and shipped to Europe. In many cases the art had more value than the yellow metal with which it was created, but that concept was too sophisticated for the invaders to comprehend at the time. The writings of the Aztecs and Mayans, including a vast storehouse of astronomical and cultural knowledge, were burned by the fanatical cleric, Bishop Diego De Landa. What is now known as the "Florentine Codex," quoted at the beginning of this chapter, was shipped to Europe where it remains today in the private library of the Vatican. Pizzaro, European invader of the Inca society, was motivated by such deficient morality that his troops were in the habit of murdering local indians and then quartering their bodies to hang from the porches for dog food. Everywhere the Spanish employed the torture techniques of the Catholic Inquisition against native people. Today the vast highways, agricultural systems and irrigation works of Inca society lie in disuse and disrepair. Even though Pizzaro could destroy Inca society and extract the gold, the Spanish were not competent to administer the region. The population in the former land of the Inca have not yet, to this day, attained the cultural vitality or living standards enjoyed in the days before the European invasion. The Aztec and Inca societies were empires themselves, in that they were hierarchical structures of power. They were also male-dominated. The Aztecs depended upon tribute from conquered peoples and it appears from what we know about them that materialism was an incipient factor in their culture. The Incas on the other hand seemed to have created an aboriginal communism. In cases, the Inca system added tribes when they petitioned for admission and in cases negotiations brought in new groups. When the Inca system came to a new group, the Inca engineers would creat new irrigation systems, roadways, storage structures for crops and other amenities for the local population. In return the locals paid a share of the produce, which was far less than the tax that was to come with the Spanish. The Incas built sophisticated highways and irrigation systems that have yet to be equalled. By transporting guano (seabird manure) fertilizer from the Galapagos Islands up into the elaborate high mountain terrace agriculture, the Incas had created an ecological niche for themselves that provided stability, much like the stability created by the flooding of the Nile Valley in Egypt prior to the construction of the Aswan Dam.

The Mayan culture as a whole was not based on military power. It was significantly different from that of either the Aztecs or Incas. It was not based upon the large irrigation systems or highways of the Incas, nor was it based upon conquest and tribute such as with the Aztecs. The Mayas were a rainforest culture that relied on sophisticated and sustainable rainforest horticulture which was primarily decentralized. The ruins that remain in Central America were not population centers with markets and administrative apparatus but ceremonial centers for native religious/cultural practices.

After the Aztec gold was gone the Spanish continued their quest for precious metals, establishing mines in any area that seemed promising. Zacatecas, Guanajuato, Ixmiquilpan, Zimapan, Pachuca, Chaucingo, Temascaltepec, Tlalpujahua and Parral, in Mexico were denuded of vegetation for the smelters and of natives for the labor. When so many natives had been worked to death that there was danger that the mines might shut down, African slaves were imported to work the Mexican mines as they had been to work the plantations of the Caribbean after the natives had expired there. The Spanish did not progress as rapidly in the tropical Central American region as they had in Aztec lands further north, because of the rainforest and because there was a relative paucity of gold amassed in the Mayan ceremonial centers. The Spanish empire did establish a thin European political hegemony all through the region on the coasts and the flat lands of Central America. A plantation economy, designed to extort the fertility of the soil with slave labor, was established in the more level areas where rainforest was cleared and the empire culture was able to gain a foothold. From these bases, exports could be shipped and European products (especially military supplies) could be received, insuring continued European domination of the region. In this manner the imperial hierarchies became rooted in the area. Human slavery is identified with the plantation slavery of Africans in the social mind of empire. In actuality, empires themselves are institutionalized coercion and slavery. The hierarchal systems of order provide significant control of people while slavery is total control. This is contrasted with our former culture in which there were no police, jails or centralized power over others. During the Spanish conquest the King of Spain would "give" large grants of land in the Americas to prominent conquistadors and colonists. All native people that existed on that land were also included. In practice the conquistadors enslaved those that were needed and killed, drove away or sold the rest. Cortez, for example, received twenty-three thousand vassals (slaves) for his efforts in the conquest.[1] Though we call it by various euphemisms, the power relationships between the oligarchy and the peasants of El Salvador have not changed since the Indians were enslaved to work the original estates of that country and this remains true in much of Latin America where Indians are dominated in a system of violence and coercion. This caste-racial system is now enforced by modern armies supplied by the industrial state. The difference in the colonial systems between "settler" countries like the U.S., Australia and New Zealand and "conquest" countries like El Salvador, Peru and Bolivia is that in the former, european settlers swarmed into the areas to create a society and economy that replicated the mother country but was centered in the colonial country. In the colonial style exhibited by El Salvador, Peru and Bolivia, the colonization was to profit by export to the mother country. This was in the style of the latifundia, the large state-owned and slave or peasant-worked farms of Roman times. The profit from this "landed estate" system goes to benefit a small elite who control the land and the masses of the population. On the other hand, in the countries that began as small-holder, settler colonies, there were not the large factory-farm systems that could profit by cheap labor. Because of this, in the places like the U.S., if the natives could not be used as cheap labor on the settlers' farms and or industries, they were pushed away and confined or eliminated by wars of extermination.

In the "conquest" areas Natives were more likely to be worked to death. Historian Alanzo de Zorita describes conditions in the occupied territories of Mexico where the latifundia system was established:

"The collective tribute and labor demands of the Spanish settlers, the Crown, and the Church far exceeded the relatively puny exactions of the Aztec rulers, nobility, and priesthood. The more advanced European economy demanded a large increase in the supply of labor. The conquistadors or their sons became capitalist entrepreneurs with visions of limitless wealth to be obtained through silver mines, sugar and cacao plantations, cattle ranches, wheat farms. The intensity of exploitation of Indian labor became intolerable. And the Indians, their bodies enfeebled by excessive toil, malnutrition, and the hardships of long journeys to distant mines and plantations, their spirits broken by the loss of ancient tribal purposes and beliefs that gave meaning to life, became easy prey to disease, both endemic and epidemic, to maladies with which they were familiar and to scourges imported by the Europeans: smallpox, influenza, measles, typhoid, malaria. A demographic tragedy of frightful proportions resulted. The Indian population of Mexico, according to a recent estimate based on published tribute records, declined from approximately 16,871,408 in 1532 to 2,649,573 in 1568, 1,372,228 in 1595, and 1,069,255 in 1608.

"Technological changes of Spanish origin contributed to this disaster. A horde of Spanish-imported cattle and sheep swarmed over the Mexican land, often invading not only the land vacated by the declining Indian population but also the reserves of land needed by the Indian system of field rotation. The introduction of plow agriculture, less productive than Indian hoe agriculture per unit of land, and Spanish diversion of scarce water resources from Indian fields to their own fields, cattle ranches, and flour mills, also tended to upset the critical balance between land and people in Indian Mexico."[2]

It is estimated that Mexico was heavily forested on over half of its land area at the start of the conquest. Now less than 10% is forested and that is swiftly being destroyed. The process of empire culture has reduced present-day Mexico to a bare skeleton. The only thing of value in that region that can be dug up and sold today is the oil from the ground. Most of the land of Mexico is in an advanced state of eco-death, while its impoverished population explodes. Population doubling time in Mexico is now 25 years. A large share of the Natives died in the mines that the Spanish quickly opened after the Aztec and Inca treasures were hauled away. Eduardo Galeano in his *Open Veins of Latin America: Five Centuries of the Pillage of a Continent,* tells of Potosí in the present country of Bolivia. Potosí is now a relic but it was once a huge city of splendor, living from the silver mines in the area. In 1650, Potosí was one of the biggest and richest cities in the world. Luxuries from the far flung parts of the empire were shipped to Potosí in return for silver. The luxuries of the Colonial Europeans were generated by the enslavement of the native society. Galeano says that in three centuries the mines of Potosí consumed eight million Indian lives. He says that: "Many people claimed mestizo status before the court to avoid being sent to the mines and sold and resold on the market."[3]

"The Indians of the Americas totaled no less than 70 million. When the foreign conquerors appeared on the horizon a century and a half later they had been reduced to 3.5 million."[4]

The land of Mexico, Central America and Latin America is still, with the exception of Cuba and Nicaragua, owned and controlled by very small but powerful elites. Large modern plantations still generate wealth for the colonial elites and their allies, the bankers and industrialists of the First World.

The Onset of Machine Culture

Modern European imperialism may be said to have begun with the Spanish and Portuguese conquests during the late 1400's and early 1500's. Originally, the European conquests simply replicated European feudalism on new continents, continuing a pattern of imperialism not unlike that of Rome, Greece, Sumeria, and other Indo-European imperial predecessors, or the Han Chinese. But something new was afoot upon the earth in the sixteenth and seventeenth centuries. As the Spanish and Portuguese consolidated their colonies in Latin America, Africa and Southern Asia, a change began to occur in Europe which is now called the Industrial Revolution. Fueled by transworld trade promoted by a new and growing class of mercantilists, the Industrial Revolution was to simultaneously alter European peasant society almost beyond recognition and to ensure the destruction of native cultures worldwide. The pattern of empire is to conquer peripheral territories, rape them, and ship the valuables to the center of the empire, to feed its further expansion. The initial purpose of the Spanish empire was to get gold. Gold was the premium article because it could be absorbed easily by the mother country. But ultimately, in order to efficiently absorb the food and fiber shipments that were being drained from the colonies, the infrastructures of the imperial centers were going to have to change. The industrial revolution solved this problem neatly by initiating the pattern of industrialism that exists today. A mechanized industrial society could use much greater inputs of imported resources than could a feudal society. Industry allowed more types of resources to be utilized. The new machines began to process those raw materials and turn them into finished, manufactured items. While most of the production enriched Europe, some was shipped back to the colonies for sale, which further exploited the colonies. Colonial governments displaced natives from their traditional means of survival, and actively discouraged European colonists and natives from developing their own cottage industries, thus forcing the colonies to purchase European manufactured goods. (This type of exploitation was eventually to spawn the Boston Tea Party in America. The famous Swadeshi movement of Mahatma Gandhi, formed in British-colonized India during the late 1800's, aimed to reclaim the economic power of the spinning wheel back at the cottage level. The British had prohibited many cottage industries including home cloth making in India because they wanted to create consumers for manufactured items like the cloth produced by the textile industry of England. The Swadeshi slogan was, "production by the masses, not mass production.")

The End of Peasant Subsistence Culture

The shift to markets and a manufacturing economy dismembered peasant subsistence culture all over Europe. The machine and its cultural accouterments was the last lever to pry Europeans away from any remaining natural relationship to the land and to organic reality. Europe in the Middle Ages was still largely an agrarian society. The feudal lords of Europe jostled each other for power, wealth and territory, but the organization of society had not yet attained complete dependence on gold as the organizing principle of the society. Currency and markets had not yet become all powerful. In their daily lives, the medieval peasantry conducted a human community-centered society with extended family systems. Despite centuries of domination by Roman and post-Roman civilized thought forms, and despite the fact that the peasants themselves had descended from invading patriarchal Indo-European tribes such as the Celts, Angles, Saxons, and others, fifteenth-century European peasant society retained significant qualities of ancient human culture. People shared food and took some responsibility for each other. Individual starvation seldom occurred. Peasant society was a subsistence community devoted to the feeding, housing and care of its members. The peasants' relationship to the land was strong and carried with it limited rights. Society had not yet become a market economy. Yet the essence of medieval peasant society had degraded vastly from tribal hunter-forager existence. These people were the inheritors of thousands of years of Indo-European divergence from Natural culture. They lived in a society structured by hierarchy and patriarchy, where the elite accumulated material wealth and power by pursuing military adventure. Peasant surpluses, "the rent" enriched an elite class of landed nobles and royalty. Patriarchy appears to be endemic to Indo-European culture. The root language, which linguists call <u>Indo-European</u>, was spoken at least ten thousand years ago by peoples in the Caucasus mountains of Central Asia. Linguist Emile Beneviste writes of the primacy of paternity over maternity, "All the facts up to now prompt us to recognize the primacy of the concept of paternity in Indo-European."[5] Beneviste finds no female counterpart to the formal word for father in the original Indo-European language. His linguistic study points to "the non-existence of any legal status for the mother in Indo-European society. The absence of a word <u>matrius</u> as a counterpart to <u>patrius</u> may be cited."[6] Strict patriarchy certainly characterizes the cultures of Indo-European linguistic groups from India to England. A steady swing of the axe had gone on in Europe for thousands of years after the ancient forager/hunters who had populated Europe were displaced by invading Indo-Europeans. Cattle, sheep, and goats, brought into Europe with the Indo-European cultural groups, cannot well utilize forests. Cereal grains, the basis of the Indo-European cultural metabolism, cannot be grown unless the forest is cut down and open fields established. Because this metabolism depends upon good soils for their agriculture, we find them in many areas where forests had formerly existed. After the Thirteenth Century A.D., when the Arabs invaded the Iberian peninsula, heavy sheep grazing became part of the culture of Spain, spreading from there to Italy. The forests of these areas went down to create grasslands for grazing, resulting in severe soil erosion. As European empires developed, the forests were increasingly decimated for smelting and shipbuilding for foreign trade and war fleets as well as being cleared for agriculture. The introduction of industrial machinery to weave cloth in England in the Sixteenth Century created a flourishing cloth and wool industry there. The English quickly became the leaders in the Industrial Revolution. As the English drew resources out of their new colonies, they manufactured items such as cloth for sale back to the colonies. Large supplies of cotton and wool were necessary. These were obtained from Europe and from colonies such as Egypt and what is now the southeastern United States. European land-based peasants and gentry alike began to be cashiered from the land by industrialists who needed the land to produce raw materials for industry, such as to raise sheep to supply the new woolen mills. Dispossessed peasants were forced into the swelling labor pool of the young industrial system. Land and humans were becoming commodities for sale on the labor markets and commercial markets of the industrial empire. People did not give themselves up to the labor market easily. The bulk of the peasantry produced most of what they needed from their own plots and by their own effort. They had little relation to the money (market) economy and little incentive to work in the horrible conditions of the factories. Commentators of the day noted that higher wages produced less work. The reason was simple if wages were high, people would more rapidly gain the little they needed for subsistence and would quit sooner. The laboring classes were still of peasant culture. They produced most of what they needed within their families and had not yet developed unlimited needs or desires for material wealth that would keep them at the wheel indefinitely. Economic historian Karl Polanyi writes:

"The Lyons manufacturers of the eighteenth century urged low wages primarily for social reasons. Only an overworked and downtrodden laborer, they argued, would forgo to associate with his comrades and escape the condition of personal servitude under which he could be made to do whatever his master required from him. Legal compulsion and parish serfdom as in England, the rigors of an absolutist labor police as on the continent, indented labor as in the early Americas were the prerequisites of the 'willing worker.' But the final stage was reached with the application of 'nature's penalty,' hunger. In order to release it [labor] it was necessary to liquidate organic society, which refused to permit the individual to starve." [7]

In England, as in many other European countries, parcels of land, and the people on the land, were divided up among landowning nobles. In cultural practice, however, feudal society functioned somewhat like a large family. The peasants had obligations to the baron and the baron had obligations to the peasantry, especially to provide military protection. In this large, somewhat communal family, land tenure was not based on the concept of private property but was held according to "traditional use," a complex of culturally sanctioned arrangements. The agreements of traditional use were destroyed by the Industrial Revolution. Suddenly the English land barons began to say, "I own this land and now I want the peasants removed." The notorious English "enclosure laws" of the sixteenth century stripped peasants of the forest and pasture lands that they had traditionally held in common with the aristocracy. The numbers of poor and wandering homeless rose. Polanyi writes of this period: "Enclosures have appropriately been called a revolution of the rich against the poor. The lords and nobles were upsetting the social order, breaking down ancient law and custom, sometimes by means of violence, often by pressure and intimidation. They were literally robbing the poor of their share in the common, tearing down the houses which, by the hitherto unbreakable force of custom, the poor had long regarded as theirs and their heirs'. The fabric of society was being disrupted desolate villages and the ruins of human dwellings testified to the fierceness with which the revolution raged, endangering the defenses of the country, wasting its towns, decimating its population, turning its overburdened soil into dust, harassing its people and turning them from decent husbandmen into a mob of beggars and thieves. Though this happened only in patches, the black spots threatened to melt into a uniform catastrophe." [8]

Vagrancy laws were also instituted at this time. It became a crime not to have money. This was particulary directed toward the self-sufficient peasantry because, though they were well-fed and housed, they participated only marginally in the money economy. Their domestic industry was land-based, not market-based. Though they were self-sufficient, according to the new laws they were vagrants, and as such were rounded up and sent to the poorhouses where they were rented out as workers to the monied landowners and factory owners. (Vagrancy laws continued to be enforced in the U.S. as late as the 1950's but for other purposes).

The slums of the new industrial towns filled with former peasants who were now little more than slaves. Polanyi describes their plight::

"Local authorities were gladly taking advantage of the unexpected demand of the cotton mills for destitute children whose apprenticing was left to the care of the parish. Many hundreds were indented with manufacturers, often in distant parts of the country. Altogether the new towns developed a healthy appetite for paupers. Factories were even prepared to pay for the use of the poor. Adults were assigned to any employer who would take them for their keep just as they would be billeted out in turn amongst the farmers of the parish, in one or another form of the roundsman system. Farming out was cheaper than the running of 'gaols without guilt,' as workhouses were sometimes called."[9]

By 1700 the wealth of Europe was concentrated in a few hands and the poverty of the masses was well-advanced. By that time subsistence culture was doomed, the power of the nobles was on the decline, and the entrepreneurial "gentlemen farmers" and wealthy industrialists had the upper hand.

Waves of social revolution swept Europe throughout the twelfth through eighteenth centuries. These various and diverse movements, including the Luddites, the Levellers, the Diggers, the Chartists, the Quakers, and others, were spiritually-based. They were usually anti-materialist in the sense that they were a move toward a social form of communalism which incorporated the sharing of meals and property. The impulse toward communalism and anti-materialism was strong. Resistance to the shredding of the last of human social environments as represented by feudalism caused constant revolt and even at times, civil war. Occasionally, whole areas and cities were taken over by these groups. The popes and royalty put these affronts to hierarchy and elitism down by bringing out armies to massacre the participants. Even so, spiritual heirs of these movements continue to attempt to return to a more natural way of life, even to this day.

The Conquest of Rationalism

"Progress," "development" and "productivity" were the intellectual banners of the new entrepreneurial class as it attacked traditional society. A social movement developed, led by the commercial interests whose rallying cry was "free markets" and "unfettered freedom of action for commerce." Then, as now, the touted benefits went largely to the new industrial class, as the numbers of the poor and dispossessed grew. As poverty increased among the masses, the industrialists secured their hold on society. Foreign trade, foreign adventurism and imperialism increased. Most of us have been taught in our schools to regard this era of industrial assault as a time of great progress but it was only "progress" for the elite.

The philosophers of the new movement were the "rationalists." The rationalists believed that human "reason" should be the basis of human conduct. They were set in opposition to the "traditionalists" of various stripes, who accepted truth based on revelation, the Christian Bible, tradition, other "non-scientific" beliefs, or on the remnants of aboriginal knowledge still in the culture. Industrial expansion was continually revolutionized by the products of mechanical invention and the new empirical-experimental science. The vitality of life came to be perceived as the rigid functioning of chemical processes and the earth was perceived as a machine, a giant clock. As scientists projected the new society's thought-forms onto the universe, the mystery and awe of life evaporated. Science and industry promulgated a world-view which turned millions of years of human culture, on its head. Now consciously seeking to "subdue" Nature, they waged social war against tradition.

Women were singled out as enemies of the new rationalism. For centuries European village women had retained and passed on remnants of the knowledge of pre-Roman, pre-Christian culture. Women were often powerful figures in peasant village life, maintaining the stability of the people's relationship to the land by practicing their knowledge of healing, of herbs, of the natural life of the earth. The power of these women had long stymied the efforts of the patriarchal Church of Rome to control the peasantry. Now the church, the mercantile state, and the new philosophers of rational "science" joined forces in a largely successful assault of torture and murder aimed at physically eradicating all remaining practitioners of natural healing arts. A bloody convulsion of state- and church-sponsored witch hunts took place throughout Europe during the sixteenth century. In the several countries for which we have records, over 100,000 people were prosecuted for witchcraft, over 80 per cent of them women.[10] In some cases, female populations of whole villages were tortured to death. The Christian hate propaganda, an early example of the cover-ups and misinformation campaigns of the type which today are used to rationalize the murder of the last tribal peoples on earth, masked, and continues to mask, the true aim of the witch hunts: to finally stamp out European Natural culture.

The concept of "progress" is really the old mythos of linear increase dressed in new clothing. People believed that commerce, science, industrialism and the conquest of the inferior by the superior, would cause the human family to continually improve its condition (and by the end of the sixteenth century the lot of most of human society in Europe desperately needed improving!). Not even the most rash would say that there would ever be any end to the linear increase of wealth and its benefits created by marketing and technology. It appeared that progress would be infinite, even to the stars. Thus Europeans, en masse, fell victim to the imperialist belief system and the subliminal justification for empire became ingrained in the culture.

Europe Explodes Across the Earth

In 1800 well over half of the earth was populated by tribal, hunter-forager people. These people had maintained their cultural patterns since Pleistocene times. These cultures, which emphasize balance with the natural world, had stable populations. It was against this background of stability that the European empire exploded.

In Europe the social and environmental disruption caused by empire culture was accelerated dramatically by the Industrial Revolution. It created a population explosion. Demographers estimate that, prior to the Industrial Revolution, the doubling time of the "civilized" world population was approximately once every 250 years, a rate of increase that had generally remained stable back into the distant past. Between 1850 and 1930 world population doubled —in 80 years. The populations of the U.S., Canada, Australia and Argentina tripled between 1850 and 1900. During the nineteenth century the world population of Europeans, including both the inhabitants of the European continent and the overseas colonials increased between three and four times as fast as the native populations of other continents.[11] Today, in the 1980's, the world population doubling time is estimated to be only 33 years and is falling. The reasons for this human population increase may be discerned by studying natural life. Stability prevails in undisturbed natural systems. Species populations of a stable ecosystem remain in balance with one another. When the ecosystem is injured or destroyed, food sources are thrown out of balance. Some foods become more abundant while others disappear, causing the populations of some species to expand while others diminish or become extinct. For a time the ecosystem experiences upheaval, as out-of-balance populations experiencing unchecked growth, swell, exhaust food sources, and crash. Slowly, after a natural disruption, such as a volcanic eruption, the system heals and stability returns.

In Europe, centuries of human disturbance had depleted the land, and human populations had already suffered several large expansions followed by dramatic crashes caused by plagues. By the sixteenth century, human populations of Europe were just recovering from the decimation of the latter waves of medieval plague. During the time when human populations had plummeted, the resilient European landscape, especially the forests, had recovered somewhat from the depredations of farming, and mining inflicted upon it in previous centuries. With the arrival of the Industrial Revolution the commercial interests quickly exploited the health of the land of Europe but there was a new development, the imported raw materials. The new inflow of raw materials from the colonies swelled the productive capacity of European society beyond anything previously imagined. Despite the general misery, the population of Europe increased. One of the great services the colonization of North America performed for Europe was the export of European population. Had not massive transfers of the exploding European population occurred, sooner or later the progressively impoverished masses of Europe may have achieved their growing demands that the rich share food and wealth. By exporting masses of population the European elite could keep its wealth and control, and the colonists would generate even more wealth from abroad to enrich the empire. This is one of the reasons that elites of all empires demand growth. If there is a growth situation, the people experience increase and don't demand what the elite have. At the same time, if the pie is growing, the elite's percentage share grows faster and the new shares at the bottom come from growth and not from the accumulations of the elite.

Between 1820 and 1930 Europe exported more than 50 million people, one-fifth of the population.[12] Thirty-five million people were exported from Europe in the last half of the Nineteenth Century alone. During approximately that same period, Natural culture tribal populations worldwide declined precipitously. Anthropologist John H. Bodley writes:

"...It might be conservatively estimated that during the 150 years between 1780 and 1930 world tribal populations were reduced by at least thirty million as a direct result of the spread of industrial civilization. A less conservative and probably more realistic estimate would place the figure at perhaps fifty million." [12] The varying estimates of world tribal populations are partially a result of newer research. As the European conquest proceeded, there were many areas into which they spilled that were "empty." Like the wild horse that proceeded the European-human arrival on the Great Plains of North America by centuries, human diseases from Europe raced ahead of the conquerors. In his work, *Ecological Imperialism,* Alfred W. Crosby shows that when Cortez was retaking the Aztec capital of Tenochtitlán, the Aztecs holding the city were already and at the same time undergoing a severe epidemic of smallpox. By the time Pizzaro came to ravage the Incas, smallpox had already been there and decimated the population. Crosby states that:

"The disease often spread far beyond the European frontier, often to people who had barely heard of the white invaders. Smallpox probably reached the Puget Sound area on the northwest Pacific coast in 1782 or 1783, a part of the world then as distant from the main centers of human population as any place on earth. When the explorer George Vancouver sailed into the Sound in 1793, he found Amerindians with pockmarked faces, and human bones scattered along the beach at Port Discovery - skulls, limbs, ribs, backbones - so many as to produce the impression that this was 'a general cemetery for the whole of the surrounding country.' He judged that 'at no very remote period this country had been far more populous than at present.' It was an assessment that he could accurately have extended to the entire continent."[13]

The toll of the human massacre that was the European -industrial colonization of the earth was in the multiple tens of millions. The conservative anthropological guess that makes estimates from tribes now existing is thirty million. From the public health view of Crosby this may be boosted to well over one hundred million people. Whatever the monstrous statistics are, we should be alerted that this is the most incredible murder of human populations that has ever happened on the planet. Also it should be noted that in our cultural reality this has gone into the memory vacuum. The significance of this mass murder occupies little space in history books and the public has little understanding that their colonies are based in such dimensions of death.

Given the respective cultural assumptions held by invader and native about life and reality, there was and is no way that the two views of life could live side by side. The one lives stably in its habitat, the living world. The other eats up the living world for its growth. The European existed in a mental-cultural realm of products and beliefs attached to the cultural centers of Europe. The tribal native represented the antithesis of what European culture described as the "proper" way to live. In many cases it was difficult for the Europeans to view the natives as actual human beings. In some areas the natives were consciously worked to death, and in many areas were hunted like game animals. In the early Anglo settlement of California, for example, parties of gentlemen hunters often gathered in San Francisco to go out "hunting" the peaceful natives in the northern part of the state. The programming and conditioning of the culture of empire is so profound that even today it is difficult for the person of industrial culture to see a human being of another culture who is lacking money or high-priced manufactured possessions, as significant. The truly horrible things done by the Nazis to the Jews, Gypsies, homosexuals and anti-fascists during the holocaust are held up to the world as an extreme example of human inhumanity to human, and deservedly so. This inhumanity happened to white-skinned people of European culture and so is deemed nightmarish by the civilized mind. Little notice is taken by the "official" histories of the tens of millions of native victims of the atrocities during expansion of the European empire. The colonizers of the empire on the frontier periphery functioned in a vacuum of official attention, and in many cases enjoyed official complicity while doing their killing and torturing of natives. The "frontier" industrial-culture settlers were armed with the latest machine made weapons from the factories of Europe. Native people of the world were little prepared to roll back the invasion. There were those back in the capitals of Europe and in the colonies who began to clothe these thefts of land and killing of alien people, in theological, moral and legalistic phrases. In his study of the legal relationship between Native Americans and the U.S. government, *Behind the Trail of Broken Treaties: An Indian Declaration of Independence*, Vine DeLoria Jr. points out that the early Puritans claimed the biblical edict of "go forth and multiply" as the reason that they should take native land. As there was no room in Europe to "go forth and multiply," therefore God must have meant them to come to North America.[14] To a European of that time and to a transnational corporation of our time, the idea that human beings can live on the earth without substantially altering and "developing" it is absurd. When empire culture people encounter tribal hunter-forager people who live on the earth without altering it, they assume that the land is not being "used." They refer to it as "wilderness" and abhor this condition. To the European, it is clearly justifiable to take land not being put to "proper use" in order to make it "productive" through farming or herding. DeLoria exposes one of the big myths in European culture- the myth that when native people are exposed to the "obviously superior" culture of the empire they will voluntarily give up their culture and join the invader's culture. This myth contradicts the world-wide warfare with native people which has taken place throughout the impe-rial-industrial expansion. This myth is supported by the basic assumption of the imperial psyche that its own culture is superior to all others. This in turn is supported by the competitive social Darwinist view, which further twisted the nineteenth-century notion of "survival of the fittest" into the idea that those who muscled their way to the top of social hierarchies were obviously the "fittest" to rule. (Naziism and fascism developed logically from this thought.) DeLoria goes to the heart of the matter when he says: "One of the final and more sophisticated arguments for taking the lands of the aboriginal peoples involved the transmission of the benefits of civilization to the uncivilized. Taking the lands by whatever means possible was justifiable because, in return, the Indians were receiving the great benefits of Western Civilization, which had allowed the European peoples to create such military and economic power as to make it possible for them to dispossess other peoples."[15]

The advancement of the frontier of the empire of industrial civilization took a uniform pattern throughout the world. First, all easily-transported valuables were shipped to the mother country, then settlers were needed to work the land and obtain the raw materials of the area. Finally, the labor of the enslaved natives was necessary if that was appropriate to the use that the land was to be put. When plantation agriculture was instituted, when mining was to be pursued, or rubber gathering carried out, it was planned and presumed by all colonial authorities that this labor would be carried out by involuntary native service. The justification? John H. Bodley recounts an opinion delivered in 1921:

"The American legal authority, Alpheus Snow, pointed out that natives simply lack the acquisitive drive characteristic of civilized man, and doing virtually anything that will correct this mental deficiency is permissible and even a moral duty of the state."[16] The global expansion of the industrial empire was proceeded by armed violence and was followed by missionaries and government administrators who performed the function of destroying native culture. In the U.S., the practice of any religion other than Christianity by the subjugated natives was outlawed for many years. In Soviet Russia, Bodley describes how the Soviet industrialists actually created a Lenin-Stalin cult that was used to destroy native cultures of the East, deemed inimical to "progress." Soviet government functionaries circulated printed material and pictures representing Lenin and Stalin as all powerful solar deities to replace tribal shamanism.[17] All over the world where the European empire intruded, mil-lions died. In the 1890's, Germans swarmed over the cattle-herding Herero tribes of the Southwest African region now known as Namibia. By 1906 the original Herero population of 300,000 had been reduced to 20,000 landless fugitives, following numerous massacres and unequal battles between tribespeople with spears and German soldiers with guns and cannons. One of the leaders of that territorial government, Paul Rohrbach, proclaimed the imperial position in 1907, after ordering native herdsmen to turn over their grazing lands to white European settlers:

"...The native tribes must withdraw from the lands on which they have pastured their cattle and so let the White man pasture his cattle on these self-same lands. If the moral right of this standpoint is questioned, the answer is that for people of the culture standard of the South African Natives, the loss of their free national barbarism and the development of a class of workers in the service of and dependent on the Whites is primarily a law of existence in the highest degree. For a people, as for an individual, an existence appears to be justified in the degree that it is useful in the progress of general development. By no argument in the world can it be shown that the preservation of any degree of national independence, national prosperity and political organization by the races of South West Africa would be of greater or even of equal advantage for the development of mankind in general or the German people in particular than that these races should be made serviceable in the enjoyment of their former territories by the White races."[18]

This is an example of the types of encounters that happened daily on a world-wide basis, for centuries- and still continue wherever there are aboriginal people remaining.

Slavery and Empire

In the culture of empire, with its social hierarchies, the society is a system of extortion of humans and nature. Given this reality it is difficult to establish a set definition of slavery other than the outright chattel slavery of the plantation system where masses of humans were purchased solely as labor power. The mass system of slavery which powered the Roman empire eventually ended but the serf system of European land tenure, in its hierarchal nature, was a system of coerced labor to a considerable degree. Some actual buying and selling of European people continued into the times of the Middle Ages. European slavery in the pre-industrial days was more akin to indebted servitude or debt peonage. Slaves of European origin were sold in the port cities of the Mediterranean, traded into North Africa and the Mid-East. For their part, some stratified societies of Africa also sold slaves into North Africa and Europe. In those stratified societies of both Europe and Africa, the social definition of a slave was not what it was with "plantation slavery" or "industrial slavery." The authority on the history of slavery, Basil Davidson describes the type of slavery that existed just prior to the development of the mass African slave trade that paralleled the development of the industrial revolution:

> "As in Africa, so in Europe: the medieval slave, in one as in the other, was a captive who could win access to a system of mutual duty and obligation that bound noble and commoner together. And what went for the manners of society went for the morals of the merchants too - whether in Europe or Africa. European traders sold their fellow-countrymen to the overseas states of Egypt and North Africa. Pressured by the need for European goods, the lords of Africa began to sell their own folk to the mariners who came from Europe."[19]

When the Europeans and in particular the Portuguese, arrived in the 1500's on the west coast of Africa they encountered "kingdoms" in some places, stratified African societies. These were peoples who generally had been influenced by the patriarchal/hierarchal cultures of Islam. They were generally contiguous to the Islamic influenced areas of Sahara, Sudan and Ethiopia. These stratified African societies were by no means universal. Many African societies had evolved without kingships or other centralizing institutions of political or economic power.[20]

It was from the stratified African societies that the modern colonial slave trade began. The early beginnings of the trade in the mid-1400's began to dwarf any slave trade that had gone before. No longer were a few slaves on a ship filled with cargo but whole ships full of slaves began to infuse the trade. The Portuguese trade began by purchasing slaves from the Kingdoms on the west coast of Africa. These kingdoms held slaves, most of whom were captured in war. This grew into industrial slavery, not the kind where a few people were added onto a feudal barony but the kind of mass system where the millions of slaves were absolutely enslaved in an imperial plantation and production system in the money economy. As native populations of the New World dwindled, in areas of mass slavery such as the mines of Mexico or the plantations of the Caribbean Islands, colonialists imported human slaves to help them enslave the earth, as it were. They turned accessible flat areas into huge monocultures to produce products for export to Europe. After the purchase price, the labor of slaves was practically free. The great demand for slaves made super profits for the slave traders. One of the first Englishmen to develop the market in African slaves (in the mid-1500's) was John Hawkins, rumored to be Queen Elizabeth's lover. After he spent many energetic years in the slave trade, Elizabeth knighted him for his efforts. During the award ceremony, she described his labor in the colonies as: "Going every day on shore to take the inhabitants with burning and spoiling their towns."[21]

When the supply of slaves purchased from African kingdoms was not large enough, slavers began to raid the coast. At first the slavers, English, French, Dutch, Spanish, Danes, and Portuguese, could simply put ashore on the coast of West Africa and begin raiding villages. As the coast became devastated they began to move inland. E.D. Morel in his classic, *Black Man's Burden*, says that::

"The trade had grown so large that mere kidnapping raids conducted by white men in the immediate neighborhood of the coast-line were quite insufficient to meet its requirements. Regions inaccessible to the European had to be tapped by the organization of civil wars. The whole of the immense region from the Senegal to the Congo, and even further south, became in the course of years convulsed by incessant internecine struggles. A vast tumult reigned from one extremity to the other of the most populous and fertile portions of the continent. Tribe was bribed to fight tribe, community to raid community."[22]

There is no accurate count of the number of slaves taken. Morel indicates that the British alone transported three million between 1666 and 1766, to British, French and Spanish American colonies. One quarter of a million people died on the voyages when these three million were transported and it is estimated that one-third of those on the land route to the slave shipment ports on the coast of Africa died. We may assume that many millions of lives were involved and the lives of many others were disrupted or extinguished after their villages were devastated and crops ruined. Some slave raiding by Arabs in Africa, for the Mid-East market runs far back into history and that total will never be known either, but the medieval and later era can be traced somewhat by historians from written records. The historian Basil Davidson estimates that the complete toll of humans transported out of Africa over the many years into slavery, from the fifteenth to the nineteenth century, may run up toward fifty million people.

Slavery was institutionalized within the social system of Europe. Given the belief in their superiority and the general ideology of an expansionist, conquering empire, civilized people committed the most horrifying acts. E.D. Morel quotes a personal report, an account of a day in the life of a slaver:

"Then might you see mothers forsaking their children and husbands their wives, each striving to escape as best he could. Some drowned themselves in the water, others thought to escape by hiding under their huts others stowed their children among the sea-weed, where our men found them afterwards, hoping they would thus escape notice.... And at last our Lord God, who giveth a reward for every good deed, willed that for the toil they had undergone in His service they should that day obtain victory over their enemies, as well as a guerdon and a payment for all their labour and expense for they took captive of those Moors, what with men, women and children, 165, besides those that perished and were killed. And when the battle was over, all praised God for the great mercy He had shown them, in that He had willed to give them such a victory, and with so little damage to themselves. They were all very joyful, praising loudly the Lord God for that He had deigned to give such help to such a handful of His Christian people."[23]

In a culture where the lot of the common English sailor differed from that of a slave only by degree, and the condition of a child laborer working 15 hours a day and living in the slums, was similar it was easy for the European population to accept slavery. Slavery was widely accepted and condoned. Even religions got into the business. Morel says that at least one missionary offshoot of a major church was involved. He says that the, "'Society for propagating Christianity,' including half the Episcopal bench, derived, as masters, from the labour of their slaves in the West Indies, an income which they spent in 'teaching the religion of peace and goodwill to men.'"[24]

European slave traders constantly fomented wars between tribes. They thus created lucrative markets for European-made arms while reaping a harvest of slaves for sale from the victors. At times guns were traded to one group in order to create markets with other groups who scrambled to get guns to redress the balance of power. Like the slave trade, the arms industry produced super profits for imperial exploiters.

Apologists of slavery have said that the slave's lot was good because they were cared for and protected as property, something that the lowly wage laborer was not. Morel gives a short report from one slave holding region: "For a hundred years slaves in Barbadoes were mutilated, tortured, gibbeted alive and left to starve to death, burnt alive, flung into coppers of boiling sugar, whipped to death."[25]

Many areas of the world that were once used in the plantation/slave production system are now ecologically destroyed. The island of Haiti, prior to the European expansion for example, was once a rich and dense tropical rainforest inhabited by Natural culture people. First the new invaders' plantations worked virtually all the native labor to death. African slaves were then imported and replaced by more African slaves as they in turn were worked to death. The replaceable cheap labor provided by the slave trade enabled exploitation of the land to intensify at an unprecedented rate. Finally, toward the end of the era of mass slavery, the slaves of Haiti revolted and established their own government. The population began to grow and as it grew the last of the natural ecosystem was eliminated. To survive, people were forced to cultivate more and more fragile areas. As the mountainsides were deforested, severe erosion began.

The island of Haiti is now a barren ecological sink, populated by hungry people who can only drive it into further ecological collapse in their attempt to survive. Similarly, soils in the southeastern U.S. have not recovered from the overuse and erosion engendered by the plantation slavery-driven cotton plantations of the same era. In many cities of the Greek empire more than half the population were slaves. The same condition obtained in the Babylonian empire. We see the dynamics of the culture arranged so that it is a monolithic system of extortion of biological energy. The energy comes from the soil, the plant world, animals and the human population. The modern industrial system is simply a refinement of these dynamics. The semantics have changed but the patriarchal/ hierarchal system continues to funnel energy to the elite though they may be called office workers, factory workers or even scientists who labor in the laboratories of "defense" contractors.

The World-Wide Extermination of Natural Culture

In the last quarter of the Nineteenth Century, while the "mopping up" of the tribal populations and the invasion of their habitats was in progress in the U.S., a similar war using the Remington rifle, was going on in South America against the Araucanian, Puelche and Tehuelche tribes of the pampas and the Araucanians of Chile. These tribes were almost exterminated outright, leaving only a handful to dwindle away. Human slavery had been abolished in many countries in the mid-to late, 1800's because of the outcry by sympathetic groups in Europe and the U.S. Because of rising awareness of brutality in the colonies, the activities on the "frontier" and military conquests such as Cuba and the Philippines were increasingly described to the public as "civilizing," "opportunities for primitives to work and learn the value of money," and "moral and material regeneration." A large protracted war, primarily fought by settlers from England and Scotland was conducted against the native Maori of New Zealand in the 1860's and 1870's, while the British and other colonialist countries fought wars against hill tribes all across Southeast Asia, through the foothills of the Himalayas and into the Hindu Kush toward Afghanistan. In Bangladesh and in India efforts are still underway to dominate the last remaining tribal peoples which the British Colonial Administration was unable to subdue completely. In Southeast Asia the assault on tribal groups continues to this day. In Formosa, in the early 1900's, the incipient industrial empire of Japan used their armed forces to invade the land of the aboriginal Formosans who had been holding out against the Chinese settlers. After conducting warfare against the natives for some years they finally ended the native resistance by using heavy cruisers at sea to bombard the villages with cannons. In other areas such as Australia, the South Sea Islands, Siberia, Tasmania, Lapland, Africa, the cold regions and equatorial regions of the Americas and the rainforest regions of Southeast Asia there were many little wars or in other cases Natural people were simply overwhelmed and pushed aside. Even with increased public awareness of what was taking place in the colonies, the slave trade known as "blackbirding" captured native South Sea Islanders and sold them for labor in the plantations of Queensland, Australia. This trade endured for 50 years, between 1860 and 1910. The anthropologist John Bodley estimates that 60,000 people were successfully enslaved. A large percentage of these were killed or died from diseases brought by the slavers. These practices were presented to the public mind and world press as "contract labor."[26] The genocide of native tribal hunter-foragers goes on today in India, Bangladesh, Southeast Asia, Paraguay, Chile and in the Amazon jungle, carried out by militaries, industrial interests or settlers. The perpetrators continue to justify their behavior in the traditional manner, as the modern empire assaults life in its manifold forms. Human slavery is only an extreme form of what is basic to imperial society itself, the overt or subtle coercion of the masses to produce surpluses for the elite. It is the purpose of empire to conquer and enslave. Some modification of coercion was used on all native peoples who were needed as labor for the productive process. The whole intent was to conquer other lands and make them rewarding for the imperial elite, either by native labor or the labor of the exported poor of Europe. Even without personal, private ownership of other human beings, the very existence of colonies, where the native people are forced into a style of life that serves the material and social interest of the invaders, is a form of slavery.

Historically, the super-profits from guns, drugs, rum, sugar and slaves have driven imperialism. When we look at the vast amount of historical detail we see that there is no limit on murder, torture, pain and destruction that the culture of empire will impose in order to further its ends. It has finally culminated in a situation where whole imperial societies are dependent for their survival upon the ravishing of other societies and other land masses. A culture that will murder millions in the process of looting whole continents will stop at nothing. Substances that have a compulsive and addictive chemical reaction in the human body have been especially profitable. Galeano says that the Inca empire distributed coca leaves during ceremonial days but that when the Spanish had established themselves they began to push the drug and tax it. He says:

"In Cuzco four hundred Spanish merchants lived off the coca traffic. Every year one hundred thousand baskets with a million kilos of coca-leaf entered the Potosí silver mines. The Church took a tax from the drug."[27]

In Asia the imperialists found opium. They took this addictive substance, greatly increased its production and turned it into an instrument of foreign policy.

Opium and Empire

The old degenerate empires of Asia fell to modern colonialism, just as did the world's tribal populations.

After Britain's colonial concessionaire, the East India Company, had consolidated control of India, it began to import tea from China. In 1715, the English established a trading center outside the city walls of Canton. The English empire soon became habituated to Chinese tea. By 1830 the East India Company was making a profit of one million pound sterling per year from the

China tea trade. The tax on tea levied by the British government was beginning to represent a substantial base of the government budget. The importation of tea soon became a fundamental element of the British economy, but the other side of the equation was deficient. The English could find very little that the Chinese were interested in buying. There was nothing that the Europeans had that the Chinese wanted. The English had tried selling wool and cotton in China, but the Chinese already had fine silks and cotton of their own. The New England Yankees did strike a small bonanza when they discovered that the Chinese would buy seal pelts. In twenty-seven years they nearly wiped out the seal populations of the Falkland islands and the Aleutian islands. By 1830, when the seal breeding grounds had been destroyed, that trade collapsed.

As the tea trade grew, the English treasury began to be drained of its silver, which was the only currency the Chinese traders would accept. The balance of payments problem became severe. The English searched for something that they could sell in China to get the silver back. Opium became the answer to the English dilemma. Not only could opium return super-profits from those addicted to the drug but it helped soften-up Chinese society for the penetration of English imperialism (and the other colonial empires trying to nudge their way into the massive "China market").

The French and Dutch had been the first in the opium trade in the mid-1700's, purchasing huge volumes in Bengal. The Dutch in particular used it as a political tactic against Indonesia whose populations were resisting the imposition of the plantation system in their area. The Dutch flooded Indonesia with opium and then after the social disintegration, were able to take it over. The English saw the success of this tactic. When Bengal fell to the English Empire the East India Company then had a monopoly on the opium trade and they encouraged additional production in new areas of India. Jack Beeching, in his history, *The Chinese Opium Wars*, says: "In 1782 there had been no sale for the cargo of Bengal opium that Warren Hastings had sent hopefully to Canton. By 1830, the opium trade there was probably the largest commerce of its time in any single commodity, anywhere in the world." [28]

The East India Company was not inclined to miss a chance for profits. They began also to import opium into England for the home population. Soon opium was sold in England in packets of powder and in liquid elixirs called generically, laudanum. Commercial preparations at the retail level were wearing such trade names as Godfrey's Cordial and Mother Bailey's quieting Syrup.[29] In the United States where the drug was also legally sold, there were 120,000 opium addicts by 1875.[30]

By 1700, Chinese society had become stagnant under foreign Mongol rulers. From 1700, until the take-over by the cadres under Mao Tse-Tung after World War II, the European powers plus Canada and the U.S., pummeled the closed society of China breaking in at the edges, trying to create markets for their goods. Armed outbreaks and at times small wars were fomented, the whole period is referred to as the "opium wars." At the time of the opium wars, Chinese society was governed by an administrative class of Manchus. The Manchus were invading mongols who continued to maintain close relations with their original homeland, Manchuria. At times they even brought in horse cavalry from the steppes to fight the various groups busily dismembering the huge decadent Chinese empire. China was twenty times the size and population of England.

China, being a culture of empire, resembled European imperial culture in many ways and it was much older and the cultural images were more thorough. There were few ideological divisions. In China the emperor was the Son Of Heaven, the ruler of the Middle Kingdom, the center of the universe. The rigid patriarchy was culturally bolstered by the Confucian doctrines of ancestor worship and submission to the emperors and those more elevated in the hierarchy. The Han chinese, the ethnic group that makes up 97% of China, consider themselves culturally and racially superior to all others, who they refer to with a term equivalent to "barbarians." Though the throne of China had been captured several times by the nomads from the north, Chinese society had never been completely shattered in war. China had remained for thousands of years as the center of gravity of east Asia. For thousands of years the fortunes of individual Chinese dynasties have ebbed and flowed. They have enslaved the geographical areas adjacent to them in Southeast Asia and to the north of them, but they seldom absorbed anything cultural in excess of the material extortion of the peripheral satraps. The Chinese culture is so thoroughly imbued with super-race feeling that especially in the early days of European contact, "barbarians" were kept out of the walled cities as much for the convenience of the Chinese as for the safety of the foreigners. The simple sight of a non-Chinese caused immediate riots among the population. When the powerful european religious organizations began attempting to penetrate Chinese society for their own organizational motives, the missionaries met with little success because they were so restricted and confined. The simple sight of a European missionary on the streets of a city would provoke riots that posed serious physical danger.[31]

The elites of many powerful social structures within the European empires were getting benefits from the opium poisoning and disintegration of Chinese society. The Catholic hierarchy and the protestant hierarchies also moved with many strategies toward furthering their growth and power in China. The East India Company was a major force in exploiting China and smaller trader groups from many countries were loitering around the sidelines picking up what crumbs they could.

Because of internal decay and because of the pressures exerted by the outside powers, the decadent Manchu regime finally dissolved in the first decade of the 1900's. The battle to rule China was picked up by indigenous Chinese warlords under the leadership of Sun Yat-Sen and the foreigner assisted Koumintang under Chaing Kai-Shek. Although opium importation (officially) stopped after the fall of the Manchus, the Japanese empire revived it when they invaded in 1938 as a method of extorting money from Chinese society. This was certainly not the end of drug pushing as an instrument of foreign policy. Alfred W. McCoy, Professor of History at the University of

Wisconsin and author of the books *The Politics of Heroin: CIA Complicity in the Global Drug Trade, The Politics of Heroin in Southeast Asia* and *Drug Traffic: Narcotics and Organized Crime in Australia,* traces opium to the present in Southeast Asia:

> "In Indochina, you have to understand first of all that the extensive opium trade, mass consumption, particularly in the cities, was a result of European colonial policy. It's only in Southeast Asia that colonial governments paid for their very dynamic development: irrigation, massive road networks, rail networks by direct taxes upon indigenous consumers, taxes on alcohol, salt, and particularly opium. In British Malay 40 percent of colonial taxes came from opium. In French Indochina it ranged about 15 percent from the period from the 1870's up through the 1950's, when as a result of UN pressure, all of these governments abolished the state opium trade. Thailand was the next to last to do it. It didn't abolish its state opium monopoly, rather like an alcohol beverage control that a lot of states have, until 1957. Laos didn't abolish theirs until 1961. So you have mass opium consumption in Southeast Asia as a result of the colonial policy of making the colony pay with opium.
>
> "Most of the opium was not produced in Southeast Asia. It came from abroad, either southern China or India."[32]

In the early 1960's the U.S. agency, the CIA, sponsored the creation of what became the world's largest opium growing industry in Southeast Asia. They did this to create an economic base for their "allies" in the secret wars of the 1950's and on into the present. The first group of allies were the Nationalist Chinese generals and their troops who were chased into Southeast Asia by Mao's Red Army. Others were different tribal groups that were forced by various elites: Chinese Generals, indigenous elites and the employees of the CIA to create an economic infrastructure based on opium and their males for use as cadre in the wars. In the present all areas of opium poppy and coca production are also areas of historic U.S. government and CIA contacts. These are the Andean nations who have for many years received U.S. military equipment, money and training, the Syrian generals who control opium growing in the Bekka Valley, the opium growing Afghanistan mujahadeen, the Pakistani Generals, and the military and political elites throughout Southeast Asia.

In the old imperial culture of China, Mao Tse-Tung and the peasant rebellion represented the resurgence of Chinese imperial culture. Although they had a new ideological twist, they essentially reunified the old imperial culture and campaigned against foreign "contamination." The Communists under Mao succeeded in ridding China of missionaries, traders and other remnants of the "barbarians." China has now rejoined the "family of nations" as a modern imperial state.

There appears to be nothing that the controlling elites of the imperial hierarchies will not do to service their greed and their craving for power. Guns, drugs, slavery, torture, massacre, assassination, and the most massive destruction, ecologically and socially are the stock in trade. Because public education and awareness was growing in the industrial countries in the 1800's, we see also the beginnings of the relationship of the elites to their own First World populations in terms of the control of information to which they are allowed exposure. We see in one example, with the "rubber boom" experience of the Congo, that it is possible for the elites of the industrial societies to literally alter history. We see this also in the opium wars.

Because of the distasteful nature of the colonial activities in the Far East, the facts about the creation of a market for opium in China were downplayed if not obscured. Jack Beeching in his history, *The Chinese Opium Wars*, recounts one public disinformation campaign conducted by the opium traders. William Jardine was head of one of the largest groups importing opium into China. He spearheaded a media campaign financed with a self-imposed tax on each chest of opium imported into China by all importers. In a letter to Jardine, at that time, in London, a fellow trader instructed Jardine, "You will not, however, be limited to this outlay, as the magnitude of the object can well bear any amount of expense ... you may find it expedient to secure, at a high price, the services of some leading newspaper ... we are told there are literary men whom it is usual to employ ..."[33] The opium smugglers had abundant cash to bribe newspapers and politicians.

Beeching indicates that the disinformation campaign in the London media worked well. He says, "subsidized or not, sensational pamphlets and news items multiplied. All London was rapidly made aware how honest British [opium] merchants in Canton had been besieged, imprisoned, deprived of food, and actually threatened with death." In fact this was the inflated description of an incident in Canton that was no more than an ultimately failed attempt by one Chinese official to stop the importation of opium.

The Rubber Boom

With the invention of the automobile, demand for rubber increased enormously. In the tropical regions of the Amazon and the Congo, the "Rubber Boom" of the late 1800's and early 1900's resulted in the deaths of millions of people. There were few "laborers" to be found in the rainforests where the extraction of the sap of the rubber tree took place. When the boom began, the industry was faced with the problem of finding a labor supply. The solution to this problem adopted by the rubber companies, like the early industrial revolution, was to force natives out of their subsistence culture in order to turn them into "slave labor." In the western Amazon the British-owned Peruvian Amazon Company sent armed gangs to capture natives. Bodley reports that "rape, slavery, torture by flogging and mutilation," and "mass murder by

shooting, poisoning, starvation, and burning," were practiced against the
native people. The colonial government of Peru never acted to restrain the
British company. Similar atrocities took place in other areas of the Amazon
where rubber was gathered, ending when rubber plantations of the East Indies
took over the market after 1915.[34] Though the Amazon exported rubber, the
richest source was the Congo Basin in Africa. The Congo River drains most of
the watershed of the African equatorial rainforest. Villages and tribes ran for
several thousand miles along its banks. Most of the native people lived in settled
villages where they maintained rainforest gardens, raised tree crops and
foraged in the forest for additional sustenance. Native trading all over the
Congo was active, although the culture did not support any kind of empire-
style market economy. As in the rainforest-Mayan culture of Central America,
no hierarchical superstructure of commercial trade or region-wide military had
developed. The stability of the many different tribal cultures up and down the
Congo river and into the expanse of forest was maintained by thousands of
years of complex bartering agreements. By the late 1800's, most tribes of the
rainforest of Central Africa had become dominated by European colonial
powers. One man, King Leopold II of Belgium, personally owned one million
square miles of the Congo, along with everything on it, including the people. As
a private estate, the Congo Free State, as the area was known, was subject to no
law or scrutiny of any government. It was this peculiar ownership that helped
the rulers of the Congo Free State shield their activities from public view, even
from the view of the Belgian government.

In the Congo, companies that were financed by the sale of stock in Europe,
were given rights by the King to exploit specified sections. The King retained
one-half the shares in each company. Stock in these incredibly profitable
companies was distributed around elite financial circles, political circles and
the diplomatic circles, cutting many of the "well placed" of Europe into the
game.

European merchants had traded up the Congo for many generations
exploiting a lucrative European market for red-wood, camwood powder, wax,
ivory, tin, copper, lead, and palm oil. But the big new stockholder-owned
companies were interested solely in the super-profit trade in two items, ivory
and rubber. All other trade was prohibited. The company controlling each area
hired gangs of thugs, detribalized and marginalized natives, criminals, and
mercenaries to collect a "tax" payable only in ivory or rubber, which had been
levied on the natives by the companies themselves. Trade was abandoned in
favor of out-and-out extortion. For twenty years, the mercenary hierarchies in
each region assaulted native Congo villages, burning, killing, raping, looting,
burning down gardens and fields and killing orchard trees. One popular
method to get a village to pay the tax was to imprison all of the women and
children of the village until the men paid the tax by gathering rubber or by
ravaging elephant herds for ivory. In areas where the rubber plant did not grow,
the people were forced to give fish or agricultural products to support colonial
administrations in the areas where rubber was tapped.

Soon the rubber and ivory trade began to rival other colonial bonanzas such as the gold and diamonds of South Africa that were produced by quasi-slave labor. By 1900 the French Congo, just west of the Belgian holding, had been parceled out to 40 concessionaire companies. In both the French and Belgian Congo, mercenaries were routinely awarded bonuses for bringing back hands, sexual organs and ears to the local administrators after a punitive raid on native people designed to compel them to gather more- by terror. One missionary reported:

"It is blood-curdling to see them (the soldiers) returning with hands of the slain, and to find the hands of young children amongst the bigger ones evidencing their bravery.... The rubber from this district has cost hundreds of lives, and the scenes I have witnessed, while unable to help the oppressed, have been almost enough to make me wish I were dead...."[35] E.D. Morel, founder of the Congo Reform Movement, reported that, "in one region 6,000 natives were killed and mutilated every six months."[36] In all, Morel reports that some nine million natives were forced to, "spend their lives in the extremely arduous and dangerous task of gathering and preparing india-rubber in the virgin forests...." [37] The population of the Congo Free State, which in 1884 had stood at an estimated 20 to 30 million, had shrunk to nine million by 1911.

The huge dividends on the shares in the concession companies were causing a furor in Europe. Morel writes, "French finance was excited by the wild wave of speculation in Congo rubber shares which swept over Belgium, and by the prodigious profits of the great Belgian Concessionaire Companies."[38]The power of the dozens of concessionaire companies reached from Africa into the political and diplomatic circles of England and the Continent. They and their political allies who profited by the outrage in the Congo conducted a constant disinformation operation in the European press through their own statements and the assistance of compliant pundits and politicians. The line was that the Congo natives were, "...little better than animals, with no conception of land tenure or tribal government, no commercial instincts, no industrial pursuits, 'entitled,' as a Belgian Premier felt no shame in declaring, 'to nothing.'"[39]

Reformers in both France and England worked for years to expose the crimes committed against the peoples of the Congo. The publication of Joseph Conrad's *Heart of Darkness* and Morel's book, *Red Rubber,* in 1906, spawned vocal protests over the activities in the colonies. But the evidence was well concealed. Though the French government did not use the words "National Security," popular today, it nonetheless suppressed all evidence held by the government concerning the Congo. Thousands of church people and other concerned citizens, primarily in England and on the Continent, became involved in the Congo Reform Movement. They visited the Congo, interviewed travellers, surreptitiously obtained suppressed government reports and yet the European elite succeeded in altering history. Governments set up "commissions of inquiry" which themselves were actually a damage control and disinformation tactic. When the reform groups finally accumulated voluminous damning evidence, the elite press would not report it. Many in the press held concession shares. The murder of ten or more million people in a twenty year period by the most grotesque butchers was excised from the history of Western Civilization by the cheerleaders and profiteers of imperial conquest.

By 1915, human society came to an end in the Congo. All trading stopped. Villages were deserted. The forest grew back over the gardens. Any survivors were either enslaved as farmers, porters, mercenary fighters- or they were in hiding in the frontier areas and the deep forest. By 1910 the rubber tree plantations in Southeast Asia were beginning to take over the trade. As World War I began, few paid attention to events in the colonies. Though a veil continued over the deep Congo, the manipulation by outside, covert forces has never really stopped to this day.

NOTES

1   Open Veins of Latin America: Five Centuries of the Pillage of a Continent. Eduardo Galeano. Monthly Review Press. New York. 1973. p.53.
2   Life and Labor In Ancient Mexico. Alonso de Zorita. trans. & intro. Benjamin Keen. Rutgers U. Press. 1971. pp. 8,9.
3   ibid. p. 51.
4   Galeano. Open Veins of Latin America. op. cit. p. 50.
5   Indo-European Language And Society. Emile Benveniste. Elizabeth Palmer, trans. U. of Miami Press. Coral Gables, Florida. 1973. p. 175.
6   ibid. p. 175.
7   The Great Transformation: The Political and Economic Origins of Our Time. Karl Polanyi. Beacon Press. Boston. 1957. p. 165.
8   ibid. p. 35.
9   ibid. p.116.
10 The Death Of Nature: Women, Ecology And The Scientific Revolution. Carolyn Merchant. Harper & Row Pub. New York. 1979. p. 138.
11 Man's Role In Changing The Face Of The Earth. Thomas, Jr. ed. Vol. 2. U. of Chicago Press. Chicago. 1956. "The Spiral of Population," Warren S. Thompson. p. 974.
12 Ecological Imperialism: The Biological Expansion of Europe, 900-1900. Alfred W. Crosby. Cambridge U. Press. New York. 1974. p. 5.
13 ibid. p. 203.
14 Behind The Trail of Broken Treaties: An Indian Declaration of Independence. Vine Deloria, Jr. Dell Pub. Co. New York. 1974. p. 93.
15 ibid. p. 94.
16 Victims Of Progress. John H. Bodley. Cummings Pub. Co. Menlo Park, Ca. 1975. p. 130.
17 ibid. p. 115.
18 ibid. p. 55,56.
19 The African Slave Trade. Basil Davidson. Little, Brown & Co. Boston. 1980. p. 42.
20 ibid., pp. 36-37.
21 The Black Man's Burden: The White Man in Africa from the Fifteenth Century to World War I. E.D. Morel. Modern Reader Paperbacks. New York. 1969. p.17.
22 ibid. p. 20.
23 ibid. p. 15.
24 ibid. p. 21.

25   ibid. p. 22.
26   Bodley, op. cit. p. 35-36.
27   Galeano. The Open Veins Of Latin America. op. cit. p. 58,59.
28   The Chinese Opium Wars. Jack Beeching. Harcourt Brace Jovanovich. New York. 1975. p.39.
29   ibid. p. 28.
30   ibid. p. 178.
31   Saving China: Canadian Missionaries In The Middle Kingdom 1888-1959. Alvyn J. Austin. U. of Toronto Press. Toronto. 1986. p. 13.
32   Z Magazine. January 1991. "The Politics Of Drugs: An Interview with Alfred McCoy." pp. 65-66.
33   ibid. p. 83.
34   Bodley, op. cit. p. 31-32.
35   Morel, op. cit. p. 121.
36   ibid. p. 123.
37   ibid. p. 141.
38   ibid. p. 128.
39   ibid. p. 115.

CHAPTER 12

COLONIALISM IN THE MODERN WORLD

Zaire: The Congo Atrocity Evolves

Following the end of the rubber boom, the French-Belgian created blood-bath in the Congo basin subsided somewhat but the basic extraction of profits went on. By 1960 the Congo, now called Zaire, was being readied for independence like many African colonies. Independence was to be with a Belgian-chosen leader and with continuing outside ownership and control of the rich resources of oil, cobalt, copper and other minerals. As independence day neared an indigenous leader, Patrice Lumumba arose and began to win elections. By the day of independence he was the acknowledged leader of the new country. Soon a former sergeant in the Congolese army, Mobutu, who had been handpicked by Belgian Intelligence and the U.S. CIA to be the leader, had much of the military behind him and Lumumba murdered. By 1965, Mobutu Sese Seko became the absolute dictator and continues to rule this hapless land to this day under the direction of the Israeli Mossad and the CIA who oversee security affairs while the industrial elite is represented by such groups as the international oil cartel and Union Minie're, owned at the time of independence by the Belgian Corporation, the special Board of Katanga and the company well known in South Africa, the Anglo-American company, Oppenheim de Beers.[1]

Prior to independence the Belgian directed export agriculture had also made the country food self-sufficient (prior to colonialism the area had been food self-sufficient for thousands of years). The money making export crops were sugar, rice, corn, millet, cassava, bananas and other minor crops. As the society disintegrated under the Mobutu dictatorship, food production fell. In 1988 the country imported 60% of its food.

Like other U.S. backed dictators such as Marcos of the Philippines, Somoza of Nicaragua and the Shah of Iran who were super thieves, Mobutu has simply thrown open the country to the trans-nationals who pay a sum to Mobutu for the resources. The Mobutu government occupies itself with robbing the people of what little is left while Mobutu travels to his many palaces, including 26 luxury apartments, villas, chateaux and palaces in Europe. Some place his personal fortune at $8 billion, all of it stolen from the impoverished people of Zaire.

Journalist Steve Askin reports that despite Zaire's being one of the richest countries in Africa, the country is $5 billion in debt to the international banks. The Zairian people are the ninth poorest on earth yet they must struggle to bear up under a typical International Monetary Fund "austerity plan." "Zaire has fired 40 percent of its government workers, withheld wage increases from those still on the payroll, [and] drastically cut its already meager social service spending. By this economic bloodletting of the population, Zaire is able to pay the international bankers 30 percent of the national budget for debt repayment."[2]

Three billion dollars of the loan money that incurred this debt went to the Trans-National construction company of Morrison-Knudson to build a power line 1,100 miles long from a dam near Mobutu's capital of Kinshasha, to Katanga province where the cobalt and copper mines are located. Even though there is hydro-electric potential near the mines, this $3 billion was spent so that Mobutu could "turn off the lights" from Kinshasha, 1,100 miles to the north, in case of any secessionist effort. Mobutu is used by the U.S. for votes in the U.N. and the Organization of African Unity. The country is used as a staging area for CIA warfare, projected into other African states and Mobutu's army is used as a U.S. surrogate for invading other African countries according to the needs of U.S. strategy. Torture, including the CIA's favorite, the electric shock machine, is widely used against both political and criminal detainees. Total fascism is the form of government under the dictator and total neglect is the social policy. Estimates are that less than 10% of the roads that existed on independence day remain and indigenous commerce has all but stopped. After three hundred years of colonial plunder Zaire still has riches to loot, the people continue to starve and the living conditions deteriorate under the "neo-colonialism" of the industrial order.[3]

The reason that Zaire is not a matter of household conversation in the U.S. is that the situation is not reported by the corporate media of the U.S. The mass information media is essentially controlled by the state in the socialist countries and in the capitalist countries it is owned by the capitalist class. In the U.S., according to Ben Badgakian, in his study, *The Media Monopoly*, the whole of television, films, radio, newspapers, magazines and book publishing is essentially owned by less than twenty-five huge conglomerate corporations. As Michael Parenti explains in his recent book, *The Mass Media*, the corporate owned media do not so much alter the facts, but frame the facts of each event within the social and ideological framework of the national security state- the militarized juggernaut. Within the context of the national security state the CIA has significantly infiltrated the ranks of the media as we began to learn in the late 1960's. In addition to subsidizing various book publishings, there are working writers on the payrolls, or the payrolls of CIA front groups, as well as media workers who are conduits for information that the agency wishes to be presented to the public. Because of the CIA infiltration of journalism, especially in Third World countries, it is possible for them to conduct world-wide disinformation campaigns.

Antarctica: Empire at the End of the World

Nothing describes the needs and motives of the present industrial empire so well in this era, as the final rape-Antarctica. This beautiful and mysterious land is literally the end of the world. It is the south end of the planet and it is the last piece of the planet that has not been plundered by the culture of empire.

Because of the convection currents and because Antarctica is exposed to all oceans, it occupies a pivotal place in the planetary cycles of weather and biology. Barney Brewster in his Friends of the Earth book about Antarctica says that;

"Although the Southern Ocean represents only five per cent of the world's oceans in area, it accounts for 20 per cent of the total marine photosynthesis and plays a major part in deep-ocean water circulation, influencing waters far to the north. Antarctic deep-ocean water carries nutrients which feed economically important fisheries in many parts of the world - Argentine hake, Brazilian tuna, South African pilchard and the remnants of the Peruvian anchoveta fishery."[4]

Ocean upwellings around the periphery of Antarctica provide the nutrient to charge the food chain. The phytoplankton feed the masses of krill. Krill are a small shrimp-like organism that grow up to three inches long and exist in the Antarctic waters in the amounts of millions of tons. They are the basic energy of the simple food chain of Antarctica. They directly feed the baleen whales, squid and small fish, crabeater seals, adelie penguin, and the sea birds. The next level of the food chain that feeds on the krill eaters are the large fish, weddell and ross seals, killer whale, leopard seal, gull and emperor penguin. The whales in the southern waters were early hunted to near extinction as they migrated in, seasonally, to feed on the krill. Now, "It is estimated that blue whales are less than 5 per cent of their original stock, humpbacks 3 per cent, and fin whales less than 20 per cent."[5] The fur seals around South Georgia and the South Shetland islands have been slowly increasing since the devastation for the Yankee trade to China but some authorities believe the small population is now going down again because of the initial krill fishing in the area which is impacting the food chain.[6] In the islands north of Antarctica, especially toward Australia, there have been industries that boiled seals and penguins for the oil in their bodies but so far as is known, no complete extinctions have been the result of that practice.

The land mass of Antarctica has not yet been devastated by human activities. Most of the visitors have been "scientific expeditions" who are there to do science as well as to bolster their respective country's claim to a piece of the action by their presence- as well as look for industrial valuables. Approximately 700 people winter over at Antarctica and the population rises to 4-5,000 in the summer. This population is scattered at 33 year-round bases and other temporary sites. Two thousand tons of cargo and food come in each year as well as 20 million litres of fuel. Very little is taken out.[7] Most of these human settlements are on the rocks or other spots bare of ice. This has created a conflict with the animals and birds who themselves heavily use these scarce sights for nesting and other life activities. Because there are no land animals larger than three centimeters in size (mites), the living population is centered on the ocean and the shorelines which are essential to them. This is also the location where the human exploiters will congregate as they arrive and set up operations.

Increasing human populations are a threat to the Antarctic environment. Another continuing threat is human stupidity. In 1962 the United States Navy brought in a nuclear power plant in violation of the Antarctic treaty. After ten years of trouble and leaks the reactor was shut down. It was shipped back to the U.S. with 101 large drums of contaminated earth and was followed later by 11,000 cubic meters of radioactive rock. After six years of work, the site was declared sanitized.[8]

That the industrial predators are preparing to dismember the Antarctic is plain. The most serious threats at the present are krill fishing, whaling, sealing, oil drilling and mining. Krill fishing has been commenced by Japan and the U.S.S.R. Other countries are testing products made with the krill to try to find ways to make money from it. The krill catch was estimated by the FOA at 20,000 to 40,000 tons in the early 1970's and has been rising steadily. The life habits of the krill are quite complex and little is known about them and little is known about the whole complex of krill and krill eaters. Nonetheless, the industrialists have charged ahead. Harvesting the krill could have serious effects. The nearly extinct whale species need it to revive their numbers and other krill feeders depend on it.

There are pirate whalers who have connections with the Japanese fishing fleets in the area who are still killing the nearly extinct large whales. The large scale whalers of recent years, the Russians and the Japanese, are taking minke whale in the area but have not killed the endangered fin, blue, humpback or southern right whales as far as is known. Because of the expense of operating in Antarctica, exploiting the area is to a great extent dependent upon how desperate countries become for protein, minerals and oil. As ecological catastrophes and exhaustion of resources progress outside Antarctica, the validity of industrial exploitation of Antarctic increases.

A very serious possibility is a rush for the "black gold." A number of countries have had oil exploration teams and programs in Antarctica. If oil production begins, Antarctica will be finished. Already there are reports of penguins covered with oil from local spills from ships in the area. The biodegradation rate in the area is far longer than in warmer areas. All garbage, equipment and other debris left since the first humans came there is still there.

Oil spills and the locating of human communities that would be needed for the work on Antarctica could finish the life that needs the sea and the strip of land close to the sea. The krill, the baleen whales that filter sea water to catch the krill, the penguins, seabirds and seals which travel from land to water would all be devastated. In an environment like the Antarctic, clean-up would be almost impossible and if a blow-out occurred it could be under conditions that would make it difficult to stop and if it could not be stopped, (in mid-winter for example) it would simply continue to drain into the sea.

The approach of the industrial countries to Antarctica demonstrates that the essential dynamics of empire culture have not changed since the time of the Sumerians. The motive of immediate gain continues to take precedence over all other values.

Empire in the Modern World:Managed Opinion

The evidence of history suggests that as the public awareness increased in the First World countries, the imperial elites found it necessary to manage domestic opinion and sources of information. The motives and methods of extorting the colonies did not change but the sensibilities of the public in the imperial countries became more acute. The French revolution, the American revolution and other changes brought a more sophisticated view of the rights of citizens and the functioning of elites. The motives and strategies of colonialism do not change but the justifications and explanations to the public of the First World have became a smooth integral part of the operation. In the Sixteenth Century no explanation to the European public was necessary but later imperialism became a phenomena of cultural opinion. It became a social ideology. As this change occurred it became necessary for the elites to reflect back to the public the charitable and beneficial effects on the colonies and to conceal the basic motives and methods. In the U.S. it was clothed in "Manifest Destiny," God was often said to have given the new world to the deserving Christians and this encouraged the "missionary fervor" which was encouraged by the elites. All this combined into a jingoistic support for empire. In the present the continuing enterprise to extort valuables from the colonies and to ensure control of them, is clothed in a mythology of "anticommunism" and "antiterrorism." The competing elites of the industrialized countries have managed to thoroughly militarize human society. The elites often say that the reason that we must have such tight police control of civilized society is because of "human nature." That is, humans are so violent and savage that there must be outside control of their behavior. On the world scene, the justification for the military control of the planet is said to be the threat of "capitalist imperialism," "communist subversion" or "guerilla insurgency." The reality is, however, that empires expend the effort to have colonies because they are getting something from them - money- markets and resources. Now, with the huge government debt of Third World countries, the elites of the capitalist group can literally take over these countries. When the debt cannot be paid and the country is desperate for capital, the International Monetary Fund or the World Bank will extend another loan if the country agrees to allow the bankers to send in its own teams to run the economic planning and commerce departments of those countries. The "austerity" programs that the bankers subject the country to are designed to squeeze money out of the country to pay the debt. The foreign exchange to pay the debt is generated by exporting the country's resources. This impoverishes the workers, the ecology and tends to centralize the remaining economy in the hands of the elite.

Controlling the Colony

In a world of empires, colonies and competing "spheres of influence," there is the threat that some competing empire may steal a colony but there is also the greater threat that the population of the colony may try to stop the extortion and throw out the invaders. This threat of "nationalism" is dealt with by preventing any social development in the colony that is not under the control of the colonial elite. The colonial elite, in turn, ultimately is under the control of its handlers, in the First World industrial elite.

Just after the close of World War II the centers of imperial power began to consolidate their turf. The U.S.S.R. surrounded itself with dominated colonies, China began to assert its old imperial dominance and the U.S. and European capitalists moved to manage the control of the old colonial structure. This colonial control exercised by the capitalists often took the form of "giving independence" to a colony run by a colonial elite but covertly maintaining control of that former colony's military and economic infrastructure. One technique of control used in the U.S., "banana republic" colonies is revealed by a Central America study group who say:

"In 1870, US banks began the practice of offering to pay a Central American nation's entire European debt in a lump payment under the condition that the nation would agree to place itself under a customs receivership in which the US would control the nation's foreign trade and many aspects of its domestic economy. This economic relationship replaced political colonization with an equally effective method for controlling the trade, resources and labor of another country. Nicaragua was under a US customs receivership until 1949."[9]

After the close of World War II, first Britain, then the U.S. assisted in fighting a war in Greece against indigenous and left leaning forces that had been the anti-Nazi resistance during World War II. These populist Greek forces were defeated and a puppet (and Fascist, in the case of the military dictatorship) colonial elite was installed. The old colonial empires then fought the indigenous guerrillas, the "Huks" of the former U.S. colonial possession of the Philippines to a standstill in the 1950's and wiped out a peasant revolt in British controlled Malaysia in the same era. Eventually a war was fought in Vietnam in an attempt to regain the French colony that had been taken over by the anti-Japanese resistance under the leadership of Ho Chi Min.

In the post-World War II era, a system of conflict and competition evolved wherein secret government agencies were used as the spearhead of covert war. This system exists and evolved because of this same motive- to conceal these foreign activities both from the "enemies" and the First World domestic populations. The home populations would not approve of them, or the policies they serve, if they were known. That is the functional reason for the shroud of secrecy of the "National Security State." Honorable government actions are not kept secret from the people. Secret covert action agencies like the U.S., CIA and Russian, KGB exist now in many governments of the earth. After World War II, the imperial governments used their secret war agencies to set up secret police and covert action agencies in their colonies. The KGB assisted the creation of secret police in Eastern Europe and the CIA helped create secret police agencies like the hated Savak in the Shah's Iran and the KCIA in Korea. These agencies carry out domestic and foreign activities. These foreign activities are usually acts and atrocities that the elite would not want to be associated with publicly.

At times the clothing of "anti-communist" rhetoric was not used but some other negative image such as "nationalist," as in the CIA overthrow of Mohammed Mossedeq of Iran to get the oil fields. Generally, such as in the overthrow of Arbenz, the nationalist leader of Guatemala in 1954, with CIA assistance, all of the drumbeaters and "anti-communist" cheerleaders in the corporate controlled mass media were called out to manipulate the mental images of the populace of the empire. By the time of the CIA's war in Vietnam, the control of empire was being called "counter-insurgency warfare." Not only the control of the colonial elites was necessary but it became necessary to control the infrastructure of society itself. In Vietnam, the CIA discovered that they were fighting the very society itself, in a war of colonial domination. The response to this was the perceived need to destroy indigenous social leadership. Operation Phoenix and the strategic hamlet concepts came out of this. Operation Phoenix was a program to murder or imprison persons who occupied positions of social leadership not controlled by the empire. Strategic hamlets were created usually by forced relocation of peasant populations and imprisonment in guarded "villages" that were under military control.

These strategies have developed into the present such that colonial militaries and police forces that are trained in the First World, maintain "death squads" who's task it is to eliminate any indigenous leadership that may compete with the controlled cadres of the empire. Farm cooperative leaders, labor leaders, church leaders who advocate compassion for the poor, doctors, teachers who may teach self-help or assist the dispossessed are all seen as creating the possibilities of social power outside of imperial control and so are kidnapped, tortured and murdered. These assassination team members have often been trained at the U.S. base in Panama or at the torture schools at U.S. bases in Texas and Louisiana maintained by the CIA. "Low-intensity warfare," the new name for imperial control, is not always intended to have dramatic winners, often it is used simply to "soften-up" a country for some policy strategy. This amounts to simply bashing the target country with terrorism, divisiveness and sabotage until the country is shredded and its people suffering and easily controlled. What is called low-intensity warfare is not really warfare but simply the covert management techniques of the empires. This does not necessarily have anything to do with violence but involves such things as manipulating the local media through journalists, militarists and politicians who are on the foreign intelligence agency's payroll. There is usually foreign participation in elections above ground, such as through the U.S. National Endowment for Democracy, the AFL-CIO and CIA linked American Institute for Free labor Development, and the CIA-U.S. Chamber of Commerce linked Center for International Private Enterprise. There are also underground conduits of cash, supplies and experts offered to selected candidates and parties. Books are published clandestinely and widely circulated, serving covert strategies. Particular social groups and institutions are organized and financed within the target country, which serve particular strategies. In effect only the imagination limits these covert action agencies who have huge budgets hidden within their own home government's accounting.

There is the motive to protect the investments and profits in the colony and there is also the motive to prevent the example of independence of a colony, its escape from a "sphere of influence."

Creation of the "Internationalist" Empire

Although we now have the imperial centers of the U.S., Europe, U.S.S.R. and China, the coordination of the capitalist powers has integrated into a powerful elite under the auspices of the Rockefeller/Kissinger created Tri-Lateral Commission. This group includes some of the richest men in the world, leading military figures (not always in uniform), the major international bankers, and high government officials especially from the U.S., West Germany and Japan. Membership in the organization is centered on corporate entities who do business in from several to many countries. This "Commission" has developed along with a homogenized elite that owns and controls the international class of Trans-National corporations.

In a country such as the U.S., which being 6% of the world's population and consuming more than half the entire planet's resources each year, much which comes from outside its borders, the matter of the need to control the resources and markets is obvious on the face of it. As with the old slaving days and the opium days, the masses of the First World countries must be convinced that the activities of the First World governments are absolutely altruistic. "Helping," "economic development," "winning hearts and minds," and of course the "communist menace" are images used to camouflage what is really happening, which is the control and operation of an industrial empire who's vast flow system needs massive amounts of raw materials and equally massive markets for the products. Much of the control, planning and execution of these policies is out of view of the electorate and often are performed by clandestine groups such as CIA, the Israeli Mossad, the KGB and the covert action groups of the other industrial states. The structure of power that has developed from the earlier colonial empires is one of complete militarization of the world through alliances such as NATO, ASEAN, Warsaw Pact, and other military aid and currency loan connections. This has spawned the largest arms race the world has ever seen. Countries that cannot feed their people can always get loans for armaments from First World states.

The struggle for planetary supremacy is conducted with secret strategies and it is conducted in the minds of the people through the mass media. The control of sources of information is an important factor in domination of each empire's "sphere of influence."

(A full bibliography is included for those interested in the covert management of the contemporary empire.)[10]

Although industrial investment in the colonies generally returns large profits (25% per year being the standard), super-profits since World War II have come from guns and drugs. The U.S. has been the largest armaments producer, with other countries now catching up rapidly. Alliances and militarization have been encouraged all over the world and this has seen the militaries take power (overt or covert) in most societies. The petroleum industry is the largest planetary industry but it is closely followed by the armaments industry in size and production. The armaments industry mushrooms as all forms of colonial exploitation grow. A modern example is the [1989] Iran-Iraq war, where 42 arms-exporting countries sold weapons to the combatants and 36 sold to both sides.

Some now estimate the planetary drug market to be $500 billion per year. The sources of opium are Turkey (where the plant originated), Afghanistan, Pakistan, India, Burma, Laos and Mexico. The huge volumes of this valuable substance are not controlled by a few peasants in remote areas. Peasants are not seen transporting the trainloads of cash involved in this trade. It is not difficult to see that a commerce of this importance requires people of equal importance to conduct it. This super-profit trade is controlled by some of the more powerful people in the world. Governments of origin get cuts, international transporters get cuts and controllers of distribution in the rich countries get cuts. The opium poppy growing regions are (with the possible exception of portions of the Golden Triangle of Southeast Asia) substantially under the control of the U.S. In many regions such as with the Meo tribesmen of Laos, the tribals of Afghanistan/Pakistan, and the colonial elites of the cocaine producing countries of Colombia, Bolivia and Peru, there are strong historical contacts with the U.S. CIA.

The economic trade relations of empire are simple. The price of manufactured goods produced in the industrial countries rises faster than the price of raw resources sold by the Third World countries. This is the basic economic relationship. This has historically been the case. In the field of economics, the studies that developed this information are called the Prebisch Thesis, named after Raul Prebisch. Prebisch worked at the United Nations in the 1960's when he developed these statistical studies. Because of this export/import disparity and because of the energy price rise of the 1970's, the Third World has gone heavily into debt with the international bankers. This gives the bankers the opportunity to manage the economies of the Third World. In return for new loans the country must accept an economic plan that effectively bleeds the country and destroys remaining healthy ecology in the name of "resource extraction." In 1990, the net flow of money from the developing world to the developed nations was over $100 billion (U.S.) per year. This is a net figure, meaning the excess over the flow from the developed to the developing nations.[11]

The possibility of Third World countries taking over their own countries for their own benefit is slight. The overwhelming destructive power of secretly maneuvering covert action groups, an economic blockade by First World governments, a "capital strike" (the withdrawing of funds from the colony), strangulation by the international banks and a cutoff of funds by the International Monetary Fund and the World Bank is almost certain to smother any indigenous movement. Just as workers can withhold their labor in a labor strike, so can capital withhold investment. Though the remaining and remote forager/hunters of the earth can still survive nicely without the industrial empire, everyone in the money economy, who's survival systems are dependent on industry, are subject to those who control the money, guns and industrial production.

NOTES

1   <u>My Country, Africa: Autobiography of the Black Pasionaria</u>. Andre'e Blouin. Praeger Scientific pub. New York. 1983. p. 267.

2   <u>National Catholic Reporter</u>. July, 29, 1988. vol. 24, no. 36. "Rule by Kleptocracy in Zaire wins Mobutu U.S. backing," Steve Askin. p. 9.

3   ibid. pp. 7-11,14.

4   <u>Antarctica: Wilderness At Risk</u>. Barney Brewster. Friends of the Earth. San Francisco. 1982. p. 97

5   <u>Let's Save Antarctica!</u>. James N. Barnes. Greenhouse Publications. Victoria, Australia. 1982. p. 18.

6   ibid. p. 19.

7   Brewster. <u>Antarctica</u>. op. cit. p. 49.

8   ibid. p. 56,57.

9   <u>EPOCA UPDATE</u>. Summer 1990. Earth Island Institute. San Francisco, CA. p. 2,3.

10 Sources of information on the conduct of covert strategies of the modern empire.

RELEVANT PERIODICALS:

<u>Intelligence/Parapolitics</u>. monthly, $20/yr. P.O.Box 50441, Washington, D.C. 20004 or 16 rue des Ecoles, 75005 Paris, France.

<u>The National Reporter</u>. quarterly, $13/yr. P.O.Box 21279, Washington, D.C. 20009.

<u>Covert Action Information Bulletin</u>. quarterly, $15/yr. P.O.Box 50272, Washington, D.C. 20004.

<u>Lobster: Intelligence-Parapolitics-State Research</u>. published occasionally, $14/yr. 17c Pearson Ave., Hull; HU5 2SX; United Kingdom.

RELEVANT BOOKS:

The World War II era.

The War Lords of Washington: The Inside Story of Big Business Versus The People in World War II. Bruce Catton. Harcourt, Brace & Co. 1948.

The Luciano Project: The Secret Wartime Collaboration of the Mafia and the U.S. Navy. Rodney Campbell. McGraw-Hill Book Co. 1977.

Who Financed Hitler: The Secret Funding of Hitler's Rise to Power 1919-1933. James Pool and Suzanne Pool. Dial Press. 1978.

Trading With The Enemy: An Exposé of The Nazi-American Money Plot 1933-1949. Charles Higham. Delacorte Press. 1983.

Kennedy and Roosevelt: The Uneasy Alliance. Michael R. Beschloss. W.W. Norton & Co. 1980.

The Last Testament of Lucky Luciano. Marin A. Gosch and Richard Hammer. Little, Brown & Co. 1974

The Post-World War II era.

Klaus Barbie: The Shocking Story of How the U.S. Used this Nazi War Criminal as an Intelligence Agent. Erhard Dabringhaus. Acropolis Books Inc. 1984.

Aftermath: Martin Bormann and the Fourth Reich. Ladislas Farago. Simon & Schuster. 1974.

The Bormann Brotherhood: A New Investigation of the Escape and Survival of Nazi War Criminals. William Stevenson. Harcourt Brace Jovanovich. 1973.

The Belarus Secret. John Loftus. Alfred A. Knopf. 1982.
(When John Loftus was an Assistant Attorney General working for the Justice Department he was assigned to investigate the existence of numerous Nazi war criminals living comfortably in the U. S. When little action was taken, he wrote this account of the case.)

The Nazi Legacy: Klaus Barbie and the International Fascist Connection. Magnus Linklater, Isabel Hilton and Neal Ascherson. Holt, Rinehart & Winston. 1984.

The General was a Spy: The Truth about General Reinhard Gehlen. Coward, McCann & Geoghegan, Inc. 1971. (How part of Hitler's intelligence apparatus was merged with the CIA.)

The Super-States, The Korean War and the present era.

The Hidden History of the Korean War. I.F. Stone. Monthly Review Press. 1952.

Global Rift: The Third World Comes Of Age. L.S. Stavrianos. William Morrow & Co. 1981.

The Age of Surveillance: The Aims and Methods of America's Political Intelligence System. Frank J. Donner. Alfred A. Knopf. 1980.

The CIA: A Forgotten History/ US Global Interventions Since World War 2. William Blum. Zed Books. 1986.

The Washington Connection and Third World Fascism: The Political Economy of Human Rights. Vol. I Noam Chomsky and Edward S. Herman. South End Press. 1979.

After the Cataclysm: Postwar Indochina and The Reconsideration of Imperial Ideology. Vol. II. Chomsky & Herman. South End Press. 1979.

The Geography of Empire. Keith Buchanan. Bertrand Russell Peace Foundation pub. 1972.

The War Conspiracy: The Secret Road to The Second Indochina War. Peter Dale Scott. Bobbs-Merrill Co. 1972.

Torture In The Eighties. Amnesty International Report. 1984.

War Without End: American Planning For The Next Vietnams. Michael T. Klare. Alfred A. Knopf. 1970.

Deadly Deceits: My 25 years in the CIA. Ralph W. McGehee. Sheridan Square Pub. 1983.

In Search Of Enemies: A CIA Story. John Stockwell. W.W. Norton & Co. 1978.

Endless Enemies: The Making of an Unfriendly World: How America's Worldwide Interventions Destroy Democracy And Free Enterprise And Defeat Our Own Best Interests. Jonathan Kwitny. Congdon & Weed, Inc. 1984.

The Secret Team: The CIA And Its Allies In Control Of The United States And The World. L. Fletcher Prouty, Col., U.S. Airforce (Ret.) Prentice-Hall. 1973. (Excellent introductory volume by an official who served many years at the highest levels of the U.S. government/military.)

None of Your Business: Government Secrecy in America. Norman Dorsen and Stephen Gillers, Editors. Viking Press. 1974.

State Secrets: Police Surveillance in America. Paul Cowan, Nick Egleson and Nat Hentoff. Holt, Rinehart & Winston. 1974.

Agent's Of Repression: The FBI's Secret Wars Against The Black Panther Party and The American Indian Movement. Ward Churchill & Jim Vander Wall. South End Press. 1988.

Inside The Shadow Government: Declaration of Plaintiffs' Counsel Filed by the Christic Institute, U.S. District Court, Miami, Florida, March 31, 1988. Edith Holleman, et. al. Christic Institute Pub. 1324 North Caitol St. N.W., Wash. D.C. 20002.

On The Trail of the Assassins: My Investigation and Prosecution of the Murder of President Kennedy. Jim Garrison. Sheridan Square Press. 1988.

High Treason:The Assassination of President John F. Kennedy: What Really Happened. Robert Groden. Conservatory Press. 1989.

The Yankee and Cowboy War. Carl Oglesby.

Crossfire: The Plot That Killed Kennedy. Jim Marrs. Carrol & Graf Pub. 1989.

The Assassinations: Dallas And Beyond: a guide to cover-ups and investigations. First edition. Peter Dale Scott. Random House. 1976.

Works concerning the corporate sector of the same era.

In Banks We Trust: Bankers and Their Close Associates: The CIA, the Mafia, Drug Traders, Dictators, Politicians and the Vatican. Penny Lernoux. Anchor Press/Doubleday. 1984.

Trilateralism: The Trilateral Commission and Elite Planning For World Management. Holly Sklar, ed. South End Press. 1980.

The Bohemian Grove And Other Retreats: A Study in Ruling-class Cohesiveness. G. William Dumhoff. Harper Torchbooks. 1975.

Inside Job: The Looting Of America's Savings and Loans. Stephen Pizzo. McGraw Hill. 1989.

Drugs and the International elite.

The Iran Contra Connection: Secret Teams And Covert Operations In The Reagan Era. Johnathan Marshall, Peter Dale Scott and Jane Hunter. South End Press. 1987.

Out Of Control: The Story of the Reagan Administration's Secret War In Nicaragua, the Illegal Arms Pipelines, and the Contra Drug Connection. Leslie Cockburn. Atlantic Monthly Press. 1987.

The Great Heroin Coup: Drugs, Intelligence and International Fascism. Henrik Kruger. South End Press. 1980.

The Politics Of Heroin In Southeast Asia. Alfred McCoy. Harper & Row. 1972.

The Politics of Heroin: CIA Complicity in the Global Drug Trade. Alfred McCoy. Lawrence Hill/Chicago Review Press. Chicago. 1991.

Of Grass and Snow. Hank Messick. Prentice-Hall. 1990.

The Great Heroin Coup: Drugs, Intelligence and International Facism. Trans. from Danish. Henrick Kruger. Black Rose Books. Canada. 1990.

Cocaine Politics: Drugs, Armies and the CIA in Central America. Peter Dale Scott, et. al. U of Calif. Press. March, 1991.

Deep Cover: The Inside Story Of How DEA Infighting, Incompetence
And Subterfuge Lost Us The Biggest Battle Of The Drug War. Micheal
Levine. Delacorte Press. N.Y. 1990.

Elite Control of the Mass Media.

A Dangerous Game: CIA and the Mass Media. Vitaly Petrusenko.
Interpress, Prague, Czechoslovakia. 1977.

Even The Gods Can't Change History: The Facts Speak for Themselves.
George Seldes. Lyle Stuart pub. 1976.

The Pentagon Propaganda Machine. Senator J. William Fulbright.
Vintage Books. 1970.

Inventing Reality: The Politics Of The Mass Media. Michael Parenti.
St. Martin's Press. 1986.

The CIA And The Media: How America's Most Powerful News Media
Worked Hand in Glove with the Central Intelligence Agency and Why
the Church Committee Covered it Up. Carl Bernstein. Rolling Stone
(magazine). 20 Oct. 1877.

Manufacturing Consent: The Political Economy of the Mass Media.
Edward S. Herman and Noam Chomsky. Pantheon. 1989.

11   EPOCA UPDATE. Summer 1990. "Are Debt-for-Nature Swaps the
Answer? Earth Island Institute. San Francisco, CA. p. 3.

BOOK TWO

THE SEED

OF THE

FUTURE

CHAPTER 13

THE PRINCIPLES OF LIFE

The Moral Basis of the Life of the Earth

We live at a time of dissolution of human social bodies as well as the unraveling of the life force of our planet. This gives us all a sense of confusion and contradiction within existing social realities. Our response must be to turn to the enduring cosmic patterns of life, toward the healing of life. Because of the depth of the crisis our response must be equally fundamental. We are proposing to create no less than a completely new human culture that relates to the earth in a completely different way. We seek power, the power to endure. We are coming out of a position of weakness in which the power to kill and coerce was seen as the road to utopia. Now that the weakness of that conception is displayed in the planetary suicide of this final cycle of empire, those who choose to respond in a positive way need gather the seeds of Natural cultures and the truly beneficial things created by civilization and carry them through the apocalypse.

Our effort is to regain personal, social, ecological and cosmic balance. We propose to do this by adopting the natural pattern of life on this planet as our guide. The natural world is a world of shared energies. The life giving sunlight is captured by the green plants for transformation into living vegetation, the life energies circulate, transform and continue to circulate through the vegetational and animal food chains. With this circulation, a slow build-up of the soil occurs to provide for the planet's further ability to support green plants that can capture more energy, driving the system to its climax of biological succession, its dynamic balance within the life of the planet. Just as the balance of energies within the human organism is consciously maintained among a vast array of different substances and nutrients, dynamic balance is maintained in the planetary organism by multi-billions of constantly interacting life processes. Just as the intellect alone could never guide and administer the functions of the human body, there is no way that human intellect could make decisions about the life of the earth that would be superior to the cosmic intelligence that has created and maintained it.

The life of the planet is able to cover the earth in its extremes of temperature, pressure and moisture variation through its creativity. The creativity and adaptability of planetary life combines with the thrust toward diversity of form and function that allows life to express its intelligence on all parts of the planet's surface. The hallmark of the whole life is diversity within unity. The planetary life functions with the paradox of unities within unities such that each life form is a unity unto itself but yet is a part of a greater whole.

The unities of the planetary life as well as innumerable and constantly acting life processes all maintain relationship with each other. Everything is connected and any adjustment of one effects others so that they adjust simultaneously to the new conditions of their existence. Creativity, balance, adaptability, shared energies, unity-diversity, transformation and relationship are modes of behavior that we find fundamental to life. These behaviors of living things occur within a context of consciousness. Each life form is a conscious entity. Consciousness is the glue that holds the form together and animates it. When consciousness departs in death, the form disintegrates.

These seven principles and their subsidiary effects, are drawn from observation of the behavior of the web of living things. This is the behavior of life on earth. This is its moral pattern. From this we may draw moral principles for the behavior of human society. When we create human culture that is patterned on these principles and integrated with the web of life then human thought and action will be consonant with the purpose of life on this planet. Humans will represent the life of the earth at the level of human activity. Life does have a moral basis and the moral obligations are clear. If we are to create a sustainable society, we must follow Natural Law. With the crisis and dissolution of empire we see the sanctions of the law. In creating new culture we must be aware of the need to conform to the law so that our kind and others may endure. Following our path back to the source we see that the elements of our new culture need contain balance, self-regulation (responsibility to self and others), an expanded view as to the functioning of the wholes, a foundation in cooperation and an institutionalized creativity. If our social pattern is grounded in the paradigm of life then our actions expressed from that base will be resonant with cosmic patterns.

Balance is the Foundation of Life

In a social sense maturity is seen as self-regulation, that point at which we are not dependent upon parents or others to conduct our affairs. In the organic world beings also exhibit self-regulation. It is the self-regulation of each species that gives the eco-system its balance. Because each being lives according to its nature the whole functions in resonance. The balance of the human population in a forager/hunter band is self-regulating. This ecological maturity is fundamental. The cosmos exists in balance, the life of the earth exists in balance. Within this we see by contrast that the theorists of empire culture invented ideologies of linear increase, ideologies of imbalance. When the new edition of the myth of linear increase was being formulated in Darwin's time, the rationalist philosophers searched for a motivating dynamic in the natural world. They looked for a cause of change which they could hold up as the force for linear increase. Darwin and Malthus found the motor in population increase. For Darwin, the balance of species is maintained mechanically by predators and starvation. As this flood of population continues it is the "survival of the fittest" that culls out the weak and selects the strong, whose descendants then become the new "evolutionary wave." Imbedded in this perspective is a total irresponsibility, a complete immaturity. No being is responsible to the whole. Each being is only obligated to fight others for its own survival. This pattern is in fact reflected in the culture in which we live. This is why we face planetary suicide. No one is responsible for the life of the earth. One simply struggles for the "individualist" power and wealth held out by the culture.

This scheme fit in with the theories of "free markets" propounded by Adam Smith in his tome, *An Inquiry into the Nature and Causes of the Wealth of Nations* (1776). In Smith's theory, many sellers and buyers in a free market would choose the best product at the least cost, thus constantly moving efficiency and social benefit forward as the inefficient died off. In this scheme, no one is responsible, "the natural order," "the hidden hand of the market," brings the "good things" to society. No society was ever configured this way. Powerful social forces, cartels and monopolies set prices and control supply, but Smith was creating a myth not describing reality. This is similar to Darwin's myth of the population motor. The claim is made that it is not human directed, that it fits the pattern of the cosmos. As this mythos expanded, "social Darwinism" then became welded onto it. The linear thinker Hegel with his "dialectics" also thought he had discovered some kind of "natural" law. The "dialectic" is simply the clash of two opposing forces that result in a synthesis. As interpreted by Karl Marx in *Das Kapital*, the "dialectic" was focused on social changes in the imperial tumor body. The force of the industrial ruling class is contradicted by the force of the class of industrial workers. In Karl Marx's adoption of this theory, this would represent the thesis and antithesis. This contradiction of the ruling class and the working class is resolved in the synthesis which in Marx's view would be the dictatorship of the industrial proletariat. In Hegel's linear dialectic, the synthesis becomes the new thesis and then a new antithesis arises. This is resolved into a new synthesis in order to keep the train of linear events going.

This culture bound theory looks good when applied to human social change within empire because the culture is based in competition/conflict, but this is an artificially created situation. If one tried to apply these linear theories to the natural life of the earth, they would not correspond to reality. The body of capitalist myth has allowed individuals in empire culture to believe that they have no moral responsibility, because, in their conditioned way of thinking, it is "natural" and "just common sense" that there be the rich and the starving, as that is how evolution progresses. Ignoring the dynasties of inherited capitalistic wealth and the power of an entrenched elite, people will say that it is natural for some to have more than others. Just as it is natural for the more highly evolved industrial societies to control and aid those less able to modernize.

The body of Marxist myth can only work if there is industrialization. In this theory of imbalance, one accepts the cult of science and the poisonous and destructive process of industrialization as the path to utopia. Like the capitalist variety industrialist, the radiation poisoning and ecological degradation of Marxist lands is seen only as a "management" problem.

By focusing on the matter of balance in the cosmos and on earth we see that some of the basic assumptions by which all of us in empire culture are conditioned, are at great variance from cosmic patterns. The matter of population balance is fundamental to our understanding.

Robert Augros and George Stanciu in their important new book, *The New Biology*, survey recent biological studies that describe the self-regulation of populations. They show that elephants, for example, regulate their populations according to food supply and living conditions by raising or lowering the age of puberty and by shortening or lengthening the duration of the period of sexual fertility of females. Augros and Stanciu say that, "Evidence from other field studies indicate that the birth rate or the age of first reproduction depends on population density in many large mammals, including white-tailed deer, elk, bison, moose, bighorn sheep, Dall's sheep, ibex, wildebeest, Himalayan tahr, hippopotamus, lion, grizzly bear, dugong, harp seals, southern elephant seal, spotted porpoise, striped dolphin, blue whale, and sperm whale."[1]

There are many different ways in which species regulate their populations. One interesting study showed that all of the birds of the same species, in the same region, can vary the number of eggs in the nest in any one season according to food availability and species population density. In a certain year of low food supply all of the birds' nests would have three rather than the usual four eggs. Augros and Stanciu quote biologist V.C. Wynne-Edwards who says:

"Setting all preconceptions aside, however, and returning to a detached assessment of the facts revealed by modern observation and experiment, it becomes almost immediately evident that a very large part of the regulation of numbers depends not on Darwin's hostile forces but on the initiative taken by the animals themselves; that is to say, to an important extent it is an intrinsic phenomenon."[2]

In the popular mind the image of ecological balance is the wolf pack and moose herd. This image does represent the balance of the food chain but eliminates the cooperative and wholistic elements of ecological functioning. While the wolf, cougar and eagle are dramatic and fit the imperial image of power and violence, these predators are only a handful while there are millions of other species from micro-organisms to redwood trees, whose populations are not impacted significantly by predators.

Life is wise, mature and self-regulating. The myth of the "red in tooth and claw" has distorted our understanding of nature, but by a review of recent biology we are able to adjust our images to the way nature really works and the way a creative and stable human culture could fit into it. In the contrasts that we have been examining we see that there is a profound shift of image from mindless organisms driven to maximize their numbers, to responsible, intelligent self-regulating living beings. These are not academic biological questions; they are political questions of the theology of empire. They control the definition of what life is, and define appropriate behavior for humans.

Reductionism is the prevalent method of science. The "Newtonians" who dominate the sciences except for the new "relativity" school of physics, say that the universe is like a giant clock built of "dead" matter. We take apart the pieces and examine them down to their quarks and discover what makes the world tick. This is the dominant scientific view and the "conventional wisdom" of empire culture. But the rare scientists such as Augros and Stanciu propose a wholistic view in which the cosmos and each of its components relate as whole but interrelated bodies.

The Cycles of Life

Balance and cycle are the basic processes of the cosmos. Events are circular, cyclical and vibrational- from one pole and back around to the other. We are born to cycle and motion. From the time that the reproductive cells are formed in each of our parents, we are in motion. When a sperm makes its journey to our egg, we are in motion. When we are later carried in the womb, we are in an amniotic sea of motion. After the cycle of gestation, we are finally born out of the body into a world of motion where winds blow, seasons cycle, and cycles of our own growth occur.

Each of us has been born onto a sphere travelling in space, called the Earth, which is spinning around the central sun. The central sun with its planetary companions travels in a circle within our galaxy which itself is moving around a supercluster of galaxies. From the moment our first cell is created, we are part of the whole, and we never cease being in motion. We are a process, part of increasingly larger processes. There is no such thing as linear expansion toward some static impregnable security. The motion we experience is not random, but is cyclic. The circles of the Milky Way Galaxy, the solar system, our earth and the moon around us, occur in cycles so finely balanced and timed that they may be computed exactly, far into the future or into the past. These invariable motions are the Law. These impeccably tuned, harmonious cycles are imposed upon us by forces so powerful that there is no question that they are Cosmic Law, Natural Law. Within these celestial cycles the planet spins in a constant cycle of sunlight/darkness that is functionally a day/night alternating current. Each point on the planet's sphere is saturated with energy, then shadowed from it in precisely timed measures. Within the diurnal/nocturnal cycle and the energy cycle of the seasons, organic life on earth proliferates. The life of the earth was able to grow and develop because it remained in a state of dynamic balance. There is certainly change in the earth's life but this occurs within a context of balance. The earth's poles do tilt which causes the seasons. If the earth tilted even a few more degrees or if there were any deviation of the earth's orbit around the sun, the life of the earth would be greatly altered or non-existent. The organic life of the Earth has developed its cycles within the womb of the solar system. The sun, the principal energy source, is itself a cyclically pulsating body which experiences periodic expansion and contraction. The sun revolves in a 27-30 day cycle, its heat output fluctuates in a 273 month cycle, sunspots occur in a 22.22 year cycle, and the magnetic poles of the sun reverse themselves every 22 years. The widely varying energy fields of the sun encompass the earth, as it vibrates within what might be called the solar energy body. Could we visually perceive magnetic energy fields, we would see the teardrop shaped body of the earth and its magnetosphere speeding around the sun. Within this teardrop of the magnetosphere we would see a stronger doughnut-shaped magnetic energy field with depressions at the north and south poles. Further within this energy envelope are layers of tenuous matter called the atmospheric strata: exosphere, ionosphere, mesosphere, stratosphere, and troposphere. As with organic cell membranes, each of these layers is composed of different elements and performs particular functions for the inner body of the planet. The ozone layer is a barrier allowing certain energies to pass and preventing others from entering. The skin of all biological cells performs this same function.

The earth, the complex blue and white speckled egg, is alive, and its life processes vary constantly as it spins. Its colors change with the seasons; its cloud layers whirl and circulate in rhythmic cycles. Not surprisingly, an Italian chemist has discovered that the speed of the chemical reactions varies according to a number of planetary situations.

"More than 400,000 experiments, covering a ten-year period, by Professor Giorgio Piccardi, of Florence, Italy, show that the time required to complete various chemical reactions varies with the time of day, the time of year, the sunspot cycle, and whether or not the chemicals in his test tubes and flasks are protected from external electromagnetic forces by metallic shields."[3]

Uncountable numbers of organic events occur each second on earth, conditioned by celestial events within the body of the solar system. The sunspot cycle, the solar cycle, the moon cycle, the alternation of light and dark, all these events and more, trigger or impress themselves on organic events on the earth. Everything is in relationship, everything flows in cyclic adaptation according to its nature and place in the universe. Organic events such as the metabolism of plankton in the oceans, the migration of salmon, the growth of forests, the annual migration of caribou, the cycles of sexual reproduction and innumerable other events all are influenced by cyclic forces utterly enmeshed in a flowing whole so intricately balanced that a relatively small eruption on the sun, a solar flare, can create multiple effects in the process of the life of the earth.

Whether viewed from the energy metabolism of the solar system or from the vantage point of the various kinds of living molecules in the cell, life unfolds in a series of wholes, each fitting into and forming an integral aspect of a larger whole. The many parts whose functions combine to create the cell are also a part of an organ, which in turn is part of the whole body. That body may be part of a tribe, a school of fish, or a deer herd whose social body then fits into a larger food chain. The pattern of the cosmos is form integrated within form and mind within mind.

The various habitats across the surface of the planet comprise the body of the earth, which itself is involved with energy flows (metabolism) that are solar, galactic and cosmic. The mind of the cell exists within the mind of the organ which exists within the mind of the body. Form exists within form, mind within mind and life within life.

Life Cooperates

Our subconscious conditioning leads us to believe in the ubiquity of violence. We see the culture of violence of the empire as natural. Nonetheless, there is no mindless, gratuitous violence in nature. There is eating. Predators eat prey and the prey violently resist but organisms don't go around attacking each other for no reason. There are territorial challenges and mating challenges but these seldom reach the stage of violence and death. Our conditioned belief in the violence in nature is so deep that the Hollywood film makers who create "nature" movies train animals to fight for the films. Wild stallions kill each other and bears attack each other in the movies because it adds drama and it lends an air of "authenticity" to the film. People expect it, so it is faked for the audience.

Darwin said, "All nature is at war, one organism with another, or with external nature."[4] This struggle for survival follows his original assumptions of scarce resources and exploding populations. This assumption of the violence of life has been shared by many of the original rationalist philosophers as well as the general conditioned population, most of whom, no doubt grew up in the artificial environments of cities and had little contact with natural reality.

Ecology is sometimes called the "subversive science" because it assumes interdependence in the living world. Ecology is the study of the inter-relationships of nature. As these cooperative inter-relationships became more apparent through study, the new science became more subversive to orthodoxy. It is now demonstrable that nature is a vast cooperative enterprise. There is no war. Each being functions according to its own nature and its nature fits its ecological niche. Organisms aren't out in nature battling over the same grass seed. Each feeds according to its own niche and these niches are highly refined. Ecologist Robert MacArthur did a study of five species of warblers, all about the same size, all occupying the same territory and all eating the same food- spruce bud worms. He discovered that their niches were so finely and cooperatively tuned that each species predominantly used a different portion of the tree for their feeding. That is, one species would go to the top portion of the tree, another would concentrate on the base of the tree, another one quarter of the way from the top and so forth. These finely tuned niches exist throughout nature.

Not only are organisms careful about their niches but they work cooperatively together in all sorts of symbiotic ways. Biologist David Kirk says, "It is doubtful whether there is an animal alive that does not have a symbiotic relationship with at least one other life form."[5] This is also true in whole communities. The succession from primary to climax forest is an array of symbiotic relationships as species prepare the way for others. Authors Augros and Stanciu cite the work of marine biologist Conrad Limbaugh, who has studied cleaner-client relationships. Involved in this startling activity, so far known, are forty-two species of fish, six shrimps, and Beebe's crab. In these cases one species takes parasites from the body of another for food. Limbaugh says, "'I saw up to 300 fish cleaned at one station in the Bahamas during one six-hour daylight period.' The client fish approaches the station and poses, allowing the cleaner to forage within its gills and even to enter its mouth without danger. No one yet knows what prevents ordinarily voracious fish from eating the cleaners."[6]

The Consciousness of Life is Creative

The beauty and wealth of the life of the earth is its diversity. "...Two billion different kinds of organisms have at one time or other inhabited the earth."[7] The creativity of life forms is such that some live at the bottom of the ocean and some in the coldest arctic regions. The diversity of forms and the diverse ways in which they cooperate together to form one unity demonstrates overwhelming, creative intelligence. The "evolutionary transformations" show this creativity. There are huge disjuncts in the proliferation of the forms. Such a disjunct is the transformation from the spore bearing plants to the flowering plants that appeared, suddenly, world-wide. Gerbert Grohmann in his study of plant form, entitled *The Plant*, states, "To conclude - as the evolution theory does - that lower forms of life developed into higher ones means to get lost in theories and thereby violate the fundamentals of science. We have proof of the fact that the higher organisms follow after the lower ones, not that they descend from them."[8]

Augros and Stanciu say that::

"Whole new orders appear suddenly and simultaneously, with no evidence of intermediate stages. These sudden bursts of new flora and fauna, so typical of the fossil data, are called radiations since the ancestral stock develops at one time many new body plans and diversifies in several directions at once. Mammals are a fine example. During the early Cenozoic era some 50 million years ago, mammals suddenly diverged into about twenty-four different orders ranging from bats to whales, kangaroos to elephants, and rodents to rhinoceroses."

"The pattern, then, is great clusters of diversified organisms appearing like Athena, full-blown from the head of Zeus. This typical pattern of radiation dramatically contradicts Darwinian gradualism. Darwin himself recognized this and called the sudden appearance and early diversity of flowering plants 'an abominable mystery.'"[9]

Mechanistic theories such as Darwin's gradualism or the doctrine of uniformitarianism (slow earth changes over long periods of time) in geology, have endured not so much because of the logic of the theory but that they fit the prevailing social ideology so well. The increasingly "powerful" civilized human, "man the toolmaker," acting on inert, mindless matter is a welcomed image. The conscious power of an intelligent and balanced earth that creates the forms of life in which the human is one, is not welcome news. To think that all of the life forms are part of the whole intelligent life of Earth like all of the forms in a cell are part of a cell's life, would frame a new ethical view. That image would come dangerously near causing us and the empire to question our way of life.

The mechanists of science have gone to great lengths to suggest that life has little power of conscious creativity. Their efforts to deny that animals think is laughable to anyone who has lived on a farm or ranch. Another intellectual sleight of hand is the creation of the concept of instinct. Instinct is a meaningless word that has long served the mechanists as an explanation for what could not at the time be explained or admitted. Is the honey bee society so conscious and intelligent in its own way that it can do the activities and constructions that it does? No, is the mechanist reply, "it's instinct." In creating new human culture we will be creating an assemblage of ideas, a thought form, which will be linked with biology. An expanded view will be taken of what mind is and how it fits with culture, biology and the earth.

The Psychobiological Perspective

The mind-set of industrial culture is conditioned by the cult of scientism. The reductionist view that matter is the only reality has become the cultural "common-sense" view. This is not in fact what the scientific method says. Empirical science observes, measures, quantifies and performs tests on things, with the understanding that the "things" have to be matter or none of this could be done. The actual scientific method makes no comment on anything outside the realm of matter that it tests. What has happened is that the body of repeatable experiments and "scientific laws" (one must be aware there is much dubious material travelling under this banner) has been raised to the level of "truth" and dogma. Science has become the bible by which truth and reality is verified by a mass culture influenced by years of classroom conditioning. Love, creativity, hope, consciousness, in fact much of the real non-material reality of life and activity has been relegated to insignificance by the cult of science.

The quest for power (military and other) through science has become the central focus of the industrial empire. In the broad view, science is the means to power whereby the empire culture more efficiently extorts the life force of the planet. (Scientific agriculture does not concentrate on building the life of the soil, it concentrates on producing heavier tonnages for market). The reality that science is an integral component of the imperial social system is shown by the fact that more than half of the working scientists of the U.S. are employed in the military-industrial sector. This is hardly a dispassionate search for truth as the propagandists would have it. The scientific establishment is deeply implicated in the social apparatus of coercion and death as a means of political control.

The control of the public definition of reality, human nature, and of nature, even life itself, is not just a matter of scientific dialogue, it is an item of central importance to the power of empire itself. If the context of reality in the public mind is narrowed to a chemical reaction, people will more willingly march in lock-step than if they were to realize the mystery, awe and immensity of reality. If the public were to understand that each of us is a conscious being living within other conscious beings, such as Gaia, the whole life of the earth, the purpose of public life would change, as would the status of the scientific/military/industrial elites who now control the production of material goods.

Materialist science, is a cult. It is a mass social institution and also a method of knowing. It continues the split between Being and Doing. When we look at Natural cultures we see great attention to Being- in relationship to the world. When we look at the scientific ideology we see great attention devoted to abstracted Doing, with little attention paid to our inherent being. Da Free John (a.k.a., Franklin Jones) summarizes this difference which underlies the struggle of empire to control the life of the earth:

"The scientific establishment has been organized in league with the highest levels of concentrated political, economic and propagandistic power in the world today. Science is simply the primary method of knowing in modern societies, and its rule is established in no less an irrational and authoritarian manner than was the case with any religious or philosophical principle that ruled societies in the past.

"The method of science has now become a style of existence, a mood or strategy of relating to the world and to other human beings. That method now describes the conventional posture taken by 'Everyman' in every form of his relationship to the conditions of existence. Science has become a world-view, a presumption about the World-Process itself. It has become a religion, although a false one. And modern societies are Cults of this new religion. Can this new religion establish us as individuals and communities in right relationship to each other and to the World-Process? Absolutely not! Science is only a method of inquiry, or knowing about. It is not itself the right, true, or inherent form of our relationship to the conditions of existence, we cannot account for existence itself. And we are, regardless of our personal and present state of knowledge about the natural mechanics of the world, <u>always</u> responsible for our right relationship to the various conditions of experience, to the beings with whom we exist in this world, and to the World-Process as a whole. <u>Relationship</u> is inherently and perpetually a matter of individual responsibility, founded in intuition, prior to the analytical mind."10

The cult of scientism and empire has brought us to the brink of the death of the planet and the cult figures have no adequate response. The sad, one-dimensional leaders of empire challenge any new strategy meant to lead to health. If they don't like ecological restoration, what do they have to offer our collective grandchildren? If they don't like permaculture, let them then defend industrial agriculture. If they don't like population control, let's hear from them what they have to offer in view of the reality that we all see. Every patriarch in a position of power in every mass institution bears responsibility. It is obvious now that their refrain of growth and material wealth is not the answer.

We need to maintain perspective on the cult of scientism. It is discredited by its works. We live on a rapidly dying planet. We can't let the group that has led us to the brink of annihilation convince us that more of the same is a solution.

All Is Mind

The philosophical materialists of the modern empire, including mechanist/reductionist science, Marxist and Capitalist political theory and even such things as modern industrial medicine, would have us believe that we are simply the manifestation of chemical reactions in the cells. In the estimation of the philosophical materialist, the knowledge that seeds have of when and where to germinate, the migration of birds, the complex self-regulation of organic bodies comes about because of chemical reactions. That is, they assume that awareness is a result of chemical reactions in the brain.

This, we would say is part of the whole accomplishment of empire culture to denature and de-sacralize life to the point of meaninglessness. If we are conditioned to experience our lives as only marginally meaningful, we certainly will invest little meaning in the life around us. The awe, mystery and wonder of the teeming life of our earth is reduced to a meaningless movement of substance.

Yet it is precisely the non-material that makes life real and meaningful. The test is in our awareness. Do we intuitively feel that our conscious awareness is some unexplained process of chemical and electrical reactions? It is joy, ecstasy, love and other feelings that make life worth living. In opposition to the dry pronouncements of science there is a rich fund of inherited wisdom. The large bulk of forager/hunters and aboriginals say they perceive a non-material, spiritual reality. They give varied impressions and descriptions of non-material dimensions.

Hindu yogis of ancient tradition, Hermeticists and others assert that all is mind.[11] All is mind say the ancients. Form is created by the imaging power of consciousness. Form is created using consciousness as material. Consciousness is light. Form is congealed light vibrating at a lesser vibration than pure light.

When one looks out into the cosmos at night, one sees points of light. This light is the refraction of pure light striking the cells in our eyes. We know intellectually that the cosmos is full of pure light going in all directions from those stars but most of us cannot perceive that light. We see darkness.

From the Unseen to the Seen: The Manifestation of Material Reality in the Hopi View

We picture reality and its meaning through language. The inspection of the languages of different cultures reveal that each lives in radically different worlds. The semanticist Stuart Chase says, "There is no one metaphysical pool of universal thought. Speakers of different languages see the Cosmos differently, evaluate it differently, sometimes not by much, sometimes widely. Thinking is relative to the language learned." The languages of the world-wide materialist empire, which are generally Indo-European languages, contain world pictures. They contain specifications of what a human is and contain specifications of what each human should aspire to become, in a linear manner. All of these word images are conditioning agents of the world view held by the culture of empire.

On the other hand, the Hopi belong to a loose language group called Uto-Aztecan. Their language reveals a world that is much different than our own and to show the contrast, their language is closer to the concepts in Einstein's Theory of Relativity. According to some physicists, the Hopi language could have been used to express Einstein's theory which at present can only be fully described in mathematics.

Because this whole matter of linearity and linear increase as a cultural fundamental is so important it is productive to contrast the Hopi view with the one in our own heads. All humans are involved with the concept of time, or duration. One type of time is psychological time, which the Hopi would emphasize. This is duration as we experience it in consciousness, our conscious experience of what was and what is now. All of us have experienced altered states of consciousness to some degree and know that our experience of duration changes according to our level of concentration and other factors. The other concept of time is actually measurement. When we look at a watch we are looking at a measurement of cosmic movement. The circulation of our planet around the sun is divided into months, weeks, days, hours, minutes, seconds and so forth. The time on the watch face is not psychological time but measurement of the earth's travel and thus often, is not the time that we experience.

To the Hopi, there is the reality of the Here and Now manifest material world and then there is the unseen, not yet manifest world from whence this present world came. In this part especially, the Hopi view reflects the basic pattern of our ancient cultural view that the material world is manifest from an unseen spiritual world with which we can be in communication and which we can influence according to our behavior. Philosophy students will remember Plato's Idealism. This is a refined reflection of the view that was general in Natural culture. In Plato's view the material world with all of its forms is a more or less imperfect reflection of perfect ideas of form held in unmanifest dimensions of Being.

In any language into which this document could be successfully translated, there will be the concept of linear time. There will be past, present and future. This is the very psychological cornerstone of the myth of linear increase. Nonetheless in the time that is measured by distance of planetary travel, the earth doesn't really go anywhere but around in circles. Our mental appreciation of "time" that we gained from that measurement is turned into a linear progression that we think of mentally as starting in the remote past and moving through to a remote future in a linear manner.

Benjamin Lee Whorf, one of the early scholars of linguistics, examined the Hopi language intensely. He describes what he discovered of Hopi metaphysics:

"The metaphysics underlying our own language, thinking, and modern culture (I speak not of the recent and quite different relativity metaphysics of modern science) imposes upon the universe two grand COSMIC FORMS, space and time; static three-dimensional infinite space, and kinetic one-dimensional uniformly and perpetually flowing time—two utterly separate and unconnected aspects of reality (according to this familiar way of thinking). The flowing realm of time is, in turn, the subject of a threefold division: past, present and future.

"The Hopi metaphysics also has its cosmic forms comparable to these in scale and scope. What are they? It imposes upon the universe two grand cosmic forms, which as a first approximation in terminology we may call MANIFESTED and MANIFESTING (or, UNMANIFEST) or, again, OBJECTIVE and SUBJECTIVE. The objective or manifested comprises all that is or has been accessible to the senses, the historical physical universe, in fact, with no attempt to distinguish between present and past, but excluding everything that we call future. The subjective or manifesting comprises all that we call future, BUT NOT MERELY THIS; it includes equally and indistinguishably all that we call mental—everything that appears or exists in the mind, or, as the Hopi would prefer to say, in the HEART, not only the heart of man, but the heart of animals, plants, and things, and behind and within all forms and appearances of nature in the heart of nature, and by an implication and extension which has been felt by more than one anthropologist, yet would hardly ever be spoken of by a Hopi himself, so charged is the idea with religious and magical awesomeness, in the very heart of the Cosmos itself. The subjective realm (subjective from our viewpoint, but intensely real and quivering with life, power, and potency to the Hopi) embraces not only our FUTURE, much of which the Hopi regards as more or less predestined in essence if not in exact form, but also all mentality, intellection, and emotion, the essence and typical form of which is the striving of purposeful desire, intelligent in character, toward manifestation—a manifestation which is much resisted and delayed, but in some form or other is inevitable. It is the realm of expectancy, of desire and purpose, of vitalizing life, of efficient causes, of thought thinking itself out from an inner realm (the Hopian Heart) into manifestation. It is in a dynamic state, yet not a state of motion—it is not advancing toward us out of a future, but ALREADY WITH US in vital and mental form, and its dynamism is at work in the field of eventuating or manifesting, evolving without motion from the subjective by degrees to a result which is the objective."[12]

The world of the Hopi is manifest or unmanifest. The manifest is that which has been "made", "solidified." That which is not yet "made" nonetheless exists in potential, in a world that is yet to work itself out into the objective "hardness" of this objective world. The Hopis in their effort to maintain the "balance" of the world, "work" on the inner subjective in the Kivas. Later, they will do the same in the elaborate ceremonials in the village plazas. They do this in order to "help" that which will become "made" in the objective world. A fundamental understanding of Hopi, and generally most Natural cultures, is that each person and tribe are conscious participants in the consciousness of the whole world. Thus the thinking, intention and balance of each person and tribe has an effect on the balance of the life of the whole. This is one of the aspects of what the Hopi mean when they say they are keeping the world in balance. The meaning of this statement is not that they are keeping the north and south poles in their places. The statement is a simplification of a vast complex of meanings involved with the balances and manifestation of life.

The culture of empire has made the ability to create tools that more and more efficiently extort the life force of the earth, the basis of judgement of what peoples are "advanced" along the linear road and what peoples are not. When we look at the complexity of languages we see another way of viewing the richness of human culture.

From a linguistic point of view, Whorf says:

"It causes us to transcend the boundaries of local cultures, nationalities, physical peculiarities dubbed "race," and to find that in their linguistic systems, though these systems differ widely, yet in the order, harmony, and beauty of the systems, and in their respective subtleties and penetrating analysis of reality, all men are equal. This fact is independent of the state of evolution as regards material culture, savagery, civilization, moral or ethical development, etc., a thing most surprising to the cultured European, a thing shocking to him, indeed a bitter pill! But it is true; the crudest savage may unconsciously manipulate with effortless ease a linguistic system so intricate, manifoldly systematized, and intellectually difficult that it requires the lifetime study of our greatest scholars to describe its workings."[13]

One does not think about the structure of the language that one is using when a conversation is going on and neither does one think of the subconscious assumptions of culture when viewing reality. In 1975, Dr. Freda Morris, clinical hypnotherapist and author of *Hypnosis With Friends & Lovers*, first began discussing the hypnotic nature of acculturation. In a recent book she says, "The absorption of our own cultural traits as we grow up is itself a process of slow hypnosis—as powerful posthypnotic suggestions are built up by the slow deep implantation of certain cues that vary from culture to culture."[14]

The Illusion of Matter

The cosmos is energy in motion. As some recent physicists say there is no "thing" there- in matter. Those "things" wearing the labels of neutrons, electrons, quarks and so forth are simply energy in motion at such speed that to us it appears hard and real. "THE ALL is MIND; The Universe is Mental," declares the *Kybalion*, an esoteric text of ancient lineage. "Nothing rests; everything moves; everything vibrates," it says.[15]

Form, is held in consciousness. Form is held in consciousness by the memory power of mind. Just as the operations of typewriting or piano playing are at first highly conscious but then become habits on a less conscious level, it is proposed that biological form exists in cosmic consciousness as "habits of mind."

Although orthodox biology has been dominated by the mechanist/reductionist and Darwinian schools of thought there have been a few vitalist biologists through the years maintaining that, in addition to matter, there is a non-material, vital element present in life. Through each decade there have been a few of these biologists on the periphery of orthodoxy. Recently new developments, that could be looked upon as related to Vitalism, have occurred in biology. These researchers seek to explain the elaboration of the form of each organism by means other than the physio-chemical. Rupert Sheldrake has created a body of thought concerning fields leading to the creation of biological form.

Sheldrake participates in a school of thought called Morphic Resonance. The biologists of this school say that biological form is created by immaterial morphic fields, fields of force that create forms. Sheldrake, advances this notion in two recent books, *A New Science of Life: The Hypothesis of Formative Causation* (1985) and *The Presence of the Past; Morphic Resonance and the Habits of Nature*, (1988).[16]

What is it that Creates Forms?

A serious problem has existed for the mechanist scientists for many years in their attempts to explain the development of form from embryo to maturity. What is it that guides the development of the form? What is it that holds the form in its shape as the cells and other substances change in the body? Recently the lay persons have been led to believe that it is the DNA code that does this, but when we get down to specifics, we find that the genetic researchers do not go so far as to say that DNA completely controls the development of form. They only say that DNA is related to the final characteristics of form. The DNA in the arm is the exact copy of the DNA in the leg. They are duplicates, there is nothing different in them that could explain the differential development of the form of the arm or leg. Recently science commentators have compared the DNA code to a computer program and have made the analogy from the computer codes, to the computer output, but even here, in this case, some person created the computer and the software.

Author Edward W. Russell wrote the book, *The Fields of Life*, which discusses the work of Dr. Harold Saxton Burr, which concerns immaterial force fields that participate in creating biological form. Russell points to the logical problems involved in the confusion of the creation of form and DNA. He states:

> "A part cannot be a matrix for a whole; a simple design cannot be a blueprint for a more complicated one. As a functioning organization, the body is more than the sum of its components. Genes and DNA molecules are simpler organizations than the organization of the body <u>as a whole</u>.
>
> "It is true that DNA-fans credit molecules with anthropomorphic powers, in much the same way as primitive tribes attribute human attributes to idols of stone or wood. They solemnly assure us that Molecule A has all the information needed for heredity, that Molecule B passes this on to the cells while Molecule C assesses the needs of the cells and restrains A and B from getting too enthusiastic. But nobody has so far explained <u>how</u> Molecule A got the information in the first place, <u>how</u> Molecule B distributes it and <u>how</u> Molecule C can judge anything, let alone check A and B."[17]

Author Richard Moss, a medical doctor reports on this matter of the development of the form of fetuses:

> "...There have been experiments with the developing frog embryo where, at a point in its development when it has begun to differentiate the left and right arm buds, the embryo can be cut in such a way as to rotate the arm buds. The left arm bud ends up on the right and the right arm bud is on the left. Yet, instead of going on to develop the displaced left and right arms, the embryo matures and that which began as a left arm turns into a right arm and that which would have been a right arm turns into a left arm.

"There is nothing in the genetic material as we understand it that should account for the interruption of a normal process by a human experimenter. If life unfolds simply through the material maintained in the genetic pattern then this realignment should not occur."[18]

Cells are individual conscious entities that participate in collective consciousnesses at various levels. There are many varieties of one-celled beings who do not live in cell communities but spend their lives free and self-regulating. When cells join in cooperative association they do not lose consciousness any more than a fish in a school. Although not popularized by the mechanist orthodoxies of the universities, there is a body of empirical evidence indicating that there is more to organism than simply chemical reactions. Dr. Harold Saxton Burr has spent much of his life experimenting with electrical fields that envelop all organic forms. We need keep in mind that all form is of a field nature. When we put iron filings around a magnet we see the shape of an immaterial field. When we examine matter we see an atomic field that assumes many forms. The nature of form is that it has boundary. Organic forms have the familiar material boundaries (skin) that we see and then there is an electrical envelope outside this boundary that has been studied by Dr. H.S. Burr. This envelope is an extremely weak, direct current electrical field, extending out less than an inch. This field exists around all organic forms. There are also other energy fields such as the alternating current fields of electricity extending out from various regions of the human body, but none of these encompass the whole body. Dr. Burr was interested not so much by the fact that such a field exists but by the fluctuation of energy potential in these fields which resonated with terrestrial and extra-terrestrial events. By monitoring the direct current field around living things, Dr. Burr found that the change in potential energy of this field correlates with specific events both internal and external to the body. This energy field that Burr studied is the same as the energy field that is monitored by the lie detector (Electro-Galvanic Skin Response Machine). The lie detector monitors fluctuations of the emotions. It is important to note that the field of electricity itself is probably not the emotion but a by-product of its functioning. The symptomatic fluctuation makes it possible to monitor the actual phenomenon. By his study, Burr found that each of us is participant in the metabolism of the solar body through this field. Fluctuations in energy potential of this direct current field correlate with the lunar cycle and the sun spot cycle. He also discovered that by monitoring the field, the ovulation of the human female can be spotted exactly, a matter of extreme importance to the human family. The electrical monitoring indicates an immaterial force that both controls and is controlled by the material. It is an integrated whole. It has long been a question in biology of how the form of cellular organization maintains itself while the substance changes. The question of how the cells of the foetus create the form of the child or the cells of an organ recreate its form after an injury has remained a mystery. Living organisms are a flow system with intake of material being transformed into proteins, cells and fluids. The rule of thumb is that the entire human body is cellularly replaced in a seven year period. Although the materials of the body are in constant flux, the form of the whole does not change, except slowly with age.

Dr. Burr found that the control field which he was monitoring electrically is a guiding field, or more specifically a partially guiding field. He sets out a hypothesis which he states in the following manner:

"The pattern or organization of any biological system is established by a complex electro-dynamic field which is in part determined by its atomic physio-chemical components and which in part determines the behavior and orientation of those components. This field is electrical in the physical sense and by its properties relates the entities of the biological system in a characteristic pattern and is itself, in part, a result of the existence of those entities. It determines and is determined by the components.

"More than establishing pattern, it must maintain pattern in the midst of a physio-chemical flux. Therefore, it must regulate and control living things. It must be the mechanism, the outcome of whose activity is wholeness, organization, and continuity."[19]

Burr's research led him to the discovery that by monitoring the energy field he could determine the longitudinal axis (spinal column) of an unfertilized salamander egg. As he monitored it after fertilization his monitoring of the immaterial guiding field indicated that the spinal column remained congruous with the electrical polarity throughout its development. That is, the guiding field was there before fertilization and remained there as the guiding field, as the biological form unfolded. Burr went further and demonstrated that the guiding field not only participates in guiding the development of form but is always at work with the living organism. Burr used a rudimentary protoplasmic being called plasmodium for his experiment that indicated activity in the immaterial field before activity was seen in the material. He explains:

"Under the microscope, it is simple to demonstrate that every 60 or 90 seconds the protoplasm in the veins reverses the direction of flow. The electrical pickup from the vein, combined with the moving picture, reveals that in the majority of instances polar reversal of the voltage occurs before there is a directional change of the plasmic flow, but also there are many instances where the change in both phenomena seem to occur simultaneously."[20]

Although Burr's work never gained the attention of the orthodox, whose view would deny this possibility, it nonetheless gives us a direction to proceed. What Burr's work indicates is that we are intimately involved with unseen fields of energy. With Burr's methods of monitoring, the depth of a trance state can be followed while a person is in hypnosis. In the experiments done with hypnosis, Burr and his associates found that having the hypnotized subject remember highly emotional situations caused the electrical field to change (therefore its value as a lie-detector). Burr also found the cosmic fluctuations of moon cycle, sun cycle and sunspots caused changes in the electrical potential of field, thus giving us evidence of the intimate connection of our bodies and emotions to cosmic events. In addition to being simply another piece of evidence that everything is connected, the Burr material shows an interaction between a force field that can be monitored by its electrical side effect and the physical organism. It suggests even further that important aspects of the control of the material form exists in this field.

The Creation of Form - Morphic Resonance

Mechanistic science does not emphasize consciousness. Consciousness and any of its possibilities are unmentioned aspects of life that still are left in mystery. For example the kind of problem that might come up is how to explain memory. The molecules, especially proteins, of our bodies are replaced in days or months, at most. So how does the memory of early childhood continue to exist in the proteins of the brain cells of an elderly person? Is it encoded somehow in a chemical reaction? Mechanistic science because it does not acknowledge the immaterial will not consider consciousness and its abilities, but continues to dissect brains and molecules attempting to fashion an answer. With his hypothesis of formative causation Rupert Sheldrake has pointed a way out of the dead-end and looks at "effects" then argues back to causes. Though he does not mention consciousness, he suggests fields as an explanatory term. Sheldrake says that fields are non-material regions of influence and he points to gravity as an illustration of this. Gravity holds us to the earth. Because of the precise force of its pull our own bone structure is engineered. If our bones were longer or thinner or of weaker substance we would not be able to function on the surface of the earth. In this manner we and all other things on the earth's surface are structured by this field.

The energy field of the solar system has been discussed. This field with its many different types of energies certainly has an effect on the forms within it, such as the nature of biological life on earth.

Electro-magnetic fields are familiar non-material force fields. These fields of electrical vibration bring us radio and television. Physicists measure electron fields, neutron fields and there are force fields even within atoms, they say. These recognized fields are non-material with effects in the material that can be experimentally measured. Though immaterial, these fields can be seen as controlling the material in some manner. Sheldrake says:

"The nature of fields is inevitably mysterious. According to modern physics, these entities are more fundamental than matter. Fields cannot be explained in terms of matter; rather, matter is explained in terms of energy within fields. Physics cannot explain the nature of the different kinds of fields in terms of anything else physical, unless it be in terms of a more fundamental unified field, such as the original cosmic field. But then this too is inexplicable-unless we assume it was created by God. And then God is inexplicable.

"We can, of course, assume that fields are as they are because they are determined by eternal mathematical laws, but then there is the same problem with these laws; how can we explain them?"[21]

In Sheldrake's thinking, the shape of each organism is guided by a morphogenic field. (The coming into being of form is morphogenesis). The morphogenic field of that organism resonates with the other fields of that species of organism that have gone before. Form resonates with form irrespective of the time frame in which it occurs. In his thinking, these fields are beyond our "normal" experience of space and time.

Each individual organism is in a guiding field that resonates with all others of that specific form that have gone before. Here Sheldrake says that the inherent capacity of memory and habit is instrumental. Just as many of our daily routines were learned with conscious attention but have now fallen below the level of conscious awareness and become habit, Sheldrake says it is memory and habit that are essential to the functioning of these formative fields of living things. The forms of organisms are in continual flux, says Sheldrake. As the flow of biological life goes on, new habits are slowly formed and go on to be incorporated into all newly developing organisms of that species. He offers many examples of the functioning of the morphic resonance of behavior patterns within species and a clear example is of the well documented development of a habit among a bird species residing in England, the blue tits.

Sheldrake says that in the case of the blue tits, they are very territorial, seldom straying more than a few miles from their breeding place. Yet a new habit resonated through the species all over England.

In Southampton, in 1921, a blue tit was observed to peck through the foil cap of a milk bottle, tear the foil back and drink from the bottle. The spread of this habit was recorded at regular intervals from 1930 to 1947. There are eleven species to which this habit has spread but it is most frequently confined to great tits, coal tits and blue tits. After the first observation of this "milk poaching," the habit was seen to spread rapidly through England where sometimes flocks of tits would follow milk delivery people through the neighborhoods waiting for the milk bottles to be put on people's porches. The detailed studies of this phenomenon show that the habit was independently "discovered" by individual tits 89 times in the British Isles. In the view of morphic resonance, this habit pattern resonated within the tit species and the pattern was then increasingly manifest by individual tits. During World War II milk deliveries in England stopped for the duration which was longer than the normal tit lifespan, yet when milk deliveries commenced again, tits all over England again began to take up the habit. After the war, "It seems certain that the habit was started in many different places by many individuals," researchers said. The habit also spread to Sweden, Denmark and Holland.[22]

The case of the blue tits is of behavioral form, or behavioral morphology. It also shows the resonance of habit over space and time. In the matter of the physical form itself, Sheldrake's other major point is that forms, themselves are habits of nature. We have the example of what in orthodox science is called "parallel evolution" which relates to habits of form. There are many examples of "evolutionary convergence" where biological forms from dissimilar species and different continents end up having similar or almost identical form or function- or both. There is also the popular illustration of the parallelism between the placental mammals and the marsupials of Australia. In Australia there is a marsupial flying phalanger that is almost a duplicate of a mammalian flying squirrel. In the southwestern U.S. there is a rodent called a kangaroo rat. In Australia there is a marsupial that is the same form. There is even a mole-like marsupial (except it has a chitinous beak like a duck-billed platypus) in Australia that lives and behaves like mammalian moles. The mechanists have gone through many intellectual contortions to explain these similarities but it is difficult when one assumes the life on earth to be "chance chemical reactions." Morphic resonance on the other hand gives us a much better tool with which to think about this subject. The group consciousness of aggregates of discrete, individual organisms further shows that there must be something other than chemical reactions directing organisms. There are many invertebrate organisms that live in colonies such as ant hills or bee hives that are so highly organized and differentiated that they appear to be unitary organisms. Sheldrake points to the order Siphonophora which resemble the unitary, multicellular jellyfish but contrarily, are actually made up of individual organisms acting in concert. These assemblages live in open oceans. He says that <u>Nanomia</u>, a member of this order;

> "...consists of many specialized individual organisms. At the top is an individual modified into a gas-filled float. Below it are organisms that act like little bellows, squirting out jets of water which propel the colony; by altering the shape of their openings they are able to alter the direction of the jets. Through their co-ordinated action the <u>Nanomia</u> colony is able to dart about vigorously, moving at any angle and in any plane, even executing loop-the-loop curves. Lower on the stem there are other organisms which are specialized for the ingestion and digestion of nutrients for the rest of the colony. Long branched tentacles arise from them and are used to capture prey. There are also bracts, consisting of inert, scalelike organisms that fit over the stem and help protect it from physical damage. Finally, there are sexual organisms, which produce gametes which through fertilization can give rise to new colonies."[23]

With <u>Nanomia</u> we have the extreme blurring of the distinction between colony organization and "unitary organism." We see also the difficulty of explaining how all of these "individual unitary organisms" instantaneously coordinate if all they are is a mass of chemical reactions. The <u>Nanomia</u> poses some difficulty of explanation for the DNA influenced mechanist but none for a viewpoint of morphic resonance where fields are "nested" within fields. A molecule is a community metabolism, a cell is a community metabolism, and so forth for groups of cells as organs and organs as bodies, insect communities, particularly ants and termites, and we then carry this cooperative metabolism through whole ecosystems, ultimately to the being of the planet itself.

There are many examples of group consciousness in the natural world. Another fascinating group-being is in the family of fungi. It is <u>Dictyostelium discoidium</u>, a slime mold. Individual organisms of this species live spread out in local areas of a forest floor where they live separately, and survive by eating bacteria. Each of them is about 5 microns in diameter which means it would take some 200 of them to cover the dot of an "i." Because of their size, researchers say, to move twelve inches would be like a seventy mile trip for humans.

After some generations of moving about feeding on bacteria, the organisms' food supply becomes exhausted. When this happens a hormone-type substance is released from a few key individuals which constitutes a signal and the individuals all head for that spot. Then, they mass into a clump that may number 100,000 individuals, measuring a few millimeters across. When the mass is assembled it resembles a slug complete with individuals that function as "eyes" and others who serve as "feet." When all is ready, the slug goes off across the forest floor looking for greener pastures, travelling on a coat of "slime" that the assembled group excretes. When it reaches an area to its liking it tips up on end and the slug changes into a form resembling a tiny mushroom with a long thin stalk. When it has achieved this new, similarly highly organized and complex structure, the small bulb at the top of the stalk emits spores, which begin a new cycle of individuals who multiply both by splitting and sometimes by sexual congress. Biologists have learned that the voluntary assembly of the slug can be artificially broken apart and the individuals can go back to being individuals if there is food nearby but, by the time the slug reaches the stalk and spore cap form, the individuals cannot return to their previous life as individuals. After reaching this point when spores are put out to create the new generations, the old body with all of its individuals dies.

Here again the importance of consciousness is dealt with in biological functioning. The slime mold and <u>Nanomia</u> are examples where the distinction between individual and group consciousness becomes very blurred. Nonetheless the primacy of consciousness in each individual is paramount in order to coordinate the physical actions of the colonial being and its group consciousness.

It has been proposed that the earth is a conscious entity as are all biological forms and that the consciousness of individuals can co-mingle in community, or colonial beings. It is plain that the colonial organisms have a purpose (to continue their lives by feeding themselves) and there are indications that Gaia itself has purposive intent.

Human scholarship has not focussed on the functioning of conscious wholes the way it has focussed on the behavior of the inert parts in atomic physics and molecular chemistry. Even so, we do have some hints that the consciousness of the whole earth functions even in an anticipatory way.

Does the Life of the Earth Have A Plan?

Gerbert Grohmann, who was a student of Johann Wolfgang von Goethe and of Rudolph Steiner, suggests that biological form, when looked at as a project of the planetary whole, has undergone simultaneous change across the whole world at the same time. There have been periods during the development of biological forms on the earth during which form changed en mass. An example is the leap from spore bearing to coniferous and then to flowering plants. This is akin to the body of the earth undergoing transformation. These periods represent leaps in the change of biological form. Pertaining to the plant family Grohmann says:

"All phylogenetic [phylum=race or strain] development is discontinuous. Leaps are made and gaps divide the different stages. The facts demonstrate this clearly. The materialistic principle of the continuity of substance and force applied to the history of evolution inevitably leads to contradictions. The crest of the first wave of the development of plants growing in soil is the carboniferous flora; however, with the end of the Paleozoic Era, which for the plant kingdom lies between the Lower New Red Sandstone and the Permian Limestone period, this highly developed flora with its many very distinct species has vanished almost completely. One could hardly have a more impressive fact than this. After the Triassic Red Sandstone period, which is characterized by its scanty plant growth, a new beginning is made: the flora of the Mesophytic Era. The former vegetation, however, did not develop further.

"During the Mesophytic Era we again find highly developed plants of a special character, particularly in the Jurassic and Chalk formations. But this climax is also an end. In the Upper Chalk the rich variety of forms has disappeared. Suddenly, flowering plants spring up without warning, simultaneously in many different parts of the world. We need not violate palaeontological facts in order to find, for each of these great periods, one characteristic plant organ. In the carboniferous period it is the leafy vegetative shoot, corresponding to the fern. In the middle period (Mesophytic), with the predominance of conifers, Ginkgoes and Cycads, the leafstalk type of plant has risen to the stage of seed bearing. In the next period, Upper Chalk and Tertiary, the real flowering plant finally appears."[24]

Grohmann points out that the change of form occurs across the biological spectrum during these "evolutionary leaps." As the fern series comes to its end it begins to show form that is anticipatory of the cone bearing plants but the substance of the fern cannot carry the trajectory on because the actual tissue material could not sustain it. Grohmann says; "Organic evolution does not entail only progressive transformation of forms, but the very substance must be developed from stage to stage in order to create the conditions suitable for a certain level of organization."[25]

As the form of the fern reaches its end and it begins to develop form prophetic of the soon to appear cone bearing plants, the ferns do not continue to transform and become cone bearing plants. The ferns die out as predominant plants and new plants appear that are the cone bearing plants with substance organized appropriately to support the new form.

Grohmann's work points to avenues of thinking that are even beyond the morphic resonance of Sheldrake- that the resonance of form shows evidence of some plan that precedes the creation of form- anticipatory, creative thought on a grand scale. This goes beyond Sheldrake's careful documentation to suggest an active intelligence involved in creating the forms of life. What is being considered here is an inversion of the civilized perspective. What happens in consciousness is instrumental in events in the material, biological world. Without this understanding we will be greatly hindered in creating new human culture.

The Social Conditioning of Human Health

We of contemporary society have been conditioned with the image that health is a personal problem. Beyond that we are led to believe that health is a matter of chemistry. Being chemistry, health can then be ministered to by the vast establishment of the chemical/pharmaceutical industry. The medical establishment which is the third largest industry in the United States, just behind petroleum and war machines, is a direct expression of the structure and ideas of empire and the manner in which that culture relates to living things. Much like modern agriculture, the medical industry is a vast array of industrial institutions which produce chemicals, medical machinery, design and build hospitals with specialized architecture, produce computer programs for doctors offices, and operate massive medical education establishments and so forth. Because health care in the view of the scientific establishment, is chemistry, the focus of attention is on blood samples, tissue samples, biopsies and such. Within the system little attention is given to the person, their dietary habits, the air they breathe, their living conditions or other factors. The establishment exists for profit and the aggrandizement of those who direct it. The personal life and well-being of the client is unimportant. It is chemistry (called molecular medicine in the trade) that the medical establishment focuses upon. In fact, within the functional operation of the medical establishment the more unhealthy the population, the higher the profits. For decades the damage from birth trauma caused by hospital birthing practices have been known. Little has changed because those practices are there for the convenience and efficiency of the institution itself.

Public health researchers, by and large, are not part of the medical establishment. They have a much more wholistic perspective in that they look at the statistics of the health of whole populations. By looking at their work we begin to see to what extent the individual is shaped and conditioned by the group consciousness of the tribe or in this case a mass society. We begin to see that ideas held in the mind-culture-effect biological systems. We see the importance of creating new human culture with great attention.

The tumor body of empire is a planetary medical problem. It is progressive disintegration of the life system. The "material advancement" of "man the toolmaker" is held out to the public mind as a symbol of "progress." Meanwhile, in real terms, we have seen that health, diet and longevity severely declined when empire began.

The reality is that culture can condition us so that it actually causes disease. On the positive side of this we find that culture, if it is properly formed, can lead us to health and positive emotional condition.

Leonard A. Sagan, who is a scholar of Public Health has authored a study that argues convincingly that individual health has little to do with industrial medicine but is a reflection of the quality of social experience. In his study, *The Health of Nations: True Causes of Sickness and Well Being*,[26] Sagan demonstrates that the increase in population and longevity began before the rise of modern medicine, childhood death from infectious diseases began to decline long before anti-biotic chemicals and that modern medical care has little effect on public health. Sagan convincingly demonstrates that psycho-social changes have been responsible for the increase in life span and the increase in immunity. His study shows that social conditions directly effect human health. With the expansion of the world empire, the economic condition of Europeans and those of the European colonies began to improve and the personal and social expectations of the people began to rise. The stability and strength of what we know as the "modern family" increased. The conditions of life of the Industrial Revolution period began to fall away as working people forced demands upon the elite for the eight hour day, better working conditions and a greater share in the social benefits. As the masses forced an opening in the social fabric, the people had more hope and aspiration in their lives. They began to throw off the slave psychology and hold themselves in more esteem, which is what Sagan sees as the key to personal health, a strong sense of self esteem built upon a social foundation that provides at least for the necessities of life. In the larger context this means that the elite of civilization, by sacrificing the life of the earth, have climbed back up to conditions Natural people already enjoyed. But what is being explored is how social conditions affect health.

Sagan shows that the decline in mortality rates began prior to the great sanitary movement of the nineteenth century. He states,

"It was not the decline in infection that caused the decline in mortality rates but rather a decline in death rates of those who were infected."

High rates of infection persisted until very recent decades. The majority of deaths among infants are not due to microbiological agents transmitted through the food and water supply but rather are from microbiological agents commonly present in the environment; the deaths are the result of infection with viruses and other ubiquitous organisms, which will inevitably result among infants with lowered resistance.

"The decline in mortality from infectious diseases has been as dramatic among those diseases that are spread from person to person, such as tuberculosis, where sanitation efforts are ineffective, as among those that are spread through the food and water supply or through insect vectors."

Sagan continues by saying, "Finally, there is another explanation for the decline in deaths from infectious diseases, namely, an improvement in human resistance."[27] Sagan introduces public health studies to show that modern medical care has little correlation with public health and that nutrition (above the malnutrition rate) does not correlate with public health. It will be a surprise to all of us who have been subjected to a lifetime of propaganda conditioning by the medical establishment that numerous studies show that the less food people have the healthier they are and statistically, the more doctors there are per capita in First World countries, the higher rises the infant mortality. A comparison of eighteen present industrial societies shows that higher infant mortality correlates with the increased number of doctors. Further, studies show that there is no correlation between public health expenditures and decline in death rates in these countries.[28] To add another startling series of statistical studies, he points out that although there have been mortality rate changes concerned with specific organ sites, the risk of dying of cancer once it starts is no different than it was fifty years ago. The incidence of cancer has gone up tremendously but once one has cancer, the risk of dying of it has not changed in fifty years even given the tremendous investment in cancer research and treatment.

So what has caused the increase in health according to Sagan? His studies point to the increased strength of the nuclear family. In the larger context we saw the destruction of the tribe, the clan, extended family and finally the Industrial Revolution wiped out communal peasant existence. The slow climb back to simply a nuclear family for Europeans has been at the expense of the colonized world because of increased wealth trickling down to the masses in the imperial centers. Beginning with the Industrial Revolution and lasting up until well into twentieth century, what there was of family life was grim. Child labor took them out of the family at an early age. Labor hours for everyone were long and continuous; housing, wages and the conditions of life almost precluded a stable, nurturing family. Sagan points out that only recently has any attention been devoted toward the nurturing of infants and children. Many studies have shown that nurturing during infancy affects infant mortality, I.Q. levels, physical stature, and illness rates. The loss of one or both parents, indicating family influence, is even more well known because of the greater ease of statistical comparison. For example, for a person who has lost both parents the suicide risk is seven times greater than a person from an intact family. In another study that Sagan cites, of college students who had been separated from a parent during childhood, nearly half had serious thoughts of suicide, whereas students who came from intact families only demonstrated a 10% incidence of such thoughts.

In a study from Johns Hopkins Medical School, 1,337 medical students were studied. In this study it was found that closeness to parents and the father's age (the older the father, the greater the incidence) at the time of the subject's birth strongly correlated with later suicide, mental illness and tumors. In a study at the University of Pittsburgh it was found that parental loss- death of a parent, separation or divorce of parents, correlated with a 25% increased chance of gastric neurosis, 35% for duodenal ulcer, 36% for psychoneurosis, 38% for alcoholism, 45% for rheumatoid arthritis, 55% for accidents, 55% for tuberculosis, 62% for delinquency and 70% for suicide.

Not only does early childhood experience in the family affect health and mortality but the strength of the fabric of society affects the health of the family. In Natural culture the clan social environment was the norm. Now, the nearest thing approaching the clan are therapy and support groups. Though these groups have been only a fragile reflection of the clan, they are never the less of great aid to the individual members. Sagan finds that married people as a whole, have lower death rates than people of the same age who are single or widowed and the death rate for married persons is half that of divorced people. An elaborate study conducted in Alameda County, in northern California, clearly demonstrated that social isolation, "... Was associated with increased mortality from ischemic heart disease, cancer, cardiovascular diseases, and all other diagnoses, including suicide and accidental death."[29] In reality living in the social conditions of an empire is as destructive to humans as war.

While the military is an instrument of war and death, in reality, simply the socialization it provides in human camaraderie, actually decreases its members mortality rates (outside the battlefield). Individuals who actually experience military society have better health ratings than others. Sagan cites studies showing that, "... Mortality rates of servicemen are significantly below that of the U.S. population generally. For all personnel ages seventeen and over, the death rate is only 57 percent of that of non-military people of the same age."[30] Another study, in Massachusetts, indicates the influence of social disintegration on health. It has shown a correlation between poverty, social isolation and cancer risk.

The relatively small group of people in industrial societies who have statistically better health and longevity also have social advantages well above the norm, Sagan finds. This is the group who have a firm social foundation as infants, who have avenues of advancement and who have, because of social privilege or unusual families, been enabled to gain optimism and self esteem.

Studies from many industrial nations show that longevity is, looked at as a whole, a function of social class with the longest living group being the wealthiest. Studies in England, where universal health care has been in place a long time, show that the provision of health care makes little difference in these statistics, before or after the institution of a universal health care plan. Further to the point that health is a psychological matter influenced by social conditions, is the link between education and health. Sagan says:

"The mortality differences between those of the least and those of the highest [educational] achievement are very great, more so for women than for men, and are greatest among the middle-aged; females who have had four or more years of college have half the death rate experienced by those with little or no education. Differences in mortality among educational classes exist for a broad spectrum of diseases, the greatest differences occurring in deaths due to infectious diseases. Men with the least educational achievement experienced death from tuberculosis at a rate 776 percent higher than those with the highest educational level."[31]

The link between mental-emotional state and health is much stronger than the simple wealth-health link Sagan says. "The studies seem to favor literacy as being <u>directly</u> linked to health rather than as a proxy for other variables. That is, the statistical association between literacy and health is consistently stronger than that between health and income."[32]

Following his review of social/personal health in modern industrial societies, Sagan details the personality attributes of those who live the longest and have the least illness. First, he says, they have a high level of self-esteem. They have a high regard for themselves but they are committed to goals other than their own personal welfare. These healthy people place high value on health and survival. They are future oriented. They are trusting and easily enter into social networks. They relish companionship, yet are not uncomfortable when alone and seek periods of contemplation and aloneness. Finally, he says that these people seek knowledge beyond formal education. He quotes Aaron Antonovsky of the Ben-Gurion University who says these people have a sense of coherence,...a global orientation that expresses the extent to which one has a pervasive, enduring though dynamic feeling of confidence that one's internal and external environments are predictable and that there is a high probability that things will work out as well as can reasonably be expected."[33]

The pattern that is described fits well with what we know about the situation of forager/hunter tribes who relate to the ecological and spiritual whole around them.

Sagan shows quite adequately that health in a cosmic context is related to the question of identity and to positive emotional level. These factors exist in consciousness. Culture also exists in consciousness. An individual can be injured - the effect of the mind upon the body - simply by being conditioned into empire culture. The world industrial empire has passed the cusp of its development. The easily grasped "resources" are gone and the population explosion is in full acceleration. The flow of resources that floated the wealth of the First world populations up to the standard of Natural human culture are now declining and the disintegration of the family, especially in the U.S. is increasing. Sagan shows that the breakup of the nuclear family is showing a rapid increase, teenage pregnancy is increasing rapidly, as well as child abuse. All of these factors will have definite effects across the population. Sagan states that morbidity is increasing, particularly among children and that the evidence is that the health of the U.S. population is now going down. He concludes by saying; "As the modern nuclear family has come unglued, crime, suicide, and drug use have soared, just as have divorce and teenage pregnancy while scholastic achievement has declined. These associations and causal relationships have yet to be widely appreciated."[34]

The Medical Question of Identity

While Sagan offers the knowledge of a specialist concerning the statistics of health and social relationships, there is a larger context. This context is of true organic identity. We are seeing the rise of illness that is associated with psychological stress and with the auto-immune system. Psychological stress is a function of the reality one identifies with. If one is thoroughly conditioned and identifies closely with the immediate day to day social reality, such as the daily crises on t.v. news programs, one experiences more stress than if one identifies oneself as an organic being functioning among other organic beings on the planet earth. In the case of the auto-immune system a deeper level of consciousness is at work. AIDS, cancer, allergies, asthsma, candida albicans, lowered resistance to infection and other illnesses are related to the functioning of the auto-immune system. For example in the case of cancer, people get cancer every day. That is, a few cells in the body malfunction and do not replicate as they should. These cells are normally then consumed by the body. The consciousness of the body decides that they are not self- but other. The auto-immune system is directed by consciousness, not chemistry.

The same situation exists with the populations of the micro-organism candida albicans. Normally, the population levels of the candida in our bodies are maintained at a beneficial level but in some cases, such as after over-doses of anti-biotics, the auto-immune system seems not to know its identity, the difference between self and other. When this happens the populations of candida explode without the auto-immune system controlling them. At that point serious illness develops. Here we have society and the person, living out of cosmic balance and then the vegetative consciousness of the individual body becoming out of balance. The problem on all three levels is that the being does not know what it is. Like the cancer cell, it has lost its sense of identity within the cosmic pattern.

Life and its consciousness cannot be fooled. We may act in an objectified, machine-like manner, we may begin to resemble the machine artifacts that we have created, we may even begin to believe that we can live in a machine culture with no more humanity than an internal combustion engine, but we cannot escape the fact that we are organic beings with a unique birthright and ancestry just like other species. What Sagan's material shows is the necessity of focussing on social environment in our new culture. There is also the necessity of having that social environment grounded in the pattern and principles of biological life. We must first know that we are within the body of Gaia. As we heal as a social body from the disease of empire, it is particularly the children upon whom we must focus. As we adults begin to create the new culture in a healing, therapeutic environment, we must be able to have fewer children but focus more attention on them.

We are discussing a leap that will be generations long. The present crisis is so profound that it will be many generations before "normalcy" returns. We are creating healing cultures whose basic patterns are such that we expect them to weather the events. It is the children and their children who will be living through this. We want these children to have the best possible opportunity. It is obvious from the material that has been examined that the clan structure is without doubt the most important ingredient in a person's later life. Given these considerations a new culture would be child centered and secondarily focussed on women of child bearing age. This is our hope for the future, the children. If we can function in therapeutic community to create a positive emotional environment and raise children without emotional crippling, then we will have provided the foundation for their lives.

It is not we who will be the final result of the cultural creation but they who must climb upon our shoulders, who will teach their children of the illness we have suffered and the positive direction that they must follow. In nurturing the children, we nurture the new culture.

NOTES

1   The New Biology: Discovering The Wisdom In Nature. Robert Augros & George Stanciu. New Science Library. Shambala pub. Boston. 1988. pp.125,126.
2   ibid. p. 128.
3   Cycles: The Mysterious Forces That Trigger Events. Edward R. Dewey and Og Mandino. Hawthorn Books. New York. 1971. p. 200.
4   ibid. p. 89
5   ibid. p. 105.
6   ibid. p. 114.
7   ibid. p. 155.
8   The Plant. Gerbert Grohmann. Rudolf Steiner Press. London. 1974. p. 198.
9   Augros & Stanciu. The New Biology. op. cit. p. 173.
10 The Transmission Of Doubt: Talks and Essays on the Transcendence of Scientific Materialism through Radical Understanding. Da Free John. The Dawn Horse Press. Clearlake, Calif. 1984. pp. 95,96.
11 A view from modern physics is given in:
    Space-time And Beyond: Toward An Explanation Of The Unexplainable. Bob Toben, in conversation with physicists Jack Sarfatti, Ph.D. and Fred Wolf, Ph.D. E.P. Dutton. New York. 1975.
    Many examples are given in written works of yogis. A recent treatment is:
    Nuclear Evolution: Discovery of the Rainbow Body. Christopher Hills. University of the Trees Press. Boulder Creek, Ca. 1977.
    An example from Hermetic tradition is:
    The Kybalion: A Study of The Hermetic Philosophy Of Ancient Egypt And Greece. by Three Initiates. The Yogi Publication Society. Masonic Temple. Chicago, Ill. 1936.
12 Language, Thought & Reality. Benjamin Lee Whorf. M.I.T. Pub. 1956. pp. 59,60.
13 ibid. pp. 263,264.
14 Hypnosis With Friends and Lovers. Freda Morris. Harper & Row. San Francisco. 1979. p. XIII.
15 The Kybalion. op. cit.
16 A New Science of Life: The Hypothesis of Formative Causation. Rupert Sheldrake. 2nd. ed. Blond & Briggs. London. 1985.
    The Presence of the Past: Morphic Resonance and the Habits of Nature. Rupert Sheldrake. Times Books. New York. 1988.
17 Design For Destiny: Science Reveals the Soul. Edward W. Russell. Ballantine Books. New York. 1971. pp. 36,37.

18   The I That Is We. Richard Moss, M.D. Celestial Arts, pub. Berkeley,
      Ca. 1981. p. 31.

19   The Fields of Life: Our Links With the Universe. Dr. Harold Saxton
      Burr. Ballentine Books. New York. 1972. p. 29.

20   ibid. p. 81.

21   Sheldrake. A New Science of Life. op. cit. p. 99.

22   ibid. pp.177-180.

23   ibid. p. 226.

24   The Plant: A Guide to Understanding its Nature. Gerbert Grohmann.
      Trans. K. Castelliz from Die Pflanze, Vol. I. Rudolf Steiner Press.
      London. 1974. pp.195,196.

25   ibid. p. 201.

26   The Health of Nations: True Causes of Sickness and Well Being.
      Leonard A. Sagan. Basic Books Inc. N.Y. N.Y. 1987.

27   ibid. p. 41.

28   ibid. p. 81.

29   ibid. pp. 135,136.

30   ibid. p. 138.

31   ibid. p. 175.

32   ibid. p. 177.

33   ibid. p. 188.

34   ibid. p. 110.

CHAPTER 14

CULTURE AS ORGANISM

The Cultivated Life

Human culture is usually spoken of as the totality of ways of living of a people that are passed down the generations. Prior to the era of empires, human cultural knowledge was concerned in large part with the earth and its manifold life. Humans foraged upon the earth for their sustenance and the lore of the earth was their code of adaptation to that life. Their culture taught each generation how to live on the earth. Culture taught what to eat, how to eat it and when to eat it. Culture taught the ways to create shelter. Culture taught the meaning of the world, the explanation of what it is and how it came to be. Culture also taught how the tribe was to fit into that world. It taught the appropriate mating and the form of the extended family relationships. Importantly, it taught identity.

Human culture is an autonomous thought form, carried in the consciousness of the cultural members, that proceeds through time, more or less independently of any single individual. The culture is essentially held in the consciousness of individuals but it is not created by those individuals. It is learned from the group. This flow of individuals through the cultural form is similar to the flow of individual cells through an organ. As individual cells are replaced in the body, the body maintains the integrity of its form and in a similar manner the cultural form maintains its integrity.

The meanings inherent in the English language indicate the ancient understanding of the process of culture. The words cult, culture, cultivar and cultivate all indicate a process of effort toward the continuance of the ideas and forms of life and knowledge. There is also the implication that the living things are learning and adapting. A cult is an assembling of people around some idea, especially a religious idea. It is a process in which the people learn certain ways of living and certain beliefs about the world. This body of knowledge is then passed on within the cult. When one cultivates a plant or crop, the living things are given attention and their lives are guided in certain ways. A variety of plant that has been cared for and whose optimum individuals have been selected over many generations is called a cultivar. "Domesticated" plants are cultivars.

This type of "cultivation" happens in the natural world. Of course there are no humans guiding the plant families and cultures, but families of plants do learn to modify their forms in order to adapt to the differing conditions of the earth. The willow-poplar-aspen tree family is a good example. This family is very important in semi-arid environments on the North American continent. They can propagate by seed transported by wind, water or animals. They can even propagate by pieces of themselves. For example, if a branch is torn off in a flood and comes to rest in a pile of flood debris, the branch will often take root and create a new colony. Once established, their main means of increase is by the root system. They establish a dense web of roots in an area and an upright tree or bush may grow out of any particular root area. This plant grows in stream courses or in areas where underground water is abundant and near the surface. Because floodings- or fire, especially in the case of aspen,- may clear off the above ground stems, the plant's continuance is based in the root system. If its above ground stems are cleared, it simply sends up new shoots. Its main body is the extensive root system underground. This important plant holds the soils of riparian habitats and also creates fertile micro-climates, adapting its shape and behavior to the amount of moisture it can get and to the elevation in which it grows, which relates then to the temperature that it must endure. Some members of the willow family are large in moist, hot, low elevations. As elevation increases or moisture decreases, the form of the plant will modify but the essential characteristics of the family remain. The modifications, each which have separate scientific names, vary, but the essential characteristics of the family are unchanged. The modifications of the family are the indication of the families' learning to adapt to different conditions. It is the indication of the family's culture. Opuntia, the familiar elephant ear cactus that grows the savory prickly pear fruits, is another example of a family with a rich culture. Opuntia will grow in a desert near sea level and up elevation to 6,500 feet. In some modifications in its low elevation desert home it can grow to ten feet tall, with wide and succulent leaves. In more moist, higher and colder elevations it may only grow six inches tall with small shriveled leaves. It has acculturated itself throughout the spread of the land and its conditions. Animal culture shows this type of modification as their culture adapts to the differences of the land. In the past, some of the members of the bear family would be out on the great plains foraging on bison and elk carcasses. Others, especially the black and brown bears, would be high in the Rockies, concentrating on berries and insects. In the Pacific Northwest the bears would depend heavily on salmon runs. In the arctic the polar bears have a much different culture.

The salmon are an example of fish culture. They migrate from their birth places out to sea and then return after an extended period of time back to their exact place of birth to spawn. Individuals return to destinations which are spread all over the watershed. Due to the differing of soils, moisture abundance and vegetation mix, the taste and smell of the water coming from their birth place directs them home. Each of the different cultural groups such as coho, steelhead and sockeye have different times and styles in which they run to spawn in the upland streams, but each of their cultures show a similarity of adaptation to the earth.

Natural human culture has grown out of the earth as an adaptation to it. The earth, its life and metabolism have provided the pattern and ideas for human culture. Human cultures show a rich variety of adaptation to the differing conditions of the earth but the basic pattern of culture fits the basic life principles and pattern of the planetary life as a whole. The Natural cultures and their divisions were cultivated over eons of time. In the far north, where there is less sunlight and the lighter skin-colored people are found such as Lapps and Inuit (or eskimo), the complex of culture is adapted to the cold and the darkness. The Lapps of northern Scandinavia, like the former Inuit, inland from the Hudson's Bay of Canada, have adapted to the deer family, reindeer and caribou, as their main energy source. Most of the other Inuit live from the sea.

In terms of human cultures, there are people who live primarily from the fish in the sea, cultures that were dependent upon the salmon runs of northern Europe, the British Isles, and both coasts of North America. There were cultures dependent upon massive deer and bison herds. There were the cultures of the complex rainforest ecosystems. Each of these variations of human culture were highly adapted and very ancient, as are the adaptations of the willow family or the prickly pear family. As the invasion of the world by the European empire was ongoing, the Cossacks of Russia broke over the Ural mountains into the Siberian region. At that time there were more than one hundred different cultural groups in the Siberian areas. Each of these groups was ecologically adapted to their local region and each had a different language or dialect and differing manners. This same condition obtained in California at the onset of the European invasion. Like the Siberian region, there were more than one hundred tribes in California differentiated into languages, dialects and ecological adaptations. If takes many thousands of years for languages and human social systems to differentiate into distinct groups. This shows that natural human existence offered stability over long periods of time and that warfare and tumult were not characteristic. When one views the intricacies of adaptation of the San in the Kalahari or the Inuit of the far north, it is apparent that the huge body of knowledge that enables these human cultures to adapt to such extremes was cultured over immense lengths of time.

The rainforest regions are considered by most people knowledgeable in the subject, to be the womb of organic life. Here light, temperature and moisture conditions have produced dense and complex patterns of life. Catherine Caulfield in her book *In The Rainforest*, explains that,

"Between 40 and 50 percent of all types of living things —as many as five million species of plants, animals, and insects, —live in tropical rainforests, though they cover less than 2 percent of the globe.... Tropical forests contain from 20 to 86 species of trees per acre, whereas a temperate forest has only about 4 tree species per acre. The forests of the North American

Temperate zone have fewer than 400 species of trees.... Mount Makiliang, a forested volcano in the Philippines has more woody plant species than all of the United States. Tiny Panama has as many plant species as the whole continent of Europe." [1]

The rainforest is also considered to be the womb of the human species. Many of the last remaining examples of our ancient human family exist in rainforest environments. These cultural groups have worked out intricate balances with the life around them. Many of them combine planting, gathering and hunting in their way of life. These cultural forms are without doubt the oldest and the most sophisticated on the planet in terms of their biological survival value, the ultimate test. Natural culture people live in a materially simple environment. Their food and shelter needs are simple and the tools that they need to accomplish this are few. This is especially true of nomadic people who would obviously keep any materials to a minimum because they would have to transport them. Transporting heavy loads of household goods, when the materials to create them existed everywhere would simply not make sense. This same functionalism applied to gaining food. Natural cultures sought food in the simplest way they could. They were not ideologically wed to hunting, gathering or planting but would use whatever was most efficient in any ecosystem. The White Mountain Apaches of the present State of Arizona, for example, were basically gatherer/hunters but they would plant at times, and they could be keen planters. On occasion a clan or larger group would stay in one area for a whole season to raise a crop. Others would return on the migratory gathering cycle to combine both gains. At other times seeds would be planted in certain areas from which harvests could be obtained when the group cycled back on the gathering route. In some seasons, in some ecosystems, planting would be more efficient than migrating. In some years of the climatic cycle, planting could be more efficient than hunting. Among the Jicarilla Apaches who formerly lived in the area of present northeastern New Mexico, there were band divisions who lived in two different ecosystems. The Olleros lived out on the edges of the Great Plains and were adapted to the herbivores there, the migratory herds. The Llaneros lived in the foothills and upper elevations of the Sangre de Cristo range. These groups would come together periodically, especially at fall harvest to share the gain of the seasons. In this way the bounty of a number of ecosystems circulated through the tribe.

We have some examples still remaining of highly complex rainforest acculturations that combined planting, gathering and hunting. Catherine Caulfield reports that:

"Ed Price, an agricultural economist who works for the International Rice Research Institute in the Philippines, spent three years with small farmers in a village called Cale, in Batangas Province. Cale was not in the really steep and difficult highlands; it was more rolling hills, but there was no irrigation. In three years he identified more than 160 different crops and crop combinations grown by those farmers. They performed more than one hundred different technical operations. Whereas if you talk to a year-round irrigated rice farmer, he grows probably only one or two varieties of rice. And you can certainly number on two hands every operation he does to those crops. Its very simple, cut and dried.

"But then, if you leap to tribal peoples in the hills, the agriculture is even more complex. They know the names of far more plants, and they grow far more plants. Their pest control strategies are more complex and their planting and harvesting timetables more finely tuned. They are more aware of wildlife in general. Forest species are one of their resources. In fact that is one of the distinguishing features of tribal people, that they depend partly on the forest itself for what they need. They forage, collect resin, gums, rattan, in addition to growing rice and other crops."

Caulfield gives an example of another tribal people who have the characteristic complex knowledge of their environment; "The Hanunoo people of the Philippines are hunter-gatherers who divide the plants in their territory into 1,600 categories, although botanists can only distinguish 1,200 species."[2]

One might say that natural human culture grew organically upon the life of the earth much like the culture of the willow family, opuntia or mountain lion. It fit into the energy pathways of the earth life much as an organ fits into a body. Human culture became part of the energy web of the living planet. The wisdom of Natural human culture is demonstrated by the endurance of the human family's adaptation over millions of years.

Culture is an Energy Code

All culture, even empire culture, contains an energy code. It informs the individual about what one eats, how one gains shelter and how one uses the materials of the earth for culturally important purposes. There is that part of the cultural knowledge that has to do with the practical everyday functions such as cooking, hunting and housekeeping. In a larger context there is the consideration of the environment and the culturally important stories, the myths and legends connected with it. This aspect of culture usually involves ceremonies and rituals having to do with such things as the seasons, the growth of life and the hunt. The encompassing cultural context is the cosmology. This framework of ideas is called by many names, myth, legend, story, religion and so forth. It gives an account of how material/immaterial creation came to be and what its purpose and meanings are- and the meanings of the human lives and destiny within it. This is the creation myth that sets the framework for that which has value and meaning. Human culture has an organic being of its own independent of any individual member of the cultural group. The culture and its teachings is the effective means by which the individual members maintain life. The culture sustains itself over time, though a succession of individuals are born and die within it. Culture is a body of knowledge, a framework of ideas, a thought form, held in the consciousness of individuals. The ideational thought form of culture is reflected in the material world. This reflection is the knowledge of how to build an atl-atl, bow and arrow or how to gather the acorns, leach out the acids and make them into a nutritious foodstuff. Culture teaches identity- one's place in the food-chains, the biological energy pathways of the earth no less than the cultures of the willow varieties allow their adaptation to many environmental conditions.

The culture of humans and certain other mammals, we know without dispute, is held in conscious memory and we are suggesting that the culture of other biological forms results from morphic resonance. Life forms are a psycho-biological phenomenon. Culture, whether it is plant, mammal or the culture of any biological form, is an organic and natural part of the life of the earth. Even in the case of the culture of empire it is organic, however pathological. Culture is part of the planetary life. It is not simply a human creation for humans. Many types of animals have an individually transmitted culture. That is, the culture is transmitted to them by parents or older individuals of that family of beings. Most are familiar with the story of the baby lions that are taken from their parents at birth. Growing up with humans, the lions adapt somewhat to human culture but they do not learn their own. Therefore they cannot simply be let loose in the wilds or they will die. Specifically, they do not know how to hunt nor what to hunt, as this knowledge is taught to them by their parents in nature. This phenomenon can be seen in mountain lions, bears, primates and many other animals that humans capture for pets. In the natural world each species carries an immaterial, ideational, thought form. The thought form is the energy code of the species life, or tribal life, that "informs" by generational transmission, the individual of its energy code of adaptation and survival. From the rainforests, the womb of humans and their culture, people ventured out onto the grassy plains and beyond. As they moved, their adaptation became refined to areas as difficult as the arctic and the Kalahari. The wisdom of adaptation allowed them to survive. Human cultural forms experienced diverse florescence. In many tribes, song, dance, ritual, and oral literature became so rich that specialists were needed to learn the many parts and many persons would be required in order to contain and transmit the whole tribal cultural form. In a world of living beauty, culture developed to the rich level of some Native American tribes who had specific songs for most daily activities and certainly for all important cycles of one's life. To the bird songs and the wolves' howl was added the richness of human culture.

In the remnants of Australian aboriginal culture or the existing Pueblo culture of the southwest U.S., as well as many other surviving tribal groups, we see beautiful and elaborate ceremony dramatizing the life of the earth in cultural form. The themes of ceremony relate directly to the living reality of the earth and cosmos. In Pueblo culture there is the buffalo dance, the green corn dance, the deer dance and so forth. In Australian aboriginal culture there are equally complex rituals related, as are the Pueblos, to participating with the creative force in the natural cycles of existence. Until the time of empire, human culture grew out of the living earth. Cultural ceremony was the living earth in human dramatization. The living earth was its habitat, its home. Culture was a holographic thought form held in the consciousness of individual humans. This form was a reflection and re-presentation of the life of the earth, which is itself a reflection of the effect of cosmic forces, i.e., all of the energy forces that have resulted in the planet earth being what it is and where it is and the solar, magnetic, atomic and other forces that sustain its being.

Human Culture is the Womb that Bears the Individual

Just as local conditions in the Solar body have created the environment for our type of life to be born on the planet earth, human culture creates what we are. But we are not products of human culture simply, we are the result of the efforts of life's adaptation since the first cell. In our being is contained the memory of an ancient past. Each of us in our embryonic development pass through stages that begin with the most ancient fish and end with our full development. Each human embryo at the initial stages closely resembles that of a fish. A little later in development at the point where the fish embryo is developing gills, our embryo also develops folds which if not differentiated further would be gills. As all the vertebrate species embryos develop they recapitulate the line of origin. As their embryos near maturity each continues on to form its individual species' differentiation but in the first few weeks of life the embryos of all vertebrates are nearly indistinguishable.

The habits of the first cell continue through space and time as transformations of form and substance until a human baby is born. At that point the baby is bonded to the mother and to the earth, as Joseph Chilton Pearce points out in *Magical Child*. The phases of bonding that Pearce describes involve being secure and bonded with, for example, the mother, while exploring the world and then being secure and bonded with the mother and earth while exploring oneself. This is the way that the thought-form of culture functions also. The Solar body is the womb in which the earth grows as the cell grows within the conditions of the earth. The manifesting culture of organic life bears human culture and it finally bears the individual. In each step one is born within the other as if in a womb. From culture the individual learns identity and reality-view.

In tribal society there is a kind of individualism and paradoxically there is an understanding and acceptance of the interdependence of the human family and tribe. Jamake Highwater speaks of these unities of individual, tribe and cosmos. He explains:

"In tribal religions there is no salvation apart from the continuance of the tribe itself because the existence of the individual presupposes the existence of the community. Every element of tribal experience is necessarily understood as part of the largest meaning of life insofar as life...does not exist without the tribe which gives animation to its members. Yet the deviations of the individual are taken for granted because each person is part of the whole.

"It is through relationships that Native Americans comprehend themselves. Such relationships are richly orchestrated, as we have already seen, by elaborations of languages and ritual activities. Underlying the identity of the tribe and the experience of personality in the individual is the sacred sense of place that provides the whole group with its centeredness. The Indian individual is spiritually interdependent upon the language, folk history, ritualism, and geographical sacredness of his or her whole people. Relationships between members of families, bands, clans and other tribal groups are defined and intensified through relational and generational language rather than through personal names, which are considered to be sacred and private to the individual. The relatedness of the individual and the tribe extends outward beyond the family, band or clan to include all things of the world. Thus nothing exists in isolation. Individualism does not presuppose autonomy, alienation, or isolation. And freedom is not the right to express yourself but the far more fundamental right to be yourself."[3]

The realism of tribal society is that individual humans do not simply fall out of the sky but that each individual exists and in fact becomes what they are because of relationships to larger bodies of life both human and non-human.

The Birthright of Identity

Every human child should have the right to be culturally informed of who, what and where they are. To know that they are the most recent of an immensely long history of biological form and that biological form is a vast interrelated system of life. What the nature of biological form is and where it is in terms of location in a bioregion, continent and planet should be the beginnings of education. Children are entitled to know the true organic reality.

In Natural culture people were conditioned as children by the living world within which they existed. The elders took them out onto the earth and pointed out how the various species lived, because first, this was survival knowledge. This also meant that they were being conditioned with a reality view that was based in the truth of the cosmic pattern of life. Conditioning of consciousness is not a negative occurrence, this is how we learn. The argument is with civilized conditioning. It is that it is self-injuring and ultimately suicidal.

The spirit's task in the material world is the manipulation of energies. The adaptation of various forms of life to the interrelated system of organic reality leads to their success and maturity. Power is endurance, to be able to continue existence. This power is created by successful adaptation to the flows of energy of the cosmos. When human cultures offer the platform information-identity that enables them to endure for hundreds of thousands of years, then individual and group creativity can be sponsored beyond that firm basis.

The Morality of the Cell (Our Ancestor)

Adaptation and cooperation are the premier standards of behavior of the cells. The principles of life's functioning are a cooperative energy flow. Shared energies, transformation, diversity-unity, balance, creativity, adaptability and relationship are patterns of life and also can be called the morality of life. Life in all its forms stretching from the cell to the human tribe have followed this general functioning, this value system of life. As the culture of empire has erupted within the life system there has been a tension between the natural system of morality- this natural wisdom of life- and the diseased morality of empire. The various religions of empire represent, in a broad way, the resurgence of life habits (morality) into the imperial arena, opposing the dominant trends of empire. Through the history of empire there has existed a tension between the basic life perpetuating morality of the cells and the life defeating morality of empire. Though the pathology of empire has increased geometrically, the life morality continues to exert itself in the positive values imbedded in religion, charitable agencies, nature preservation groups, and some social ideologies. The tension exists also in each of us as the whisperings of the cells tell us the positive impulses such as kindness, helpfulness, cooperation while the structure of the social system of empire forces us toward self advancement, cynicism and cruelty at the expense of other Beings.

NOTES

1   Quoted in <u>Friends of the Trees 1988 International Green Front Report</u>.
     May, 1988. Friends of the Trees, P.O. Box 1466, Chelan, Washington
     98816. p.32.
2   <u>In the Rainforest</u>. Catherine Caulfield. Alfred A. Knopf pub. New
     York. 1985. p. 130.
3   <u>The Primal Mind</u>. Jamake Highwater. Harper & Row. 1981. pp.
     171,172.

CHAPTER 15

THE LIFE OF THE TRIBE

Flow, balance and cycle had been the basis of human experience for eons, until the present civilization arose. For several million years, humans were primarily nomadic gatherer/hunters, flowing with the seasons and the game. When the fruits ripened in the valleys, they went there. When the berries ripened in the mountains, they gathered them. Generally, they maintained a somewhat fixed migration route within their territories which followed the seasons of the food sources. Even on the islands in oceans, foods changed according to the seasonal shifts of ocean currents and the different species of life each brought. Experience of reality flowed with the cycles of the seasons. Social life flowed in cycle also. Social rituals were timed with cycles of star movement, seasons, birth and death, and fluctuations in food abundance. People saw the cycle of birth, maturity, marriage, old age and dissolution of each individual but also saw that the integrity of the tribe and the body of knowledge of the tribe endured over time, as the individual people flowed through it. The purpose here is not to look at all of the interesting variants of human culture around the earth but to observe the general and basic pattern which allowed humans to survive over such a long period of time, and then to investigate what suddenly happened that put people in the extreme situation in which they are now. There were and still are habits and practices of Natural culture people that are offensive to animal rights activists, to liberal intellectuals, to religious conservatives and many others of present day empire culture. This often leads people to reject wholesale any useful knowledge aboriginal cultures offer. So that these statements are clear, it is necessary to clarify that resuming forager/hunter culture intact is not necessarily being advocated. The immediate problem is the apocalypse of civilization. This has come about because the culture is out of balance. The first task is to learn how humans can endure on earth. The effort is to look at examples of our ancestors who had a sustainable culture so that ideas may gained of how we can create a new culture of balance. Cannibals and headhunters lived in balance with the earth, this is what the focus is, not necessarily their dietary habits. With the same respect, because empire has produced such monstrous suffering on the earth, this does not mean that throughout the course of civilization, methods, artifacts, understandings, and practices have not been created that are of great value, now and in the future. None of this should distract from our basic search which is first, to understand how to live in balance. This is the test to which any plan or method must be submitted. First it must be asked- does this add or detract from ecological balance?

Living in Harmony

Prior to their absorption by empire culture, an unimaginably rich variety of human Natural cultures circled the earth, each reflecting in its unique cultural consciousness the complexity and magic of life on Earth. The Natural cultures and divisions were cultivated over eons of time. Primal, or Natural peoples —those who exist in harmony and stability with the cycles of the Natural life— generally experience a deep subconscious sense of psychic security that is based in the Natural abundance of the earth ecologies. Rarely do they experience scarcity. Food is all around them.

Primal societies tend to be egalitarian, non-coercive, and non-hierarchical. The tribal culture of the human family did not have jails and police. In tribal society there was generally some form of consensus government operating, some kind of common agreement before actions are taken. In many tribes no action is taken unless everyone agrees. A tribe is a group of cooperating people, any one of whom could, ultimately, go off alone and still survive. Yet the culture of the tribe holds them together.

The food and shelter needs of Natural people are simple and the tools that they need are few. Rather, the wealth of tribal cultures is non-material. The human relationships are rich, the relationships with the surrounding living things are complex, and the learned culture including the oral literature is vast.

The Tukano: A Primal Adaptation

Anthropologists studying the remaining primal cultures of the earth have discovered numerous tribal cosmologies and world-views. In the mid-1960's, anthropologist Gerardo Reichel-Dolmatoff, of the Universidad de los Andes in Bogota, Columbia, studied an intact tribe in Amazonia who call themselves Wirá —"wind", or, Wirá- pora —"sons of the wind." They are part of a larger, linguistically-related group known as the Tukano, which probably numbers no more than a few thousand people. This tribe is an excellent cultural group to examine because the pattern of social and ecological balance is so explicit in the culture, rather than implicit as many other Natural cultural systems are. Reichel-Dolmatoff has had the alertness to see the ecological implications of Tukano culture. Prior to the present ecological crisis anthropologists tended not to recognize such concerns.

The Wirá/Tukano live in the northwest part of the Amazonian rainforest in Colombia, near the border of Brazil. The Wirá territory borders the Rio Vaupés on the north and east, which is also the Brazilian/Colombian border in that locality.

The Tukano homeland is a diversified ecosystem which includes hilly uplands, some grassy savanna with sparsely scattered trees, and some tropical forest in its lower elevations. The Wirá live in large communal shelters called malocas, each of which houses an extended family made up of four to eight nuclear families. These shelters are widely scattered over the tribal lands. Part of the group subsistence is from horticulture that is practiced in small clearings. Manioc in its numerous strains is the most important staple. Plantain, banana, yams, pineapple, chili peppers and maize is grown, although maize is of minor importance in this area. Cotton and tobacco are also grown. Reichel-Dolmatoff lists thirteen edible fruits which the Tukano gather from the area. They also gather a large number of wild foods, medicines and materials from the ecosystem.

The Tukano hunt mostly small animals and birds and take an occasional deer, peccary and tapir as well. The environment of the Tukano is just on the edge of the deep Amazon forest and Reichel-Dolmatoff states that the edible species are not as abundant or diverse as in the deep forest but foraging is certainly important. The Tukano fish the plentiful rivers of their homeland; symbols related to fishing play an important part in their culture. The Tukanos' deep knowledge of the life of their homeland indicates that they have been in this location for a very long time. Every feature of the landscape is alive with symbolic meaning for the Tukano, passed down to them from their ancestors. The Tukano area is sparsely populated but they are bordered on all sides by other tribes. Reichel-Dolmatoff does not mention any conflicts between the Tukano and neighboring tribes.

The Tukano believe that the creative force of the universe, the Sun-Father, continually creates a limited number of plant and animal beings. His energy causes plants to grow and bear fruit, and animals to grow and to bear young. His masculine power continually energizes and gives form to a feminine world. His energy illumines and creates on both biological and spiritual levels. The energy of the universe is limited, as determined by the creativity of the Sun-Father. This energy flows in a circuit through all beings, between people, animals and plants, between tribal society and Nature.[1]

The Tukano perceive their universe as a giant flow system whose ability to produce energy is directly related to the amount of energy that it receives. They believe that an important way that humans can energize the system is to conserve, or repress, sexual energy. The "conserved" sexual energy returns directly to the total energy available to the whole of existence, enhancing its vitality. Human health and well-being, attained by controlling the consumption of food, also creates an energy input to the system. The energy of human well-being influences the stars, the weather, and other components of the system which are neither plants or animals but spirit forms. A fundamental tenet of Tukano cultural instruction is that human beings should never disturb the equilibrium of the finite flow system, but should return whatever energy they remove from the system as soon as possible. For example, when an animal is killed or when a crop is harvested the energy of the local fauna and flora is thought to be diminished; however, as soon as the game or fruit are eaten by humans, the energy is conserved, because the consumers of the food thus acquire the reproductive life force that previously belonged to the animal or plant.[2]

The matter of ecological, social and personal balance is a major focus of the culture. Reichel-Dolmatoff writes:

"This cosmological model of a system which constantly requires rebalancing in the form of inputs of energy retrieved by individual effort, constitutes a religious proposition which is ultimately connected with the social and economic organization of the group. In this way, the general balance of energy flow becomes a religious objective in which native ecological concepts play a dominant organizational role. To understand the structure and functioning of the ecosystem becomes therefore a vital task to the Tukano. It follows that the Indian's ethnobiological knowledge of the Natural environment is not casual and is not something he assimilates through gradually increasing familiarity and repeated sense experience; it is a structured, disciplined knowledge which is based upon a long tradition of enquiry and which is acquired of necessity as part of his intellectual equipment for biological and cultural survival."[3]

In the Tukano view, the goal of life and of the human activities and attitudes is to assure the biological and cultural continuity of Tukano society. "This goal can only be achieved by a system of strict reciprocity in all relationships that man establishes in the biosphere, be they in the framework of his own society or with the animals."[4] They believe that Tukano society will prosper only if all other life forms are able to prosper and to manifest according to the needs of each species.

Three important practices help to maintain balance within Tukano society, and between the Tukano and their environment. These are: population control, control of the exploitation of the Natural environment and the control of human aggression.

Population control is maintained by oral, herbal contraceptives, long nursing periods, abstinence, and by abandonment of the aged and infirm. Because food and sex are so closely related in ecological symbolism, control of conception is quite well regulated. The Tukano are fully aware of the balances between their population and the carrying capacity of the land area that they occupy.

The medicine people of the tribe, called payé regulate human impact on the environment and act to control social aggression. Illness is considered by the Tukano to be caused by personal, cultural and/or ecological imbalances. Such imbalances might include overhunting, waste of resources, or meddling with certain types of sexual energy discharge. The shaman, in dealing with individual illnesses, is concerned with individual behavior, and with cultural practices. An important function of the shaman is to communicate with the Spirit Beings who watch over the animals and the world of plants. As the shamans carry out their duties, they function as ecological guides. Whether the subject is encouraging cooperation or controlling aggression, the hunting of game, planting of fields or considering whether to move the village periodically to preserve the ecology, the shaman, through divinatory means, decides the issue.

Using mind-expanding vegetable substances to aid in communication with the Spirit Beings and with the deep consciousness of individuals or species of plants or animals, the shamans work to balance supra-individual social and ecological structures that have been disturbed by the sick person or by the tribe. The Tukano concept of the flow of life energy, appears generally to correspond to the prana of the Hindus, the chi of the Chinese acupuncturist, Wilhelm Reich's orgone energy, or the kurunba life essence of the Australian aborigines. To divine the flow of the life energy, the shaman goes into a divinatory trance:

"To the shaman it is therefore of the essence to diagnose correctly the causes of the illness, to identify the exact quality of the inadequate relationship (to be adultery, overhunting, or any other over-indulgence or waste), and then to redress the balance by communicating with the spirits and by establishing reconciliatory contacts with the game animals. To mention just one example of how a diagnosis is established: a man who has killed too many animals of a certain species will appear in the shaman's dream or trance states in the shape of that animal and the image will be accompanied by a certain luminosity, a certain degree of light. It is quite remarkable that differences in high or low light intensity are recognised to be very important in the flow of solar energy, as understood by the Tukano, and that shamans will mention in their spells and incantations up to seven shades of 'yellow light' that energize the biosphere."[5]

The Tukano observation of the Natural world has aided them in maintaining a culture of sustainability and equilibrium. They exhibit very little interest in acquiring the type of new knowledge which would aid them in exploiting their environment for short-term gain, or in obtaining more food or supplies than they actually need. "But," writes Reichel-Dolmatoff:

"There is always a great deal of interest in accumulating more factual knowledge about biological reality and, above all, about knowing what the physical world requires from man. This knowledge, the Indians believe, is essential for survival because man must bring himself into conformity with nature if he wants to exist as part of nature's unity, and must fit his demands to nature's availabilities.

"Animal behavior is of greatest interest to the Indians because it often constitutes a model for what is possible in terms of successful adaptation.... The Indians have a detailed knowledge of such aspects as seasonal variation and microdistributions of the animal and plant species of their habitat. They have a good understanding of ecological communities, of the behavior of social insects, of bird flocks, the organization of fish runs, and other forms of collective behavior. Such phenomena as parasitism, symbiosis, commensalism and other relationships between co-occurring species have been well observed by them and are pointed out as possible methods of adaptation."[6]

The Tukano, like many native cultures in the western hemisphere, believe that the world is running down, deteriorating since its time of initiation. To assist the universe in re-creating itself and in maintaining its vitality, the Tukano regularly participate in ritual ceremonies where past, present and future generations are joined together. These rituals, in which plant and animal spirits are also believed to participate, appear to reinforce the motivation of each Tukano tribe member to walk in balance on the Earth.

Today, the Tukano world of perpetual balance is evaporating. Shell Oil company is exploring and drilling in the area. The land and rivers are becoming poisoned by oil and by the toxic chemicals used in the drilling process. Settlers from other parts of Columbia are being encouraged by the Columbian government to settle in the region, in order to relieve the population pressures within other areas of the country and to secure the remote border against possible Brazilian expansionism. The settlers and the oil workers continually assault and kill the Tukano, and push them off their lands. The Tukano/Wira' have also been assailed by missionaries, particularly by priests of the Monfortian Congregation of Dutch Catholics, the Catholic Order of San Xavier. Recently the (protestant) New Tribes Mission and the (protestant) Summer Institute of Linguistics have moved in. Their base of operations is the "Bible Belt" of the southern U.S. They focus on destroying tribal culture. By destroying tribal communalism and other elements which they describe as "primitivism," they hope to lead the natives into "the free enterprise economy."[7]

Peace With the Earth

It is important that we look at the emotional content of culture. We live in a culture of muted desperation. We are inculcated with a grasping nature because of the competitive basis of the culture and because of the arranged scarcity. In contrast, the emotional tenor of many forager/hunter cultures was distinctly peaceful and emotionally positive. A small, blonde woman named Florinda Donner, for example, went to live recently with the Yanomami tribe of the Amazon. She met an elderly woman at a trading post who agreed to guide her through the rainforest to the tribe's location. In her book *Shabono* she details her pleasant time with that tribe. In this case as well as many others, we see the inversion of the images we have been conditioned with. Here a lone woman joins a "savage" tribe and stays a lengthy period without receiving a scratch. Had she simply walked through the seamier parts of any large "civilized" city her safety could not be nearly as secure.

Part of the emotional security of our Natural culture was no doubt due to its holism. Rather than live in a narrow, "mentalized" social world, in that culture people lived in the universe, so to speak. The earth, the sky, the stars were the context of their life and they accepted and identified with them all. Natural culture teaches that we are an integral part of all life. Black Elk, Holy Man of the Oglala (Sioux), who shares in a line of inheritance unbroken since the Pleistocene and beyond, states this viewpoint. He speaks of a "threefold peace" which he says, is the only true peace:

"The first peace, which was the most important, is that which comes with the souls of men when they realize their relationship, their oneness, with the universe and all its Powers, and when they realize that at the center of the universe dwells Wakan-Tanka, and that this center is really everywhere, it is within each of us. This is the real Peace, and the others are but reflections of this. The second peace is that which is made between two individuals, and the third is that which is made between two nations. But above all you should understand that there can never be peace between nations until there is first known that true peace which, as I have often said, is within the souls of men."

This cultural understanding that we are children of the universe is extremely important. With the realization and acceptance of this fact comes maturity and responsibility to oneself and to the cosmos. One heritage of early culture is consideration for other life forms. The Apaches of the Southwestern U.S. would not kill animals at water holes because it was unfair, since all beings need water. When the !Kung San (Bushmen) of the Kalahari find a clutch of ostrich eggs, they take only part of them out of respect for the ostrich. Examples like these are numerous in reports about Natural culture people. The sharing, the cooperativeness, the wisdom and understanding- the concern for that which is outside of self- are attributes of self governing human maturity. In 1977, the traditional elders of the Six Nations Iroquois Confederacy, the Hau de no sau nee, issued a statement appealing to the United Nations for help in maintaining their identity in the face of the continued destruction of their culture by U.S. and Canadian society. In the statement, later published under the title, *The Hau de no sau nee Address to the Western World,* they describe their past prior to the invasion of empire culture. The former abundance of their lives is evident. Many points of correspondence with Tukano thought emerge from the Hau de no sau nee statement as well. Clearly, reverence for life and cooperation among tribal members were seen to assure continued abundance:

"We were a people of a great forest. That forest was a source of great wealth. It was a place in which was to be found huge hardwoods and an almost unimaginable abundance and variety of nuts, berries, roots, and herbs. In addition to these, the rivers teamed with fish and the forest and its meadows abounded with game. It was, in fact, a kind of Utopia, a place where no one went hungry, a place where the people were happy and healthy.

"Our traditions were such that we were careful not to allow our populations to rise to numbers that would overtax the other forms of life. We practiced strict forms of conservation. Our culture is based on a principle that directs us to constantly think about the welfare of seven generations into the future. To this end, our people took only as many animals as were needed to meet our needs. Not until the arrival of the colonists did the wholesale slaughter of animals occur.

"We feel that many people will be confused when we say that ours is a Way of Life, and that our economy cannot be separated from the many aspects of our culture. Our economy is unlike that of Western peoples. We believe that all things in the world were created by what the English language forces us to call 'Spiritual Beings,' including one that we call the Great Creator. All things in this world belong to the Creator and the spirits of the world. We also believe that we are required to honor these beings, in respect of the gift of life.

"In accordance with our ways, we are required to hold many kinds of feasts and ceremonies which can best be described as 'give-aways.' It is said that among our people, our leaders, those whom the Anglo people insist on calling 'chiefs,' are the poorest among us. By the laws of our culture, our leaders are both political and spiritual leaders. They are leaders of many ceremonies which require the distribution of great wealth. As spiritual/political leaders, they provide a kind of economic conduit. To become a political leader, a person is required to be a spiritual leader, and to become a spiritual leader a person must be extraordinarily generous in terms of material goods.

"Our basic economic unit is the family. The means of distribution, aside from simple trade, consists of a kind of spiritual tradition manifested in the functions of the religious/civil leaders in a highly complex religious, governmental, and social structure.

"The Hau de no sau nee have no concept of private property. This concept would be a contradiction to a people who believe that the Earth belongs to the Creator. Property is an idea by which people can be excluded from having access to lands, or other means of producing a livelihood. That idea would destroy our culture, which requires that every individual live in service to the Spiritual Ways and the People. That idea (property) would produce slavery. The acceptance of the idea of property would produce leaders whose functions would favor excluding people from access to property, and they would cease to perform their functions as leaders of our societies and distributors of goods.

"Before the colonists came, we had no consciousness about a concept of commodities. Everything, even the things we make, belong to the Creators of Life and are to be returned ceremonially, and in reality, to the owners. Our people live a simple life, one unencumbered by the need of endless material commodities. The fact that their needs are few means that all the peoples' needs are easily met. It is also true that our means of distribution is an eminently fair process, one in which all of the people share in all of the material wealth all of the time.

"Our Domestic Mode of Production has a number of definitions which are culturally specific. Our peoples' economy requires a community of people and is not intended to define an economy based on the self-sufficient nuclear family. Some modern economists estimate that in most parts of the world, the isolated nuclear family cannot produce enough to survive in a Domestic Mode of Production.

Ours was a wealthy society. No one suffered from want. All had the right to food, clothing, and shelter. All shared in the bounty of the spiritual ceremonies and the Natural World. No one stood in any material relationship of power over anyone else. No one could deny anyone access to the things they needed. All in all, before the colonists came, ours was a beautiful and rewarding Way of Life." [8]

When Europeans first arrived on this continent, Hau de no sau nee territory covered the land from Vermont to Ohio and from Quebec to Tennessee. There were hundreds of Indian camps throughout this region. This culture functioned under a constitution called the "Great Law of Peace." *The Hau de no sau nee Address to the Western World*, describes this body of law as, "a law which recognized that vertical hierarchy creates conflicts...They dedicated the superbly complex organization of their society to function to prevent the rise internally of hierarchy."[9]

This governing form was the inspiration for the concepts of separation of powers and checks and balances, found in the United States constitution, concepts which have now spread throughout the world. The Address states that, "It is the oldest functioning document in the world which has contained a recognition of the freedoms the Western democracies recently claim as their own: the freedom of speech, freedom of religion, and the rights of women to participate in government."[10] The "checks and balances" constitution of the United States has the express purpose of controlling centralized authority. The ideas for the structure of it were taken from the Iroquois Confederacy of the northeast U.S. The Six Nations Confederacy as it is also called is made up of the Mohawk, Oneida, Cayuga, Seneca, Onondaga and Tuscarora tribes. Originally there were five tribes in the confederation and their symbol was the eagle with five arrows wrapped in hide in its claws. This is the symbol that appears on back of the U.S. one dollar bill, where the eagle has 13 arrows wrapped, denoting the original colonies. At the time the U.S. constitution was promulgated it was seen by the world as a tremendous advance in "civilization," because relatively speaking it limited the power of the emperor/elite and provided representation of the people in a structure of parliamentary democracy. Though "civilization" has not arrived at the purity of democracy or the culture of the Six Nations and their "Great Law of Peace," the constitution of the Six Nations exemplifies the Natural culture tradition of control of hierarchy as worked out by these tribes. The "Great Law of Peace" also reflected gender balance that empire culture has not yet attained. Within the structure of the Six Nations were womens' councils that were an equal part of considerations. In addition to this, Clan Mothers were very powerful and in many cases held advisory powers with respect to council decisions that were close to what parliamentarians would consider a veto.[11]

Non-Hierarchal Self-Government of Natural Societies

The enterprise of the cells reaches a high level of organization and coordination of energies- power. This communal power appears to function with common agreement of the cells and without central command, as far as their own functioning. In tribal society there is generally consensus government, some kind of common agreement before actions are taken. This seems obvious on the face of it when there is a group of cooperating people, any one of whom could, ultimately, go off alone and still survive. In the imperial inversion, control is paramount. The control begins with the feeding base, e.g., agriculture or herding. One does not gather what is there, one controls the system of fertility extortion. In the same way, the hierarchy of social power controls the productive power of the human masses and their food supply with physical coercion-some kind of militarized force with the ultimate power to kill.

Mark Twain is reported to have said, "Tell me where you get your corn pone and I'll tell you what your opinions are." This is reasonable in civilized society but in forager society, most of the people except the very young and the aged can feed themselves by their own efforts- they ate what they found. When the culture of stasis broke out, the sedentary society was located in one place and social hierarchies determined the allocation of land and they determined who was to eat, what they ate and how much, because of the elite control of the mass. In Natural human culture with emphasis on relationship and cooperation, there is the ability to satisfy human needs (food-shelter-love). Power is latent in the ability of the tribe to cooperate and work together for its continuance. Power is also latent in the respect for elders' knowledge and wisdom. The youth do not know because they do not have experience. The elders do know, they have lived through the experiences. In the hunt, in foraging, in personal relationships, the youth respect and listen to the elders because that is how they have always learned since infancy. Wisdom is an extremely important factor in Natural human culture. Wisdom leads to authority. But, even though there is authority and respect there is no centralized power or coercion. Power in the tribe lies with each person; it is not centralized. It is not the power of the one to compel the many. It is the power created by the many working together. The

French anthropologist, Pierre Clastres has explored this question of "political structure" in Natural human society. What he has determined is that tribal society in the Americas, where he studied, are arranged so as to prevent centralized power from arising just as the Hau de no sau nee state. In the South American native societies which he examines, there is a titular chief, one who speaks for the tribe.

When the imperial mind encountered the Natural culture it immediately concluded that chiefs equalled emperors. Not so, says Clastres. Chiefs were the way that Natural culture prevented the formation of centralized power, the way that they controlled hierarchy. By setting up the chief as the leader and then preventing the chief from having dictatorial power, Natural culture protected itself and protected the freedom of everyone involved from the extortion of dictatorial, centralized power. Clastres says:

"Given their political organization, most Indian societies of America are distinguished by their sense of democracy and taste for equality. The first explorers of Brazil and the ethnographers who came after often emphasized the fact that the most notable characteristic of the Indian chief consists of his almost complete lack of authority; among these people the political function appears barely differentiated. Though it is scattered and inadequate, the documentation we have lends support to that vivid impression of democracy common to all those who studied American societies.... It is the lack of social stratification and the authority of power that should be stressed as the distinguishing features of the political organization of the majority of Indian societies. Some of them, such as the Ona and the Yahgan of Tierra del Fuego, do not even possess the institution of chieftainship; and it is said of the Jivaro that their language has no term for the chief.

To a mind shaped by cultures in which political power is endowed with real might, the distinctive rule of the American chieftainship is asserted in paradoxical fashion. Just what is this power that is deprived of its own exercise? What is it that defines the chief, since he lacks authority? And one might soon be tempted, yielding to the temptation of a more or less conscious evolutionism, to conclude that political power in these societies is epiphenomenal, that their archaism prevents them from creating a genuine political form. However, to solve the problem in this fashion compels one to frame it again in a different way: from where does this institution without "substance" derive its strength to endure? For what needs to be understood is the bizarre persistence of a 'power' that is practically powerless, of a chieftainship without authority, of a function operating in a void.[12]

In a text written in 1948, R. Lowie, analyzing the distinctive features of the type of chief alluded to above, labeled by him titular chief, isolates three essential traits of the Indian leader. These traits recur throughout the two Americas, making it possible to grasp them as the necessary conditions of power in those areas:

(1.) The chief is a 'peacemaker': he is the group's moderating agency, a fact borne out by the frequent division of power into civil and military.

(2.) He must be generous with his possessions, and cannot allow himself, without betraying his office, to reject the incessant demands of those under his 'administration.'

(3.) Only a good orator can become chief.[13]

This pattern of triple qualification indispensable to the holder of the political office is, in all probability, equally valid for both North and South American societies. First of all, it is truly remarkable that the features of the chieftainship stand in strong contrast to one another in time of war and in time of peace. While often the leadership of the group is assumed by two different individuals. Among the Cubeo, for instance, or among the tribes of the Orinoco, there exists a civil power and a military power. During military expeditions the war chief commands a substantial amount of power- at times absolute- over the group of warriors. But once peace is restored the war chief loses all his power. The model of coercive power is adopted, therefore, only in exceptional circumstances when the group faces an external threat. But the conjunction of power and coercion ends as soon as the group returns to its normal internal life. ...Normal civil power, based on the consensus omnium and not on constraint, is thus profoundly peaceful and its function is 'pacification': the chief is responsible for maintaining peace and harmony in the group. He must appease quarrels and settle disputes- not by employing force he does not possess and which would not be acknowledged in any case, but by relying solely on the strength of his prestige, his fairness, and his verbal ability. More than a judge who passes sentence, he is an arbiter who seeks to reconcile. The chief can do nothing to prevent a dispute from turning into a feud if he fails to effect a reconciliation of the contending parties. That plainly reveals the disjunction between power and coercion.

"The second characteristic of the Indian chieftainship- generosity- appears to be more than a duty: it is a bondage. Ethnologists have observed that among the most varied peoples of South America this obligation to give, to which the chief is bound, is experienced by the Indians as a kind of right to subject him to a continuous looting. And if the unfortunate leader tries to check this flight of gifts, he is immediately shorn of all prestige and power."[14]

Clastres makes another interesting observation of the dynamic of sharing and its highly regarded value in Natural society. He observes that when polygamy occurs, it is usually confined to the Chief and sometimes also the principal leaders, who by the cultural definition, share the most. The women, who are the real, and recognized, productive strength of the group, produce much of the material which the leaders give out. Thus, in a sense the group places a number of powerful, productive women in place with the chief and receives gifts from the Whole institution of chieftainship.

Clastres continues:

"Besides this extraordinary penchant for the chief's possessions, the Indians place a high value on his words: talent as a speaker is both a condition and instrument of political power. There are many tribes in which every day, either at dawn or sunset, the chief must gratify the people of his group with an edifying discourse. Every day the Pilaga, Sherente, and Tupinamba chiefs exhort their people to abide by tradition. It is not an accident that the gist of their discourse is closely connected to their function as 'peacemaker.' No doubt the chief is sometimes a voice preaching in the wilderness: the Toba of the Chaco or the Trumai of the upper Xingu often ignore the discourse of their leader, who thus speaks in an atmosphere of general indifference. But this should not hide from us the Indian's love of the spoken word: a Chiriguano explained the accession of a woman to the office of chief by saying: 'Her father taught her the art of speaking.' "15

"Humble in scope, the chief's functions are controlled nonetheless by public opinion. A planner of the group's economic and ceremonial activities, the leader possesses no decision-making power; he is never certain that his 'orders' will be carried out. This permanent fragility of a power unceasingly contested imparts its <u>tonality</u> to the exercise of the office: the power of the chief depends on the good will of the group. It thus becomes easy to understand the direct interest the chief has in maintaining peace: the outbreak of a crisis that would destroy internal harmony calls for the intervention of power, but simultaneously gives rise to that <u>intention</u> to contest which the chief has not the means to overcome."16

As Clastres indicates, there are occasions when the chief cannot successfully mediate disputes among the group. When this happens, anthropologists indicate, tribal groups generally solve this by fission. The group splits apart. There is no battle for the centralized power, because there is no centralized power.

These observations apply to the basic patterns of Natural human culture. There are of course permutations of the patterns of Natural human culture, but we are making observations of the basic outlines of the bulk of Natural human family and not the permutations such as for example the "Kings" of some African groups, the Andean Inca society or, for example, some societies in which castes and rampant human slavery have broken out.

The Essene Community: An Example of an Integrative Womb

Becoming personally integrated and balanced with the earth and cosmos does not necessarily mean duplicating forager /hunters, though they present immediate and sound examples. The point is to live in balance in an integrated way, on all levels. The culture of the Essenes provides an example that shows that the individual can become integrated and that human culture can be created that is in balance with the life of the earth. The point is that in the Essene culture balance is fundamental for the person and the cultural group. The fundamental requirement for the Essene or the Tukano culture to be perpetually viable on the earth, is that it exist in balance. The Essenes, until they were destroyed by the Roman Empire, created this accomplishment from around 300 B.C. to 100 A.D. The Essenes were not a tribe or an ethnic group. They were monastic communities that existed in Egypt and the Mid-East. The Essenes were mostly Jews who lived apart and did not participate in the mainstream culture other than deriving some of their philosophy from ancient Jewish teachings. They lived in the desert, but usually near bodies of water, such as small lakes or streams. They gained their food through unique forms of desert agriculture.

We know of the Essenes from the writings of Josephus Flavius, a contemporary Jewish historian and political figure in the Roman government, from Philo, the Alexandrian philosopher and writer, and the writings of Plinius the Elder, the Roman Naturalist. We also know of the Essenes from references in the Dead Sea Scrolls that were found in Qumran near the Dead Sea. Some of these scrolls contain copies of early books of the Christian bible which contain references to the Essenes, but which in later centuries were excised by the Church.

A contemporary scholar and linguist who has provided much information about the Essenes is Edmond Bordeaux Székely. There are three groups of Essene documents that he was able to translate from the original Aramaic language. One of these sets was held by the Royal House of Hapsburg in Austria, another was held in the library of the Vatican and the other set were the Dead Sea Scrolls, written in Aramaic. It is unknown how the Vatican obtained its Essene documents which are stored there along with many other unique "art" treasures. The Hapsburg texts are thought to have been brought out of Central Asia in the Tenth Century by Nestorian priests who were fleeing persecution.

The Essenes were accomplished horticulturalists and arboculturalists. Székely says that each one of them carried a small trowel with which to do gardening and to scoop up any organic material in the area for the compost. Healing had great emphasis in Essene communities and members often would travel into villages to do healings. As a spiritual community, the Essenes maintained an orderly day that was structured toward raising consciousness. They lived a simple, regular life, close to the earth with their gardens and orchards.

The information that Edmond Bordeaux Székely provides indicates that the culture of the monastic communities was directed toward centering and balancing the individual and community. The Essenes maintained a daily focus on cosmic, terrestrial and personal integration. The Essenes believed that they and everything in the cosmos existed in a pattern of energies which they consciously sought to integrate with. Székely says that, "They had the deep wisdom to understand that these forces were sources of energy, knowledge and harmony by which man can transform his organism into a more and more sensitive instrument to receive and consciously utilize the forces. The characteristics of each one of the different forces was very clear to them and they knew what the force meant in each individual's life and how it should be utilized."[17] Because of the work of Székely and others we know the form of the Essene practices but unfortunately there is no full written record of the esoteric teachings that amplified and gave substance to that form. We do know, according to Shékely's work, that the framework of these different forces was set out in a series of seven morning and evening meditations, which also included noontime "peace" meditations. Székely says that there were three immediate objectives in this practice. "The first is to make man conscious of the activities of the different forces and forms of energy which surround him and perpetually flow toward him from nature and the cosmos. The second is to make him aware of the organs and centers within his being which can receive these currents of energy. The third is to establish a connection between the organs and centers and their corresponding forces so as to absorb, control and utilize each current."[18]

The morning communions were concerned with the visible terrestrial realm of energies. The series of daily contemplations were food, topsoil, trees, beauty, sunrise, blood-rivers-water, and breath. Each of these meditations focused on a broad concept. For example the Thursday morning meditation was called the Angel of water and the concept was the liquidity of blood, rivers and so forth. The force involved is that of circulation which exists throughout the cosmos. It was the thinking of the Essenes that the day would begin with the seed thoughts and contemplations which then would be with them until evening as they dealt with the material world. At mid-day the Essenes focused on peace contemplations. The evening meditations were devoted to more ethereal concepts. The evening communions of the Essenes prepared the individual to utilize a different dimension of consciousness. As Székely says, modern life with its tension and lack of peacefulness results in the sleep state and dreaming being primarily a time to emotionally "detoxify" from the events in the waking state. The Essenes on the other hand lived isolated in very peaceful conditions and they used the sleep state as a constructive and creative faculty. Székely says, "The Essenes knew that these last thoughts influenced the subconscious mind throughout the night, and that the evening communions therefore put the subconscious into contact with the storehouse of superior cosmic forces. They knew that sleep can thus become a source of deepest knowledge."[19]

The evening communions were devoted to forces of the invisible realms that had correspondence with the terrestrial force that had been the subject of the morning communion. The subjects of the evening communions were the eternal life, creative work, peace, power, love, wisdom and the creative universal spirit. The Essenes, until they were destroyed by the Roman Empire, created this accomplishment of balanced community and won the admiration of the early historians mentioned. Josephus and the other historians referred to them variously as, " 'A race by themselves, more remarkable than any other in the world,'" "'the oldest of the initiates, receiving their teaching from Central Asia,'" and "'teaching perpetuated through an immense space of ages.' "[20]

Integrating Ourselves and the New Culture

Love holds the world together. In our Natural state we are at one with the world. We are at one with our social environment, the clan and we are at one with ourselves. It is the flow of love- positive energy, that holds this together. This is the condition that we will create in our new culture. This is the condition that our children are entitled to as their birthright on the earth. This is the baseline condition that all humans are entitled to as they begin to create their own personal lives.

Extensive studies have shown the profound effect of experiences in early childhood that carry down through the generational lines. Children who have been beaten will beat their own children. Children who have been sexually abused will be sexually abusive. The manner in which children are dealt with will condition them for the balance of their lives. This in itself is enough reason for us to establish a healing community. In a larger context, it is the lack of love and comforting atmosphere that ingrains the fear and separation that is the motor of civilization.

In our own lives it is our fear and defensiveness that we must deal with in pursuing our own wholeness, our integration. We have been conditioned into separation and contraction. Wilhelm Reich's image of the expansive phase of the body, reaching out to the world, is appropriate. It is this condition that we need move toward. Our cultural upbringing teaches us to emphasize the intellect at the expense of our emotional body. In universities across civilization, the pressure is such that students jump from the windows of the dormitories when their intellectual achievement does not meet the standards that are set up for them. Our conditioning is such that when confronted by stress, the intellect churns but the atrophied emotional body cannot respond. We are unable to respond in a holistic way because we are conditioned into fear and separation. We have learned to perceive the world and other people as a source of threat.

This conditioning is not immutable. We can cause this conditioning to evaporate by focusing the conscious mind upon it. This must be done with the concentration and vigor of the whole being. The subconscious mind holds the whole of our experience. In the familiar story of the person in a hypnotic trance state, they can remember an experience that occurred many years before and they can recall the ticking of a clock, the smells, the emotional response of that moment. Our actual conscious awareness is profound but it is filtered through the surface conscious mind which sorts out and holds in surface consciousness only that which the surface consciousness defines as important. It is in our subconscious mind, the less than fully conscious realm of mind, where the basic assumptions about our existence are held. These assumptions and conclusions of the subconscious are the groundwork of our present lives.

There are two ways in which this "posture" toward life is created. The first is simply repetition. This is the same thing as acculturation. In the field of hypnosis this is done in light trance and the suggestion is given over and over. (A trance is simply a concentrated state of attention such as one adopts when watching television or sitting in a classroom). In a classroom there is the conscious flow of events, the teacher teaches and the children respond, but there is also the emotional context that the mind perceives. That is, the competition between the students. Each is eager to receive the exclusive rewards by getting their hand up first, by having the right answer. This sets the framework of the mind to readily accept suggestions from the teacher. The suggestion in this case is the content of teaching, which is accepted uncritically. The suggestion is also the social context in which this occurs. This goes on day after day, for years. It is not any particular interaction that sets the tone for the subconscious mind, it is the emotional experience of the constant competitive, separative environment that conditions the subconscious mind. This repetition conditions the mind to view the world as an environment containing competitive threats. This in turn limits our ability to be open, loving and trusting adults. Birth trauma, family conditions, television images, school experiences, all serve to establish our basic subconscious grounding.

In the field of hypnosis there is also a second way to suggest assumptions about reality to the subconscious mind. This is done in deep trance. A deep trance is a highly concentrated state of attention. In this state the intellectual body and the emotional body are functioning in a unity and the yes/no critical faculty of surface consciousness is not functioning. In this state the being is not fragmented consciously but is completely in deep consciousness. This is the state in which early childhood trauma causes the subconscious mind to have deeply set assumptions about reality.

The birth experience is the first and most fundamental experience that we integrate into our being. Negative and self limiting suggestions as well as the positive and bonding suggestions can be easily accepted by the subconscious mind at this early point. As Arthur Janov began to work with people who had experienced birth trauma he developed a therapy that involves conscious recall of the trauma. To recall the trauma and understand it as an adult in another, more benign context, changes the subconscious mind's understanding of the event and helps dissolve the blockage of positive emotional energy and enhances the feeling of well-being. This is the key element in dealing with subconscious assumptions. They must be brought up to consciousness, relived and the effect eliminated by present understanding. In Janov's therapy, patients recall the primal event of birth. The following is an example of a primal experience of one of Janov's patients:

> "I had lost the fight at birth and felt totally defeated. Life was against me. I felt I had no control over what was happening to me. During this Primal I felt like I was being jostled about by different people. I was very scared. I'm not sure what the feelings were all about, since there were no scenes or images in my mind. But I would hazard to guess it was the doctor and nurses handling me after birth. "I felt so alone. I cried for help. Where is someone to see how much I hurt? I even felt angry that they could be so stupid to see my crying and screaming and just let me go on doing it. I just wanted someone to hold me gently and let me calm down. Then I felt I didn't want anyone to touch me if it was going to be rough."[21]

It is this type of "reliving" of primal events that allows the person to resolve a contraction that may have prevented the person from having emotionally rich relationships with other people for a lifetime.

The subconscious mind accepts deep suggestions throughout life but particulary it accepts suggestions in youth, before the personality is thoroughly armored and in a defensive posture. The accepting of a suggestion by the subconscious mind requires a highly emotional state, a state brought on by accident, punishment, fear or other emotional trauma. This is the sudden acceptance of deep suggestion as opposed to conditioning by repetition.

The subconscious assumptions not only configure one's view of reality but actively guide the daily life. If one has accepted a self limiting suggestion such, "You're no good, you'll never amount to anything," during a spanking, for example, the subconscious mind will ensure that the suggestion will be carried out. People that constantly repeat self-limiting suggestions such as, "I never could do that," "I was never any good at that," "I'll never be able to learn that," "No one likes me," are repeating and reinforcing subconscious suggestions which the subconscious mind will endeavor to carry out in their daily lives.

With considerable effort these self-limiting assumptions and contractions can be eliminated, but first we need to gain an image for ourselves as being centered on the earth, centered in cosmic reality.

That we are organic beings, living in community with other organic beings on the surface of the planet earth is not always clear to individuals in civilization. We need personal experience of this, personal images of this reality. If we go to a wilderness area or the most undisturbed Natural area that we can find, we will be immersed in, and receive stimulus from the Natural life. This is the place where we can become grounded. We may not become immediately integrated with the Natural life the first time, but we will be with the proper images, sights, smells, Natural sounds and feelings.

In a Natural area we can concentrate or meditate on our roots and origin in life. We can consciously open ourselves to any possible communication from that life. We go there with intent. Our intent is to use that time to focus on the reality of our being. We understand that we are organic beings just as the birds and the trees and that this is our home and is where we belong. This is our corporeal identity. We begin to identify with the Natural life. Given the present chaos in society and the many diversions, it may not be easy to get to a quiet, undamaged Natural area often, but it is essential. It is essential to have that experience and to gather those images into memory. This is the grounding, the realization- not just intellectually held -that one is a Natural organism, on the surface of the earth, itself which is flying through space among other large bodies such as sun, moon, planets and stars. Healing from the injury of alienation is not dependent on the cleverness of the technique but on the deep-seated intent of the person. This is because the ideas and feelings that were produced from the original conditioning influences are also deep-seated. The imprints from the original conditionings are stamped into the subconscious mind as general understandings and postures of feeling. The subconscious mind is in the realm of the vegetative mind that operates the body, keeping the body in a state of homeostasis. The intellectual mind might change itself every day but the subconscious mind receives the constant repetition of ideas and other conditioning stimuluses- over a life-time. It is this mind that develops the basic emotional posture of the being.

The experience of empire culture is to live in an abstracted manner. If one goes to the industrial medicine establishment for medical care one is dealt with on the chemical level by molecular biologists. This has no effect on peoples' life problems or their emotional health. We live at the level of our feelings. How we feel about ourselves, how we feel about the world is the state of our health. It is at this key level of the subconscious mind that the first healing must be brought about.

The direction of healing is toward healthy and Natural energy flows for the inhibited and contracted organism. In the mid-twentieth century a large body of healing knowledge has arisen which seeks to unlock the flow of vital energies.

Acupuncture, acupressure massage, shiatsu, Janov's primal therapy, hypnosis, rebirthing, Reichian massage, reflexology and many others deal with blockages of energy flows. Mental blocks, emotional blockages and physical blockages of energy are involved. This field of medicine is now called Alternative Medicine in the United States. Many of the modalities can be learned easily through workshops and seminars given in most major cities. A vast literature is also now available at many bookstores. One of these typical modalities, for example, Reichian massage, deals with both mental blocks and their location as mild cramps and zones of tension in the musculature. Reichian work has its roots in Freudian analysis and it uses this mental-analytical technique but also heavily relies on massage to help loosen and eliminate the actual body armor- areas in the body where tension is held. When the mental and physical blocks are released a phenomena occurs that the Reichian therapists call "streamings." These streamings are spasms of energy releases of the body accompanied by shuddering and definite emotional release.

As we begin to create new culture we must integrate knowledges and methods into the cultural form that address these problems of blockage of positive energy. In emerging from the disaster of civilization we understand that we have all been injured by the experience of its acculturation. New culture needs to have the qualities of a therapeutic community to assist the adults as they begin moving toward emotional healing and toward the full enjoyment of life. As we begin moving toward health, maturity and reality we will begin taking responsibility for our own lives-cosmically speaking-and responsibility for our home, the earth.

The Security of Children in the Extended Family

In Natural human culture the relational language of family identity, that is, what you call mother, father, uncles and aunts is much more diffuse than in the more atomized relationships of civilization. Often all of the mother's sisters are referred to as "mother." The same situation often obtained with the identification of the father. In a broad sense the young are looked upon as children of the tribe.

The task of raising the children was also a diffuse activity. The grandparents often participated more in raising the children than the biological parents. In some cultures the siblings of the parents had responsibilities in instruction of the children in certain areas, just as the "chief" or sometimes the shaman had responsibilities of orating the cultural traditions.

In this diffuse manner of social relationships direct coercive authority was not emphasized. Children when they engaged in disapproved behavior were usually shunned and then rewarded with affection when they engaged in approved behavior. Nonetheless the social situation of children was of a different quality than in modern industrial society families. Children were looked upon differently, they were valued and they performed valued tasks in the family from the time that they could understand. The children's work was appreciated and the children understood that they had a legitimate and needed place. This is a contrast with the situation of children in industrial society that have no more functional purpose than a pet poodle. It is apparent to the youth of industrial society that they have no functional purpose to their families (other than possibly taking out the trash or mowing the lawn). This childhood tends to reinforce the feeling that life is meaningless. Their real legitimacy is as workers in the production system. When they get a job and generate money, then they become legitimate persons and escape their dependency status.

While the teaching of the young in industrial society is done by the mass institutions of television and school, in Natural culture, ordinarily, much energy is devoted to the teaching of young people. As the young people work alongside the adults they learn all of the voluminous skills needed to transform significant items of the Natural environment into human uses. In these cultures children were taught who they are, what it means to be a human and what the nature of humans is. In the book *Seven Arrows*, Hyemeyohsts Storm kindly shares with us the type of sophisticated teaching that U.S. northern plains culture contained. In this teaching of the Medicine Wheel, the child learns of the foundation of human action; wisdom, innocence, trust, feelings, introspection, illumination and understanding. The possibilities and problems of wars, hate, love, greed, generosity and loneliness are pointed out.[22] In the Native American cultures that emphasize the Medicine Wheel as well as many other Natural cultures, voluminous teaching stories exist. Because of the style of life, the adults and youth are together and there is plenty of time for the transmission of human culture through the teaching stories and other means. These functions in Natural culture help the children learn what to expect in life and to learn the meaning of their personal experiences. In modern society this type of teaching is rarely offered a child.

In recreating human culture we will need to consciously create, in the first generation at least, groups of people who can stay together as "family." In the human past many different types of marriage and family arrangements have been created. Today the bulk of the world's people live in some kind of multiple person, marriage arrangement. Unfortunately, at this time most of these exist in patriarchal societies, none the less, group marriage has been common through human history.

Clans will be created, marriages will occur and group marriage should not be ruled out. Many severe social pathologies manifest in the present shrivelled nuclear family. The problems of control, dominance/submission and emotional dependency occur in the nuclear family. In group marriage these patterns cannot so easily endure. Group marriage causes people to be more mature, faces them with the responsibility for their actions in co-equal association where one person cannot control another and one person usually does not develop addictive emotional dependency on one other person.

Awareness is Power

It is not difficult to understand that the interests of our ancestor, the cell, is the same as the interests of each human child, each human adult, the whole of human society, the whole of the ecosystem, the whole of Gaia and the cosmos. To establish more potentiative relationships and to become more conscious of self and other is the standard. For the life-form to rest in the stable diversity of its organic niche, to potentiate that diversity and for conscious awareness to increase- is to gain power. The awareness of what one is and the context one exists in, increases the chances of enduring and increases Being. If all levels are congruent- cell, micro-organism, fish, plant, animal, human, human society, ecosystem and Gaia- then empowerment takes place. In a cosmic context, humans cannot empower themselves at the expense of the other life that supports them. For humans to truly empower themselves they must also empower Gaia.

How is this to be done? It is to be done by establishing human cultural form such that by its "housekeeping" life activities, potentiates the biological life and by its internal dynamics, potentiates that culture itself and the Being of each individual of that culture. The culture must be created so that this effort is inherent in the cultural awareness and dynamics. This is what basing the culture on the simple principles of life means. If the principles are followed, the potentiation of life will flow from that, just as when the principles of the Inversion are followed, ultimate extinction results.

Reality Conditioning

Conditioning is fundamental to the cosmos. Everything is conditioned by other cycles of energy, just as the metabolism of energy of the Sun conditions the life of the earth. Conditioning in the mental realm functions such that when first presented with an idea (such as the erroneous, imperial idea that power is simply the ability to force others or the world to bend to our desires), it is fresh and new, but by the repeated exposure to the idea it is accepted by the intellectual mind and slips below the level of conscious inspection and becomes part of our subconscious "world view." Once this occurs and that idea slips in with other complementary sets of ideas, then we do not consciously think about it- we simply know that it is right. It is through this lens of complementary ideas that we perceive the world and insist that we are seeing "reality."

When the baby mountain lion is born, its conditioning begins to predominate with conditioning from its elders. The baby mountain lion is conditioned with the facts and reality of its identity- what it is and how a being of its nature behaves, what it eats and how it socializes with other mountain lions. A human baby in Natural culture undergoes a similar conditioning with relationship to its nature and to the Natural world. We cannot escape conditioning- but we can become aware of it. As we nurture the children into their birthright, ideally we are providing them with the knowledge and conditioning of their organic identity. This must be the baseline starting point or otherwise the conflict with the cosmic cycles of energy will not allow them to endure. Conditioning into our organic identity will also create the mental image of the principles of life's behavior which organic culture will also follow. Because New culture will exist in a natural, living environment, this becomes the larger context of conditioning. Natural, non-pathological culture is an organic phenomenon. Humans become what they are conditioned to be, according to the ideas and images of the existing culture. Our healing culture needs be patterned on the true organic identity and to provide the image for further creative group development. It needs to convey the image of what the nature of human is, rather than declensing the possibilities of our lives. This needs to include all of our relations and our faculties and abilities, both physical and psychic. We humans who have conscious choice of our cultural form have the opportunity and ability to creatively potentiate our being. Out of the disintegration and crisis on the earth we may awaken enough <u>now</u> to grasp the opportunity to create the new, to create a culture in which the conditioning is conscious and we are conscious of the choice of conditioning.

Our identity is the cosmos, the same as the cell in the liver is us. We are also an interactive part of the solar being, Gaia, the bioregion, the tribe and we are the person of the physical body. While we are a fraction of the culture of our tribe, we are also individuals.

The simple principles of the behavior of life are our path. If we are in those bounds, whatever we do we will be on the path. We will develop relationship, more energy, more being, more unique individual diversity and so forth as we mimic life's pattern of beauty, ecstacy and complexity. This means that we must be severed from the conditioning of empire and its culture. That is not to say that we must fear it but that we need a firm grip on organic reality and a healthy sense of what conditioning itself is.

Certainly the amplification of our being, as taught to the children will begin with our perceptive faculties, our faculties of awareness. Awareness is power, consciousness is power. Our heightened awareness increases our power to endure and to cooperate with the cosmic project of life. The awareness to adapt efficiently to the life of the earth is power. The degree of awareness, increases that ability, that power.

Each of us have the senses of sight, hearing, touch, emotion and intellect that aid us in perception of objective reality (and our internal subjective reality). Each of these senses has a further refinement that is normally atrophied in civilization and not always emphasized in Natural cultures. With the sense of vision, there occurs clairvoyance. With the sense of hearing there is clairaudience (hearing on spiritual planes). With the sense of touch there is the faculty of clairsenscience (hunches of "feeling" of some reality not perceived by the physical senses). There is also the faculty of mental telepathy. There is the capacity of foreknowledge, knowing a thing that will happen before it occurs. There is the faculty of divination, finding answers to questions through non-intellectual means. Associated with this ability is the capacity that can be called dowsing for want of a better English word. This is an extremely important faculty to develop not only for locating the water veins in the earth and understanding one's place in that way but for dowsing many other earth energies in one's place so one begins to understand the functioning of the body of Gaia as a living being.

As the practice of acupuncture allows the practitioner to assist the beneficial movements of energies in the human body, the activities of the geomancer who dowses and understands the Gaian energy flows of her watershed is very important to the activity of integrating human activities with the life of the earth.

This is part of the womb function of culture. The pattern of culture should emphasize the cultivation of these natural abilities of the human tribe.

Communication is Relationship

We who are the life of the earth are increasing our Being. Our nature as humans allows us to amplify and potentiate what now lies dormant, waiting to unfold. Like the unused capacity of our brains, there are other potential abilities that can be cultivated. The clarity and strength of our communication is one of those. Communication is conscious relationship and also energy relationship. Communication at a telepathic level with the other beings we live with will amplify the experience of life. This is a distinct possibility of future cultural creation. The planetary life has put humans, whales, dolphins and elephants in one similar niche. They have great ability to form images and to communicate them. Because of the fold of the frontal lobes of the brain, we species are particularly suited toward complex communication. The little we know about interspecies communication in Natural culture suggests that communication with other species enjoys a long tradition.

Communication between humans on a verbal level uses the tool of language. Language reflects the focus of attention of the culture. In the language of the Inuit of the far north it is said there are more than thirty descriptive words for snow, its different conditions. In the ancient language of the Greeks there were many descriptive words for love, the various qualities of its manifestation. Language- semantics, carries the culture and becomes a tool of thought. In that respect, as we learn languages we learn the cultural nuances. In creating a new cultural form we need create new language appropriate to that cultural perception.

We find that in English as well as many other languages of civilization there is much confusion. In many cases similar sounds mean different things, different word sounds mean the same thing. Language, as we know it, is indistinct. To add to this we are now coming into the age of double-speak in which elites employ psychological operations and media manipulation teams to confuse and disinform the masses.

An example of the type of linguistic pattern that we need has been discovered by John W. Weilgart. Weilgart who had a thorough background in linguistics, psychology and philosophy experienced a revelation. In this revelation the seed ideas of a new type of human language occurred to him. 'aUI' is the name of this language. It is not the type of language that we are accustomed to. Abstract symbols like letters do not denote or connote abstract meanings. Instead there are a set of thirty-one basic symbols that reflect the basic intuitive realities of our existence. These are such things as space, movement, light, human, life, time, matter, sound, feeling, round, equal, inside, quantity, quality and so forth. Out of these basic categories thoughts are put together intuitively and analogically. The symbols for each of these categories is congruent with their meaning such that 'inside' is a circle with a dot inside of it. Feeling is a heart shaped symbol and active is a lightening shaped symbol. Next, Weilgart created the sounds for each symbol so that the sound is intuitively similar to the meaning such that the sound for inside is a guttural sound coming from deep inside the throat. The way that the thoughts are combined can be shown by the abstract thought-meaning-symbol-sound; anticipation. In aUI this becomes fore-feeling and it uses the heart symbol for feeling with the symbol for before in front of it. Weilgart has also created a sign language in which the arms and upper torso form the symbols. This provides an additional level of congruence of meaning for each symbol.

Dr. Richard S. Hanson, Professor of Ancient Near Eastern Languages at Harvard University says that:

> "In discovering aUI, Prof. Weilgart had discovered something of the nature of language in its primitive state and something essential about human communication at its beginning stages. This 'language of space' is not a concocted language like esperanto. It is a rediscovery of the basic categories of human thought and expression.
>
> To semantic theorists this should be most interesting. By working with basic categories of meaning and a simple set of aural and visual symbols for each, Prof. Weilgart has succeeded in making language definitive rather than merely denotive or conative. Basic categories are communicated through single symbols and new concepts are created by merely combining the basic symbols by way of a simple, intuitive logic. The result is language which has the simplicity of archaic speech plus the sophistication of modern thought."[23]

There are a number of cultures known to modern anthropology that use several languages within the culture. Among the Apaches of Southern New Mexico there existed a "war language" that was only used in expeditions of war. Among other cultures there are known to have been spiritual languages, used primarily for discourse on spiritual subjects. Certainly with the creation of new culture the need for new language exists. The languages of empire carry all of those definitions of reality within it. If we use a pure language that has no emotional connotations connected with it, we will be greatly aided in creating new social reality.

aUI is so intuitive and simple that Weilgart was able to teach it to many different groups. Individuals of these diverse groups such as military servicemen, children of tribal societies, and U.S. school children were able to begin communicating in the language within a few minutes. Weilgart, among other talents, was a professor of psychology. In this capacity he used this language to facilitate communication with people classed as schizophrenic. These people, who ordinarily experience confusion in communication, were able to improve their communication significantly because of the precision and clarity of the language that they learned after a brief introduction.

The Pleasure of Life

One of the ways that the psychology of empire steals individual power is by conditioning them with the sense of their meaninglessness and inferiority, as well as the fear of pleasure. The example of the Judeo-Christian heritage, the Islamic heritage and the Confucian heritage is of the masses learning that they are unworthy, inadequate and as children in need of discipline by the religious hierarchies and the emperor/elite. Christianity particularly, after the first ten centuries of being controlled by the Roman Empire, conditions the people to believe in their "sin," their inadequacy before the Pope and emperor. Christianity historically has emphasized the benefits of suffering and the sin of pleasure. Sin originally meant "missing the mark," that is, not being with God or the transcendental consciousness. Nonetheless the hierarchy brought it around to mean the inadequacy of the "faithful" in adhering to the dictates of the hierarchy. The basic human needs are food, shelter and love. Love is the wholistic feeling of attraction and is an integrative force. It is a holding together. At the same time on a personal level it is also an expansive giving force. While "man the toolmaker" emphasizes Doing to the detriment of the content of life, we need emphasize the fulfillment of life and its pleasurable quality. Love in all its aspects as a communication of energies need be emphasized. There is no reason in our quest for amplified states of Being that we cannot acculturate the enhancement, technique and knowledge of love to a more sophisticated degree than the culture of militarism has carried the strategies of conflict. We are conditioned with the emotional plague that Wilhelm Reich calls the "pleasure anxiety." Our fearful contraction prevents our liberation. The danger of having nothing to do if we stop making machines is not real. Acculturating ways to enhance our enjoyment of life is a pleasurable task and is a legitimate focus of cultural attention. In 1927, the anthropologist Bronislaw Malinowski brought out his work, *Sex and Repression In Savage Society* and in 1929 he brought out *The Sexual Life of Savages*. These books tended to corroborate Wilhelm Reich's findings. Malinowski had the opportunity to live with a cultural group in the South Seas, on the Trobriand Islands, in a culture of relative sexual freedom. In this culture nakedness and sexual activity were accepted as a natural part of life. Children were allowed complete sexual freedom, and, in fact, huts were established for them within the villages for their games and play. The only taboo was incest and this was vigorously enforced. Malinowski reports that:

"The children initiate each other into the mysteries of sexual life in a directly practical manner at a very early age. A premature amorous existence begins among them long before they are able really to carry out the act of sex. They indulge in plays and pastimes in which they satisfy their curiosity concerning the appearance and function of the organs of generation, and incidentally receive, it would seem, a certain amount of positive pleasure. Genital manipulation and such minor perversions (sic) as oral stimulation of the organs are typical forms of this amusement. Small boys and girls are said to be frequently initiated by their somewhat older companions, who allow them to witness their own amorous dalliance. As they are untrammelled by the authority of their elders and unrestrained by any moral code, except that of specific tribal taboo, there is nothing but their degree of curiosity, of ripeness, and of 'temperament' or sensuality, to determine how much or how little they shall indulge in sexual pastimes.

The attitude of the grown-ups and even of the parents toward such infantile indulgence is either that of complete indifference or that of complacency-they find it natural, and do not see why they should scold or interfere."[24]

Malinowski found the Trobriand Islanders to be free, democratic-minded, and self-governing without compulsion. He found also a freedom from violence, theft and European types of sexual perversion, i.e., sadism, masochism, rape, prostitution, sexual incompetence and inability to respond sexually because of neurotic complications. This certainly is a radically different image of society compared to the one raised by Barbara Tuchman of the Fourteenth Century European social reality. An anthropological study of people living on the Amphlett Islands nearby provides further dramatic contrast. This group, who's origins Malinowski did not report, with its patriarchal, authoritarian family structure, displayed all the signs of the European neurotic, such as distrust, anxiety, neurosis, perversion and suicide. It is interesting to see that those tribal peoples who have slid into neuroticism, authoritarian culture, and sexual imbalance in the same pattern as the empire culture, also display the same sorts of personal dysfunctions. Although the bulk of the Pleistocene cultural inheritance favors sexual balance, those tribes who, for whatever reason, have become dominated by one sex exclusively, usually patriarchy, show problems just as does the culture of empire. Love and beauty come not by fighting for it but by surrendering to it. Reich suggests that it is the ability to surrender fully in the arms of a loved one that is the primary condition of receiving the beauty of love. A deep sense of psychic security is necessary in order to accomplish this. Nature puts her template upon the flow of Life. She shows that sharing, non-defensiveness, and cooperation are the pattern of health and sanity on the level of cellular sharing, on the level of sexual sharing—and in the spiritual realm, the road to transformation has always been said to be by the route of surrender to the creative spirit of the Cosmos. To let go. To trust the creative Life to provide. To follow the pattern of nature that is created by a higher intelligence is the path to transformation and to psychic security. It lies in following the natural pattern. The path to psychic security, security while living in motion, in transformation, in the flow of a constantly changing world, is not to react defensively against change in a vain attempt to create a static, secure environment, but to surrender, let go on every level and realize that the power of the cosmic intelligence creates, guides and sustains the world. The direction toward wholeness of self, soil and world is to generalize the sexual love from the genital point to the universe through the stages of transformation of life; cellular, self, others, the planet and the cosmos. Life then becomes wholly responsive.

We are faced with a life without a future in civilization, with fear, cynicism-the programmed helplessness- and the social pattern of isolation tugging at us. We are discouraged from forming human community and creating the future. Nonetheless we have the power to do it. That is simple. The key to the power is overcoming our estrangement from others and from the world. If we can trust each other in community, that is the power. Then it can be done. If the materialist can fly around the sky in a tin can, we can certainly create a culture of increasing beauty, awareness, communication between species, cooperation between species, and communication between humans and the larger forms such as Gaia and the beings that are Gaia's neighbors.

Healthy Culture: Glimpses From the Past

The reports of novelists and travellers often give us more of the flavor of encounters with tribal people than dry academic studies. During the period of European colonization encounters were happening around the globe. Some of these "first encounter" reports carry the amazement of the Europeans who were coming from a life in a culture of tension and negative emotion, when they encountered a radically different culture. The contrast between a healthy culture and an unhealthy culture is clear. Herman Melville provides a view of a culture in which positive feelings are prevalent from his book *Typee*. The Typee, a tribe on the Marquesa Islands, are now an almost vanished group but they were in full flower when Melville visited. About his experience, he says:

> "During my whole stay on the island I never witnessed a single quarrel, nor anything that in the slightest degree approached even to a dispute. The natives appeared to form one household, whose members were bound together by the ties of strong affection. The love of kindred I did not so much perceive, for it seemed blended in the general love; and where all were treated as brothers and sisters, it was hard to tell who were actually related to each other by blood. Let it not be supposed that I have overdrawn this picture, I have not done so."

A few early explorers have provided us with insights into the day to day lives and the emotional tenor of other Natural cultures that existed before the complete expansion of the world empire. Explorer Villialm Stefannson, writing in 1908 had the following report after living 13 months with an Eskimo family:

> "With their absolute equality of the sexes and perfect freedom of separation, a permanent union of uncongenial persons is wellnigh inconceivable. But if a couple find each other congenial enough to remain married a year or two, divorce becomes exceedingly improbable, and is

much rarer among the middle-aged than among us. People of the age of 25 and over are usually very fond of each other, and the family—when once it becomes settled—appears to be on a higher level of affection and mutual consideration than is common among us. In an Eskimo home I have never heard an unpleasant word between a man and his wife, never seen a child punished, nor an old person treated inconsiderately. Yet the household affairs are carried on in an orderly way, and the good behavior of the children is remarked by practically every traveller.

These charming qualities of the Eskimo home may be largely due to their equable disposition and the general fitness of their character for the communal relations; but it seems reasonable to give a portion of the credit to their remarkable social organization; for they live under conditions for which some of our best men are striving—conditions that with our idealists are even yet merely dreams."[25]

Obviously, not all tribal cultures have arrived at the level of positive cooperation that this report demonstrates of the Eskimos, but we can be sure on the other side of it that few imperial cultures have.

So that we may fix in our minds the fact that it is possible for humans to live on the planet without jails, nuclear war, ecological ruination, valium, and the one-dimensional artificiality of suburban-shopping center culture, let us look at another report from the same area. This report is from the famous arctic explorer Amundsen. He states:

"During the voyage of the Gjoa, we came into contact with ten different Eskimo tribes in all ... and I must state it as my firm conviction that the Eskimo living absolutely isolated from civilization of any kind are undoubtedly the happiest, healthiest, most honorable and most contented among them. It must therefore be the bounded duty of civilized nations who come into contact with the Eskimo to safeguard them against contaminating influences, and by laws and stringent regulations protect them against the many perils and evils of so-called civilization. Unless this is done they will inevitably be ruined.... My sincerest wish for our friends the Nechilli Eskimo is that Civilization may never reach them."[26]

NOTES

1   Akwesasne Notes. vol. 16, #6, Winter 1983. "Cosmology As Ecological
     Analysis: A View From The Rain Forest." G. Reichel-Dolmatoff. pp.
     22-25. (Reprinted from The Ecologist, Cornwall, England)
2   Amazonian Cosmos: The Sexual and Religious Symbolism of the
     Tukano Indians. Gerardo Reichel-Dolmatoff. University of Chicago
     Press. Chicago. 1971. p.50.
3   Akwesasne Notes, op. cit. p. 22.
4   Reichel-Dolmatoff. Amazonian Cosmos. op. cit. p. 243.
5   Akwesasne Notes. op. cit. p.24.
6   ibid. pp. 22-25.
7   The Indian Peoples of Paraguay: Their Plight and Their Prospects.
     Special Report. Cultural Survival Publications, 53A Church Street,
     Cambridge, MA. 02138. $2. (contains information on New Tribes
     Mission capture of Aché Indians in Paraguay and their incarceration
     and death in a concentration camp).

     Fishers of Men or Founders of Empire? The Wycliffe Bible Translators
     in Latin America. A U.S. Evangelical Mission in the Third World.
     Published with Zed Press. December 1982. 344 pp. $12.95. available
     from Cultural Survival at the above address. (contains references to
     activities of Summer Institute of Linguistics).

     Cultural Survival Quarterly. "Health Care Among the Culina,
     Western Amazonia." Donald K. Pollock.   vol. 12, #1, 1988. p.32.
     (Contains report of Summer Institute of Linguistics selling medicine to
     Indians- which works to force them into the money economy and assist
     the campaign against traditional medicine which they identify with
     "Satanism.")
8   A Basic Call to Consciousness: The Hau de no sau nee Address to the
     Western World. Geneva, Switzerland. Autumn, 1977. Akwesasne
     Notes. Mohawk Nation. via Rooseveltown, New York 13683.
9   ibid. p. iii.
10   ibid. p. 18.
11   The Constitution Of The Five Nations or The Iroquois Book of The
     Great Law. A.C. Parker. Iroqrafts, pub. R.R. #2, Ohsweken, Ontario,
     Canada. 1984.
12   Society Against The State. Pierre Clastres. Robert Hurley, trans. Mole

Editions, Urizen Books. New York. 1977. p. 20.

13   ibid. p. 21.

14   ibid. p. 22.

15   ibid. p. 23.

16   ibid. p. 28.

17   From Enoch To The Dead Sea Scrolls. Edmond Bordeaux Székely.
     Academy Books, pub. San Diego,CA. 1975. p. 28.

18   ibid. pp. 29,30.

19   ibid. p. 79.

20   ibid. p. 14.

21   Imprints: The Life Long Effects of the Birth Experience. Arthur Janov.
     Coward-McCann, Inc. New York. 1983. p. 45.

22   Seven Arrows. Hyemeyohsts Storm. Harper & Row. New York. 1972.

23   Cosmic Elements Of Meaning: Symbols of the Spirit's Life. Dr. John W.
     Weilgart. Cosmic Communication Co., 100 Elm Court, Decorah, Iowa
     52101. preface, p. xvii.

24   The Sexual Life of Savages; In North-Western Melanesia. Bronislaw
     Malinowski. Halcyon House. New York. 1929. pp. 55,56.

25   Civilization Its Cause and Cure and Other Essays. Edward Carpenter.
     George Allen & Unwin Ltd. pub. London. 1914. p. 81.

26   ibid. p. 82.

*

CHAPTER 16

THE RESTORATION OF THE LIFE OF
THE EARTH

Few of us initially have the luxury of simply pulling out of the culture of empire, immediately denying it our energy. There is no blame. Establishing a culture that is in balance with the earth requires the cooperation of a group of people. One cannot simply go to the mountains and be a forager/hunter, the animals are mostly gone and the wild food plants are rare. We can work for social justice, we can work toward ecological sanity but we are still living in a culture and in a pattern that is destroying the life of the earth. To be actively mobilizing toward setting up what might be called "seed" communities is the really significant action. If people don't actually get out of the money economy to a significant degree, if they don't create a new land based culture that aids the earth, all the other political and environmental efforts will ultimately be meaningless. To be actively mobilizing toward setting up seed communities is what is most significant. Movement is now happening, the seed is being empowered. That we are moving toward food growing capability, land, community, emotional positivity, healing, integration of every level possible - and toward the top of the watersheds, that is the significant action- by whatever means we have at our disposal. Of course people must resist the destruction and move ahead on all the fronts that they are normally active in, but this becomes meaningless unless cultures of balance are also established. In the last decade of the Twentieth Century there are tremendous resources available. There is much food-growing expertise available and healing techniques- both personal and social, there are libraries full of information about specific ecosystems and there are libraries of knowledge about all of the diverse ways that societies have been formed in the past. We have all of the resources that we need.

In the past several decades a great intuitive movement toward healing and integration has taken place. This has taken place with the rise of holistic health and the resurgence of interest in spiritual knowledge. This has taken place on the mental and emotional levels with all of the support groups and holistic

*Mimbres pot design from Kiva culture found on Mimbres River valley and San Francisco valley.

healing modalities that have manifest. This has also taken place with the knowledge of the physical ecology and life of the planet. Not only is conservation of primary concern, but the restoration of watersheds is beginning. No funding of "projects" has done this, no elite has organized it. It has arisen intuitively from the people in response to real needs. It is the beginnings of the decentralist answer to the contradiction of civilization. In comparison with the phantasy world of the "Golden Age" of the Nineteen Fifties it is a planetary awakening.

In the field that might be called feeding oneself and the restoration of the planetary life, a similar explosion of genius has taken place. There are now many tools and resources. The important factor is to create a practical plan that answers the question, "How do we live in balance with Nature?" This is a familiar intellectual refrain and a popular concept but the practical shape of it must be drawn and then it must be done. That first step must be taken- create the method and build the image.

The Simplicity

In order to retain our sense of reality it is necessary for us to look briefly again at where we are in our understanding of food producing, so that we can appreciate the tremendously valuable advice of the elders, even if we and the anthropologists can only glimpse the larger outlines of it. Civilized agriculture is war with the spirit of life and war with the cosmos. Agriculture is an effort to force the simplicity and unbalance of the "ten world food plants" on the cosmos. When the climax ecosystem is cleared for agriculture, the earth seeks by all means at its disposal to heal the wound. It sends in the first aid crew to revegetate the area and cover the poor oxidizing and eroding, bare soil. If life finds some unnatural abundance of exotic plants there, like soybeans or designer flowers, it calls in all of the species of fungus, micro-organisms and insects that can eat up that sickly or unnatural life and reconvert it back into the life stream. What this means is, that it takes energy to fight life which is making an effort to rebalance itself. To do this requires fertilizers, poisons, petroleum, steel mills, agricultural universities, polluted waters, dead seas and on and on. When technicians look at a swidden plot in a rainforest and compare its productivity to a farm field and talk of how the "natives" might increase the productivity of the swidden plot to "help" them achieve some surpluses to sell so that they can exist on the margins of the money economy, what we are really looking at is trying to help them get some money so that they too can help poison and kill.

Native cultures are organic formations on the earth, they are not intellectual/ideological groups. We cannot expect that they understand the moral history of the steel axe and we cannot fault them for their "absurd truthfulness" and inability to refuse the invaders statement that there is a better way than the one they have always used. The historical corruption of natural culture has not been a contest of force between two groups but simply injury to organic cultural form, the same as a climax ecosystem is deformed by the bulldozer.

A system whose purpose is to extort surpluses from the soil requires a fight against nature, usually in the form of mono-cropping, and that all important pattern of empire- simplification and control. Our interest is in an entirely different perspective, an inverse perspective. Complexity, not immediate explosions of production is desired. Stability, fertility and diversity should constantly increase. When people are released from the extortion/profit motive in agriculture then the latitude for creative abilities is released and the scope of possibilities increases tremendously.

Some hints from the elders about an inverse method of producing food will be gained. Producing food by adaptation to the balance of life is the inverse of modern agriculture. While looking at the techniques of the elders, it will be kept in mind that creating culture for ourselves that envelopes the practices that we create for our watersheds is a simultaneous necessity.

The Adaptation of the Most Ancient Ancestors: Rainforest Permaculture

In the age of the great ice sheets, much of the earth became more arid. In those times the rainforest was forced to retreat to refuge zones. One of these zones, for example, is the area of the relatively small Awa tribe, straddling the border of Colombia and Ecuador, near the coast of South America. This area, like the other "refuge zones" in other rainforests, is extremely rich in localized species, ones that came through the ice ages intact. Our human family survived through those ages with them. It is easily possible that direct ancestors of the Awa came through those times. These people and the other rainforest people are the ancient ones. It is they who have the sophistication of adaptation that reaches back toward our origins. The adaptation of rainforest peoples is as diverse as is the rainforest ecosystem itself but some patterns emerge in the adaptations of many of the tribes that will be helpful hints to us. We can consider it advice from the elders. The first and most striking thing about the rainforest peoples is their encyclopedic knowledge. D.A. Posey, a valiant anthropologist-advocate who has recently been arrested by the Brazilian government for effectively assisting the Kayapó tribe of the Amazon, says that the Kayapó gather, "Some 250 species of plants for their fruits and hundreds of others for their nuts, tubers and leaves." He and a co-worker A.B. Anderson state, in their 1983 survey, that of 140 plants in the Kayapó area, "only two were not considered useful by the Kayapó. Equally astonishing is that the Kayapó claimed to have planted approximately 85% of the plants collected in ten sample forest 'islands'."[1]

The rainforest people gather their needs from the environment. They create tools, clothing, ceremonial wear, building materials, and medicines as well as food. They collect waxes, oils, ointments, ornaments, perfumes, pigments, dyes, gums and resins, as other anthropologists have pointed out.[2]

Insects and no doubt the roe of fish are also important food sources. Animals and fish of course are primary sources of protein for some rainforest peoples and for many other tribes horticulture is a mainstay of their stability.

Many Amazonian people rely on fishing for their basic diet. But the natural people don't always just fish, they have an intricate cultural relationship with the fish tribe, physically and spiritually. The pattern of these relationships is adaptation and mutual aid. Anthropologist J. Chernela writes of the Uanano tribe of the Amazon who gather fruit eating fish which subsist from fruit that falls from trees at the banks of the rivers. This creative adaptation of fish and forest means that the forest, especially along the banks must be protected for the fish. As Chernela describes it, the Uanano understand the fish who congregate in spawning are conducting a "fruit-exchange" ceremonial dance. During this period the fish are protected by the people and are only caught when returning from the dance.

It is this sophistication of cultural understanding that gives these people their power of continuance (and it is mirrored in other rainforest-fishing cultures). Not the fact that the living habits of the fish are understood intellectually, but that this understanding is integrated in human culture, is what creates the sophistication.

The Complexity

Catherine Caufield, in her work, *In The Rainforest*, tells of the Lawa living in the rainforest of northern Thailand bordering Burma. (Now, unfortunately, according to articles in *Cultural Survival*, many of these stable rainforest tribes of the area are being assaulted by the Thailand central government for the familiar "national security" and anti-guerilla reasons.)[3] As Caufield describes them, the Lawa are shifting cultivators who live in settled villages and have been in the same place for many centuries. She states,

"They grow more than eighty food crops, plus another fifty for medicine and ceremonial and household uses. In addition, they collect and use more than two hundred wild plants that grow in their fallow fields. Their system supports about 80 people per square mile, taking fallow land into account. One square mile of cultivated land supports 625 people, a ratio that compares well with, for example, Britain, which has one square mile of agricultural land in use for every 750 people. Britain, of course imports 60 percent of the fresh fruit, 20 percent of the grain, and 23 percent of the meat its people consume, whereas the Lawa are self-sufficient in food."[4]

Caufield goes on to explain that they take great care of their land in terms of fire, soil erosion and soil disturbance. She says that anthropologist Peter Kunstadter has learned that young Lawa children can recognize 84 cultivated varieties of plants and another 16 useful uncultivated plants, "Even at the stage where the plants are less than a centimeter in size."[5]

The Lawa, powerful as their cultural adaptation is, are not the most complex culturally, according to researchers in Southeast Asia and the South Sea Islands. It is the more "primitive" tribes higher in the hills who know more plants, grow even more varieties, hunt in the natural forest and gather there. It is the complexity of the adaptation and the encyclopedia knowledge, then, which distinguishes the more powerful people.

The Cultural Survival volume, *Indigenous Peoples And Tropical Forests*, summarizes the, so far, limited observations that have been made of true rainforest food growing, called swidden. (This is distinguished from the destructive and ignorant temporary agriculture practiced by "frontier" settlers at the edge of rainforests. This practice, which is destroying rainforests is usually referred to as slash and burn.) First, the matter of soils is known precisely by most indigenous people. Soil quality is judged by the type of vegetation growing on it. It is judged by its color, taste, smell and by examining its subsoil moisture during various seasons. This means not that any one spot will be chosen for a plot but that each area is appropriate for plots according to the plants that will subsist best in that environment. The food growing regime will not necessarily involve one or several plots, but may encompass many smaller ones according to the needs. During clearing of the plots, some of the plant species may be saved. Some of the tree species may be saved also for shade, wind breaks, to attract wild animals or for later use. In the planting one does not simply sow seeds but may use seeds, seedlings, cuttings, tubers and roots. In arranging the plantings, shade, light, soil, soil moisture, companion plants, nearby trees and other considerations will indicate the creation of micro-climates within the plot. All of these combinations will be transformed according to the different ecological zones that each plot has been located in. As the plot is "feathered" into the mature forest the matter of local animals is keenly considered in terms of attracting them to the area by having plants in the locale that the animals like and utilize. The anthropologists have discovered that many plots remain in some kind of use for many years. With use, the soil and the growth of different plants in the plot changes. As the years go on, different plants are emphasized, often tending more and more toward bush and tree crops. There is mention in the literature of use of plots for 20, 30 and more years. One very important observation made by a few of the anthropologists is that this transformation from cleared plot to mature forest follows to a great extent the phases of ecological succession of the natural forest - except the tribespeople substitute useful relatives or plants of similar life habits for the plant that would ordinarily be in place during ecological succession.

As the planetary ecological crisis has deepened, anthropologist have focused their attention more clearly on the ecology of natural culture and are beginning to suggest that some "wild" rainforest environments are looking more like managed environments. Animals are attracted here and there according to the plants that are planted; the shamans of the Tukano for example, monitor the species populations and help expand or inhibit hunting. The Uanano and others work together with the fish populations. Posey adds that the

Kayapó collect forest plants and replant them near camp and near main trails. This tactic he calls 'forest fields.' He says, "They use at least 54 species of plants from these forest fields, including several types of wild manioc, three varieties of wild yams, a type of bush bean and three or more wild varieties of cupa."[6] Posey says that even now in their debilitated condition a Kayapó village may have 500 kilometers of trails that are planted and managed so that travel may go on for months at a time without resort to garden produce. Posey points to one ecological zone in which forest "islands" occur in a savanna region. When he observed the forest islands closely he perceived that they had been 75 per cent created by the Kayapó through laborious methods of upgrading of the soil environment.[7] When we consider that each of these hundreds of plant species used by the rainforest people, have individual growth habits and needs and that they have individual uses within the tribe and that they may well have individual meanings spiritually in the cultural cosmology, we are approaching some ability to conceive of the complexity with which these people live. In addition to this general over-view of swidden we should keep in mind that some rainforest ecosystems may have highly specialized adaptations such as swamp draining, types of raised beds with water channelling between them and other unique combinations of plots on highly varied ecosystems ranging from rainforest to drier savanna or higher elevations which are within a tribes' habitat.

Beyond the European Row-Crop Garden: A Look at Some Recent Methods

The practice of clearing the forest, plowing, planting, exhausting the soil and moving on has enjoyed a long history in the empire. Gardening has been often a kind of mini-scale picture of the broadscale farming system. In recent generations developments have occurred that offer differing perspectives on this standard. Civilized gardeners have always followed the cultural standard of -more!- and since the Nineteenth Century popularization of soil fertilizing in Europe, there has been the production oriented effort to grow plants faster and bigger. One might call it the "biggest pumpkin at the county fair," syndrome. Finally attention began to shift (still today only with a small but vital minority of gardeners) to food value, hardiness and other values. A milestone was set when Sir Albert Howard published his book *Soil and Health*. Howard was a colonial administrator in India in the first part of the Twentieth Century. He began to experiment with soil enrichment and composted soils. During his work with the soil, he drew the conclusion that healthy soils produce healthy plants. Healthy plants in turn produce healthy people and livestock. One of his experiments was to drive a herd of his brahman cattle to the next village, among a herd of diseased cattle to show that because of his healthy soil, they would be unharmed- and they were not. Another important point that he made was that the life system will attempt to eliminate the dross and the unhealthy. He insisted that if the plant is healthy it will not be focused on by the diseases and insects, as will sickly or exotic plants that are grown completely outside their space and time, because of their economic value. The backbone of Howard's system of nutrition was the science of composting. The creation of concentrated fertility in compost was the basis of his work. The observation that healthy soil creates healthy plants seems common sense today (except to the industrial agriculturalist) but was startling in its time. J.I. Rodale, as a young man became inspired by Howard's work and started the famous magazines *Organic Gardening* and also *Prevention*. This point of view found a ready market and Rodale and his family were able to create a remarkable institution featuring a number of associated magazines, a large research farm in Emmaus, Pennsylvania and a broad readership. While *Organic Gardening* stuck with the row-cropping and annual plants to a large extent, the focus was turned effectively to soil and health. It is because of the Rodale family and their focusing the attention of a vigorous minority of gardeners, that we are able today to save some seed strains and also introduce and test cultivars such as quinuoa, teff and grain amaranth. As large numbers of us begin turning to personal food growing, a file of old copies of *Organic Gardening* will be invaluable.

Food From Trees

Civilized people and Europeans in particular live in self created boxes, often with several trees outside and a square plot called a garden which focuses on vegetables. This comes from the civilized contraction of urban life and from the feudal farm ecology inherited from Europe in particular. Trees, tree crops and forest farming are largely left out of this picture. While the soil of row crops must be fed, trees and forests of trees build soil, pump water, provide habitat for other species and do many other services for the earth life. What we have seen is that herding and industrial agriculture are often the lowest uses of the land. Using trees as a source of sustenance and to help reforest the earth makes good sense.

The authors of *Forest Farming* offer some comparisons between food raising and agricultural commerce. The herder can get an average of 200 pounds of meat from an acre of rich land. This operation is generally a for-profit business. Although there may be no market for it in the money economy, in reality that same area of land could produce one and one-half tons of cereal grain, seven tons of apples, or 15-20 tons of flour from the pods of honey locust trees. (And the honey locust flour is superior in nutritional value to any cereal grain.)[8]

Some average yields of tree crops help illuminate these tremendous differences. Douglas and Hart, in *Forest Farming* give the yields for a few of the hundreds of tree species that yield oils, gums, nuts, fruits and many other useful items: African locust beans 10-15 tons per acre; carob, 18-20; mulberries, 8-10; persimmons, 5-7; chestnuts, 7-11; oaks 10-12; pecans, 9-11; and dates, 4-7.[9]

These authors have done a world survey of trees that can produce food for people or animals. One of the valuable effects of their studies is to show us the amazing variety of trees that are useful for survival, though they may not be useful in a "profit making" farm. Trees, aside from the reforestation imperative, offer great prospect to green culture.

The two basic texts of tree gardening are *Tree Crops - A Permanent Agriculture*, Russell J. Smith (Harcourt Brace & Co., 1929) and *Forest Farming: Towards A Solution To Problems of World Hunger and Conservation*, J. Sholto Douglas and Robert A. de J. Hart (Rodale Press, Emmaus, Pa. 1978).

Spirulina: The Sunlight and Water Food

Micro-organisms are the essential life of the earth. The numbers of them, the complexity of the roles that they play and their survival abilities make the larger forms of life that humans are accustomed to, insignificant in biological terms. Students estimate that ninety percent of the species of life on this planet cannot be seen with the human eye.

One of the recent and revolutionary developments in human food is from micro-organisms. Spirulina is a blue-green microalgae that is between 62-68% protein. Chlorella is a similar microalgae which has a protein content of 40-50%. Spirulina can be grown easily with sunlight, water and small amounts of fertilizer such as chicken manure or de-natured human excrement. Being essentially a carbon compound it can be used for food or fuel.

Yogi and philosopher, Christopher Hills has been primarily responsible for bringing this food to the hungry world population at the present time. In 1965, Hills and Dr. Hiroshi Nakamura of Japan organized the Microalgae International Union composed of nearly 150 scientists (primarily microbiologists) to do research and offer information to the world about the use of algae for human food. By the Nineteen Seventies the Microalgae Union had worked out all of the systems necessary to mass produce this potent and easily grown food. Even though the Microalgae Union had found an inexpensive and potent food that could be one of the answers to the world food problem, to their chagrin they failed in their effort to get it adopted in any serious way by the world's governments. The simple reason for the failure was that the people that profit from the existing world food production system have their power and wealth from that system and the prospect of a new food or food supplement that is potent and inexpensive is not to their liking. Nonetheless all of the bugs have already been worked out of the systems of production and it is ready to be used as a help with the problem of world starvation and it can be one more technique in our inventory of food growing.

Comparison of protein content of Spirulina and Chlorella with common foods (% in dry weight)

Spirulina	62—68
Chlorella	40—50
Soy Bean	39
Beef	18—20
Egg	18
Fish	16—18
Wheat	6—10
Rice	7
Potato	2

Amount of organic substances of Spirulina in dry weight (%)

	Spirulina	Chlorella	Soy bean
Protein	62 -- 68	40 -- 50	39
Carbohydrate	18 -- 20	10 -- 25	36
lipide	2 -- 3	10 -- 30	19
Vitamins	pro,A,B1, B2,B6,B12,C	pro,A,B1,B, nicotinic acid	B1,B2,B6

Spirulina is grown by sunlight in water that does not freeze, provided it is kept separate from other water so that other micro-organisms do not begin to grow in it. It is harvested by filtration through ordinary cloth. The reproduction rate of Spirulina is 40X per 24 hour period, therefore one ton becomes 40 tons in one day under the most optimal conditions.

Spirulina was an important staple food of the ancient Mayans and the people of Chad in Africa now gather this food from bodies of water and make it into cakes. In any survival situation this food certainly should be considered.[10]

The Ecological Health Garden

Edmond Bordeaux Székely has developed a system to produce high quality food in a small space. Székely, a farsighted, renaissance person who spoke ten modern languages and was a philologist in Sanskrit, Aramaic, Greek and Latin, also translated important Mayan Codexes. Székely authored 68 books and translated many. It was his translating of ancient Essene documents from the Aramaic that sparked his interest in health, diet and in the Essene way of life, including their agricultural practices.

Székely sets out his method in the book *The Ecological Health Garden*. His method involves four units; a compost unit, an earthworm farm unit, a germination unit and a plant unit, thus the system is partly to build soil and partly to grow plants on the healthy soil. The compost unit of course is created by any organic debris that can be collected and the earthworm farm also is fed by organic debris, producing probably the highest intensity soil fertility possible and also producing earthworms in abundance for planting in the compost and in the plant boxes. The germination unit is kept in the dark and a moist medium is used for making the seeds sprout. Ten percent of the sprouted seeds are used for planting in the plant boxes and the balance is eaten. By staggering the germination times a continuous supply of sprouts can be had. The plants, which are grown in boxes, are grown in intensely fertile soil and therefore are of the highest nutritional value. In addition to the compost heap, Székely says the earthworm unit will occupy about two square yards. The germination unit will measure one square yard and for each person about 16 square yards of planting boxes will be necessary.

The principles involved in deciding what to grow in the system are: 1. maximum nutritional value; 2. plants suitable for intensive ecological gardening; 3. personal likes and dislikes; 4. preference given to plants that can be eaten in a fresh state; and plants that cannot easily be obtained elsewhere, such as in the wild state.

One of the points that is highlighted by Széckley's system is how easily we may feed ourselves in an emergency situation. This simple system that he outlines can support life. It can be even more simple if we gather the seed of selected wild plants for sprouting.

The 'Do Nothing' Farmer

Masanobu Fukuoka is a person who has caused a stir by the publication of his book, *The One Straw Revolution,* in which he advocates and demonstrates what he calls "do nothing farming." Fukuoka began a career with the Japanese government in an agricultural related job but soon quit in frustration to return to the farm that he had inherited from his family. For 40 some years Fukuoka has been developing a system of no plow agriculture. The results of his method of growing rice equals the harvest from the traditional intensive methods of old Japan and equals the modern industrial system of rice production. He advocates no plowing, no chemical or compost fertilizer, no weeding or herbicides and no dependence on chemicals.

"In early October, before the harvest, white clover and the seeds of fast-growing varieties of winter grain are broadcast among the ripening stalks of rice. The clover and barley or rye sprout and grow an inch or two by the time the rice is ready to be harvested. During the rice harvest, the sprouted seeds are trampled by the feet of the harvesters, but recover in no time at all. When the threshing is completed, the rice straw is spread over the field.

"Between mid-November and mid-December is a good time to broadcast the pellets containing the rice seed among the young barley or rye plants, but they can also be broadcast in spring. A thin layer of chicken manure is spread over the field to help decompose the straw, and the year's planting is complete. "In May the winter grain is harvested. After threshing, all of the straw is scattered over the field.

"Water is then allowed to stand in the field for a week or ten days. This causes the weeds and clover to weaken and allows the rice to sprout up through the straw. Rain water alone is sufficient for the plants during June and July; in August fresh water is run through the field about once a week without being allowed to stand. The autumn harvest is now at hand.

"Such is the yearly cycle of rice/winter grain cultivation by the natural method. The seeding and harvesting so closely follow the natural pattern that it could be considered a natural process rather than an agricultural technique."[11]

Every year that Fukuoka has used this method his soil has grown richer because the natural cycle of feeding the soil continues. This is different than even traditional Japanese agriculture that burned the straw in former times (industrial methods are now uniformly used in Japan).

One interesting and simple trick that Fukuoka has developed is to coat the seeds of the rice and vegetables that he sows with clay, simply by mixing the seed and the clay and sifting it through a wire mesh. This prevents the chickens and birds from eating the seed when it is broadcast on the surface.

Fukuoka reclaimed some of the nearby hillsides that had been abandoned after the soil had been exhausted by farming. He hauled in ferns, straw and other organic material from higher up the mountain and hauled in rotting logs to help build up the soil. He also planted a fast growing acacia variety from Australia. These trees, being legumes, help the soil at the lower levels where the tree roots penetrate. As the mountainside had previously been clear cut, pine sprouts grew from some of the stumps. Many of these he let grow. He planted a number of varieties of fruit trees in this area and also broadcast clover seed. He says that six to ten acacias per quarter acre were enough to fertilize the deep soil and help the fruit trees which he says only once needed to have the brush and trees immediately around them cut back. On the surface soil he planted clover and the Japanese radish called daikon, a strong growing plant that will reseed itself. Fukuoka also cut back the weeds periodically with a scythe to help provide more green manure. Now, Fukuoka reports, "As a result of this thick weed/clover cover, over the past twenty years, the surface layer of the orchard soil, which had been hard red clay, has become loose, dark colored, and rich with earthworms and organic matter."[12]

Fukuoka also broadcasts many vegetable seeds as he does rice. These he places on the hillsides and between the trees in the orchard. These vegetables reseed themselves year after year and change their quality for the better, Fukuoka feels, back toward their original wild ancestors.

One of the values of Fukuoka's work is to show that by following the principles of nature one can at least equal modern industrial methods. He also demonstrates that feeding the soil is the key to healthy plants and healthy people who consume them.

He says that, "Doctors and medicine become necessary when people create a sickly environment."

In Fukuoka's natural, "do nothing" farming style, time is allowed for human pursuits. He suggests writing poetry and Haiku such as did the traditional farmers of Japan. "In caring for a quarter acre field," reports Fukuoka, "One or two people can do all the work of growing rice and winter grain in a matter of a few days."[13]

He goes on to explain that if 22 bushels (1,3000 pounds) of rice and 22 bushels of winter grain are harvested from a quarter acre field, then the field will support five to ten people, along with an hour or so per day maintaining the balance of the farm. He points out that, "If the field were turned over to pasturage, or if the grain were fed to cattle, only one person could be supported per quarter acre."[14]

Fukuoka's food growing has much to recommend it simply in its Taoist-like philosophy. He says, for example:

"The farmer became too busy when people began to investigate the world and decided that it would be 'good' if we did this or did that. All my research has been in the direction of <u>not</u> doing this or that. These thirty years have taught me that farmers would have been better off doing almost nothing at all.

"The more people do, the more society develops, the more problems arise. The increasing desolation of nature, the exhaustion of resources, the uneasiness and disintegration of the human spirit, all have been brought about by humanity's trying to accomplish something. Originally there was no reason to progress, and nothing that had to be done. We have come to the point at which there is no other way than to bring about a 'movement' not to bring anything about."[15]

European Mystic Gardening

Another method created in this century is Bio-dynamic Gardening. The foundation of the Bio-dynamic method was set out in 1924 by the German mystic, Rudolph Steiner, though it draws upon the folk tradition of Europe going back to early Indo-European days. Bio-dynamic gardening is a wholistic perspective that takes into account the movements of the planets and the earth as well as the activities of the soil and plants. In an alchemical sense it asks for the discipline of observation such that the consciousness of the gardener and the surrounding life are expanded.

Bio-dynamics too, relies heavily upon composting, but, this is a composting method with cosmic significance. Wolf D. Storl, a practitioner of the method says:

"Bio-dynamics, though not disparaging of common sense, is concerned essentially with consciousness-expansion in regard to plants, animals and soil. The attempt is made to look into the deeper spirit of nature. Out of this deeper awareness, based on exquisite observation of nature, the approach calls for <u>not</u> letting things run their natural course, but for intensifying certain natural processes (creating optimal animal populations, making special compost preparations, planting selected companion plants at certain cosmic constellations), aiding nature where she is weak after so many centuries of abuse, short-cutting destructive processes, and using human intelligence, kindness and good will to foster positive developments (planting hedges for birds, planting bee pastures, etc.). Bio-dynamics is a human service to the earth and its creatures, not just a method for increasing production or for providing healthy food."

With its emphasis of right relationship to the earth, Bio-dynamics outlines a symbolic method of thought which is applied alchemically to life and its activities. Fundamental to this are the four elements of fire, air, water and earth. These "elements" symbolize tendencies of movement and condition, such as warm, dry, moist, expansive and contractive. These tendencies are seen as basic to the way the material world functions and are used as templates of thought and analysis.

Findhorn: Communication With the Spirit of Life

Findhorn, now well known in New Age circles, is located in a transformed trailer park on the north coast of Scotland. In this cold, damp, sandy, sterile and generally inhospitable area that is farther north than Moscow, a center of energies has manifest a remarkable synthesis of people and plants. The Center was begun by a retired Royal Airforce Captain named Peter Caddy and his wife Eileen, who communicates directly with esoteric spiritual levels. The couple who were living a "normal" life, with Peter working as a hotel manager, began to experience personal and marital crises. These developed into considerable anguish and stress in their lifestyle. Both of them were ultimately reduced to a point of desperation. Eileen developed clairaudience and began to be guided by a voice. Because of their experiences, they came to depend upon the guidance and perplexed as they were, they were guided to the nondescript and forbidding piece of sandy spit that is now known as Findhorn Garden. With only a tiny pension and after some crisis, these two moved out of a fairly luxurious middle-class life, into what was really a tiny trailer house slum, and in a decade, a spiritual center was functioning whose story had spread world-wide- without these two ever having to plan or worry about where the energy would come from to manifest the vision. As they adjusted to the strange environment, a woman named Dorothy MacLean joined with them and she began to be guided by nature spirits toward garden building and this Peter carried out. The various life forms that gave guidance were given the names of the traditional culture of the area such as devas, Pan, elves, sprites, nymphs and such. The word symbols put on the consciousness of these living beings are without a doubt inherited, with modification from Celtic culture which inherited it from the pre-Indo-European cultures that built Stonehenge. The arrangements of the names of these different spirits shows the pattern of lives within lives and consciousness within consciousness. There are water sprites and "elementals," who then are also part of plants. There are names for plant species and animal species and then finally there is Pan, the spirit of the whole of Nature. Pan encompasses these other "component" spirits. The inherited language shows that people recognized life functioning within life and spirits within spirits.

The humans of Findhorn put absolute faith in the advice they received from these spirits and unusual things began to occur among the living things in the garden, things like the now legendary forty pound cabbages. The fact that the whole garden rested on what would normally be relatively sterile sea shore sand with only a few inches of compost on the surface added to the amazement. As the communication developed, trees and bushes were added to the garden and a multitude of flower varieties. As human community began to manifest around these people, the gigantism of the vegetables began to lessen, but the vitality of the living garden arrangement did not. The energy then seemed to manifest in the human community that was being created and the life energies it was manifesting.

Manifesting was one of the central themes of the community. The sense was to integrate oneself with the cosmic life, accept the guidance given as to what one should do and then expect and have absolute faith that the means to achieve that guidance would manifest.

The unique neo-tribal sharing of energies at Findhorn transcended the shallow image of rules, structure and rigid community form. Paul Hawken, a visitor to Findhorn in the mid-Nineteen Seventies says:

"Although this community grows, it does not go out and work for anything it requires. Everything here is produced by the 'law of manifestation' which is the tenet that if you are following that voice within you which is the higher consciousness common to all men, then you are 'in the right place at the right time, doing the right thing' and all of your needs will be met. Your needs— not your desires. The faith that they feel is like a rock—it is immovable. Such absolute faith can have its problems when it occasionally meets the dualistic consciousness of the confused beings who stalk the earth, and I guess that is just about everybody including me. People, sometimes a little self-righteous in their ambivalent state, are sometimes shocked by the absolutes of Findhorn. This is not a community where itinerants can wander in and by invoking their presence claim 'rights'. There is no minority view here simply because there is no majority. There are not two sides to an argument because there are no arguments. What sounds wonderful to some may sound a bit frightening to others. At Findhorn, there are no regulations, there are no orders, there are no chains of command, but there is a group constantly striving to maintain an improve their receptivity to God and each other in order to channel light and truth to Earth. So there is no rule or knowing how something will come to the community and likewise there is no planning for the 'future'—there is only the simple faith that in time all needs will be met."[16]

Another encouraging point about Findhorn is that it shows possibilities of people stepping out of civilization and being able to manifest a positive emotional environment in a group. Hawken reports:

"Unfolding at Findhorn is an environment highly conducive to the transformation of consciousness. I never heard anyone at Findhorn criticize anyone else while I was there. I repeat, during my two-week stay, I never heard a single negative word about another person. There is no set of dogmas, diets, meditative techniques, or physical exercises to aid or bring about such consciousness."[17]

In the experience of Findhorn everyone was living intensely in the 'here and now', an experience akin to being able to do what you've really wanted to do for a length of time. At Findhorn, according the Hawken, they had an explanation for this:

"It is felt here that because we concentrate so much on our 'image' of ourself, we must constantly hold ourselves in check and re-adjust either ourselves or external reality to conform to this image. Since this is essentially an energy turned in on itself, it does not renew itself easily. This leads to mental and physical fatigue, self-consciousness, lack of self-assurance, and a hindered vision of true reality.

Those who are able to release this heavy burden of 'image' and personality experience a great release of energy which was formerly used to hide and conform oneself. Findhorn provides for people, young and old, a matrix within which they can rapidly undergo this process of transformation. The energy which is released is merged with the energies which come from higher levels. The merging of these two energies creates a synergistic effect where the whole exceeds the sum of the parts. The remarkable thing about Findhorn is that so many here are living embodiments of that change, yet Findhorn lacks obvious techniques, dogmas, or religious doctrines to hasten along this process or bring it about."[18]

NOTES

1   Indigenous Peoples And Tropical Forests:Models of Land Use and
     Management from Latin America. Cultural Survival Report #27. Jason
     W. Clay. Cultural Survival Inc. pub. Cambridge, Mass. 1988. p. 5.
2   Prance, Campbell and Nelson 1977. Quoted in Indigenous Peoples And
     Tropical Rainforests. p. 5.
3   Cultural Survival Quarterly. Vol. 12, #4. 1988. "Resettlement And
     Relocation," part II.
4   In The Rainforest. Catherine Caufield. Alfred A. Knopf pub. New
     York. 1985. p. 136.
5   ibid. p. 136.
6   Clay. Indigenous Peoples And Tropical Forests. op. cit. summary from
     text. Posey quotation. p. 51.
7   ibid. p. 55.
8   Forest Farming: Toward A Solution To Problems of World Hunger and
     Conservation. J. Sholto Douglas & Robert A. de J. Hart. Rodale Press.
     Emmaus, Pa. 1978. p. 5. (nutrition p. 37).
9   Douglas & Hart. Forest Farming. op. cit. p. 5.
10   Honolulu Star Bulletin. March 29, 1972. "The Solution for Hunger Is a
     Small Matter" Jocelyn Fujii. P. B-2.
     The Mass Production of Spirulina: A Helical Blue-Green Algae As A
     New Food. Dr. Hiroshi Nakamura. Microalgae International Union
     pub. London. 1970.
11   The One-Straw Revolution: An Introduction To Natural Farming.
     Masanobu Fukuoka. Rodale Press. Emmaus, Pa. 1978. pp. 42-44.
12   ibid. p. 64.
13   ibid. p. 3.
14   ibid. p. 103.
15   ibid. p. 159.
16   Findhorn - a Center of Light. Paul Hawken. Tao Pub. Boston, Mass.
     1974. pp. 27,28.
17   ibid. p. 33.
18   ibid. pp. 37,38.

CHAPTER 17

PERMANENT DESERT CULTURE

The model, the example of "living in balance with nature" that will be explored, is a watershed that exists in a semi-arid environment in the South-western United States. Because this area exists in that climate, it will be useful to survey the different strategies that humans have used to adapt to these regions. While this model applies to the near desert areas, it is suggested that a similar analysis be applied to any area in which a community of people may wart to establish.

The Forager Example

Adaptations to the desert environment have been sedentary, nomadic and variations between the two. The Bushmen people of Southern Africa are a very ancient race of people that populated the cone of Southern Africa until the very recent arrival of the negroid, Bantu people and others. These people who are as physically different from the negroid peoples as the caucasians are from the eskimos, have been eliminated in most of their previous habitat and only survive in the severe environment of the central deserts of the cone where the non-adapted could not, until recently, enter- the Kalahari.

The Bushmen people are probably equal to the northern Eskimos in the incredible balance that they maintain with the life around them. For eight to ten months of each year they have no obvious source of water. Their liquid comes from plants and animals. Their water diet is so meager that every possible drop of liquid is squeezed from each animal that they kill and saved for consumption. Yet, researchers and visitors that know the Bushmen people say that they are happy, kind, cooperative, and well adjusted to their environment.

Anthropologist George Silberbauer lived with a group of Bushmen clans in one part of the Kalahari Desert. The group that Silberbauer lived with and studied he named the G/wi for recognition in the English language. The G/wi he states, "have water for only six to eight weeks in most years."[1] The balance that the G/wi have reached with their environment is so fine, Silberbauer notes, that they often exist on the edge of heatstroke during the hot, dry seasons yet he never witnessed heatstroke. He states:

> "Many G/wi, by their lassitude, malaise, and atypical irritability manifest what appears to be the prodromal signs of heatstroke, which, although they do not develop into stroke episodes, indicate how slender the margin of survival sometimes becomes under these conditions."[2]

The earth in the G/wi homeland is predominantly covered by grasses, forbs, brush (especially thorn bushes), and some trees. The people migrate throughout their land and attempt to camp near waterholes or sources of moisture. Edible plants make up the bulk of the G/wi diet; from 75 to 100%, according to Silberbauer. He states that there are 30 odd species that are the main subsistence for the group and he further notes that there are plant species that are consumed only for their moisture value rather than for their limited value as food. The G/wi do eat meat of course, when they can. Silberbauer lists 20 species that are used ranging from giraffe, down through a number of antelope types to other species such as porcupine, warthog, rabbits, jackals, rodents, birds, tortoises, snakes and frogs. He also indicates a substantial diet of invertebrates. Silberbauer calculates the annual meat consumption at 93.14 kg. per person. Other researchers have noted that the caloric and protein value of food consumption of Bushmen peoples generally compares with that of Europeans.

As various students of the Bushmen peoples describe them, they have few possessions other than functional tools and utensils. Researchers also comment on their somewhat mystic profundity. One anthropologist who has studied other bands of Bushmen in another (and slightly wetter) area of the Kalahari says that they identified 200 plant species and 220 animal species for him and probably most were used for food, medicine or materials.[3] This encyclopedic knowledge of the life around them and the sensing of its pulsations and movements begins to take on a mysterious aura to a person who has not lived life with the natural world. For example, the arrow point poison that is used by the G/wi comes from a larva of a particular beetle. This beetle larva that exists in cocoons some 20 to 25 cm. under the ground, are only found under a certain kind of large bush, the corkwood. The poison is only active when it enters the bloodstream and can be ingested without harm. This makes it an ideal poison for hunting arrows. How the G/wi learned of the larva and learned to use the poison is a mystery which indicates the profound sense that they have of the life around them.

The life cycle of the Central Kalahari is a two phase cycle of summer rains and winter dryness. During the rainy season the seed inventory that has been dispersed over the desert floor, germinates and the plant life flourishes, animals of all kinds gestate and lay eggs and water holes fill. At this time the tsama melons, a basic staple which provide food and moisture for the G/wi, proliferate. At this season, Silberbauer estimates that there were 29 usable species of plants available. It is during this time that the families and bands come together because the concentration of people can be supported in one area. At this wet season time of May in the southern hemisphere, the grouped people travelled only a few miles foraging for food. The people have a migration pattern that fits the season, the moisture and therefore the immediate food availability. As the season begins to dry the people disperse. The concentrated group breaks up and the bands go to different water holes. Hunting involves considerable travel on the part of the men. When bow and arrow hunting, the men go on several days trek. In this case they jerk the meat, that is they sliver it into thin strips and sun dry it. In this way it can be conveniently carried back to camp, although any moisture derived from the animal must be consumed on the spot. The people do use snares to catch smaller animals but this is only done near camp where the snares can be visited several times each day, because, as the observer notes, N!adima, their word for the creator, would be offended if they caused, "One of his creatures unnecessary suffering." Clubs, used in beating and throwing are also used to harvest small game.

The people occasionally rob the lions of their kills by rushing up to the lions and scaring them away. According to observer Silberbauer; "The trick lies in correctly judging the moment; if approached too early in its feed, the lion will attack, and if left too long, until it is sated and lazy, it will stand and defend its kill rather than run."[4] An interesting sidelight is the complete sense of sharing and mutual aid in this culture. The anthropologist, Silberbauer, who came to the G/wi from another culture and pattern of conditioned perception, treats the question of private property at some length. In trying to get at this question in this Pleistocene culture, he was not very successful. He explains:

"I have equated ownership with exclusiveness of use or control of use. The concept of ownership is not highly developed among the central Kalahari G/wi and I found difficulty in discussing it with them....

Undisturbed, untouched, and unclaimed territorial assets are owned by N!adima but are subject to human ownership once the process of their exploitation has been initiated. For instance, when a man signifies his intention to hunt a particular animal, it is wrong for any other man to attempt to take the animal for himself unless and until the hunt is abandoned by the first claimant."[5]

Silberbauer says that among the G/wi only the plant food that is needed that day is collected for the household and this is shared equally by the household and elderly or invalid. When the good fortune of catching a large animal occurs, the meat is distributed between hunters, helpers and the camp at large. Anthropologist Richard B. Lee in his study, "!Kung Bushmen Subsistence:An Input-Output Analysis," states concerning the sharing of food, that hunters hunt individually or in pairs, but:

> "Cooperation is clearly in evidence, however, in the consumption of food. Not only do families pool the day's production, but the entire camp—residents and visitors alike—shares equally in the total quantity of food available. The evening meal of any one family is made up of portions of food from the supplies of each of the other families resident. Foodstuffs are distributed raw or are prepared by the collector and then distributed. There is a constant flow of nuts, berries, roots and melons from one family fireplace to another until each person resident has received an equitable portion."[6]

Silberbauer notes interesting relationships between the life of the people and the life of the land. The human manuring around camps results in seed dispersion of useful plant populations in areas that are preferred camp sites for humans. He notes that the manure is worked into the ground along with the seeds by the cooperating dung beetles so that the seeds are nicely planted and ready for the next seasonal germination.

Silberbauer observed the G/wi burning grasses to promote the growth of the ground running vines of cucurbits. The grasses were burned off and then when the moisture came in, the burn spot was the first to green up. This green growth of grasses attracted the herbivores who ate it down severely (and in being there, made themselves available as food). The cucurbits then had the sun to maximize early growth, when in usual habit the cucurbit normally started its natural cycle of growth well after the grass. In the extremely dry time when animals and birds have migrated long distances away and others are in hibernation or relatively suspended animation, the G/wi also become withdrawn in a similar manner. By this time they have broken down into the smallest family units.

Even though it may seem to many that the G/wi endure hardship and in material terms are quite poor, they display a consciousness of their place in the universe, a spiritual sophistication and a human maturity far more developed than many other cultures. They are humble and careful not to take more than they need for their sustenance. They never shoot more than one game animal due to their consideration of N!adima who owns the world and consideration of the other beings who live with us on the earth. Silberbauer notes that the much valued ostrich eggs, which the G/wi find and use for food as well as valuable water containers, are each the equivalent of two dozen chicken eggs. Nonetheless, when the G/wi find an ostrich clutch, which may number ten to fifteen eggs, they only take two or three.

Silberbauer visited the G/wi in 1958-1966. He states that soon after, the long drought in the Kalahari broke. The herders, miners and others moved in to get what surpluses existed, hence the G/wi, like many other Bushmen peoples before them are no more. He says:

"...For better or worse, the close-knit, self-sufficient organization of band society, which is described in this book, and the completeness of the band member's control of their society are gone. The 'ethno-geographic present' is now the past."[7]

A Sedentary Example

The ancient Nabateans of the Negev Desert were a people who created an organic niche for themselves within the metabolism of the earth. Rather than just live in balance like most foragers, the Nabateans actively created an organic space for themselves over and above what the earth offered. They did this without damaging the other life or taking away from it. They created a new organ that further enhanced the life of the earth toward greater diversity, fertility and refinement.

The civilization of the Nabatu demonstrates what can be done by a creative group of people. The Nabatean civilization existed in the Negev and Sinai deserts for approximately two centuries and produced an amazing and exquisite culture in a land of as little as two to four inches rainfall per year. These people had no "resources" other than their creativity. They demonstrate that right now most of the deserts of the world could be successfully inhabited. This could not, of course, be done within the context of industrial civilization.

Little is known about the origins of the Nabateans. Scholars conclude, based on the existing evidence, that they were a tribe or group of tribes coming up out of Arabia into the Sinai-Negev area. Little is known either about the natural history of the Sinai-Negev desert. The interior desert has an average of four to eight inches of rainfall in the northern part of the Negev and this becomes less toward the south into the Sinai. The land forms and climatic systems are such that rainfall-vegetation regimes can change radically in only a few miles as one travels from the Mediterranean Sea, east into the desert. Efraim Orni and Dan Yaalon, in their survey of the soils of Israel, mention that the soil of the southern Negev is covered by "reg" soil which is a dark, flinty and gravelly desert pavement. Beneath this relatively impermeable surface is "a pale, loose, loamy layer up to one foot (30 cm.) thick."[8] This fact would tend to indicate considerable vegetation at some time in prehistory. The Northern Negev in the Beersheba lowlands is a yellowish-brown loess, according to the authors, and is typical of desert fringes, being soil that is brought in from the inner desert regions by dust storms. Although many desert sections of the present Middle East were forested in ancient times, little is known about what the vegetation cover of the Sinai-Negev may have been. Though there is a long history of settlement in the Negev, it was usually also a very sparse population up to the time of the Nabateans.

Although scholars find no evidence of village life for the Nabateans earlier than the first century B.C., historians believe that they were in the region as nomadic tribes. There are indications that they were not a semitic people but were aboriginals displaced from Arabia by the present inhabitants.[9]

Nelson Glueck, probably the foremost scholar of this singular people, sums up his view of them in his study, *Rivers In The Desert: A History of the Negev*, by saying:

"Their rule prevailed for several centuries from Arabia to Syria and across the Negev to Sinai. They may be accounted one of the most remarkable peoples of history. Springing swiftly out of the desert of Arabia to a position of great power and affluence, they were thrust back by the Romans even more swiftly into the limbo whence they came. While their turn lasted, the Nabateans wrought greatly, developing almost overnight into builders of magnificent cities, which are unique in the history of the handiwork of man. They became tradesmen, farmers, engineers, architects and artists of outstanding excellence. The phenomenon of their appearance and disappearance between the first centuries B.C. and A.D. may be likened to the brilliance of a meteor flashing briefly across the skies to blazing extinction.[10]

They were indeed a wonderful people, whose abilities were directed to the arts of peace rather than to the science of war, to the fructification of deserts rather than to the sowing of their neighbors' fields with salt, to the conservation of the soil and the skillful gathering and utilization of water rather than to the squandering of natural resources and to the scorching of the good earth to prevent others from enjoying its blessings.

"They found their reward in the survival values they created for themselves and their children and their childrens' children, planning and undertaking soil and water conservation schemes which sometimes must have taken generations to complete. It was in this way that they reconquered the wilderness of the Negev, planting more agricultural colonies there than it had ever known before."[11]

The first century B.C. historian Strabo helps to illuminate more of the cultural life of the Nabateans. Describing their life at that time, he says that they were, " 'temperate and industrious,' and with stringent laws concerning thrift. Democracy, a carry-over from the desert life, still regulates social life, even to that of the king. But now they drink their wine in golden beakers, are entertained by dancing girls, have planted gardens about Petra, and their king wears purple. They have few slaves, but live in houses of stone in a city unwalled because of peace."[12]

The culture of the Nabateans was based on water concentration, containerization and soil conservation. In the Negev as well as many other semi-arid deserts of the world, rainfall comes only sporadically, but often in heavy torrents. If the area has tree cover and good vegetation cover of other varieties such as grass, the land is able to harmonize the cycles of moisture, by absorbing the water. If the land has been abused or if it is simply too dry to support much vegetative cover, the rain simply runs off in torrents to sink finally in the desert lowlands.

The Nabateans existed in a desert that was very arid and had little vegetative cover. Their strategy was not to try to build soil on the expanses of desert but to use the expanses for water catchment and then to concentrate the water runoff into areas that could be intensively worked to build the soil. Because much of the environment was rock and ground with an impermeable pavement surface, they were greatly aided in the water catchment effort and made full use of this fact.

One of their talents was the containerization of water. They often cut cisterns out of solid rock (as they cut their most important city, Petra out of rock). They also used plaster created from the burning of local limestone. Plaster enabled them to dig holes in the ground almost anywhere they might need a cistern. After the hole was dug they plastered the sides and bottom so that it would hold water. There are plastered cisterns built by the Nabateans in the Negev now that are still in use by the bedouins who water their herds from them. Some of the rock cisterns that have been found have capacities of thousands of gallons. As the Nabateans had many hundreds of villages around the area they had to preserve every drop of water possible. One ingenious way of filling cisterns, other than through simple diversion from canyons, was to find caves in the cliff faces or to dig out cliff faces in the manner illustrated below.

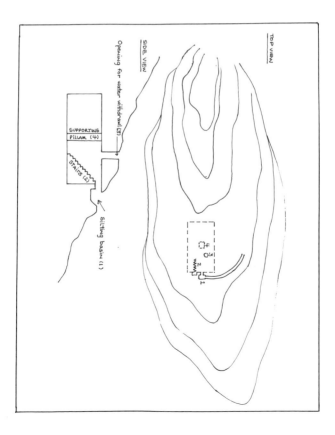

The Nabateans by the use of dams, terraces, diversionary wells, channels, aqueducts, cisterns and reservoirs, used whole watersheds as catchment areas. Their devices ordinarily went right to the tops of the valleys and canyons so that any sudden rush of water was tempered and utilized to its maximum. They used walls of rock several feet high that encircled mesa tops.

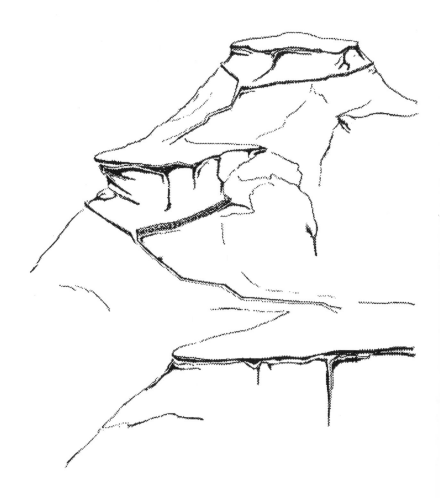

By using the diversionary walls, the water runoff could be channeled in a relatively slow moving flow onto terraces and onto flats below the mesa. An additional benefit was the topsoil suspended in the water run-off. Provided that the water wasn't cutting erosion strips, the silt that ran off would be the lighter material that had organic value in the farming areas.

After the water was concentrated it had to be spread onto the fields. Its velocity had to be checked so that it didn't dig out erosion paths in the fields. The Nabateans did this by having their fields on multiple levels. The Nabatean farmer could give some fields a small amount of water while others received more, thus making adjustment for different varieties of plants. This was done by having higher or lower spillways, thus impounding a pre-set level of water.

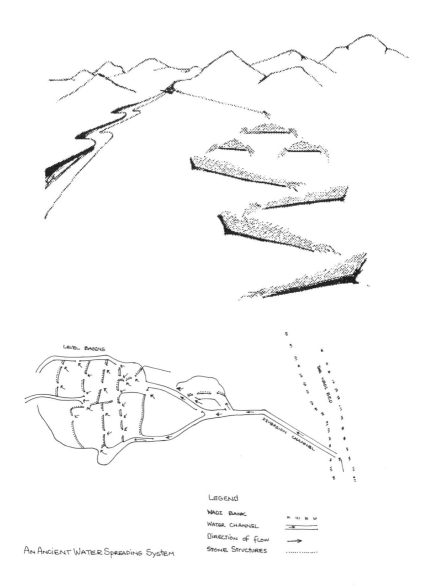

LEVEL BASINS

THE WADI BED

DIVERSION CHANNEL

LEGEND

WADI BANK

WATER CHANNEL

DIRECTION OF FLOW

STONE STRUCTURES

An Ancient Water Spreading System

In the canyon bottoms a system of basins followed each other downhill. These were constructed so that as each basin filled, the excess water ran to fill the next basin. The spillways were constructed of tightly fitted rock that was set so that the water would not run out until there was six inches of water in the basin. This slowed the water enough to prevent erosion.

The Nabateans used wells when they could reach the water table. Artesian wells still remain in the Negev from the Nabatean days. In a few instances water bearing aquifers were located. These would be strata of sandstone or other porous material that was holding water. Workers dug horizontal tunnels into the hillside until they reached the water bearing strata. Another creative technique was a combination of water catchment and well. It is called a Kanat by contemporary researchers. The Kanat system is especially used just at the point where an intermittent stream comes out of the mountains and enters a flattened area. Often, in deserts more water travels underground than on the surface and the Kanat was designed to exploit this. It functions by sinking a number of well shafts down into this layer which is usually gravel. The water seeps out of the wall of the well shaft but unlike most wells the water does not collect on the bottom. Where the floor of a normal well would be, is a horizontal tunnel. Instead the water runs down and out of the tunnel which drains all of the shafts.

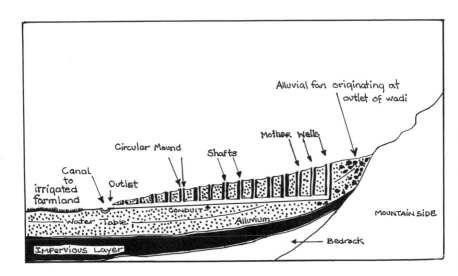

Daniel Hillel, in his study, *Land, Water and Life In A Desert Environment*, states that at the peak of the cultural manifestation of the Nabateans, there were many hundreds of farm units in the northern Negev; that "runoff farming encompassed practically all of the usable land in the northern Negev." Glueck states also that the Nabateans held "millions of gallons of water," in their cisterns and reservoirs, giving an idea of the extent of their works.[13]

The average wadi bottom planting according to Glueck was around twenty five acres. Hillel estimates the average runoff in the Negev to be from 10% to 15% of rain falling on the catchment basin and he puts the water requirements of winter crops in the Negev at about four inches of rain (or other water). From these calculations, Hillel states that the ratio of catchment basin to growing area must average 25:1. Other crops than standard field crops do better apparently. He does cite an experiment that he has done with almond trees in an area of eight to ten inches rainfall that grow well with a 3:1 catchment area to planted area.

Tree crops in the Negev are almonds, apricots, figs, olives, pomegranates, and date palms. Wheat is a winter crop and summer crops include grapes and cucurbits (i.e., melons, squash). The ancient Nabateans must have grown many of these crops. We know from written historical records that they grew barley and aracus (apparently a legume) also.

The effectiveness of the Nabateans' creativity is shown by a reconstituted Nabatean farm done by Professor Evanari of Hebrew University:

"In 1960, when this experiment was tried, Israel had the lowest rainfall ever recorded, amounting to only an inch and a half. Crops in the Negev and elsewhere failed and had to be plowed back into the soil, but to everyone's astonishment barley on the professor's ancient farm, which had lain fallow for 1,700 or more years, produced a crop that stood chest high. The secret lay in the fact that the ancient Nabatean channels, which the professor had restored, sluiced the rain down from the surrounding hills, while the walls surrounding the quarter-acre plots maintained the water at a depth of six inches when, during one sudden shower, only a fifth of an inch of rain fell. From these ancient fields the professor and his helpers gathered five hundred kilos of barley per acre, equal to the grain yield in the Dakotas.

Using the same principle of flood irrigation, Professor Evanari has converted an ancient wadi system into acres of grapes, apricots, almonds, olives, and such vegetables as asparagus, cucumbers, and artichokes. Moreover, the plants need no sprays to protect them from the usual plant diseases, as the dry heat of the desert itself bakes and sterilizes the soil."[14]

Another desert dwelling people, the Kiva People, who all used underground ceremonial chambers called Kivas, lived in ancient times and many villages still exist in the southwestern part of the North American continent. The names of their ancient groups were Anasazi, Hohokam, Mimbres and Mogollon according to their place of residence and each of the contemporary pueblos usually carry Spanish names. The ancient Kiva people constructed some hydraulic works on the order of that done by the Nabateans. Most of the land where the ancient Kiva People lived received between 10 and 20 inches of rain per year so they did not have to go to the extremes of the Nabateans in their engineering and design. They did use terracing, channeling-off water catchment areas and dams in their agriculture, even though they were able to farm dry land to a greater extent without the water concentration devices. Probably the majority of effort was flood-plain agriculture. This is simply planting flood plains with flood water channelled on to it. They had additional techniques that the Nabateans are not known to have used. One of these techniques was to find sandstone cliffs with a spring at the base. This indicated that the sandstone was an aquifer holding water. The Kiva People constructed dams on the mesa top and the impounded water would sink into the aquifer rather than run over the side. This increased the spring flow and insured a dependable water supply.

Another ingenious technique works very well. Any impermeable material laying on desert soil will cause water to collect beneath it. It will protect the soil from oxidation and also act as a mulch. The Southwestern Kiva people placed flat, dark colored rocks out in fields in a checkerboard design. The fact that half the area is covered means that the rest gets twice as much water. The dark color of the rocks also absorbs heat during the day thus moderating the cold at night.

There must have been many micro-environment techniques used by various desert dwellers. One that we know the Essenes used and no doubt which was used by the Nabateans was the earthen vessel. A pottery vessel is very water efficient when used as a planter. In this way the moisture is containerized. Another use for the pottery vessel is to bury it with its rim at ground level with plants encircling the jar. It is filled with water which slowly seeps out of its porous sides to water the plants and its top can be covered to prevent evaporative water loss.

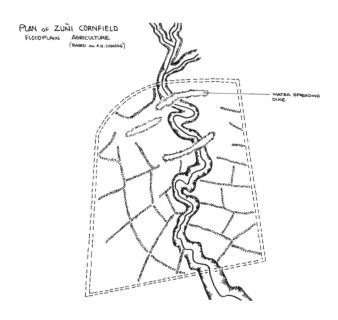

PLAN OF ZUÑI CORNFIELD
FLOODPLAIN AGRICULTURE.
(BASED ON F.H. CUSHING)

WATER SPREADING
DIKE

NOTES

1   Hunter and Habitat in the Central Kalahari Desert. George B. Silberbauer. Cambridge U. Press. 1981. p. 221.

2   ibid. p. 277.

3   Environment and Cultural Behavior. ed. Andrew P. Vayda. Natural History Press. 1969. "!Kung Bushman Subsistence:An Input-Output Analysis." Richard B. Lee. P. 67.

4   Silberbauer. Hunter and Habitat. op. cit. p. 216.

5   ibid, p. 232.

6   Lee. Environment ánd Cultural Behavior. op. cit. p. 58,59.

7   Silberbauer. Hunter and Habitat. op. cit. p. 1.

8   Israel Today: Reclamation and Conservation of the Soil. #26. Efraim Orni & Dan H. Yaalon. Israel Digest pub. P.O.B. 92. Jerusalem. 1970. p. 15.

9   The Nabateans:Their History, Culture and Archaeology. Philip C. Hammond. Paul Astrom, Pub. Gothenburg, Sweden. (Other scholars of note concerning the Nabateans are Professor Evenari of Hebrew University and Archaeologist Avrahan Neger, both of Israel.)

10   Rivers In The Desert: A History of the Negev. Nelson Glueck. Farrar, Straus & Cudahy. New York. 1959. p. 193.
See also: Land, Water and Life In A Desert Environment. Daniel Hillel. Praeger pub. 1982. And:
The Negev; The Challenge of a Desert. 2nd. ed. Michael Evenari, Leslie Shanan, Naphtali Tadmor, et. al. Harvard U. Press. Cambridge, MA 1982.

11   ibid. p. 202.

12   Hammond. The Nabateans. op. cit. p. 13.

13   ibid. p. 211.

14   World of the Desert, Slater Brown. Bobs-Merrill. New York. 1963. p.75.

CHAPTER 18

CHOOSING REALITY

Claiming Our Birthright

Civilization is a mental/material world of culturally transmitted illusion. It is suicide on a vast historical scale. It is indeed a self-fulfilling prophecy of linear increase until the final exhaustion is reached. The behavior of the swelling tumor body fails all tests of common sense and of feelings that come from the heart. When we look out upon the earth at the confusion and the dying, the results of this pattern of behavior cannot be denied. We are living out the dissolution, the degeneration and the separation on a psychological level. We are living it out on a social level and a political level and we are existing within the body of an organism that is experiencing it on a planetary level.

The conditioned illusion of the "march of progress" will fade as desperation begins to enter even for First World populations. The exponential increase of linear growth is now entering the phase in which we will see forms- mental, social, political and industrial- begin to shatter. The swelling energies of the trends of history triggered, centuries and millennia in the past, are reaching their logical culmination. As the swelling energies exceed the ability of the pre-arranged forms to contain them, the forms will disintegrate. The growth of population, the increasing prevalence of poison, the rise in background radiation, the increase in severe weather disturbance from the greenhouse effect, the increase in conflict from the militarists rabid to corner the last resources; these and many other trends of increase will ultimately insure the demise of the final world empire.

As the crises increase, the world military order of empire will attempt in the last gasp, to consolidate, to save itself, but it cannot for long. It will fall. If one destroys what feeds them, even over a length of one hundred centuries, one will finally starve.

The period that we are entering is unprecedented, there are no roadmaps for us within the culture of civilization. There will be crises within crises, within crises and the outer boundaries will be the whole body of the earth: the ozone layer, the atmospheric greenhouse gases, the macro-ocean currents and whole bioregional ecosystems. Fragmentation and sudden crises will be the hallmark of the age.

There is a valid roadmap and that is our birthright as organic and cosmic beings. We each enjoy a nature as cellular organisms and we all enjoy a nature as life on earth, enabled by cosmic conditions on that scale. Are we to believe that this beauty, joy and intelligence that we experience is confined simply to the earth? Are we to believe that there is not an energy moving toward healing, wholeness and experiential, sensory, visual, aural, and spiritual beauty in this cosmos that even exceeds the limits of our perception? When we see our wounds heal, when we see the pioneer plants cover the injured soil, when we see the sun's rays from the heart of the solar body transformed into the beauty of an old growth forest or other matured life, can we not see that the pattern leads toward wholeness, happiness and beauty? Organic life is our birthright and our roadmap is the cosmic pattern.

The Civilized Alien

We are estranged from the whole life. We suffer from separation and to the degree that we cannot recognize that source of suffering, it increases. We need release the contraction, the defense, the barrier and re-unify. The forces and patterns that have enabled life on earth, flow when the patterns are resonant on all levels. We cannot expect sufficient power from the sources unless we are centered and balanced personally, socially and then the human group is set within the life of the earth in a balanced way. If our minds can expand so that we can see the severity of the crisis on its planetary and solar scale then we can also understand the pattern. When remission of cancer is achieved by affirmation and visualization it comes about by the cell receiving intelligent communication- "inspiration"- from the whole intelligence. Where we exist, in this here and now, on the earth, we cannot simply balance person- tribe- watershed. The organic disturbance is planetary. The energies need be spread to many points of reception over the earth. Those receptive tribes need achieve resonance on both material and non-material levels.

We must start from here, from the point of our own awakening, not as a person socially defined but as a human ecologically defined. The reality of cosmic perspective- that is our awakening. Being here, in the real cosmos, we are not separate. This is our destiny, to awaken to the cosmic identity of Gaia. If we accomplish our aim of reintegrating human culture with the life of the earth then our activities will, in important ways, structure the new culture. As we organize ourselves to aid the life of the earth, social structure, ritual and practice will flow from that.

We will return to the earth and our needs will be met by the earth. From our permacultural base we can derive food, oils, flours, fibres, waxes, woods, medicinal plants, brewing agents, lubricants, fuel, dyes, glues, wood for construction, soaps and other items. We humans need food, shelter and love to survive on earth and our new culture can provide that.

The last section of this book is a roadmap for the material plane. If we follow the map and move toward the sources of life we will become spiritually informed, resonantly. We are returning home but our absence has been lengthy. We will need introductions. I have created, with advice from the elders, a permaculture of a place, a watershed. I am presenting this in the form of a "case study" but it is only a guide, a suggestion. This is a suggested guide to creating your introduction. You must create your own in your place, to the place our grandchildren and great-great grandchildren will inhabit. We are going to marry each other and we are going to join our mother the earth. Our guide is our collective great grandchild who stands afar in paradise. At this cusp of the age, at this moment of opportunity, it is time to commence the acquaintance. This is indeed a new age and a time of decision. Persons of all tribes and all races who are moving toward balance and unity are separating out from the suicide pact. This is the palpable reality. When all falls into disintegration, with all the species on earth involved, race, creed, geography and such are immaterial, only that which has prospect of continuance becomes real. This then means that our sense of reality must change. We will trade our lives as ciphers in mass, industrial society for an opportunity to meaningfully participate in cosmic creation, spiritually, intellectually, socially and ecologically. Irrespective of the final outcome, we will reap immediate challenge and enjoyment. Our lives will become more real and fun. We will return to the earth and create peace among us, for the children. We will create a human focussed society that emphasizes the expansion of human Beingness. Human abilities, talents and human focussed activities will be important rather than marginalized as in the present culture of materialism that focusses on social power and on the production of material goods. In order to succeed we must focus on the children as our most important task. Simply creating a positive emotional base in our culture and raising children in that environment will help them immensely when they face the increasing difficulties of their generations.

Our focus is on the living things. This is our cultural reality. We will become informed about the life of the earth, we will be involved with living things on a daily basis. Houses, freeways and factories as a focus of reality will fade away. Living things are the cosmic reality on earth. The growth and condition of life is our focus. We live on watersheds and in bioregions. These areas are organisms on their level of being just as the earth is an organism on its level. Our basic reality is sun, soil, water and air because those four items and their conditions are the basic reality of life on earth. We focus upon the condition of those life giving elements.

When we live at the top of our watershed and are expanding downward, a basic test of our culture and the legitimacy of our occupance on earth will be that pure air and water are emitted from the area that we inhabit. This is a simple and real test. This does not mean that we have to go to the tops of high mountains. Many rises, hills and ridges are at the top of their local watersheds.

Gaia's History

Because rock conditions soil, it is important to know the geology of one's place. In the valuable book, *The Secrets of the Soil*, Tomkins and Byrd report on several people in different locations who have discovered and used crushed rock from unique rock deposits as amazingly beneficial soil conditioners.[1] There are no doubt many of these deposits of uniquely balanced minerals scattered over the earth.

Knowing the "bones of the mother" also leads us to other knowledge. Through our dowsing and other sensing abilities we will come to know the circulation of energies within the hard body of the earth. This relates to aquifers, springs, underground streams and rivers and it also relates to the finer <u>chi</u> energies of the earth and places of power. Dowsing for underground waters is an easily learned ability. Probably the premier work in this area is the book *Supersensonics*, by Christopher Hills.[2] Other works giving instructions in dowsing techniques are also easily obtained. The dowsing ability is not confined to water but is an ability whereby one's area of consciousness that deals with that talent can inform a person of answers to many questions such as the most efficacious herb to use in specific healings, the location of minerals, the paths of the various earth energies, as well as the course of underground streams and rivers.

Geology books and academic studies can serve as introductions in this matter but observation (with all senses receptive) over time, is the final source of knowledge.

The mosaic of life that exists on the surface and which is integral with the energy flows of the hard body must be known intimately. On the watershed of the San Francisco River, the location of our case study, these mosaics of large biotic zones, or life zones, are divided in a general way by elevation and the areas where two zones intermingle, which are called ecotones, are especially important because there, the diversity is even greater. Some lore of the birds and animals can be found in books. If the life in one's place is not completely gone, older people may know some lore of the wildlife. Here again there is no substitute for observation. One reason is that birds and animals do have individual characters which are sometimes very pronounced and generalizations about whole species are only that- generalizations.

The natural history of one's area may be difficult to discover depending on the length of colonization by empire and the use that culture has made of the land. Generally, much was eliminated before any systematic gathering of biological information was begun. Some academic sources are usable, some information can be gleaned from historical libraries and works written by first settlers. On the watershed of the San Francisco River, trappers were early arrivals and several left journals. A meat hunter who sold game animals to the miners and also several early ranchers left books about their experiences. From these types of sources one gains an occasional plant, vegetation or animal description to begin putting together a picture. To gain a sense of the truly teeming life on a broad scale, one can search out studies such as Farley Mowat's *Sea Of Slaughter*. (Bantam 1986), about the north Atlantic coast or Peter Mathiesson's *Wildlife In America* (1959). The bibliographies of this type of book offers further sources that are helpful.

Understanding the natural history of the area helps understand the potential of the land and helps understand the climax ecosystem that may, but probably does not now exist.

Understanding the human occupancy of one's watershed is imperative. Again, unless there are Native people who either live now- or have cultural memories of how their ancestors lived, one must resort to books. This applies to all who have lived in the place, not simply the last native group. Other historical sources also may offer some clues to the native ethnobotany. Not only foraging systems but knowledge of the entire life ways of native people need to be focussed upon. Tools, materials, migration patterns, sacred places, "myths" and much more is of interest to those who expect they and their great-grandchildren will live with the place.

Identification manuals for plants, trees, birds, animals, mushrooms, fish and any other life forms in one's place are a must. It is important, at least initially, until we develop our own language, to use latin names for precise identification as common usage names vary from person to person and region to region (and even between some garden seed catalogues that do not use latin names). One should be out on the earth much of the time identifying food plants, medicinal herbs and generally beginning observations. Watching the plant habits is essential. Where do they grow, the north slope, south slope, canyons, ridgetops? What soils do they like? Dig into the soil, examine it periodically in different areas to keep track of soil moisture through the seasons. Smell the different soils, taste them, become familiar with them. Watch for plant associations. Notice the patina of plant groups. This often tells of underground water courses, soil types and even favorite spots where birds or animals visit often and drop seeds. If one is in a heavily impacted area, search for places that are difficult for livestock or people to get to and study that relatively undisturbed area intently. If one is in a place that is completely obliterated, try to find areas in that watershed that are somewhat natural and use them to get ideas for a permacultural restoration at the place that has been obliterated.

Begin to create seed inventories. Store them carefully with adequate note of plant description, place of residence on the watershed, date and other relevant information. Excellent books exist which explain wild seed gathering and wild plant propagation. There are books such as *American Wildlife And Plants: A Guide To Wildlife Food Habits*, by Martin, Zim and Nelson (Dover, 1951) which can greatly aid our practice of observation. This will also give us clues to the creation of wildlife habitat. In this matter one should not ignore "Fish and Game" bureaucracies. Though they focus on species important to the "trophy hunting" industry, they often have some information on other species. There are now a few books, pamphlets and magazines focussing on ecological restoration. These are very useful.

One of the important considerations that we will have is to help Gaia feed herself so she can feed us. To help her ingest sunlight we will be making effort for the climax ecosystem to restore itself. In those areas where there is no ecosystem remaining we will use permaculture. This method builds in complexity, aid to the soil and aid to the general life. Then we will live from that increase. With the world-wide damage from empire there is no way that Gaia can return to her pristine condition. We're discussing scar tissue in the case of obliterated zones. In view of the geographic transfer of plants, animals, diseases and all the rest in the past ten thousand years, what our effort must be is to simply create a facsimile ecosystem that is as complex and as close to the original as possible using what genetic materials we have at hand. Many of these species may have been unknown to the original climax ecosystem. Then we must let Gaia do the further healing growth. Hopefully the weeds will help us by overgrowing the civis problem, the villages, towns and cities that do not fit in the solar budget and are extorting other life to subsidize their energies.

The Moment of Opportunity

There is no reason that some of the remaining energies of the empire cannot be used to assist in our transition to balance. Indeed, we would hope that the entire remaining energy of civilization could be used so. The "time of purification" is now upon us. We need move swiftly. We have solutions. This must be made clear to those who will respond. Though we must use whatever strategies we can to resist the destruction of the best that remains, the forward direction of our solutions are not political, religious or ideological- they are simply the patterns of life.

The permaculture that follows is a case study. It has been created as an example, an introduction. Please use it in gaining ideas to help our mother, the earth, in your place. As we all tune into the frequency, we will be in touch.

NOTES

1   <u>Secrets Of The Soil: New Age Solutions For Restoring Our Planet</u>. Peter
     Tompkins & Christopher Bird. Harper & Row. New York. 1989.
2   <u>Supersensonics: The Science Of Radiational Paraphysics</u>. Vol. III. Chris-
     topher Hills. University of the Trees Press, P.O. Box 644, Boulder Creek,
     Calif. 95006. 1975.

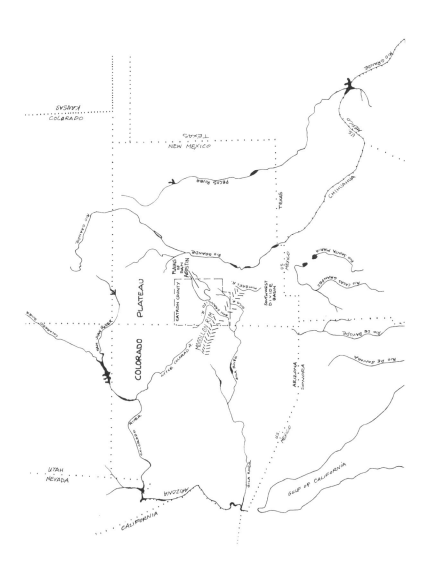

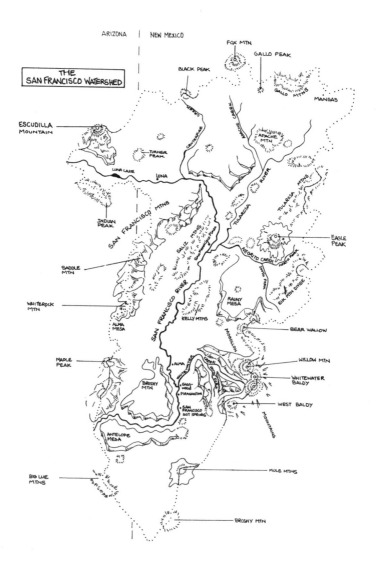

THE
SAN FRANCISCO WATERSHED

CHAPTER 19

THE NATURAL HISTORY OF
THE WATERSHED OF
THE SAN FRANCISCO RIVER

Very early in time, shallow seas covered the Southern part of New Mexico, Arizona and Northern Mexico. As the tension of the North American tectonic plate colliding with the East Pacific Rise increased, the surface of the land across the American West began to crumple, shift, and rise.

The Mogollon Rim, which is the southern border of the Colorado Plateau, was part of a stable platform related to the Great Plains and the Colorado Plateau for several hundred million years. More than a hundred million years before the present, (B.P.), the area south of the Mogollon Rim began to fall because of the geosyncline that runs southeast to the Gulf of Mexico, elevating the Colorado Plateau to the North. Somewhere in the neighborhood of seventy million years B.P., the era of late dinosaurs, the positions reversed and the southern portion again became higher than the Colorado Plateau. By the time period of twenty to thirty million years B.P. the two sections had again reversed themselves and became as they are today with the Mogollon Rim being the border area between the two.[1]

Once the surface of the earth had settled into the general contours that it now has, the Rio Grande began emptying into a large lake located in Southern New Mexico and Northern Chihuahua. The Mimbres River and the Gila River also emptied into this sump. Sometime later the Rio Grande found the outlet in the gap between the mountains where El Paso is today and began to flow to the sea at the Gulf of Mexico. The Gila found another route out through Southern Arizona to meet the Colorado at Yuma. This left the Rio Mimbres to continue to run into the sump that has been called the Southwest Divide Basin, a basin 124 miles wide from which no water exits to either ocean.[2]

The great ice sheets of the last glacial period extended not much farther south than Santa Fe, New Mexico and as they receded the climate changed. As the ice sheet receded and after it was gone, the desert ecosystem progressed

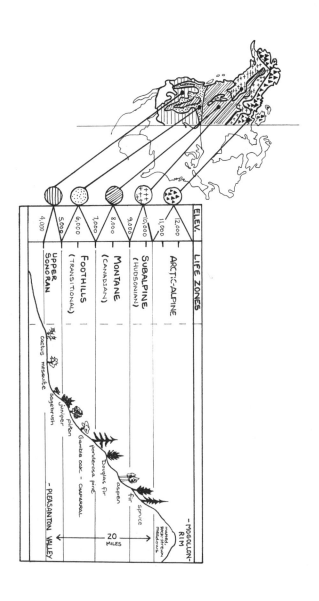

eastward and northward out of what is now the Sonoran desert. The montane system made up of pines, spruce and fir receded ahead of the piñon-juniper regime, which was followed by the desert regime.

Twenty-two thousand years ago the San Francisco watershed was probably entirely covered by forest of the pine-spruce-fir variety. As the desert regime expanded, the piñon-juniper zone began to move up in elevation. As the piñon-juniper zone began to move up in elevation and northward, grass lands followed behind and ahead of the present desert system. Grasslands dominated the northern Sonora-Chihuahua deserts for several thousand years before the present desert and the higher piñon-juniper zones were set around eight thousand years B.P.

The Elevational Life Zones

The watershed of the San Francisco River is a unique region where within a distance of roughly 20 miles one can travel from the Sonoran-Chihauhuan desert type eco-system to an alpine ecosystem or life zone characteristic of Northern Canada. This is possible because the Rim rises out of the desert with peaks that are almost 11,000 feet in elevation. The life zones of the semi-arid desert in the Southwestern U.S., like other areas, are conditioned by elevation. As one goes up elevation, the temperature and moisture regimes become cooler and more moist. Because of this the same effect will occur if one goes long distances northward. Travelling north thousands of miles, one will cross the same life zones that one crosses by going up elevation along the Mogollon Rim. This abundance of life zones creates a fertile place for forager peoples because of the seasonal variety of foods available and also because it allows humans to avoid the effects of summer heat in the desert and the winter cold in the high mountains.

The lowest elevation of the San Francisco watershed is in the Chihuahuan Desert. The Mogollon Rim is the northern boundary of both the Sonoran Desert life zone and the Chihuahuan desert to the east of it. Phoenix, Arizona is in the Sonoran and El Paso, Texas/Ciudad Juarez, Chihuahua, being in the Chihuahuan. Though both are deserts, there are significant qualitative differences between them. The big differences are that the Chihuahuan is generally higher in elevation and the Sonoran has more species diversity. From the spot that the San Francisco river joins the Gila near the border of New Mexico/ Arizona, back up toward the rim, is area that is transitional. It is the intermingling at the edge of two biogeographical regions. These are the Chihuahuan Desert to the south and the Colorado Plateau to the north. Even though the bottom of the watershed is in the Chihuahuan Desert and has those characteristics, these larger mega-zones both condition it.

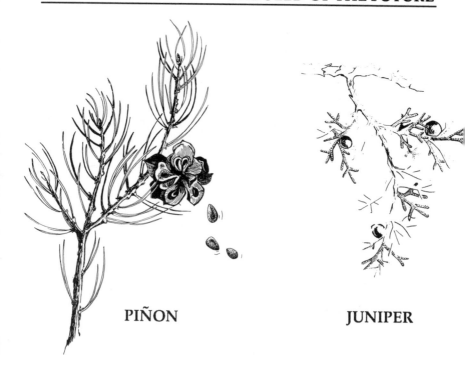

PIÑON   JUNIPER

The piñon-juniper life zone begins at roughly 5,000 feet elevation. This life zone predominates in the identifying tree species, smaller nopal cactus, and some grass species, bushes, as well as some forbs peculiar to this zone.

At the upper border of the piñon-juniper life zone is the ecotone called chaparral. Ecotone is the word that describes the intermingling of two life zones at their borders. This is a very rich ecological area that also contains oaks and manzanita as prevalent species along with the ponderosa pine which is the life-zone above it. The chaparral it should be emphasized, like other ecological specifics, does not occur at all places of the ecotone. Only where sun, soil and moisture are right will these large areas of chaparral appear.

At roughly seven thousand feet elevation the ponderosa pine forest begins. This is the zone of the cool summers and quiet nights.

Between 8,500 and 9,000 feet that life zone begins to shade into the fir-aspen zone. This is the high elevation of snow, springs, abundant fungi, boggy meadows and the beautiful aspen forests of autumn.

Above this zone is the spruce-aspen zone. This zone is everything that one would find in a northern Canadian forest. Above this zone at roughly 10,500 feet elevation we find the tree line and then hardy grasses and shrubs above at the top of Mogollon Baldy and Whitewater Baldy, the same type of areas of moss, grass and low bushes that one sees in the arctic. Each of these life zones is a general approximation as to elevation, and vegetation cover. The zones vary; for example, a warm, drier, south facing slope would have characteristics of a lower elevation than a north slope which is colder and on which the moisture evaporation is not as great. There will be areas also that are in the rainshadow of high ranges and so receive more moisture than would the same face in an area that was not in a rainshadow. Narrow canyons, especially on a north face can vary the life zone considerably. Soils also have an effect on these zones. Often if soil is poor a zone will reflect species that are characteristic of the next zone lower. Generally speaking, the life zones do maintain the given elevations with the proviso that the farther south one goes, the higher is the elevation of each life zone.

Though certain species are identified with particular life zones, it should be kept in mind that there are seasonal migrations of birds and animals and that also plant species will migrate into any area to their liking. A good example is the ponderosa pine which has its own life zone but in the days before the empire when they were not felled, they would flow down the moist canyons and stretch along the live streams at lower elevations far out into the desert as long as their roots could reach water. The elk who now live cloistered in high mountains everywhere, are naturally more of a plains and meadow animal (they are predominantly grass grazers, rather than browsers). Since the coming of empire they too have retreated.

The Moisture

Generally, precipitation on the Watershed increases about four inches for each one thousand foot rise in elevation, but there are exceptions that modify this rule. The watershed receives weather from both the Atlantic (Gulf of Mexico) and the Pacific in seasonal alternation:

"Winter is the driest season because much of the moisture from Pacific Ocean storms moving inland is removed over the mountains to the west. The seasonal difference is less pronounced west of the Continental Divide than to the east. The main source of moisture in the summer is the Gulf of Mexico. Moist air enters New Mexico in the general circulation from the southeast about the westward displaced Bermuda high pressure area. Two-thirds of the annual precipitation falls during the warmer six months, and half the annual average precipitation falls from July through September. This is mostly from brief, but often heavy, thunderstorms."[3]

Even though the low end of the watershed should follow the altitudinal pattern for rainfall it is nearer the air flow of the Atlantic out of the Gulf of Mexico which brings it more moisture. Also rain clouds headed north sometimes back up against the escarpment of the Mogollon Rim which is thousands of feet high. This also helps cause rain.

The two phase, winter-summer alternation of moisture is significant. The effects of this can be seen particularly among the grasses and the forbs, which are plants that are smaller than bushes but that are not grass or grasslike. The dual wet periods bring on cool season plants that achieve their growth during the winter rainy season and warm season plants that are adapted to the summer rainy season. The bulk of the plant species are warm season. Nonetheless, the life of cool season plants assist in feeding the browsers and grass eaters during the cold winter months and forbs such as filaree and the cool season perennial grasses help cover the exposed soil when other plants have died back because of the cold.

The summer thunderstorms not only bring in moisture but there exists a complex relationship between the organic life of the area and the moisture-electrical nature of the earth and of the upper atmospheric layers. In controlled tests it has been discovered that plants in the desert will grow significantly faster if they have natural rain from thunder storms than from the same amount of water from irrigation. When weather systems move about the planet, they carry their own electrical natures. The stories are well known of people with arthritis or old injuries who can predict the weather several days in advance because of pains. According to the study, *The Ion Effect: How Air Electricity Rules Your Life and Health*, by Fred Soyka and Alan Edmonds (Bantam, 1977) the "devil winds," the dry, hot winds like the Santana in Southern California, the Sharav in Israel and other such winds around the globe, show that the positive ionization that causes the feelings in the bones, arrives several days before the winds and weather fronts arrive.

The earth at the surface is more predominant in negative ionization than the upper atmosphere which predominates in positive ionization. Negative ionization, laboratory tests with plants show, is very life enhancing and oppositely, environments that predominate in positive ionization can actually make plants wilt as well as making people ill and irritable, because of its effect of triggering the adrenal glands which after prolonged elevation throws humans into depressions and anxieties because of the upset of the hormonal balance and blood sugar levels.

When a thunderstorm comes through the region, lightning equalizes the positive and negative charges of earth and atmosphere. As the thunder storm begins with its increase of negative ionization on the surface of the earth, most people experience an euphoric feeling, as they do in showers or when sitting near waterfalls or seashores (aerating water is one producer of negative ionization). This is caused by the heavy negative ionization amassing just before this tremendous energy exchange between the upper atmosphere and the earth - the lightning. In sum, the watershed of the San Francisco river is connected to the whole earth through these and many other macro-events.

Life Before Empire

Prior to the invasion of empire, palmate antlered Merriam elk grazed out on the lowland flats and up into the edges of the ponderosa. Mule deer too would be seen far out on the flats as well as the predominant animal of the grasslands, the pronghorn. The pronghorns were the most abundant on the grassland flats, their herds often numbering in the tens of thousands. The open grasslands, which were much more in evidence then because of grass fires, supported other animals such as the coyote and the wolf, which followed the herds.

Prairie dog towns were numerous and each contained hundreds if not thousands of the small animals. These burrowing rodents numbered in the millions in the area and provided a subsistence base for the coyote, wolf, raptors and the black footed ferret as well as the human occupants of the area, who found them especially easy to catch during summer downpours when the prairie dogs would drown out in their burrows and come to the surface of the ground where they were easily caught. The drowning of their burrows helped the earth accept and hold the sudden downpours of water and deterred sudden runoff.

The riparian habitat along the streams, the most fertile life of the desert, was originally much different. The cottonwoods were very few because they made such good food and construction materials for the beaver, but there were more willows and other trees. The beavers stretched from the Colorado River at Yuma, Arizona, up the Gila, then in all of its tributaries to the tops of the watersheds. Partly because of their activities, the water ran slow and the pools were many. The cienigas (marshes) that they created became home for many animals, water birds and waterfowl and the abandoned beaver ponds eventually dried and became beaver meadows. The beavers also created environments for other human food such as the tules (cattails), the arrow leaf potatoes and all of the animal life that visited that oasis.

The riparian habitats were the real fertility generators. These streams, such as the San Francisco, carried life out into the desert and enabled life to migrate upstream. The ponderosa were found in the canyons and valleys many miles down out in the desert as were the bears, especially grizzly.

Dr. John P. Hubbard, formerly of the Rockbridge Alum Springs Biological Laboratory and now Supervisor of the Endangered Species Program of the New Mexico Department of Fish and Game describes this ribbon of verdant green that drains the Watershed:

"Biologically, the San Francisco Valley, may be likened to an arm of the sea penetrating the midlands and highlands of southwestern New Mexico as a corridor from the lowlands to the west. The 'ocean' which it represents is the extensive, sub-tropical region of the southern Arizona and adjacent Mexico, which may be termed the plant and animal province of the Sonoran Desert, or simply the Sonoran biota. It is mainly along the San Francisco River and it's sister stream, the Gila, that the Sonoran biota penetrates southwestern New Mexico and between the two valleys an impressive representation of such plants and animals is found. Among plants included are such dominant species as the Fremont Cottonwood, Arizona Sycamore and Arizona Walnut, while some examples among the fauna include most of the native fish, the Gila Monster, Arizona Coral Snake, Arizona Cardinal, Albert's Towhee and the very rare Coati-Mundi. Not all of these have been found in the San Francisco Valley, but studies there are far from comprehensive and all may well occur, along with other Sonoran forms.

The San Francisco and other such valleys are also what might be thought of as oases for plants and animals which require permanent surface water or for the habitats that it fosters. Besides fish, animals needing an aquatic environment include many amphibians, turtles, water birds and such mammals as the beaver. Some of these and many other species require the riverside woodland and other habitats that the valleys sustain. The differing availability of surface water from the floor and up the slopes of the valleys results in a great diversity of habitats within a relatively small area. Such habitats range from stands of broadleaf trees and marshes to grassland and desert-like growths of mesquite, yucca and cacti. This large array of habitats in turn produces a diversity of animal life, so that valleys such as the San Francisco and Gila sustain a great many kinds of organisms. For example, in the Gila Valley some 115 species of birds breed, which is almost a fifth of the species regularly breeding in North America north of Mexico, and the as-yet-incompletely-surveyed San Francisco Valley will probably prove to be nearly as rich. The diversity of birdlife and doubtlessly of other groups of organisms in the vicinity of these two valleys is greater yet when one considers the very large array of habitats existing from the valley floors to the peaks of the Mogollon Mountains directly to the east. For example, within a 25 mile radius of Glenwood almost 200 species of birds may be expected to breed, a figure equalled or exceeded by few nonmarine regions in temperate North America.

The San Francisco Valley seen from afar, is a narrow ribbon of verdure through the usually brown hills and plateaus of southern Catron County, but in places it has been changed by settlement and agriculture. The open woodland along the river is predominantly cottonwood and willows, with other, less numerous trees including box elder, ash, walnut, sycamore, hackberry, oak, desert willow and others. Interposes between this riparian woodland and the river is often a fringe of the evergreen, shrubby composite called batamote or seepwillow. Beyond riparian woodland on the floodplain are thickets of mesquite and catclaw and these give way to chaparral and an evergreen woodland of oaks and junipers on the slopes.

Canyons opening into the San Francisco Valley are numerous and frequently support interesting and different assemblages of plants of their own. For example, in Whitewater Canyon are Arizona Alders, Netleaf Oaks, and Narrowleaf Cottonwoods - plants typical of the foothills rather than of the low Sonoran valleys. Towering over the San Francisco Valley are the Mogollon Mountains, which support pine, fir and spruce forests. All of these habitats combine with plains, cactus flats and others to provide the great biological diversity in the region centering on the San Francisco Valley, truly a natural treasure."

The Fire Regime

Another macro-dynamic of the watershed was fire, a cyclical occurrence with the grasslands before they were grazed down by cows. They burned often when set by lightning in the fall when the tall grass was dry. The fires helped the grassland maintain itself by burning back the other types of plants that would like to live there themselves, such as the cactuses, the larger forbs, the juniper and the piñon. High in the mountains, forest fires still become widespread in July. One period between the two-phase rainfall regime, the months of April, May and June, are quite dry. As this annual mini-drought continues into the summer, everything becomes desiccated and the humidity drops very low. Toward the first of July the dry electricity in the air begins to crackle and thunderheads begin to appear. Small at first, these thunderheads grow and finally the shock of thunder is heard, first in the highest mountains. Through the coming days as the dryness crackles and the thunderheads become larger, the fires begin. It seems that until it primes itself sufficiently, the thunderhead tribe cannot drop any rain and so the first lightning storms come through and there is lightning but no rain to put out the fires that are caused. Each July the Mogollon Rim has the highest fire rate of anywhere on the continent.

It is usually a week or ten days before the system can get itself primed and finally begin to drop rain. As the high mountains begin to get drenched, the phenomenon begins to generalize into the lower altitudes. Finally the immense flats stretching out toward Mexico are receiving a little rain. As the rain begins, the fires decrease sharply in number but continue sporadically until fall when the lightning storms cease. The view of a native, undisturbed ponderosa stand is the view of a park. From a grassy meadow one can look into the forest for a long distance past the giant, "yellow belly" ponderosas. Ordinarily, the fires that come through are ground fires that move along the ground rather slowly and ignite a bush here and there or a patch of bunch grass. The fire may singe, but never burn down the ponderosa, whose branches don't begin until fifty feet up. The effect of the fire is to open the forest and to prevent the ponderosa from entirely taking over so that a variety of other life can have space also. This is especially true in brushy chaparral where the fires are a common and natural occurrence. Fires actually help the fire-adapted varieties of that fertile zone.

The fires also help the aspen which can be forced out by the stronger fir and spruce at that higher zone. In a sense the aspen are nurse trees that come into an area first after disruption, along with the bushes with berries and other high elevation forbs and grasses. In a burned over area the aspen will resprout and hold the soil, help cool the area and help keep it moist until the evergreens can regenerate themselves.

The Human History

Humans were present at least 13,000 years ago in the southwest as indicated by the "Folsom Man" archeological find. Along with these humans were giant ground sloths, the dire wolf, the short faced bear, the saber-toothed cat, the mastodon, the mammoth, the giant peccary, camels, pronghorns of two additional species other than the one that exists today, ancient bison, the forest ox, the mountain goat, the tapir and several species of early horses. Like the large mammals world-wide, these species have disappeared during the last 10,000 years as the climate changed from grasslands in the lower areas and flatter areas of New Mexico to a more piñon-juniper regime.[4]

It is difficult to say how long humans have been in the Southwestern U.S. Most Native American people say that they have always been here. The academics cling to the Bering Strait Migration orthodoxy.

In the Mogollon Rim country we know that humans managed their longevity partially by corn. Although there were no doubt humans in the area earlier, small corn cobs have been found that date back 5,000 years. The archeological work at Bat Cave and Tularosa Cave, on the Watershed, show that corn came into the area at least that early and beans followed several thousand years later. Because some remains survive from 2,500 years B.P., we know that humans were then living in pit houses in the area. There is evidence of pit house people receding back many hundreds of years earlier in what is called the "Cochise Phase" in the Southwest, but no sites of that nature have been excavated on the San Francisco watershed.

On the San Francisco watershed there has been one major excavation of a 2,500 year old pit house village, which is called the SU site (after the large ranch with the SU brand). This site contains eighteen dwellings and it is considered by the principal archaeologist to be the only one within a fifteen to twenty-mile radius.

The archeologist, Paul Martin, describes the dwellings:

"Mogollon houses of the Pine Lawn phase lacked antechambers, partition walls, slab-linings or firepits. Furthermore, the roofs of early Mogollon houses were not supported in any standard fashion, as were the Anasazi roofs. Instead, one finds anywhere from one to six primary roof supports set apparently in higgledy-piggledy fashion (except the single roof support, which was placed near the center of the house) and never twice in the same way. Early Mogollon houses are irregular in shape, resembling an amoeba and are very shallow. Lateral entrances to Mogollon houses are not always present but when these entryways are found they may be short and stubby, or long with upward-sloping floors, and are oriented toward the east. Deep pits, sometimes several to a house, are frequently found in Mogollon houses."[5]

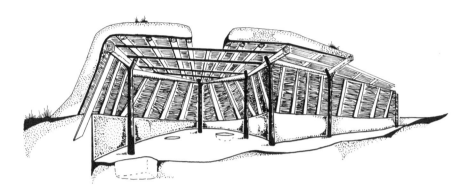

PIT HOUSE
BASED ON MARTIN

Most of the Pit House remains on the San Francisco watershed have been found in the chaparral area. The chaparral and the riparian habitats along the live (year around) streams must be considered the real fertility generating "islands" of the watershed. That we find the pit houses in this zone should be no surprise. From the chaparral zone the pit house people had the ecological zones above and below them available for forage. There is no doubt that the pit house people were sure to be in the chaparral in the fall when the natural harvest comes in. When the acorns drop in the fall and the piñon nuts are ready, the service berry, sumac, manzanita and rose hips ripen. Yucca bananas can also be found in the chaparral as can the smaller agaves. When the harvest is ready in the chaparral, the life of the area comes in to eat. Deer, bear, peccary, turkey, squirrels, pack rats, jay birds and others feast on the bounty. These animals attract others, coyotes, wolves, bobcats and mountain lions, who eat the herbivores.

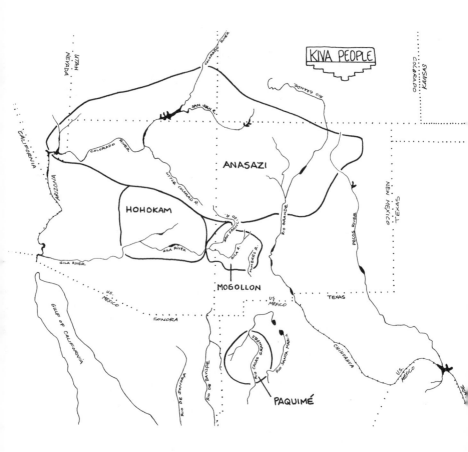

Transition to Sedentariness: The Kiva People

Food sources of the Pit House people as shown by excavations over a wide multi-state area differed according to the area and its availabilities. Subsistence shaded from almost pure hunting and foraging to almost exclusive farming. Anthropologist David Stuart gives some clues about the relative value of nomadic versus sedentary lifestyles. He says:

"It took field work among remnants of the world's nomadic peoples and in remote agricultural villages to discover the reasons. Under conditions of very low population density, nomadic hunter-gatherers earn a living with only 500 per capita hours of labor each year-and malnutrition is surprisingly rare! Unsophisticated agriculturalists required more than 1,000 per capita hours annually to do the same-but malnutrition and infant death are more common. So are crop failures."[6]

"Work time" stands at near 2,000 hours a year for the average industrial worker.

Beginning in 500 A.D., the San Francisco watershed was populated by the Kiva People (popularly known as "the Anasazi"), who, through change from the Pit House people or introduction of another strain of humans, were living in above ground "Pueblo" style buildings and all conducting spiritual activities in underground Kivas. These people are estimated to have remained on the Watershed until 1250 or 1300 A.D. They were closely related to the Mimbres subgroup nearby, one hundred miles to the east, as shown by the large number of "Mimbres style" pots dug up on the Watershed of the San Francisco.

One can hardly walk around on the Watershed at the chaparral level or below, on any suitable housing site, without finding pot shards, stone tools, arrow heads or other remains of the Kiva People. Archaeologists estimate at least 30,000 people lived in the area before the disappearance. Archeologist Christopher Nightingale who has done the most extensive survey of the area puts the figure at a level, "In excess of 30,000." No more sharp contrast could be drawn in cultural land use patterns than the fact that 2,700 people live in the same area now and only marginally, within the definitions of the industrial society.

The culture of the Kiva people was no doubt very similar to the nineteen native pueblos in New Mexico today. The adaptation to the land was by village. The village was located generally near live water so that water could be channelled in to the crops. The basic subsistence crops were mother corn and her daughters beans and squash. Beans and corn provide a complete amino-acid combination. Particularly, in the New Mexico region, green chiles were also a part of the inventory. There was tremendous variation within each of these species. The strains of corn held even today by contemporary pueblos vary according to color, water needs, temperature needs and other considerations. This same situation applies also to the bean and squash varieties.

There probably were also ancillary cultivars, such as there are in the pueblos today. Domesticated types of the wild groundcherry are grown, sunflowers are often seeded around fields, devil's claw is often domesticated and grown as well as many other useful plants. It should be mentioned that various "weed" species are usually kept around the field areas for various purposes also.

CORN   OAK

Pollen analysis of archaeological digs in Central America indicate that for nine thousand years the Mayan adaptation diet has predominated in corn, cucurbit (squash), beans, meat, agave, chili peppers, ceiba (a tree fruit), bristle grass (setaria-seeds ground to flour), cactus and amaranth.

Mother corn and her daughters are the Meso-American adaptation. In reality, the Anazasi were suburbs of the centers such as Copán and Tikal of the Central American Mayas. The pueblo cosmology, especially the Hopi, shares major patterns with the Meso-American. In Frank Waters's definitive work, *Mexico Mystique: The Coming Sixth World of Consciousness*, (Swallow Press, 1975), the similarities are clearly laid out. In the pueblos today the traditional shell necklaces called heishi are made of shell from both the Atlantic and the Pacific. The old trade routes that connected the oceans, Central America and the pueblos to the north are known. In some Kiva ceremonies, parrot feathers are still required. Just below the center of modern nuclear war at the city of Los Alamos, New Mexico, is the ruin of an ancient pueblo. As one walks up the trail approaching the mesa where the ruin is located, a long serpent is visible on the cliff face. It is the symbol of Quetzal Coatl, the redeemer and symbol of the life force of Meso-America.

From diet flows social structure in natural culture and then in the industrial inversion, diet becomes the result of what plants mass machine production methods can most profitably grow and harvest. Because of mother corn and her daughters, the pueblos must stay in one place, thus houses. The irrigated varieties of these plants require flat land near live streams. This means that some authority must apportion the scarce water and land resources. This all results in something of a stratification in the pueblos but this is not the hierarchy of the empire with which we are familiar. In most pueblos today there is no permanent leader. Leadership is rotated annually in a complex formula the precludes complete elitism. Rotation of responsibility among other "offices" and even rotation of different groups is customary. The cultures of the pueblos, which are each self-governing entities, are extremely complex. It is this complexity in addition to the cultural values that mitigates the solidification of exploiting elites.

Often in the pueblos there is an equal division into two parts, that anthropologists call moieties. One is born into their moiety. In several pueblos these are called the summer people and the winter people. This carries with it certain ceremonial obligations that relate to the seasons as well as others. One is born into a clan such as turtle, eagle, or bear. One is often born into one of several divisions in the moieties. One often joins a secret spiritual society that may or may not be related to one's birth line. One then, may marry. This will double the relational web of one's life. Finally, as an individual, one will become distinguished for talents or style and that will produce its own conditioning of all relationships. Though this listing may seem long, it by no means is exhaustive of the tremendous complexity with which the pueblos function. We must add to this a calender cycle that includes both functional acts such as ditch cleaning, the first deer hunt, the time of bean planting and such. The other important calendar cycle is the ceremonial cycle which is winter to winter and includes many ceremonies large and small, public and private.

One of the big reasons that jobs in industrial society destroy pueblo culture is that the functioning of this great swirling, ever-changing mandala of culture requires- time. In this mandala, all is integrated, the cosmos- through the star movement timing of certain ceremonies, right down to the seasonal bean dance. It is this constant flux of responsibility and the dense web of human relationships that have prevented any pueblo culture in known history from being taken over and eradicated in any permanent way.[7]

This is the culture that typified the Kiva People of the San Francisco watershed. The Kiva People of the San Francisco left at about the same time as the other "Anazasi" in the southwest, from 1200 to 1250 A.D. Some questions remain. Why did they leave? Did they exhaust the soils? Did they deforest they area for firewood during their long tenure? Did they deplete the animals and wild foraging plants to the point they have no supplemental food sources? We don't know, we can only speculate. Their disappearance could have been something entirely social, following a vision or prophecy.

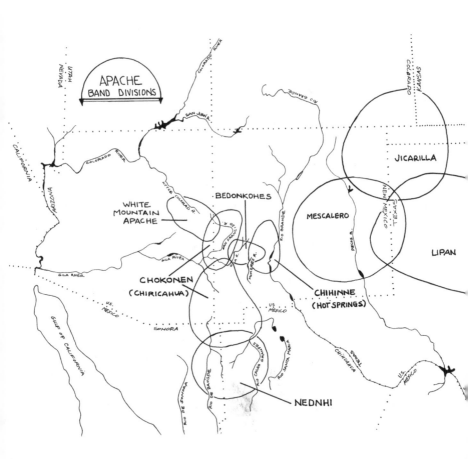

Forager/Hunters: The Apache

The forager/hunter people commonly known as the Apache came into the watershed soon after the exit of the Kiva People. The groups popularly known as Apache are Athabascan. They are part of a sizable language group that includes the large Athabascan tribe of northern Canada, the Navajo, the Hoopa on the coast of northern California and the decimated group who lived near Grants Pass in southwestern Oregon.

Just as the G/wi, living in one part of the Kalahari Desert used tsama melons as the basis of their food sustenance, the !Kung living in another part of the same desert used the ground nut, mongongo, for their primary subsistence. In the same way the various Athabascan tribes of the Southwestern U.S. maintained different lifestyles based upon the different ecologies that they were integrated with, stretching from the Great Plains in the vicinity of Oklahoma and Northern Texas (Kiowa and Lipan Apache), through Northeastern New Mexico (Jicarilla), to Eastern-Southeastern New Mexico (Mescalero), then across the Mogollon Rim and into Central Arizona (Hot Springs, Chiricauhua and Western Apache). One band, the Nednhi lived in the northern part of the Sierra Madre in Mexico. Each of these groups and areas maintained a life style based on the particular life system with which they lived.okonen band

It was the northern branch of the Chokonen (Chiricahua Apache) that specifically occupied the San Francisco watershed. This band was led by Chihuahua in the last days. This is the northern division of the Chokonen and the southern band was led by Cochise. Though we say that a band is specifically identified with an area, it may be more accurate to say that they were localized there. Bands ebbed and flowed and often entered each others customary area to visit and forage. On the east of the Watershed along the Mogollon Rim and on its back side, to the north, lived the Bedonkohes. These people are popularly identified by their famous son by marriage (he was actually born into the Nednhi Apaches of the Sierra Madre) Geronimo. Just to the northeast of the Bedonkohes, along the Black Range and north on the west side of the Rio Grande to the vicinity of what is now Truth or Consequences, New Mexico, lived the Chihinnes- Hot Springs Apaches, popularly identified with the last free leader, Victorio.

The bands were identified with these areas, though they ranged widely. In the last days of the resistance it is known that they ranged from southern Colorado to south central Mexico. Mobility was the key element in their ecological adaptation. They harvested the surpluses of the land and they had to know where these would be and when. The ethnobotanists, Morris E. Opler and Edward F. Castetter give this summation of the Apache forager lifestyle and it certainly could be applied to all of the forager people, in general, that have lived on the earth:

The Apache; "Moved with the seasonal change of weather and followed the wild food harvests as they occurred.... When colder weather came he (sic) removed to a lower altitude; in summer he (sic) was in the highlands again. When the mesquite and screwbean ripened on the flats, parties of Apache were there to gather them; when the hawthorn hips were ready in the highlands, Apache were nearby to take them. These people knew nature's calendar by heart, and no matter whether a grass seed ripened or a certain animal's fur or flesh was at its best at a particular time, the Apache was present to share in the harvest."[8]

The integration of the forager people with the life of the earth is essential and natural, so that the weather, the daily habits of the animals and plants and one's own intuition vis-a-vis the natural world make up a composite of perception in which one becomes part of the life of earth- becomes natural life.

James Kaywaykla was a grandson of Nana. Nana was the elder who rode with Geronimo. Kaywaykla was a Chihinne. The tribal name of Chihinne means Red People, referring to the red band of clay that the tribespeople put across their faces just under the eyes to cut the glare of the sun. (In modern day usage they are called the Ojo Calientes or Hot Springs Apaches.) Kaywaykla tells of the foraging habits of his people. He says in translation:

"My people spent their summers in the mountains of New Mexico, carefree, untrammeled. They migrated to Mexico in the fall, living off the land as they went, killing game, harvesting fruit, and giving thanks to Ussen for the good things He had given. They knew the land of jungles and of tropical fruit. They knew the people whose land they crossed. They were on the very best of terms with Cochise and his band. They penetrated the fastness of Juh, Chief of the Nednhi, and were received as brothers. When they in turn came to us we gave freely of our best."[9]

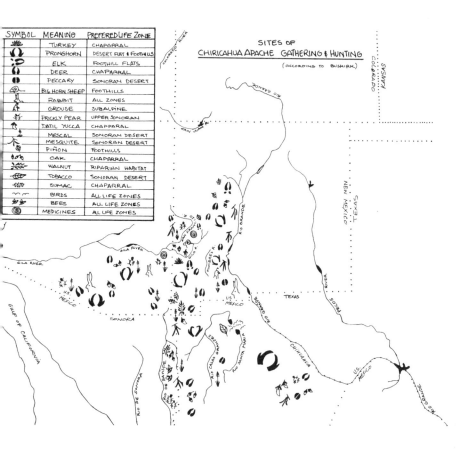

SYMBOL	MEANING	PREFERRED LIFE ZONE
	TURKEY	CHAPARRAL
	PRONGHORN	DESERT FLAT & FOOTHILLS
	ELK	FOOTHILL FLATS
	DEER	CHAPARRAL
	PECCARY	SONORAN DESERT
	BIG HORN SHEEP	FOOTHILLS
	RABBIT	ALL ZONES
	GROUSE	SUBALPINE
	PRICKLY PEAR	UPPER SONORAN
	DATIL YUCCA	CHAPARRAL
	MESCAL	SONORAN DESERT
	MESQUITE	SONORAN DESERT
	PIÑON	FOOTHILLS
	OAK	CHAPARRAL
	WALNUT	RIPARIAN HABITAT
	TOBACCO	SONORAN DESERT
	SUMAC	CHAPARRAL
	BIRDS	ALL LIFE ZONES
	BEES	ALL LIFE ZONES
	MEDICINES	ALL LIFE ZONES

SITES OF
CHIRICAHUA APACHE GATHERING & HUNTING

(ACCORDING TO BUSKIRK)

Each mountain range was a repository for many of the items that the Apaches used. On the northern edge of the Sierra Madre Occidental, the stronghold of the Nednhi Apaches, lastly led by Juh, the high mountains and foothills provided agave (agave palmerii), deer, walnuts (juglana rupestris, var. major), acorns (quercus emoryii, q. reticulata, q. turbinella, q. grises, and q. arizonica), honey, nopal fruits (opuntia phaeacantha) and mesquite (prosopis juliaflora). The Chiracahua band, popularly identified with the leader Cochise, were centered around the Dragoon, Chiracahua, Peloncillo and Hatchet mountain ranges and they had similar food with the addition of datil yucca (yucca baccata), palmilla yucca (yucca elata) and sumac. Pronghorn (often called antelope but they are not antelope, they belong to a family that is neither deer nor antelope) were available on the flats separating the ranges. The Bedonkohes, Geronimo's tribe, were centered on the headwaters of the Gila and San Francisco Rivers. This area provided mountain sheep, pronghorn, elk, deer, acorns, mescal (agave), datil yucca, nopal fruit, mesquite and piñon nuts. The Chihinnes, who centered around Ojo Caliente, enjoyed a variety similar to the Bedonkohes just south of them. These are primary items and dozens of other items of less importance were used.[10]

Probably the most important items of the Chokonen and Bedonkohe diet on the Watershed were the pronghorns, mesquite, mescal (also called agave), and acorns. The pronghorns existed from the desert area up to at least high ponderosa forest. More important than elevation is the pronghorns' need of flat land. With their amazing speed of 50-70 mph and binocular vision it is necessary for them to live in flat areas at whatever elevation they can find them. The flats must be sufficiently expansive to allow them the distance to run from their pursuers and the flats also must be smooth topsoil without rocks. As these animals existed from the desert up to the higher regions, they were a favorite animal food of the native people.

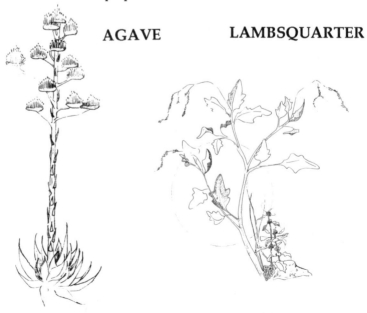

AGAVE   LAMBSQUARTER

The agave was probably the most important plant food of the Apache.[11] The agave grows best in the desert region but will grow up into the piñon-juniper to the ponderosa, although the form of the plant found there is smaller.

Anthropologist Winfred Buskirk says that the agave could be used at any season, although because the plants were abundant in an area that was the Apache's wintering environment this was normally when they were used. Any of the plants would suffice, but the best were the ones that were preparing to flower. The agaves, which are sometimes called the "century plant," only bloom once and then die. The northern agaves may bloom at ten to fifteen years, but agaves farther south in Mexico may go as long as thirty years before they flower and die:

> "In the fall and winter good edible plants could be selected by observing the leaf bases and the terminal shoot, a thickening of which indicated that the plant would bloom the following spring. The best time for gathering was in the early spring, usually in April, at which time some of the plants blossomed. At this season enough mescal was prepared to last through the summer or longer."[12]

The root was severed under the bulb and the plant taken out of the ground. The leaves of the plant were trimmed off and it was ready for roasting. The crowns average twenty pounds each and as many as forty would be roasted at one time. Basehart, who studied the Apache subsistence cycle, states that the Chiracahua gathered forty to sixty crowns per year per family, and that a month or more might be spent gathering the food.

The agaves were roasted in an earth pit, up to twelve feet in diameter and two to four feet deep. The pit was filled with oak and then fired. Small eight inch diameter lava rocks were layered over the coals, some beargrass put in as a cover and the agaves were then put into the pit. Beargrass was again put over the top and the pit was sealed with earth; an additional fire on the top of this earth appears to have been optional. Kaywaykla says that his people put the long narrow leaves of the agave down into the pit, standing them upright as they filled the pit. As the cooking progressed, they were able to check on the progress of the cooking by pulling out a leaf. The condition of the leaf indicated when the agave was cooked. Various references indicate that the agave was cooked from one to two days. After baking, the agave was pounded flat into sheets several inches thick and dried like jerky (sun dried meat). The food in this condition could be kept for a matter of years. A one-quarter cup serving of prepared agave provides thirty calories and more calcium than does a half glass of milk.[13]

Agave is very sweet and could be used with pemmican, mush, mixed with flour for breads or used in many other ways in addition to eating the dried material without further preparation.

Another use of the agave was for sewing. The sharp spine on the tip of the agave leaf can be used as a needle and the strong fibers of the leaf are used as a pre-attached thread. The leaves are simply dried and the pulp of the leaf pounded out so the remaining portion, the fibers, are used in braided or twisted fashion with its own sharp needle. Kaywaykla mentions that it is an effective method with which to sew rawhide soles onto moccasins. The juice of young agave leaves is also used medicinally when signs of impending scurvy are detected.

Both types of yuccas, (elata-narrow leaf and baccata-wide leaf) were used in the same life zone as the agave. Elata is the familiar soap yucca and its stem and flowers were also used as food. Baccata or datil yucca bears a fruit of exquisite taste which grow from five to seven inches long. These fruits are called yucca bananas and they can be eaten fresh, roasted, dried or ground into meal. The young inner shoots of this plant can also be used.

YUCCA BACCATA   PRONGHORN

The nopal cactus is a prolific plant in the desert and up into the piñon-juniper zone where its varieties grow smaller. The elephant ear leaf can be eaten as well as the fruit which is called "prickly pear" or <u>tuna</u>, in Spanish. In Mexico and in Latin groceries in the U.S., the chopped leaf can be purchased as "nopalitos". The fruit of this plant was especially used by the Apaches.

NOPAL

MOUNTAIN SHEEP

Mountain sheep were abundant in the desert ranges and in the foothills of the Mogollon Rim. These animals gain security by their unusual agility in the rocky heights of steep hills, mountains and cliffs. While not necessarily bound by life zone, it occurs that this type of terrain exists primarily in the desert and piñon-juniper regions.

Like many of the animals, the Apaches migrated seasonally, but this did not mean that they moved <u>en masse</u> everywhere they went. Basehart says, "Not all... would move any great distance in a given year, nor would the same families and larger social units travel in identical directions and distances from year to year. Thus, a group might remain close to a central base throughout one year, and travel a considerable distance the next; alliances between families were not permanent, but could shift from season to season."[14]

The Apaches did much grinding of flours. Seeds are the obvious basis of flours but seed coatings, pollen and other plant parts can also be dried and ground as flour either by itself or mixed with other desirable flours. Sources of

Apache flours were mesquite, screw bean mesquite, agave, acorn, piñon, sunflower seeds, walnuts, juniper berries, grass seeds of many types, chia in the lower elevations, devil's claw seed, coyote melon seed (calabazia), tule pollen, and amaranth seeds.

SUNFLOWER

AMARANTH

Prominent among the greens used was the amaranth (amaranthus palmeri). (Gary Nabhan says of the plant; "The raw Amaranthus palmeri greens [one hundred grams] contain nearly three times as many calories [36], eighteen times the amount of vitamin A [6100 international units], thirteen times the amount of vitamin C [80 milligrams], twenty times the amount of calcium [411 mg.], and almost seven times the amount of iron [3.4 mg.] as one hundred grams of lettuce.")[15] The immature rocky mountain bee plant (cleome serrulata) was also a staple green. Other plants known to be favored by the Apache were wild potatoes (solanum jamesii) and wild onions (allium cernuum), both which grow prominently in the chaparral.

BEE PLANT

CANAGRIA

The Apaches did some planting in the canyons and river bottoms. The detailed knowledge of the different corn colors and strains shown by anthropologists' informants, demonstrate the fact that there must have been considerable farming. The crops raised were essentially corn and beans but, of course, the seeds of wild food plants were often scattered around camp so there would be an abundant supply near.

Anthropologists estimate that the Apaches used nearly fifty species of food plants comprising 40-50 per cent of their diet. Because anthropologists were visiting the Apaches long after they had been concentrated in the reservation camps and long after the methodical and planned destruction of their culture had begun, it would be difficult to inventory their complete knowledge and lifestyle. We could suffice it to say that the Apaches probably made use of everything that was reasonably edible and used a large inventory of what they found on the land for materials to create the shelters, tools and the basic necessities of their life. Humans of course do not live in a vacuum of simply eating. The Apache display of humility and sophisticated ethical cultural perception of much of the rest of the Pleistocene inheritance. Kaywaykla, for example, speaks of the consideration for the animals and other life of the earth. He points out that animals were never killed at waterholes because of the consideration that all beings were put on the earth and that they must drink, too. They were not killed there out of fairness to them.

Geronimo (Gothlay)

Nah-thle-tla

Nana

Chihuahua

Naiche

Victorio

COATI-MUNDI

Arrival of Empire: The Story of the Last
Native People on the Watershed

Santa Fe, the Capital of what originally was called the Kingdom of New Mexico, was already a thriving village when the Pilgrims reached Plymouth Rock. Spanish immigrants, many of them from northern Spain, reached New Mexico by the Fifteen Hundreds. They first attacked the various pueblos in order to enslave the people and usurp the bottom lands for agricultural use. The blood flowed freely. The Spanish recreated the feudal culture of Spain in New Mexico with landed estates in the form of land grants given by the King of Spain. These land grants featured the landed aristocrat on the choice land surrounded in the village area by the non-landed spanish and then in an outer area lived the "coyotes," mixed-race people and detribalized natives. They were the buffer against raiders. This "Rancho Grande" colonialist structure was based in agrarian pursuits and occupied the best bottom lands of the Southwest. The "Rancho Grande" of the colonialist cattle baron such as existed across northern Mexico and is fixated in the balance of the Latin American mentality, could not be established in the open spaces of New Mexico because the nomadic tribes could not be exterminated or subdued as were the sedentary pueblo people who were based mostly in the river bottoms. Centuries passed in New Mexico with the Spanish holding the fertile bottom lands and the nomadic tribes moving freely in the surrounding area. The tribes raided the Spanish and the

Spanish in turn raided the tribes for slaves. Slaves were held in New Mexico society as well as being sent south into Mexico from the slave markets of Taos and Abiquiu. At the time of the Civil War, a Senate Investigating Committee found that New Mexicans held one-third of the Navajo tribe in forced slavery in their semi-feudal society.

The Chokonen, Chihinne and Bedonkohe bands first encountered Spanish near the watershed of the San Francisco river in Southwestern New Mexico in the Sixteen Hundreds. They came to work the mines in the Silver City area, south of the Mogollon Rim. The first groups of miners left, but later, others arrived for the silver metal. Like the personality pattern of other parts of the empire, swelling around the globe, the people invading the southwest carried the stamp of empire culture. These conquerors had light colored skins which they believed inherently superior, they were part of the flock of the Christian God, creator of the universe. They were part of a rising tide of machine makers and importantly they had the superior knowledge to "develop" the land and cultivate its ability to "produce." They also came from a culture whose central value was material goods and they were being offered the prospect of land and the "resources" on it including the native slave labor. The magnetic dream that pulled them was akin to winning the status of the landed, aristocratic nobility of Europe, on the lottery. It was this Christian/imperial mind-set that helps explain the gigantic moral atrocities these people committed upon the "godless savages." The native people and the land were there to be plundered.

As we would guess, the first significant contact between Apaches and the Europeans in the area of the Watershed was tragic. The first significant event occurred at the mines at Santa Rita, between the Mimbres and Gila rivers. Mangas Coloradas (Red Sleeves) was chief of the Chihinnes. At that time the Governor of the Mexican state of Chihuahua was offering money for Apache scalps. A man named Johnson and a number of his friends invited Mangas Coloradas and his band, reported to be several hundred, in to the mining camp for a feast. When the Apaches had begun the feast, the miners opened up on them with either a gatling gun or cannons (reports conflict). A large number were killed. Mangas Coloradas was wounded, but he escaped, carrying only his son Mangus who had not been killed.

Later, in mid-Eighteen Hundreds, when the Americans had taken the Southwest from Mexico, a Colonel Carleton came out of California leading a group called the California Column who were going to fight in the U.S. Civil War, in the east. By the time these men reached Arizona and New Mexico it appeared that their services would not be needed as the war had ended but ambitious to make a name for themselves, they began to attack Apaches. At about this time Mangas Coloradas went into the camp of these Americans to attempt to make peace with the new kind of Europeans. As he was there under a flag of truce, nonetheless he was killed. His head was then cut off and boiled. Later the skull appeared on the east coast where it was exhibited to curious crowds in a touring carnival. Victorio then succeeded as chief. In 1870 the Chihinne lead by Victorio were "given" a reservation at Ojo Caliente, west of the present Truth or Consequences, New Mexico, by Executive Order of the President of the United States. Shortly after this promise, they were forced out of that area and marched eighty miles west to Fort Tularosa on the San Francisco watershed and held over the winter by the military. The promised supplies did not arrive until spring and then they were of the characteristic inferior quality. Many died that winter of starvation and exposure. After this experience, the government allowed them to return to Ojo Caliente but shortly they were given orders to go to the death camp at San Carlos where hundreds of Apaches had already died of malaria and starvation with full knowledge of the United States government. Victorio and his group went there, some in chains, never again to have their promised reservation.

Members of the Chokonen, Chihinne and Bedonkohe bands several times broke out of the concentration camp at San Carlos. During the last escape of Victorio, many Chihinne and members of other bands went with him. From this escape they never returned. They were trapped by the Mexican Army at a range of mountains called Tres Castillos southeast of El Paso, across the border in Mexico. Almost all of the Chihinne and Bedonkohe, including Victorio, were killed at that time except for a few who escaped in the dark. During the last days of the Apache resistance, the Spanish had consolidated their hold on the bottom lands of the watershed and the Texas Cattle Barons were already swarming in. The invaders and their strident newspapers demanded that the last "renegade" Apaches either be killed or locked up on reservations. Nonetheless, several small groups stayed out and on the run for five long years as the press and the settlers remained in hysterics over the "savages". The main group was led by Geronimo and Nana of the Bedonkohes and Naiche, son of Cochise of the Chokonen. This small band of people who numbered less than 30 (25 men, the rest women and children) faced as high as 5,000 U.S. Army troops (one quarter of the U.S. Army at the time), scattered through the southwest, who rode grain fed horses and were securely supplied with food and other necessities from the U.S. Treasury. The Apaches had only their Pleistocene knowledge of the life of the area to sustain them, but because they were so pursued, they could not follow the seasons or even effectively hunt for the dwindling game of the area, yet, still they persisted by finding what they could on the land and by raiding the invaders.

Finally, the small band surrendered, September 3, 1886, to General of the U.S. Army, Nelson A. Miles who lied to the Apaches and promised them a reservation and much else that he could not deliver. The small band, who had been enticed away from their stronghold in the Sierra Madre of Mexico by General Miles' lies, were led ultimately to the Southern Pacific railway tracks north of the border. There they were loaded into boxcars along with all of the Chokonen, Chihinne and Bedonkohe people that still survived on the San Carlos reservation. Based on the lies of the U.S. government, other leaders, Mangus, the son of Mangas Coloradas of the Bedonkohes and Chihuahua, leader of the northern division of the Chokonen tribe, both separately brought small bands in at that time. They too were loaded into boxcars.

This group of the last hold-outs and the remainder of those four tribes who were living peaceably on the Fort Apache and San Carlos reservations were all put on railroad trains and shipped to a military prison in Florida. More than 400 prisoners of the Chihinne, Bedonkohe, and the two tribes of Chokonen Apaches were confined as prisoners of war for 27 years. The duplicity was such that 14 Apache scouts who had turned on their own people and in fact were the only reason that the U.S. Army could get close to the holdouts, were also imprisoned. When the government in Washington, D.C. finally realized they had also imprisoned these 14 U.S. Army enlisted men (the Apache scouts) the government ordered them mustered out of the service and kept them imprisoned along with the others. Later, the remains of the tribes were confined at an army reservation at Fort Sill, Oklahoma. In 1913 an act of Congress allowed those who wished, to return to the Mescalero Reservation of New Mexico, but due to loud protests from the people of Arizona who now occupied part of the traditional home of the Apache, they were prohibited from moving to Arizona.

The Apaches were the human casualties of the march of Empire, and it was their resistance to invasion that is responsible for the Mogollon Rim country being even as relatively undamaged and uninhabited as it is, because they kept the settlers out and then when the Apaches were removed the cattlemen who had a sparse population moved in.

In 1913 some of the Apache men who had been young boys at General Miles "peace parley" when Geronimo surrendered, returned to their homeland to decide whether they wanted to come to the old original Chihinne "reservation" at Ojo Caliente or whether those returning would like to go to the Mescalero reservation in east-central New Mexico. Jason Betzinez describes the return to Ojo Caliente of the last handful of Chihinnes after many years of imprisonment and after the invasion of the cattle barons:

"In the morning we resumed our journey to Monticello. This was where the Apaches had made their first peace with the Mexicans. We did not stop, because we all were anxious to get on to our old reservation. From Monticello the route led up the dry creek bed which previously had been such a nice little stream. Now it was all filled in with gravel, which made it twenty jumps wide instead of the one jump which it had been before.

"We arrived at the old agency after dark but got up early next morning in our eagerness to look around at our old homeland. What a depressing sight it turned out to be! The whole country, once so fertile and green, was now entirely barren. Gravel had washed down, covering all the nice valleys and pastures, even filling up the Warm Springs, which had completely vanished. The reservation was entirely ruined. Looking around bitterly, I said to myself, 'Oklahoma is good enough for me.'"[16]

There are now, no native people on the watershed, though there are many reservations within a one hundred-fifty mile radius, the White Mountain Apache, San Carlos, the large Navajo reservation in northeastern Arizona, Hopi, Zuñi, Ramah Navajo, Acoma, Laguna, Cañoncito, Alamo Navajo reservation near Magdalena, New Mexico and the Mescalero Apache reservation.[17]

The Ecological Effects of Colonization

Spanish herders began moving into the San Francisco watershed even before the Apaches had been eliminated. By the 1870's the wealthy Luna brothers of Los Lunas, New Mexico south of Albuquerque were grazing the area heavily with tens of thousands of head of sheep. At this same time, Spanish settlers were coming into the mountain valleys from the Los Lunas-Belen area bringing herds of cattle, sheep and goats. Some of the first were the Aragon family of the village of Aragon and the Benevidez family who settled near the present Village of Reserve. The first settlement, Plaza de San Francisco de Asisi del Medio was created near the confluence of the Negrito and San Francisco Rivers. Then the Jirón family came from Belen to establish Plaza Abajo, (Plaza San Francisco de Asisi de Abajo, or Lower Plaza). In the early days of Spanish settlement the relations with the Apaches were somewhat peaceable with only several Spanish people being killed (there is no historical record of how many Apaches may have been killed). The Chihinnes in the Ojo Caliente area had maintained cordial relations with the Spanish people of Monticello for many years, trading and visiting back and forth. The Spanish store at Monticello had sold guns and ammunition to the Apaches for years and that may have influenced the Apache perception of the Spanish people on the Rio San Francisco.

The Spanish headed for the most fertile lands in the area. They settled in the riparian life zone and by their occupancy extirpated most of the rich life of that area. The lush riparian zone rapidly gave way to the culture of empire as the beavers were killed out, the large ponderosas were cut for domestic use and the stock ate the willows and other vegetation. The riparian zone, except for a few areas almost inaccessible, was denuded and the rich soil that remained became pasture and agricultural fields. Much of this soil is now gone and much that does not have irrigation or seep water can hardly grow what the culture terms weeds. The sad remnants of the beaver tribe which in the past stretched down the San Francisco and then down the Gila to the Colorado river at Yuma, Arizona are now found only at two headwater tributaries of the San Francisco. There is a colony on Apache Creek and a strong colony at the top of the Watershed above Alpine, Arizona. The descendants of some of the beaver families try to branch out and establish new homes but persecution from the humans and the flood problems usually defeat them.

The only way that they can really re-establish themselves is to start from the top down. In that way they have some control of the water volume. If they try to build homes and environments in the lower elevations they are flooded out by the water coming off the overgrazed, undammed watershed above. As all of the flatter areas higher up are grazed by confined livestock, everything is eaten down to the low grass and there is nothing along the streams for the beavers to build dams with or to eat. Even in the higher areas the domesticated cow will tend to stay in the canyon bottoms and eat them out rather than forage the hillsides.

Throughout North America the extirpation of beavers has had a generally unmentioned and unrecognized but severe negative effect on the ecology. Beavers and their works are a main pillar of the life system. The dams of beavers affect the hydrology of entire life zones. This provides beaver marsh habitat in many areas of watersheds. It also helps insure live water in the streams year-around rather than the swift run-off. Beaver marshes create habitat for innumerable species, fish, frogs, insects and many others. Due to the micro-environment created, plant species are able to come into the area. Cattails and arrowleaf potatoes are types of small plants that are very useful for humans and animals. The trees that take root in these marshes, often willows, cottonwood and aspen, also lend their help in further enhancing the habitat.

Many species can be easily seen to engage in life activities that prepare and assist their environment for their benefit. With the beavers it is the creation of the marsh, that allows the water retention, that in turn encourages their preferred food trees to come in and live there. Never the less, the basic populations of Beavers were wiped out prior to 1900.

Following the Civil War at mid-century, a great push west occurred. Militarily freed-up from the civil conflict, the cavalry was turned on the native people. Military campaigns to confine or exterminate the native people served to "open-up the west." The prospect of super-profits had drawn the "mountain men" and businesses like the Hudson Bay Company west. At times as much as 1,000 % profit could be realized between what the traders gave the indians for beaver pelts and what they would bring on the New York and London markets.

When the Civil War closed, settlers rushed to grab the best of the free land. Mines and timbering were started where possible, but the quickest money came from cattle. As the Yakimas, the Nez Perce, the Paiutes, the Shoshones, the Blackfeet, the Cheyenne, the Navajo, Apache and many other tribes were confined, cattle swarmed onto their lands by the millions. With a herd of cattle and enough guns a cattle baron could move west onto free grazing land. The land of the American west was covered with good grass. In the Great Basin area there were the bunch grasses, in the Southwest there were the nutritious gramma grasses. With little investment other than a herd of cows and a crew who were handy with guns to scare off any settlers who might want to invade the range, a cattle baron could have a "cattle empire" for free. The herd would increase by the number of bred heifers each year and more western grass could be turned into yankee dollars.

Most of the herds that hit the Southwest and specifically the Watershed in this era came out of Texas. Rancher William French established a "spread" early on the Watershed before the Apaches were completely confined. He was the scion of an English colonial family whose children were spread from India to New Mexico as colonial administrators or "owners," and his comments on the invasion of Texans reflects his "social station:"

"During the years between 1882 and 1885 a number of cattle-men moved their herds, and occasionally their neighbors' herds, from Texas to New Mexico. This migration was generally in the way of business, but sometimes its object was to avoid unpleasant consequences of a not too strict observance of the law. A new brand, a new name, and a new country covered a multitude of sins. Amongst those whose absence from Texas was tolerated only on the grounds of saving expense to the State were many cowboys who lost no opportunity of displaying their hatred of Mexicans. To them all Mexicans were 'Greasers' and unfit associates for the white man."[18]

The racism on which French comments is held by what is now the "Anglo" majority of the area, to this day. The Spanish hatred of Native Americans also continues.

The effect of the massive over-grazing of the West was first to extirpate much of the bunch grass and gramma from its usual habitat. Most of the other native grasses followed such that today it is rare to find an area anywhere in the West where there is a natural mix of native grass species like the original grass cover.

Not only did the grass suffer but the native wildlife declined. The cattle Barons continued massive campaigns of extermination, not just against the settlers and sheep herders but against the coyotes, wolves, mountain lions, grizzly bears, black bears, kangaroo rats, prairie dogs, snakes of all kinds, eagles, hawks, badgers, bison, pronghorn, wild mustangs and any other living thing that might by any stretch of the imagination threaten the life of or eat the food of- the sacred cow.

For example, prior to the 30-30 Remington repeating rifle of the cowboy and the "sod busters" of the plains, the herd of pronghorn in North America is estimated to have been 20 to 40 million. By 1908 only 17,000 remained.([19]) The elimination of the beavers and over-grazing, especially of the riparian habitats, altered the hydrology of the continent. As the water run-off increased and flooding began, the narrow, shaded and slow flowing stream beds were torn out and became wide, dry washes filled with gravel and occasional "flash floods." As flooding increased, arroyo cutting began. The flood of water washes out the bottom of the stream bed in a lower elevation causing a small "waterfall" on its upper side. As flooding continues the small cliff face of the "Waterfall" successively crumbles away and the cliff face moves up the watershed. This causes the deep trenches that are termed "erosion canyons." As these canyons develop, what water there is, flows at a much lower level. What groundwater there was in the soil seeps out of the cliff faces on the sides of the erosion canyon thus dropping the water table for the whole area. Then much of the remaining plant life dies because their roots cannot reach water.

The life of the desert and semi-arid desert travels in many cycles. The cycles of the annual and perennial grass is such that it can survive drought - if it has been able to build up a sufficient sod layer in the good years. It is the storage of nutrient and life force in the elongating root system that allows the grass to revive its green parts after a fire or being eaten. When it must sacrifice the root to rebuild the green matter, the root shrivels correspondingly. If the green part of the plant is cropped down too often so that it cannot rebuild the root system, the plant will die. If there has been severe damage to it, then it will not be able to pull through the dry years.

There was a drought on the San Francisco watershed in 1892-1893 as there was in much of the West. It was so bad that many cattle died. Many natural animals no doubt also died. Another drought happened in the period 1900-1904.

A local historian tells of those days:

"In the early days, numbers and not quality counted and in the struggle for control, the range was seriously overgrazed until the 1892-1893 drought reduced numbers and permitted the range to recuperate somewhat. However, the range again stocked up.

Another drought occurred in 1900 through 1904. A 1917 report stated, 'But the range has never recovered from this past abuse and it seems as though this last drought had about finished it. When this reconnaissance was made, the range was practically denuded and there is yet no relief in sight!

In 1927, D.A. Shoemaker made an inspection report of grazing on the forest and had this to say. 'On the whole, the New Mexico division of this forest presents as poor a range management as I have observed on any National Forest area.' "[20]

One of the functions of the vegetative life on the Watershed is to flatten out the water cycles. As in many semi-arid environments, the summer thunder showers are brief but heavy. One of the cycle harmonizers that have helped prevent this heavy onslaught of water and help it sink into the earth rather than run rapidly off, cutting erosion canyons, is the prairie dog. The burrows of the prairie dog absorb much water and this can be verified by watching them come top side during a thunder storm.

Another benefit of these small animals is indicated by the studies that show that the burrowing animals help the soil by the mixing of topsoil and mineralized subsoil into fine particles. The U.S. Biological Survey of 1908 came through, southeast of the Watershed, in Grant County. At that time they estimated 6,400,000 prairie dogs in that county alone. Now, there are no black tailed prairie dogs in that county adjoining the Watershed and a similar condition exists on the Watershed. They have been exterminated by the U.S. Fish and Wildlife agency to placate the herders who felt their range was being eaten by these animals. Because the USF&W Service has killed untold millions of prairie dogs in the West, the black footed ferret which was their main predator is now thought to be extinct. These animals have not been seen in viable numbers anywhere for some years.

Part of the government subsidy to the public land grazers is the killing of rodents, coyotes, wild dogs, bears, bobcats and mountain lions. In 1981 Catron County which covers most of the Watershed, contributed $17,000 to the U.S. Fish and Wildlife Service for predator control. This was the county portion and the USF&W Service absorbed the balance. This money was spent to kill prairie dogs, kangaroo rats and coyotes. As there are 2,700 people in the county and one percent of the population are ranch owners and one third of these are absentee owners, according to Bureau of Land Management records, this represents a healthy subsidy to the herders and a significant destruction of life.

Many areas of the West, including the watershed, were formerly covered by vast prairies. As the grass cover was grazed out, many other plants came in, so that the nature of the area changed. The biggest factor in that change is that the grasslands no longer had enough vegetational cover to carry fire. Before the overgrazing, fires, whether caused by lightening or natives, burned swiftly across the top of the grasses. This helped maintain the grasslands. It removed dead debris for the growth of new green shoots and importantly burned off other competing vegetation such as the sage, juniper and piñon pine that the government now spends millions of dollars removing for the public lands ranchers, who are the people who have overgrazed the land so it cannot carry a fire.

Plants that spread when the annual and perennial grass has been killed out by overgrazing are sagebrush, creosote bush, tarbush, tumbleweed, rabbitbrush, colorado rubberweed, mesquite and various cactuses. These emergency troops attempt to cover the barren ground but usually are battled vigorously by the herders and their allies in government. These groups call the first aid crew, "invader plants." In their view it is the fault of the first aid crew for invading the range when in reality the cow herders cause it. Simply because one sees green on the land in semi-arid deserts does not mean it is in good health. The green may be the first aid crew.

Grass seeds ordinarily cannot germinate on bare ground. They need to be blown or float into some pocket of organic detritus that will shield them from the desiccating sun and hold enough moisture so that they can get a start. Providing this organic debris is an important role of the first aid crew which the government spends millions of dollars a year to kill. Although in some cases grass has difficulty growing directly beneath juniper trees, the shading on the periphery is another important role that these trees play in helping the grasses re-establish, because it slows the evaporation of moisture from the soil so that they can get a roothold. On the Watershed, the desert plants are moving north and higher up in elevation as aridity increases, they would move back down if the abused land were allowed to recover.

Not only has the riparian habitat suffered from the agriculturalists and grasslands because of the herders, but the miners have come also, although the heyday of mining is largely over. The frenzy of mining occurred on the Watershed basically in the area of the village of Mogollon from the late Eighteen Hundreds until early Nineteen Forties. In addition to polluting the waters from mining discharge, large amounts of local wood were needed to fire the smelters.

Local historian J.C. Richards tells of one among a number of mines in the area:

"Up Whitewater Creek four miles was the new gold processing mill town of White Creek or the Graham Mill, a 30 or 40 stamp type affair owned by the Helen Mining Company of Colorado. The town had a floating population from 100 to 200 people. The mill was using the mercury amalgamation system of gold recovery, using steam and pelton wheel water power. The steam boiler furnaces burned about fourteen cords of wood a day, so you can see why the hills are so barren of juniper trees."[21]

On the San Francisco watershed, fortunately, not the high volume metals such as iron or copper were smelted but only the more precious such as silver and gold. Even so the wood cutters and also the charcoal burners who cut for the commercial market, ranged over the high mountains and down lower, cutting the piñon-juniper and oaks. Their cutting damaged some areas so badly that it has not yet recovered.

Not only did the charcoal burners ravage the area but meat hunters ranged the mountains hauling out animals to sustain the food supply of the mining towns. This was a popular way to make a dollar when a person couldn't find any gold and one old miner and meat hunter James A. McKenna tells of taking pack trains out and filling them up with turkey and deer. Mostly the gangs of meat hunters went out in the late fall and winter so that they could run the game into deep snow where they were helpless and then shoot as many of the herd as they could. He explains also that the miners wouldn't buy the front portions of the deer- only the hindquarters. To McKenna's credit he did jerk the non-salable part and then sold the jerky to the less wealthy Spanish people who had not only lost much family land but the whole U.S. Southwest to the newly arrived Americans.

Each group of meat hunters made many trips each year. A story McKenna tells of one trip gives an idea of the volume of animals hauled out of the forest in the Mogollon Rim country.

"The night before Nelson was to leave for Silver City, [to take a load in] we had on hand at least fifty turkeys. During the night we had a real break, for a flock of fifty or sixty more came to roost within three hundred yards of our camp. When they were settled in, light rain fell, which seemed to affect their flying. Opening fire, we dropped at least half of them. In the morning those that had fallen on the ground could not fly, and we got quite a few more by clubbing them as they ran by our camp."[22]

McKenna tells also of being in the vicinity of Elk Mountain on the northeast edge of the San Francisco watershed and seeing many wild horses and thousands of pronghorn feeding in the foothills, where a handful of pronghorn might be seen today and there is a complete absence of wild horses. McKenna, writing years later says:

"Looking back to fifty years, I have come to the conclusion I was using up more than my share of the natural resources which belong to all the people of the state, but you cannot put an old head on young shoulders, and at that time no laws had as yet been made to save the treasure of mountain and forest. But I never killed without good reason nor wasted the bounty of our southwestern mountains."[23]

Legend in New Mexico has it that the last Gila elk, another favorite animal of the meat hunters, died in a zoo in 1921. We do know that the last naturally occurring elk of the species *Cervuc elaphus merriami* died in 1909 and the race is now extinct. Those that exist on the Watershed now are *Cervuc elaphus erxleben*, transplanted from Colorado. These transplanted elk, although similar, are from a different ecosystem and give birth in May and June, unlike the former natural species. The fact that they give birth during the annual mini-drought is a definite problem for the transplants, but they are welcome given the circumstances.

By 1935, the grizzly bear was extirpated from the whole Southwest and of course the Watershed, where the last one was killed. Aldo Leopold killed one of the last recorded wolves in the Southwest, on the northwest section of the Watershed at Ecudilla mountain. This was the "green fire" occasion. Leopold killed this wolf while he was a Forest Service employee on the Blue River. The jaguar (Felis onca) had been extirpated much earlier as had the big horn sheep (since replanted). The sonoran river otter has not been seen in the area since 1953 and is probably extirpated. It is now an endangered species. The grizzly, otter, elk and wolf that have been extirpated were subspecies that are now extinct and do not occur anywhere.

Ben V. Lilly, a locally, legendary hunter came into the area in 1910 and remained into the 1930's. Lilly made his living killing grizzly bears, black bears and lions for the bounties offered by the herders. In the year 1912, Lilly is said to have collected on one hundred and four scalps of lion and bear. Little of the meat was ever used from this wanton destruction of life and locally, now, it is taken as an act of faith to kill any bear, coyote, snake, bobcat, eagle or lion one sees, in protection of the sacred cow.

Of the birds, the aplomado falcon is extirpated and among the fishes, the Gila topminnow and the Gila chub are gone, having become extinct. In New Mexico alone, ninety-five species of wildlife, not including vegetation, are endangered of becoming extinct.[24] With plant species the situation is equally as serious. The United States Forest Service arrived on the Watershed in 1908. That agency has done much to damage the Watershed. The vast system of roads itself creates tremendous erosion and runoff (the USFS is the largest road building enterprise in the world). The other damage is the injury to the former climax forest by logging and by suppression of the natural fires. The over-grazing of the forest is also significant and contributes to erosion.

The purpose of the USFS is primarily to furnish "resources" to the timber barons. Congress annually appropriates money for them to do this and each district is expected to meet an annual quota of timber offered for sale. Meeting these quotas is an important qualification for promotion up the hierarchy. In return the district receives various subsidies and kickbacks such as for reforestation, roadbuilding, staff maintenance and so forth, based upon the timber cut.

Here in the semi-arid desert forest, like those of most of the Great Basin, the climax forest is almost gone. It is said that sustained yield is practiced but all over the Great Basin sawmills are shutting down as the forest becomes exhausted of the high-profit old growth. This same condition obtains on the

Watershed. The fragility and growth of the desert forests are far different than in the wet ecosystems of the pacific coast and the ponderosa forest do not recover as quickly or as well.

The fire suppression has changed the nature of the ecosystem. A recent study of wildfire notes:

> "On a broad scale, the effects of fire encourage the development of vegetative mosaics and the recycling not merely of chemicals but also of communities. Under ideal conditions, a kind of perpetual migration of successional stages and shifting geographic ensembles results."[25]

One of Mother Earth's virgin ponderosa pine forests is beautiful, but there are almost none left in the West that have not been ravished by the USFS. "As early as 1902 an examiner with the GLO (Government Land Office) observed that 'when first invaded by white man the forests were open, devoid of undergrowth, and consisted in the main of mature trees, with practically no forest cover,' It was not an uncommon thing for the early settlers to cut native hay in the pine forests and fill large government contracts at the different military posts. But where intensive grazing occurred, thereby eliminating broadcast fire, woody vegetation sprang up or the grassland dissolved into desert."[26] (This speaks of strictly ponderosa regions, not chaparral).

Of all of the kinds of damage logging does, the worst is removal of potential topsoil. The forest like all other places where growing things flourish, has a topsoil that is a circulating phenomenon. As the trees, the biomass, are removed cycle after cycle, the soil becomes poorer. Just like a corn field, where formerly the organic nutrient fed back into the soil, it is now hauled away to market. There is no way to escape the fact that the cropping of the forests of the earth and of the Watershed in particular, is damaging the soils. The cycle of the life of the soil is an obvious fact just as in Fukuoka's barley field. To add to that, the USFS allows cutting of trees without replacement. As of 1974 there was a backlog of 4.8 million acres of U.S. forest from which trees had been cut with no replanting.[27]

Overgrazing is the perennial problem of the empire and it also occurs in the forest. Approximately seven million head of stock graze the National Forests in place of other life that had existed there. "According to Earl D. Sandvig, a retired senior official of the Forest Service who has continued to monitor National Forest management in the West, 'Overgrazing by domestic livestock and to some extent by game animals on our public lands is creating more soil erosion and denudation of land surfaces than all other uses put together.' "[28]

In the year 1982, poisons were used on the Watershed by government agencies. These poisons are used for various industrial agricultural strategies that are applied to forests. Strychnine, phostoxin tablets and zinc phospide were used by the USFW Service to kill rodents. Spike, a dangerous herbicide is being tested for use by the BLM. The USFS used on a substantial number of acres of the Watershed: Diquat Dibromide, Dalapon M, Dicamba, Tordon 10K, and 2,4-D, all vegetation killers.[29]

Other secondary effects of the invasion of the empire has been the drying up of springs and the reduction of live water in many stream courses that ran year around in the memory of Spanish people now living on the Watershed. The alteration of the balance of the forest's life continues and the poor San Francisco River, in addition to having its riparian life severely crippled has now been channelized in some places to protect those who do not know any better than to build a house on a flood plain and to protect the fields of agrarians who are victims of the progressive denudation of the higher watershed that causes the floods to become larger each time.

In our survey of injury to the watershed we should not forget the fragmentation that has been caused. Because of private property and barbed wire fences the flows of energies, the metabolism, the migrations of plants and animals has been seriously impaired. Barbed wire on the Watershed prevents the pronghorn from effectively migrating. In pronghorn country the herders put extra wires along the bottom of fences (even on privately grazed public land) to keep out the few remaining pronghorns that the herders have not completely killed out. (Pronghorns can't jump over fences like deer, they try to go under the wire.) The elk no longer are able to come onto the lower flats and they spend their lives hiding in the higher mountains, prevented from migrating as they would normally. The secondary effect of this contraction is that the animals are not able to perform their energy sharing function of seed dispersal (nor are even the cattle) because they cannot migrate over wide areas such as they once did. The plant community uses many strategies to disperse seeds. Seed dispersal in a manure pile of an herbivore is one of their paramount strategies. In addition to all of the other damage to the photosynthesizing life, this reduction of seed dispersal is serious and adds to the self-perpetuating downward spiral.

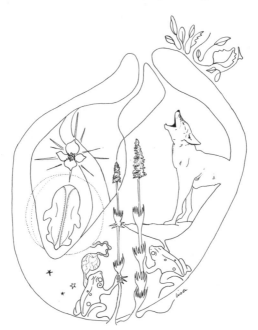

NOTES

1   Origin and Evolution of Deserts. Stephen G. Wells & Donald R.
     Haragan. eds. "Physiographic Overview of Our Arid Lands in The
     Western U.S.," Charles B. Hunt. 1983. U of NM Press. Albuquerque.
     1983. p. 30.
2   ibid. p. 33.
3   Soil Association And Land Classification for Irrigation-Catron County.
     vol. 117. #17. p. 2. U.S.D.A. Soil Conservation Service.
4   Mammals of New Mexico. J. S. Findley, A.H. Harris, D.E. Wilson & C.
     Jones. UNM Press. Albuquerque. 1975. p. 341.
5   Field Museum of Natural History, Anthropological Series, Vol. 32,
     Chicago, 1940-1947. "#1, The SU Site: Excavation At A Mogollon
     Village, Western New Mexico, 1939." Paul Martin. #2, Second Season,
     1941. Paul Martin. p. 130.
6   Socorro Defensor Chieftain. (Newspaper, Socorro, New Mexico).
     "Catron's Populous Past," David Stuart. Vol. 117. #17. p. 2.
7   Among the nineteen pueblos of New Mexico, there are three basic
     cultural divisions, Towa, Tewa and Tiwa. Each of these is a different
     language group and is qualitatively different. (There are other pueblos
     such as the Zuñi and Hopi that are, again, each another variant but
     certain basic patterns apply to all.) One excellent and basic introduc-
     tion to pueblo culture is: The Tewa World: Space, Time, Being and
     Becoming In A Pueblo Society. Alfonso Ortiz. U. of Chicago Press.
     Chicago. 1969.
8   Chiricauhua Apache Subsistence and Socio-Political Organization:
     Section Two. (quoted in) A Report of the Mescalero-Chiricauhua Land
     Claims Project. Harry W. Basehart. Contract Research #290-154.
     UofNM. 1959. p. 93.
9   In The Days of Victorio: Recollections of A Warm Springs Apache. Eve
     Ball. (James Kaywaykla, narrator). U of Arizona Press. Tuscon. 1970.
     p. 45.
10   Basehart. op. cit. provides information of gathering areas and
     Kaywaykla op. cit. provides band identification.
11   Western Apache Subsistence Economy. Winfred Suskirk. Dissertation
     for Ph. D. in Anthropology. UNM. 1949. p. 297.
12   ibid. p. 298.
13   American Indian Food and Lore. Carolyn Niethammer. Collier Books.
     New York. 1974. p. 4. (This nutrition information is quoted from
     Winifred Ross, "The Present Day Dietary Habits of the Papago Indi-
     ans," masters thesis, U. of Arizona. 1941). pp. 43,44, (in Ross).
14   Basehart. op. cit. p. 103.

15 The Desert Smells Like Rain: A Naturalist In Papago Indian Country. Gary Paul Nahban. North Point Press. San Francisco. 1982. p. 97.

16 I Fought With Geronimo. Jason Betzinez. Bonanza Books. New York. 1969. pp. 194,195.

17 The fundamental texts of this era are the following two volumes by Eve Ball which are eyewitness accounts of Apache survivors. The volumes by Barrett and by Betzinez are also important. Other histories of the era tend to be written by U.S. military participants or imperial minded historians who while shedding light on historical events within U.S. society, relate little about the native experience and nothing about the actual life of the land.
In The Days of Victorio. Eve Ball. U of Arizona Press. 1970.
Indeh: An Apache Odyssey. Eve Ball. Brigham Young U. Press. Salt Lake. 1980.
Geronimo's Story of His Life. S.M. Barrett, editor. Corner House pub. Williams-Town, Ma. 1973.

18 Some Recollections of A Western Ranchman: New Mexico 1883-1889. Vol. I. William French. Argosy-Antiquarian Ltd. New York. 1965. pp. 42,43.

19 American Wildlife & Plants: A Guide To Wildlife Food Habits. Alexander C. Martin, Herbert S. Zim & Arnold L. Nelson. Dover Pub. New York. 1951. p. 274.

20 Do You Remember Luna: 100 Years of Pioneer History 1883-1983. The Luna Ward. The Church of Jesus Christ of Latter-Day Saints. Adobe Press. Albuquerque. 1983. pp. 130,131.

21 Catron County Firestarter. "Ode To An Old Road." J.C. Richards. Vol. 3 #40. Nov. 21, 1983. Glenwood, New Mexico. p. 3.

22 Black Range Tales: Chronicling Sixty Years of Life and Adventure In The Southwest. James A. McKenna. Rio Grande Press. Glorieta, New Mexico. 1936. p.54.

23 ibid. p. 51.

24 John Hubbard, personal communication & Handbook of Species Endangered in New Mexico. M.C. Conway, H. Campbell, G. Schmitt & M.D. Hatch. NM Dept. of Game and Fish. Santa Fe. 1979.

25 Fire In America: A Cultural History of Wild Fire and Rural Fire. Stephen J. Pyne. Princeton U. Press. 1982. pp. 35,36.

26 ibid. p. 523.

27 The Last Stand: Nader's Study Group Report On The National Forests. Daniel R. Barney. Brossman Pub. New York. 1974. p. 8.

28 ibid. p. 7.

29 Catron County Firestarter. Vol. 3 #9. no date. p. 3.

CHAPTER 20

PLANETARY RESTORATION-WATERSHED RESTORATION

Forage Farming: A Permaculture of the
San Francisco River Watershed

To become healed is to become unified with our whole existence. We have dynamic balance within our whole.

We are the world, inextricably. We are three billion years old in this cellular form. We were the amoeba, the reptile, the mammal. We are they and we are our relations the trees and the grass. We are separate within ourselves only in the faculty of intellect.

If a few cells in an injured organ received enough energy that they become motivated to heal, they would have to follow the guideposts, to re-unify with other cells, the organ, the body and the organic environment that the body exists in.

We are all detribalized natives of the Pleistocene family. We are that part of the human family who have lost their way and do not know what or where their home is. Bill Mollison, the leading creator of the concepts of Permaculture went to learn from and help a group who were in a similar situation. In his book, *Arid-Land Permaculture,*[1] he shares the experience and the creative ideas that came about while working with Australian Aborigines. They desired to leave the European culture areas and go back out onto their land. Unfortunately, their native land has become so altered and destroyed that they could not exist by using their own culturally inherited survival skills and knowledge. The ecosystem had been altered by the animals imported by Europeans, which have gone wild, overgrazed and disrupted the natural life. Mollison states that 60% of the plant species on aboriginal lands are extinct; the rest are "greatly decreased." The feral camels, rabbits, cattle, horses and burros have ravaged the landscape. Mollison gives the estimate of 6,000 cattle and 20-30,000 horses on aboriginal land.[2] Because of the alteration, they asked Mollison's participation in creating a permaculture on their land. Permaculture is an ecologically integrated system of permanent agriculture that would offer the Aborigines a sustainable food basis. Like the aborigines, all of us are returning to the injured earth.

Although the watershed of the San Francisco River is not as pillaged as Central Australia, there is restoration to be done. In order to do this we must reinhabit the earth as our home in a balanced way. Unless we are placing ourselves in a wilderness area or some other unique place, we will find that restoration is called for- aiding the living earth to heal itself.

In a semi-arid region, aiding the soil's ability to absorb water and shading it from the sun is critical. For example the rule of thumb in a semi-arid desert is that fifty percent of water in open surface dams is lost to evaporation! In any area where bare soil is exposed, that soil is being oxidized and moisture is evaporating from it. We must help get the moisture into the body of the earth by helping it get into the layers of organic soil on top of the earth. The premier workers in this area are trees and grasses. Trees are our first consideration because of all of the services that they perform. They create rain by evapotranspiration. They create moist micro-climates and habitat around themselves. They bring up minerals from the subsoil and deposit this on the soil in their leaves and dead bodies and importantly they shade the soil.

The absorbent carpet of live soil is the important element in water retention. It allows the rain to be absorbed and infiltrate as well as holding moisture for the plant community. The initial effort is to slow down the water and help it soak into the earth.

One of the fundamental concepts of Permaculture is to help arrange plants, animals, insects and whatever life one can find in a manner so that each provides services for the other and a self-energizing pattern may be begun. No better example of this can be found than our friends the beavers. The massacred and battered beaver tribe are the hydrologists of nature. Their dams provide services for such a wide spectrum of life that much study would be needed to discover them all. First they dam the headwaters high in the mountains, slowing it down. Their dams back up silt which, when the beaver family moves on, becomes a beaver terrace, or beaver meadow. That is, when the dam finally silts up and dries out, a bench of soil remains which becomes fertile habitat for other species. While the dam is in use the body of water causes the subsoil water level of the whole valley floor to rise, making it available to plants. This is one important factor in the beavers' preparation of their environment for their favorite foods, willow, cottonwood and aspen which proliferate on the underground water. It is important also because all open water needs to be shaded. This prevents evaporation and cools the water so that it is compatible habitat for the local aquatic life. This is another reason why narrow, deep streams and not wide, eroded channels are needed. This growth of the glade creates micro-habitat for other species of plants and animals. There can be no more dramatic restoration than to help the beaver tribe restore their rightful place on the Watershed. One immediate method is to fence off the riparian habitat from grazing. This does two things. It allows the grass and vegetation to come back so that subsoil water can build up and then seep into the stream bed so that the stream begins to flow all the time, a necessity for the beavers' survival. The second big effect is that without the grazing, the trees and bushes that the beavers prefer to eat can come back. Some shovel work and some hand planting would speed up this restoration. As the sources of live water increase, all life immediately around increases. Animals will be able to spread out more to areas that they formerly could not reach because water was too far. Most of the animals need to come to water at least once per day. By cultivating the food trees in preferred places we can encourage the beavers to stair-step the dams downward from the top of the Watershed. They must begin at the top with their water control project or they will be flooded out lower down.

We should build relationship with the beaver tribe, communicate with them, find out as much as we can about their way of life in order to help them out. They are a primary totem of the Watershed. We can learn valuable adaptation techniques from them.

Combating erosion is the first line of defense in helping the soil community build back up. As Bill Mollison says, "mulch, mulch, mulch, mulch." Plant trees, plant bushes, plant grasses-cover the bare soil. On the Watershed the natural mixture of native grasses are all but gone on the broadscale but isolated stands can be found. When we are going about our activities on the Watershed we will know each of these varieties and it is a simple matter to gather seed here and there for our inventories.

In addition to helping the beavers, seeding is a primary activity. We collect and plant seed to create habitat for the animals and birds and also we collect seed for our inventories. Plants seed heavily and have remarkably complex strategies to get their seed to compatible habitats. Much of the strategy is based on a huge production, using random chance to get a small percentage of seed to the "right" spot. Humans, because of their mobility and intelligence can be of great help to the plants. We can learn what soil type each needs, we can understand the sun exposure and micro-climate needs. We can plant much more seed than the stationary plant, and exactly in the spots it needs to grow. By helping them, we can create an exponential leap in their growth and thus their aid in the restoration work.

The strategies of seed dispersal by the plant families is a complex art. Plants basically use wind, water, animal and bird dispersal as well as mechanically throwing their seeds out from the seed pod. The basic methods of wind dispersal are by wings on the seeds or pods and tufts or umbrellas as on the dandelion. The second important method of seed dispersal by wind is smallness of seed size, sometimes down to dust. Seeds that are primarily transported by water have generally light hulls sometimes with built-in air pockets.

Animal or bird distributed seeds use two strategies. The first is to entice the creature to eat the seed by surrounding it with attractive fruit or food of some kind. The seed then travels through the digestive tract and is often distributed with its own supply of nutrient (manure). Some seeds cannot germinate unless they travel through the proper digestive system that contains the acids that can begin to breakdown the tough seed coat. The other method of creature transfer is to get the seed or the pod to stick to the hair or feathers. This is done by putting hooks on the seed in some fashion so that they catch on the creature. Some plants do this by putting sticky substances on the seed or pod. There are plants also that throw their seeds. This strategy usually uses some kind of tension in the pod so that as the pod dries, the tension increases until the seeds are expelled. Sometimes the seeds of the explosion variety also have hooks or sticky substances that will adhere to an animal who has brushed against the plant and triggered the expulsion of the seeds.

Dispersing the seeds is only part of the plants' problem. After the dispersal it is necessary that the seeds germinate in the right soil, moisture and temperature. The factor that helps in this strategy is the tremendous production of seed by each plant, especially in arid or semi-arid deserts. In a semi-arid region, such as the Watershed, many of the plants produce seeds that are timed in various ways so that the germination of a seed crop produced in any one year may be spread over a period of many years. This is done by uneven ripening of seeds, uneven shedding of seeds from the plant and by coating the seeds with coats that have different thicknesses or seeds with different resistances to germination. The net effect of these strategies is to cover the land with millions of seeds. In any one square foot of space there may be hundreds or even thousands of seeds, within and on top of the soil, each waiting its appointed time for the beginning of life. With some seeds it may be many years before they germinate. There are even seeds that remain viable for thousands of years. Some seeds that are artificially germinated have to have a groove put in the seed coats with a file or have to be soaked in acids. This takes the place of years of wear while being transported along with the bottom gravel in a stream or setting out on the surface of the soil exposed to the elements.

The seeds in the desert have the intelligence of which year to sprout. Of the coverage of seeds on one square foot, some may be plants that are very drought resistant. A portion of these seeds would germinate in a drought year while others waited for a later drought year. On the other end of the spectrum, plants that could only survive during the wettest years would broadcast seed, some of which would germinate during a very wet year and some would wait until another wet year came along later. The net effect of this strategy is to insure or attempt to insure that the soil will be covered in all but the most extreme years and it creates a pattern of variety of the vegetation during different years which allows the maximum efficiency of the photosynthetic process of the whole plant cover.

Overgrazing inhibits seed dispersal on the Watershed. When land is grazed too closely the plants cannot make seed because the stock eat the plant bodies. By this simple fact- the lowering of seed production- widespread damage has been done to the efforts of the plant community to perpetuate itself. Inasmuch as seed germination is often spread over a period of years and it takes some years for this natural inventory to run out, this fact is not immediately apparent on an overgrazed watershed, but the health of the area relies on the greatest number of seeds possible, dispersed as widely as possible and if one year or many years of seed production is cut short by overgrazing that lowers the general health of the area.

Reseeding and replanting is one of the most obvious human chores on the Watershed and one of the most important because of human ability to recognize nature's patterns. They can upgrade the efficiency of the plants' random distribution tremendously, and thereby aid the life by multiplication.

On the Watershed, seeds move downward and toward the northeast. Seeds move downward on watersheds because of gravity and water flow. On the watershed of the San Francisco river, the prevailing winds are toward the northeast and that fact provides a general drift of seeding in that direction.

In general, the most efficient grass seeding is to seed the ridges. Grasses generally enlarge themselves in patches or "stands." If they can build up a durable population and create sod they can spread. If the ridges are heavily seeded so that stands can become established, the stands can move off down the slopes under the ridges. This is very important in the beginnings of reclamation when there are limited resources. As heavy grass stands are built up, native seed can easily be harvested from them by hand for further use in the seeding process.

The seeding of grasses can be used strategically both to heal places in danger of severe erosion and in places where the soil quality is being upgraded by forbs and brush. In these areas where the soil can support grasses but there is no seed stand nearby, the humans can seed the recovering spot from their inventory.

As the human life experience integrates with the life of the Watershed the people will be able to know the healing succession of plant regimes as a basic guide. In places where one set of plants are reclaiming, the person will know the next stage of plant life that will move in and that way will be able to seed the area quickly so that the new level of succession can get itself established.

The Watershed has been and is being damaged by the U.S. Government (who own 80-90% of it) by deforestation through logging and (self-admitted) overgrazing. As we establish on any watershed we will be lobbying and working cooperatively with the appropriate "land management" technicians (as long as they exist). As we establish cottage industries and our own beneficial uses of the public lands which enhance the ecosystems, alongside the loggers and grazers, we will begin to exert a force for human maturity, responsibility and sustainable existence by all on the Watershed.

Specific Water Retention Strategies

We have reviewed water retention and containerization strategies of the Nabateans and the Kiva people. These are specific to food growing. There is also the question of broadscale work in the area of water retention that can be done as restoration projects. For these we need to turn to Bill Mollison. The major tome of Permaculture is the book: *Permaculture: A Designers' Manual*, by Mollison.[3]

One revegetation technique that Mollison suggests, is especially useful in floodplains and more level lands. This technique is to cut small swales, which are simply depressions in the ground. A farm implement called a disc is used. It is an implement with a series of plate-like metal discs across it, pulled by a tractor. With this technique all but a quarter section of each disc-plate is cut off. As the row of quarter-discs is pulled along behind a tractor, a grid of small depressions is cut in the soil.[4]

The importance of this is that seed ordinarily cannot germinate on bare ground in dry environments. The natural places that are congenial to seed are the small depressions, rocks against which rain has washed a small bit of organic debris, fallen branches behind which organic has collected and other such impediments where wind or water has made any small pile of organic material. This mound of organic can hold enough moisture so that a seed can germinate and there will be enough soil moisture so that it can get its roots down to the soil water before the surface dries. This is the benefit of these pits on the Watershed. The depressions being there in selected places, collecting small amounts of organic and eventually nursing sprouts is a benefit. If hand work is done, a small amount of compost or mulch supplied with seed in the hole, increases the chances of life.

Mollison discusses the Yeomans Keyline System of water management developed by P.A. Yeomans of Australia.[5] One of the central features of this system is a metal shaft similar to a "ripper," pulled behind a crawler tractor, used in the earth moving trade. This shaft extends 7.01 inches to 7.99 inches into the ground. There are a number of designs of this implement, but all have a foot on the bottom of the shaft, which is pulled through the soil. The shaft holding the foot slices deeply through the soil and the triangular foot is angled, nose down, so that the soil above it is pulled up and a tunnel with an air pocket is created behind it. This implement is used across the landscape much like contour plowing. The implement is put in the ground at the gully, arroyo or eroded ravine bed and pulled along the side of the hill angling away from the stream bed and slightly down downward at the point below the keyline and slightly upward above the keyline. The Keyline is the place where the sharp drop of the hill ceases and the drop lessens and levels toward the valley. These cuts would be made successively down the hillside on each side of the watercourse. The big effects of this are to aerate the soil (the soil community needs oxygen too), allow water to infiltrate and because of the opening up to the air, the soil temperature rises, causing the soil life to increase. In *Perma-Culture Two*, Mollison says that Geoff Wallace, an associate of Yeomans, has recorded a soil temperature rise of up to 11°C under his reconditioned forest.[6]

Mollison lists some of the reasons that this method builds soil so quickly:
"- friable and open soil through which water penetrates easily as weak carbonic and humic acid, freeing soil elements for plants, and buffering pH changes;

- aerated soil, which stays warmer in winter and cooler in summer;

- the absorbent soil itself is a great water-retaining blanket, preventing run-off and rapid evaporation to the air. Plant material soaks up night moisture for later use;

- dead roots as plant and animal food, making more air spaces and tunnels in the soil, and fixing nitrogen as part of their decomposition cycle;
- easy root penetration of new plantings, whether these are annual or perennial crops;
- a permanent change in the soil, if it is not again trodden, rolled, pounded, ploughed or chemicalized into lifelessness."[7]

Another use for this system is to create the above contour treatment and then space pits along each slice and mulch, hand prepare and plant tree seedlings or other beneficial vegetation. Because of the cut in the earth the new plants will find it easy to insert their roots and stored moisture will exist for them.

A basic aim of the restoration effort is to start the positive cycling toward increased fertility. To establish a small grass-sod stand so that it can spread, to dam up a gully so plants can establish and spread, to plant a mini-forest so it can spread- is a big part of the effort of aiding life and living from the increase.

Among the many specific suggestions offered by Mollison in the *Designers' Manual* section on "Dryland Strategies" is a method to help nurse trees to maturity when grown on an open hillside. In this method, criss-cross ditches are cut across the hillside looking something like a checker board turned on its corner. At each intersection of the watergathering ditches, a tree is planted with appropriate compost and mulch. The watergathering allows infiltration of enough water to support the beginnings of the new forest. Mollison calls this the "Net and Pan" method and suggests that hardier trees be planted upslope and less hardy downslope. [8]

The Trees

Trees are the major item of life on any landscape. On the Watershed there are forests down to the Chihuahuan life zone and even in that zone, scattered piñon, juniper and mesquite exist on the open hillsides. It is the deforested hills on private land and the damaged areas in the riparian habitat (where much of the private land exists) that will receive the first attention in terms of trees. First we need consider the basic native trees of the Apache foraging system. These are the pin~on, juniper, oak, black walnut and mesquite.

To the Apaches, acorns were a basic staple and their food value and the variety of ways that they can be used must be considered by others. Acorns can be eaten raw, roasted, in soups, and ground to flour for use in baking. There are no acorns on the Watershed that require leaching such as those that grow on the continental coasts.

The piñon nut must also be considered a staple, especially in the periodic years of piñon nut abundance. Piñones would be gathered to roast, make nut butter and to dry and grind into flour. Carolyn Niethammer in her book *American Indian Food And Lore*, which is a fundamental text for this area (and also contains many recipes), says that piñons are a rich source of protein, fats and contain 3,000 calories per pound![9]

Though juniper has many uses, the only food use is the berries of the one-seeded juniper. These are the type with the white powdery surface which may be eaten raw and are rather sweet though not a good source of bulk food. In the same respect the inner bark of the ponderosa can be eaten. The Apaches toasted it on campfires so that it tasted something like biscuits. This must be considered only a survival food and not a staple. Anyone gathering bark should take care not to girdle the tree (take bark from all the way around it) as this will kill it. At this point we need take only a small experimental sample and then seal the wound with beeswax. (There is the consideration that as civilized people with a life-time of conditioning of soft, refined foods, we can't simply go out and start eating the landscape raw. Good recipes such as Niethammer's book are essential, even crucial. There are also a growing number of Native Southwestern authors who have written good cookbooks based in local, Native foods.)

Mesquite and black walnut both grow very well near water or stream courses. Full size mesquite trees grow now at the San Francisco Hot Springs, toward the bottom of the Watershed and could be cultured easily above without irrigation. The mesquite roots can go into the earth in excess of 150 feet and they are extremely hardy. Black walnuts are more cold resistant and can grow up into the ponderosa zone but they have shorter roots and must live close to stream courses or other sources of water. Douglas and Hart in *Forest Farming*, state, "Good algaroba varieties or cultivars [which include mesquite and honey locust] can yield up to twenty tons of edible beans per acre annually. The meal is an excellent cereal-substitute, superior to common field grains in nutritional content,"[10] Carolyn Niethammer in *American Indian Food and Lore*, states that black walnuts are rich in fat and contain up to 76% oil.[11] Local sources say that domestic walnut cultivars can be grafted to black walnut trunks to add hardiness. Walnut cultivars can produce an average of 8,000 pounds of nuts per acre.[12]

MESQUITE   DEVIL'S CLAW

There are many tree crops that could be adapted to the Watershed. One can find voluminous listings in references such as Mollison's *Permaculture One* or the periodical, *The International Permaculture Species Yearbook* and the Friends of the Trees Society publication, *International Green Front Report*, of possible tree species that would fit well in the Watershed. We will consider a handful of varieties that can be considered basics to getting edible forests started.[13] Honey locust, a close cousin of the mesquite are very good producers and live well on the Watershed. There are several of this species at the 5,700 foot elevation on the Watershed that produce well. Both honey locust and its cousin, mesquite, are legumes. All legumes put nitrogen in the soil. Honey locust is considerably more cold tolerant than mesquite and may grow well into the ponderosa life zone at 7,000 feet. Honey locust are useful for their pods, as wind breaks and honey locust, walnut and mesquite produce fine wood. The ground pods of honey locust are rated at 27-30% sugar and the pods and seeds are 16% protein. Honey locust flour is often mixed with other flours because of its sweetness when making breads. [14]

There are common nut trees that could live well on the Watershed. Chinese chestnut, hazelnuts, cordate walnuts- a cold-hardy variety of Japanese origin and butternut, could be adapted. The difficult problem of finding sources of cooking oil might be solved by adapting the Indian butter tree, Mowra, Ceylon oak or Malfura trees to the Watershed. The nuts of these species are listed by Douglas & Hart as being high in oil.

A number of fruit tree varieties exist on the Watershed, among them pears, pie cherries, apples and apricots. The Hopis grow apricots on their mesas which are near 7,000 feet and these can be considered staples. Various apple and pear varieties can be adapted by experimentation. Wild plums grow well and domestic cultivars should be a choice. In addition, persimmon and mulberry would do well.

One other native tree should be mentioned and that is the box elder. This tree is a cousin of the maple sugar tree and it can also be tapped for sugar sap. Box elders are living up into the ponderosa zone.

Placing the Tree

On the Hopi mesas we find the people who have the longest record of inhabitation in one place of any peoples in the Southwest. While the Hopi diet is basically the Mayan adaptation, it is almost all rain-fed or dry land agriculture. It is highly adapted to the life of the area where it is conducted. Hopi fields are not randomly placed. The location of the plot is guided by the plant to be grown there. Some plots will be on top of the mesas, some on the slopes, some out on the flats and some in ravines to take advantage of flood plain agriculture. In older times these fields might be as many as twenty miles apart and even today they are often many miles apart in order to take advantage of particular soils, particular sun exposure, water run-off or micro-climate. One of the types of fields Hopis use are literally on sand hills. In certain sandy situations this is a very enterprising method. The sand acts as a mulch. Rain soaks in immediately and if one has located in an area where there is a relatively impermeable layer under the sand, a constant seep of water will exist on the top of that layer which feeds moisture to the plant. If one is in an area such as Hopiland, evaporation exceeds rainfall and minerals and nutrients tend to stay near the surface rather than being leached toward the subsoil by abundant rain. It is because of this that quite sandy soils, such as at the Hopi mesas, can be fertile.

When we begin to think about the placement of trees, we must realize that trees are the large objects in our permaculture and that where we place them will configure much of what comes later, the wind currents, the shading, the retention of soil moisture, the build-up of organic debris and various other complex considerations. Therefore we must imitate the Hopi in terms of the depth of our thinking about how we begin our system of forage farming.

Permanent agriculture is based on perennial plants and plants that can easily reseed themselves. This is not a farm labor situation. We want to arrange the pattern at the beginning so that the rudimentary ecosystem can sustain itself and "take-off". Then our role is gentle guidance, aid and observation. We do not want to be out in the field with a hoe, struggling to grow European vegetables in an environment where they were never adapted, nor do we want to be out struggling to irrigate a rice paddy because we can't give up our brown rice. Mollison's *Designers' Manual* is excellent in its coverage of concept and placement of trees. After perusal of Mollison and much thought and observation, we can begin to search through the permaculture networks for sources of cultivars to bring in and plant.

Permaculture is not simply the arranging of plants, but is ultimately a design philosophy. The philosophy is to aid the natural life in its innate pattern. While the motive of the culture of civilization is to drain the life system of its energy for profit/growth, the perspective of permaculture is to aid the life system and live from the increase, in cultural stability. In his book, *Permaculture: A Designer's Manual*, Bill Mollison offers a brief description of a complex study. He says:

"Permaculture (permanent agriculture) is the conscious design and maintenance of agriculturally productive ecosystems which have the diversity, stability, and resilience of natural ecosystems. It is the harmonious integration of landscape and people providing their food, energy, shelter, and other material and non-material needs in a sustainable way. Without permanent agriculture there is no possibility of a stable social order.

"Permaculture design is a system of assembling conceptual, material, and strategic components in a pattern which functions to benefit life in all its forms.

"The philosophy behind permaculture is one of working with, rather than against, nature; of protracted and thoughtful observation rather than protracted and thoughtless action; of looking at systems in all their functions, rather than asking only one yield of them; and of allowing systems to demonstrate their own evolutions."[15]

It should be apparent as Mollison says, <u>that without permanent agriculture there can be no stable social order</u>. It is apparent also that the earth cannot be saved unless there is a permanent agriculture. Since the industrial revolution the earth and human labor have become a commodity. Unless permanent agriculture practiced by stable populations becomes a reality, the present instability will continue to the end. The end will be a complete exhaustion of the soils and a mass die-off of the excess population. One small example illuminates the historical process. When the one-fifth of U.S. agriculture based on the dwindling Ogalala aquifer comes to an end in the first part of the next century, the soils will be exhausted and the water gone. A mass population will be dislocated. As long as land is a commodity, those with economic power can obtain it and drain it of its fertility. In socialist countries, as long as mass populations can be shifted on and off of land such as China shifts masses to Tibet and northern Manchuria and Russia shifts masses to the "virgin" lands to be exploited with mass production industrial agriculture, the earth cannot be saved and there can be no social stability. Looked at in this way, we can see that permaculture is much more than simply a new method of horticulture because it means land and culture reform in the most fundamental meaning.

In many areas of the globe there are now no ecosystems or only remnants of ecosystems. Using permacultural methods we can place living ecosystems on the land and begin guiding those systems toward integration with any remaining natural life and toward an ultimate climax equilibrium. The standard is the maximum Net Photosynthetic Production from climax ecosystems spread around the entire living earth. We will be making effort toward balancing the solar energy budget.

A Walk Up the Watershed

The San Francisco enters the Gila river near the small copper mining towns of Clifton and Morenci, Arizona. This is an area of steep and high ridges that run north-south off of the higher elevation Mogollon Rim. This range is also on the divide between the Chihuahuan desert and the Sonoran desert. On down the Gila river, going west, is the Sonoran. From its confluence with the Gila, we follow the San Francisco up through narrow, steep, high-walled canyons. It travels through this range until it opens out into wider valleys some thirty-five miles above, at the natural pools of the San Francisco Hot Springs. The long, winding canyon through which the San Francisco travels in this area is very remote and contains many viable populations not found in abundance in the surrounding area, such as, gila monsters, ring-tail cats, coati-mundis and many species of birds, especially hawks and sometimes eagles. On the canyon walls and in this range of rugged hills, live viable herds of bighorn sheep who sometimes come down to stare at the bathers in the San Francisco Hot Springs.

At the hot springs, the valley widens significantly into the area now called Pleasanton. This area is just at the northern border of the Chihuahuan desert and the climate is appropriate for low elevation berries, fruits and melons. In the early days of occupation a Mormon community had created a rich area of irrigated orchards there but as the anti-bigamy law was passed in the late Eighteen Hundreds they left for Mexico and the orchards deteriorated and are now gone.

The Chihuahuan desert-piñon-juniper ecotone extends from the San Francisco Hot Springs on up to the area now called Alma where the river turns north and begins its travel through another, rugged canyon, which is the crack through the Mogollon Rim that goes into the upper country. The area from Clifton to Alma can be considered base camp, winter camp area, with the higher areas usable more as foraging areas. This would apply especially to the spruce-aspen zone and higher.

There are a number of natural plants that exist in abundance and that could be more encouraged in the southern region of the Watershed. Agaves grow up as high as San Francisco Plaza just below the ponderosa zone, but they are found in greater concentration much lower. Agaves grow profusely in the region from the San Francisco Hot Springs down to the point that the canyon of the San Francisco joins the Gila, and on below.

Native sunflowers are natural plants that were valuable to the Kiva People and the Apache foragers. They grow up to the ponderosas and in concentration much lower. Their seeds are 50-55% protein and they are rich in vitamin B. The seeds are also 50% oil.[16] If cultivars were interplanted with natural stands, the strain could no doubt be assisted in its value by the interfolding of the variety of genetic strains.

Devil's claw, sometimes called the unicorn plant (proboscidea altheaefolia) is a plant with an interesting aura very similar to datura, which grows on the Watershed below the ponderosa. The young pods of the devil's claw may be prepared like string beans and the seeds of the mature pod may be used as food. The seed is rated at 36% oil.[17] The seeds are 27% protein and the oil resembles safflower oil in taste and texture.[18] Gary Nabhan of the Native Seeds/Search seed bank in Tucson says that this plant has a large tuber of which the portion between the skin and the core may be eaten.[19]

The perennial cucurbit called calabazía by the Spanish and called Buffalo gourd in English (cucurbita foetidissima), is a tough and useful plant which grows well up into the piñon-juniper zone. Calabazía needs as little as ten inches of rainfall per year and grows on abused soil as well as other locations. One acre of this plant can produce 3,000 pounds of seed which will contain 1,000 pounds of vegetable oil and 1,000 pounds of protein meal. The roots of the plant in the same acre will produce six to seven tons of starch. The "squash blossoms" of this plant are also legitimate food. This is a plant that herbivores will not eat, although it has medicinal use for herbivores, such as healing flesh wounds by using the crushed leaves. A closely related plant called coyote melon (cucurbita digitata) will produce soap from green gourds and roots.[20] Nopal cactus must be considered an important food plant. The elephant-ear leaves of the nopal are good food and canned nopal is a commercial product. The nopal grows well in its large form in the southern watershed and in its smaller forms it grows up into the ponderosa zone. Its gathering zone would nonetheless be considered the lower Watershed. Another nice benefit of this plant is the fruit, (tunas, prickly pears). These fruits are high in calcium. Two tablespoons of this plant contain 48 calories and have more calcium than a glass of milk.[21]

CANYON GRAPE   ## SEGO LILY

Wild grapes (vitis arizonica) may be found up to the fir-aspen zone in rocky canyons protected from livestock. Though now rare, these grapes are very useful foodstuffs. When we are sufficiently familiar with the Watershed and its life, we will be able to locate exceptional specimens of useful wild plants like the wild grape in order to plant shoots of it in likely micro-environments. Taking a lead from our elders in the rainforest we would also be searching for plants that mimic the natural succession toward climax of the riparian habitats in particular and the broadscale ecosystem in general. Most of the riparian habitat would be returning naturally to climax, but those present areas of private property where human abuse has been long, would need intensive help of the permaculture guided succession. It is especially in these areas where we would want to increase the diversity.

There are numerous plant types already existing on the Watershed that have "similar" cousins in the domestic plant inventory. Wild amaranth for example grows very well on the Watershed. The wild amaranth, which grows under good conditions to a height of six feet, has a domesticated cousin that is called alegría by the Spanish people and is a decedent of the grain amaranth of the Aztecs and Mayans. Using the principle of "similars" one would broadcast seed of the alegría as well as the central american cultivar amaranth in spots where the native amaranth grows well. The same might apply to the coyote melons or calabazía and other cucurbits such as domestic melons and squash. Care must be taken because the calabazía is so hardy that it can grow in areas where the domestics cannot survive. This same principle of similars can be used with berry bushes, grapes, plums and even wild onion, as native species of these grow in various micro-environments of the Watershed. By using the guidance of the similars, one is being guided by the natural patterns for each type of plant and it should be cultured in the micro-environment that its relative indicates that it would do well in. This is in contrast to the square field of gardening practice where plants of different species are forced to grow side by side in a single soil and micro-climate, not necessarily to their liking.

The riparian zones, a few other moist areas and some north facing hillsides, are habitats where greens are found in abundance and greens are one of the basic foods of foraging peoples. A very important green is the lambsquarter (cenopodium album), called quelítes in Spanish (this same word is also applied to native amaranth). Lambsquarter, which is a European pioneer plant, is very nutritious and said by *Prevention Magazine* to exceed in nutritional value, most of the plants grown in European gardens. Volume for volume it also surpasses milk as a source of calcium. Other important greens are the red and yellow docks, purslane, wild amaranth, tumbleweed (russian thistle), filaree, dandelion, spiderwort, tansy mustard and the bee plant. Some of the greens such as dandelion and red dock have roots that can be used for food and can be used medicinally.

As George Osawa, the originator of Macrobiotics says, one should eat from one's watershed in season. With all of the complex chemistries and electrical, temperature and moisture changes, in sum the metabolic changes through the seasons, it seems right that we should be eating the fresh foods as they come out of the ground through these cycles. After the late winter diet of stored staples such as beans, dried fruit and such, with the only fresh green being watercress, one is ready for more fresh food. Tansy mustard it is, with its filaree-like, lacy leaves and familiar yellow flour. It is the first edible green that sprouts in the spring. It is a bitter green, but with an Italian recipe one finds it more than palatable while waiting for the wild amaranth (amaranthus palmeri). As one makes do with the tasty amaranth, others come up late in June and July with a rush so that there are many choices. By that time the tansy mustard is long gone, the amaranth too large to be palatable, but there are lambsquarters, dock, filaree, and so forth.

CATTAIL   **ARROWLEAF POTATO**

Cattail and tule potato, which tend toward being autumn foods, except for the green shoots on the cattail, are important food sources of the riparian zone. The cattail exists well up into the ponderosa zone as does the tule potato or arrowhead (thus called because of its arrowhead shaped leaf). As the beavers are re-introduced to the lower part of the Watershed, the resulting fertility in that zone will sponsor many water adapted and meadow foodstuffs both directly such as these two plants and indirectly by the environment that is created which produces homes for the animals and birds.

The roots (or rhizomes) of cattails equal ten times the average production of potatoes per acre. Niethammer says that when reduced to flour, cattails produce 32 tons of foodstuff per acre which is greater than wheat, rye or other grains. The food value of the root flour is equal to corn or rice. The pollen of the tail contains protein, sulfur and phosphorus. The rootshoots, the tips of the new leaves, the inner layers of the stalk, the green bloom spikes and the seeds are all edible.[22]

This inventory of plants that exist on the Watershed is a listing of the most obvious and productive staples. There are many other plants and some of these others have food or spice uses. There are still many other uses such as gums, oils, materials, medicines an so forth that we will adapt to our needs.

We must not forget the summer gardens in the high forest where any Andean crops such as quinoa and potatoes would thrive.

Also in these high foraging regions are useful items such as the rose hips and the tremendous crop of mushrooms of all sizes and descriptions. With civilization and private property, plants are made to grow in any area where people happen to live. On the Watershed we will establish a metabolism in which the staple crops are grown where they thrive and then barter can occur between the regions. A metabolism would be created so that everyone receives what they need.

Examples of other useful self-sustaining perennial plants would be comfrey, strawberry, asparagus, globe artichokes, jerusalem artichokes, gooseberries, currants and sloe berries. Jerusalem artichokes especially, flourish on the Watershed and would grow well on beaver pond banks just behind the cattails which root under water. Watercress is a local plant that grows well in the waterways. Watercress is a rich source of Vitamin E. Watercress dried, contains three times as much Vitamin E than does dried lettuce leaves.

What is being suggested on the Watershed is not European "gardening" but the culturing of the Watershed to add to a permacultural lifestyle. Nonetheless given the success of the subsistence styles of both the Kiva People and the Apache on this same watershed, the traditional annual plants of corn, beans, green chiles, amaranth and squash of the region should be included in any inventory of survival. The Hopi grow at least 18 varieties of beans and 20 varieties of corn where they live and some of their villages have been standing there for at least a thousand years. This kind of stability is hard to deny and the food that sustains them is of high value in desert agriculture.

This inventory is not exhaustive and will be added to by the experience of those who adapt. It is meant to indicate the sound nutritional basis of the lifestyle being suggested. As experience and observation progress, the inventory of valuable perennial and self-sustaining plant species increases, as well as transformations in the life style which are assumed by the principles of the pattern of life.

Diet isolates or integrates the human and human culture with the life of the earth as we have seen. Either humans adapt to the life of the earth or they spend their lives in conflict with the forces of the life of the earth. An appropriate example is the grasshopper abundance (which some biologists argue is caused by overgrazing) that has occurred on the Watershed the past few years. Two forces are in conflict with the grasshoppers. The people who raise European gardens are in conflict with them and the herders are in conflict because they fear the grasshoppers will eat the grass. The herders have convinced the government to come in and poison them by spraying insecticide, broadscale, thus killing an estimated 80% of the insect community. none the less, the natural life benefits from the abundance. The turkeys love grasshoppers and will eat great amounts of them but of course the turkey population is only a remnant of the former bands that existed on the Watershed. The areas of greatest grasshopper abundance occur in places colonized by the humans on the flats and lower elevations. This keeps the turkeys away because in their culture they are taught to fear humans. Other animals also eat grasshoppers. Coyotes, skunks, birds of various kinds and the host of small insectivorous animals such as rodents all gain. Humans could easily avoid the conflict with the grasshoppers by culturing the turkeys and eating turkeys.

The idea that all natural animals instinctively fear humans is as old as the empire. It is not true, as is shown by explorers who go to the remote territories where humans with guns have never been seen by animals.

People that keep domestic turkeys in areas where naturally living turkeys exist, find that the natural turkeys will call to the domestics, they will come down to meet them and if they are fed a little, they will become quite friendly (provided there are no "domestic pets" around such as cats or dogs). The permacultural environment would provide feed for the turkeys and they should be encouraged to be around areas of human habitation.

To coax a few occasionally into a small, quiet, enclosure trap so that the energies can be shared would not be at all unprincipled. Animals fear humans because humans frighten them with loud noises, such as guns, and humans chase them and frighten them in other ways. There is no reason that animals will not remain around humans if the humans can only become sensitive to the animals' needs. Quiet enclosure traps are a perfect way to share energies after having improved the region so that the animals' lives are also enhanced.

The Kiva People kept turkeys and some herded them, often sending young people out daily with the herd so that they could graze in the hills.

The point is, that if the survival culture adds to <u>all</u> of the life of the Watershed and devotes its energies to the general fertility, then they can establish a planetary diet wherein they eat everything possible. If one helps a grove of wild plums and the deer come and eat the plums, then eat deer. If one grows corn and raccoons come and eat the corn, then eat racoon. If the frogs hit the top of a population cycle then eat the frogs or eat whatever eats the frogs.

The humans are the omnivores. They can manage their diet to help harmonize the cycles and do this with intelligence. Within the life of the earth, the whole conditions the harmonization of individual cycles. The humans stand, nutritionally, in wholistic relation to the life, in that they have the greatest diversity of nutritional needs and the greatest ability to span the nutritional spectrum of any other animal. This is the reason that they can and should maintain a wholistic diet. They should eat everything possible because that is the pattern that nature points to; toward the optimum level of health through diversity. It is diversity that offers the greatest stability for the human family.

The elk, the bighorn sheep and the pronghorn have been the principal grazing animals on the Watershed in the recent past (since the Pleistocene die-off). Of these, the pronghorn must be considered the premier grass grazing animal. There is grass on hillsides and in other areas but the role of this grass is crucial to the maintenance of life of the soil and a confined-annual grass-seeking animal such as a cow should never be allowed on it. Even the large grazers of Pleistocene times would not be found normally in anything other than the open flats because their defense against the grizzly and the large cats is herd formation and running. This cannot be done on a bushy hillside or other broken country (where the most danger from stripping the grass cover exists). By introducing the cow and the sheep, the empire has struck at the most vulnerable point of the semi-arid ecosystem. The skin of grass must be saved at all costs.

All the herbivores on the Watershed, both the grazers and the browsers are edible. As has been argued, the natural mix of animals, bighorn sheep,rabbit, pika, elk, mule deer, white tail deer and even the peccary- who are omnivores but depend heavily on vegetable matter, and bighorn sheep can sustain much more population without damage to the Watershed than a smaller number of the domestic cow, horse, goat or sheep alone. Part of the restoration task will be to actively seed and plant with the needs of these animals in mind and actively lobby with the government managers (while the government can still hire managers) to stop the overgrazing of the forest and grasslands of the Watershed.

PECCARY

Ringtail, racoon, coati mundi, and gila monsters reside in the lower Watershed and spread throughout the Watershed are badger, skunk, mountain lion, bobcat, many types of bats, long tailed weasel, bears, gray fox, coyote, shrews, voles, rodents, squirrel, gopher, prairie dog, mice, woodrats, porcupine, ring-neck pheasant, quail, grouse, peccary, muskrat, and turkey. These animals have varying degrees of "palatability."

In Pleistocene culture, "hunting" is a spiritual act. One does not so much go hunt for and find an animal, one participates in the spirit of the greater life and by that, one is "presented" with the animal. A great hunter often is not one who is strong or canny but one who has the appropriate "medicine."

Silberbauer, who lived with the G/wi, describes their hunting. After explaining the stalking and positioning, he points out that the final target in the herd is chosen according to something that he uses the english word "personality" to cover. After the "personality" is taken into account, that choice is targeted and the arrows let fly. Those who have observed the moose herd, wolf pack relationship have implied that there is some similar kind of unconscious communication also that takes place between the hunted and the hunter.

In this vein, Mollison speaks of the natural way that the Aboriginal people integrated into the whole in times past. He says:

"The 'tameness' of all animal species, bird and mammal, in early explorations also suggests that the aborigine moved amongst his food species more as a herder amongst a flock than as a hunter feared by all other species. Aboriginal Tasmanians lived in small tribal territories only a days' walk across, and resided there for some 20,000 years before the whites came. From such a long period of control and selection, each region was (could we have understood and had we asked) a highly-evolved permacultural region sufficient to sustain tribal life indefinitely."[23]

Even though we may talk of eating them, that does not take away from the respect that we have for each life form. We hope that the rabbit, the deer and the lambsquarter have a full and abundant life, not that their death should be prevented. All individual biological forms change and cease to exist. It should be our focus that the remains make a beneficial contribution to some other lifestream in the great circulation. Everything is food and everything is excrement. All energy flows and transforms. In an emotionally positive culture we can avoid the pitfall of the familiar focus on death prevention and shift our view to life expansion and enhancement. The use of all of the techniques that have been discussed; permaculture, those which were used by the Nabateans and the Kiva People (and some being used now by Zuñi and Hopi) will allow further diversity of the Watershed. The waterspreading, the terracing, the floodplain agriculture can all find their uses within the varied topography. As the new culture, cultures <u>all</u> life, whichever can flourish in whatever spot at whatever time, the life for all and the food for all will increase. This will make a more fertile place for the animals as well as uncovering the possibilities of allowing formerly unknown wild species the possibility of entrance into new niches because of the increased fertility and diversity, in addition to the new life forms deliberately introduced and integrated into the system by the new culture.

MEDICINES OF THE SAN FRANCISCO WATERSHED

The Habitation

The tendency in civilization is to build artificial environments and then live out our lives enclosed and conditioned by them. The tendency of people and cultures that live in balance with the life of the earth is to build shelters from climatic extremes and live on the earth.

The earth sheltered human habitation enjoys a long tradition on the Watershed. Even the Kiva People build their most sacred dwelling, the Kiva, under or partially underground and the housing that they build seems to rise right up out of the earth, being built either with adobe or with stacked stone.

The earth sheltered design is <u>the</u> survival dwelling. A properly constructed earth shelter maintains a constant temperature right at fifty-seven degrees, at the latitude of the Watershed, meaning that it is necessary only to heat it up ten to twenty degrees to have a comfortable environment. This has a very important aspect. Even if there is no heat in the dwelling a human will not freeze. Unlike many types of design, one will survive.[24]

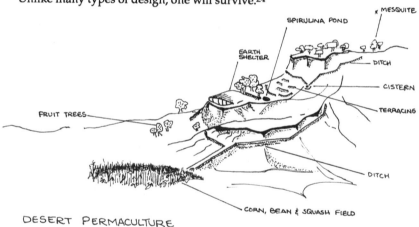

DESERT PERMACULTURE

An earth shelter can be created from local materials if necessary. With timbers, rock, adobe bricks, clay and soil, a shelter can be constructed that will be perfectly adequate.

Another important consideration in shelter design is that the elements of the design reflect implicitly the culture of the designer. It is no accident that just to the south of the Watershed, in Mexico, housing is designed with high, enclosing walls around them that often have broken glass imbedded on the top of the wall. Sharing is not a fundamental pattern in a country of great disparity of wealth. Where one does not mean to share, it is good to wall oneself in and the poor out.

Difference in design can be seen also between the sparsely populated pit house dwellers, the concentrated population of the Kiva People and their communal housing and the tipis and brush wickiups of the Apaches. Each design reflects significant conditions and lifestyle of each culture.

In present society, one of the considerations is the nuclear family. Housing is designed basically for the couple and their two point six children. The grandparents are not designed in, nor are the married children.

In our new culture with the choice of extended marriage and family, the dwellings will, of necessity, reflect the unity, relationship and sharing of energies of that culture. Ideally, individual diversity will be reflected in each individual having a private space, with the communal family space centered within these smaller spaces. Another important element of the design allows exposure out onto the earth rather than an enclosure from it.

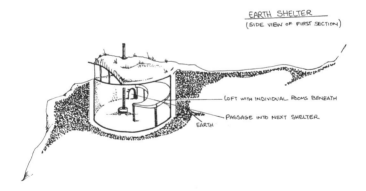

EARTH SHELTER
(SIDE VIEW OF FIRST SECTION)

LOFT WITH INDIVIDUAL ROOMS BENEATH

PASSAGE INTO NEXT SHELTER

EARTH

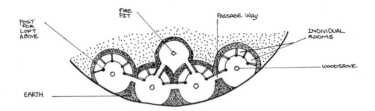

POST FOR LOFT ABOVE

FIRE PIT

PASSAGE WAY

INDIVIDUAL ROOMS

WOODSTOVE

EARTH

EARTH SHELTER PLAN
(TOP VIEWS)

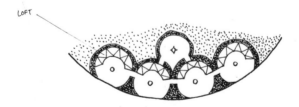

LOFT

In some countries where earth shelters are used an open patio is used, which is also underground. This is indicated in Figure #12 where a fire pit is placed. An horno, an adobe oven could well be placed in this patio also. It is envisioned that the terracing behind the shelter would be for plants that would be hand watered from the cistern.

One of the things that will begin to bring human community back into natural sympathy is the principle of sharing of energies in land ownership. Though it is absurd to think that a mere human could "own" part of the universe that they did not create, it is currently a practical reality because of the enforced social definitions. Communal ownership or land trust can restore the land toward its natural unity. Taking down the fences will assist the circulation of the metabolism to come back to a healthy level.

The Mattole Watershed: One Example of Restoration

The Mattole watershed is located on the coast of northern California in redwood-douglas fir-hardwood forest region. The Mattole river drains an area of the coastal mountains and empties directly into the Pacific Ocean. The nearest sizable town is Garberville, California. The area, like the entire coast, has been substantially logged and roaded, though the local people are actively attempting to save the last of the native forest which stands at about 10% of the original.

As in many areas, the destruction caused by "resource extraction" has had a profound effect on the ecology of the area. The hydrology of the watershed has particulary suffered. Resource extraction has caused silting of the streambeds of the river and tributaries and also the widening of the river. which exposes it to the sun, heating it up and in areas, actual landslides have swept into the river due to poor engineering of road cuts, clear cut logging and other abuse.

The Mattole people are networked through the Mattole Restoration Council.[25] The Mattole Restoration Council is made up of many other groups and networks, such as the Mattole Coordinating Council whose members are the Environmental Protection Information Center, the Mattole Soil and Water Conservation Committee, the Upper Mattole Property Owners Association, the Mattole Watershed Salmon Support Group, the Mattole Watershed Taxpayers Association, the Redwoods Monastery Community, the Coastal Headwaters Association, and the Sinkyone Council.

The efforts of these vital groups are spread over the whole watershed. The Mattole Forest and Range Lands Cooperative (soilbankers) has worked to inventory the remaining native forest, monitor logging plans and participate actively as work parties on erosion control projects. They deal as a citizens group with the timber industry, state and federal agencies. The Mattole Watershed Salmon Support Group, in one of their projects, organized the California Coastal Conservancy, the Redwood Community Action Agency and the county, to fund a bank stabilization project (rip-rap with wire netting over rock) which repaired slides caused by poor road construction and other abuse. The effort was to stop the most serious erosion problems.

Another exemplary project of the Salmon Support Group is the study of a large slide of a hillside into the Mattole river. To help fund this year-long study of the slide with constant visual, photographic and measurement observation, the Salmon Support Group corralled the General Services Foundation, Redwood National Park, Philip Williams and Associates, Department of Water

Resources (Calif.), and the Redwood Community Action Agency to assist with funding.

A locally controlled high school exists in the area called Petrolia High School. The curriculum emphasizes a strong academic program but also has teams of students who conduct their own restoration projects under the auspices of various local groups.

Like the buffalo of the Plains of old, the migrations of elk and deer through the Mogollon Rim country and the migrations of the Caribou in the north, the migrating life of the Mattole is the Salmon. Though fisheries are greatly reduced from Mexico to Alaska, there exist still, some populations of steelhead, silver salmon and king salmon on the Mattole. After their well-known travel from the mountains to the sea, the fish return to the tributary of their origin to spawn. Each of these fish species need different size gravels to spawn and these stream-bed areas exist in scattered places in the watershed. Because of logging and other "developments" many of these areas have been silted over by erosion material or the tree canopy opened up so that the water is too warm.

These species of fish function as indicators of the health of the watershed. Much of the restoration is done with these indicator species in mind. If the watershed is restoring so that the fish can come back, then it is safe to assume that the whole is regaining health. The Salmon Support Group organizes many people to help monitor the numbers and condition of these fish populations. One of the creative efforts of this group is to catch the returning salmon as they enter the river mouth. They then physically transport the fertilized eggs up to the headwaters, past the destruction and silt so that the fry will have a chance of life. The group says this allows a better than 80% survival rate from egg to fry and involves populations of in excess of 100,000 fry.

The people of the Mattole River Watershed are a developing psycho/biological community. Their creativity extends to such things as their local dance group who have created performance that expresses the watershed and selected species within it. This dance group of exceptional choreography and costumery, number approximately fifty people. They have toured the major cities of the west coast as a professional dance troupe and have received rave reviews.

Although this is a brief look at one watershed, it helps point out the reality of what is happening around the U.S. and around the world in different variations. Communities are living on watersheds and communities of various types are involved actively in planetary restoration.

When one looks at the scope of activity planet-wide, one realizes how vast is the movement toward planetary healing. Since the sixties, the direct involvement of human life toward personal/spiritual integration with cosmic life, has exploded into a multitude of paths many of which, correctly or not, are generically grouped under "New Age." There are also Pagan groups that have grown active as have Christian groups, especially the Christian base community movement. Among native people there has been a resurgence of activity in Native spirituality and life ways. In all, awareness of spiritual/non-material realities has increased much.

The movement of physical, emotional and mental healing that relies on removing blockages to positive energies, is travelling under the banner, "Wholistic Health" or "Alternative Medicine."

This movement with all of its modalities such as re-birthing, Reichian therapy, massage, accupressure massage, acupuncture, reflexology, hypnotherapy, primal therapy, macrobiotic and many others are matched by the growth of support groups that travel under various labels and all are a significant gesture toward healing the personal and social isolation of all involved.

These movements are matched by the growth in the interest in physical, emotional, mental and spiritual balance that have come from the monasteries of the Far East. Disciplines such as Tai Chi, Kung Fu, Akaido, Karate and the rest are at base, disciplines of spiritual balance.

In the past thirty years many new forms of social relating have emerged that are outside the hierarchal form of civilization. Affinity groups, collective ownership, a renewed interest in the Mondragon Plan- the cooperative economy of the Basque region of Spain, the "anarchist" production groups functioning in some other areas in Spain, the LETS system, a local currency/economic plan, and many others. These show the desire of many of us to have some real relationship to the institutions within which we live out our lives.

There are many tens of thousands of people just in the U.S., living in the old line religious communities such as the Hutterites and Amish. There are also many living in communities that may be said to have descended from the hippies of Haight-Ashbury and there are further thousands living in what are loosely termed, "New Age Communities." Information concerning the hundreds of these groups can be found in the *New Age Community Guide*. This document can be obtained from Harbin Springs Pub., P.O.Box 1132, Middletown, California 95461, $7.95+postage.

Along with these developments have come the revolutions in housing design and alternative energy. In 1950, maybe one person in ten million realized that simply sitting a house in relation to the angle of the sun could have an effect on heating bills, comfort or standard of living. Though the elites of the transnationals have tried to buy-out and stifle this field, we can now obtain much useful information about alternative design and energy.

One of the most significant movements of recent years has been feminist awareness. From the realization that brassieres were a kind of chinese foot binding, a part of the feminist movement has begun to emphasize eco/feminism and offer a serious challenge to the very foundations of patriarchy, ecodestruction and militarism in the empire. The missing female perspective through the succession of empires has allowed the growth of the crippled and distorted activities of science, religion, economics, culture and the basic way that the conditioning of imperial society causes us to see the world. The women who are struggling up through many of the mass institutions are making quantum changes in the perspectives of society. In many areas what women are pointing out seems quite simple and plain to everyone, its just that there have not been women around to point that out. Those eco-feminist women who stand outside the tumor body of empire are leading the movement toward planetary healing. It is a nurturing activity and we can expect women to lead it.

In response to the starvation of millions and the destruction of life, the alternatives to industrial agriculture have exploded in size and number. The field of Permaculture is ablaze with activity. If one looks at a Permaculture publication such as the *International Permaculture Species Yearbook*, it becomes clear that this is a planetary movement. In the directory section are listed ten Permaculture publications. Eighty-five Permaculture centers are listed that exist in Sixteen countries. Ninety-seven bioregional (watershed) groups are listed in seven countries. Eighty-five green and green oriented groups are listed in sixteen countries. One hundred and eighty-eight alternative economics groups are listed in twenty-two countries. Permaculture related organizations and publications number fifty-nine in forty-four countries. Centers where one can actually obtain seed or plant cultivars important in Permaculture work, number sixty-five sources in eleven countries.

Since the atom bomb in 1945, an awakening has taken place. A small percentage of the human family has awakened enough to intuitively go in the wholistic direction needed. By doing this (completely intuitively and with out top-down organization) we now have the framework of tools, knowledges and methodologies that we need to create a new culture and put it on the ground.

On the Watershed: Some Practical Considerations

Looking at the functional situation of extended family in industrial culture we can see the strength that it has, in economics, social health and in the storms of the future. When we look at the prospect of buying land, we begin the understand the functional position of the masses in empire. For a working class family to buy land is all but impossible. Buying a piece of land for a family is expensive but if many families go together an buy a large piece of land, the price per acre goes down radically. We can easily buy land by all of us putting our small bit into Trust and have the trust buy the land. The Trust as it grows can then buy more land. Most of us are leaking energy to landlords, food distributing systems, clothing manufacturers and such simply from inattention or because our own social institutions are undeveloped. We are all going to be paying someone for rent, food, clothing and heat. We can divert our economic energy from the sharks and use it to energize our own institutions that have survival value.

We are in the practical situation of needing to still have a connection with the money economy as we position ourselves in terms of cutting our outflow by owning our land, growing the bulk of our own food and communally putting up our own shelter. Unless we are in unique circumstance, we will have to deal with money (at least until the world debt bubble pops).

Most watersheds we now, or would in the near future, inhabit, are in remote areas. Because of transportation costs and the world energy situation we would want to be producing small items of high value in our cottage industries. We have discussed the Apache foraging system with its agave, prickly pears, yucca bananas and piñon nuts. Each of these items can be considered rare delicacies. Agave butters, prickly pear jelly, yucca banana butter and jelly and piñon nut butters, possibly flavored with natural herbal flavors from the Watershed, would compare well with any delicacies sold in any airport gift shop in the world.

The possibility of grazing bees is very attractive. By knowing the land well, it is possible to move hives to specific wild blooms in the high mountain meadows. This cropping would allow the sale of "wildflower specialty honey" (and it would also escape the northward migrating "killer bees" who can only live in lowland, warm regions).

Another splendid idea is suggested by John Kimmey who, with the direction of the Hopi elders, organized the native seed bank, 0, located in Santa Fe, New Mexico. The Center was organized to collect and save the remaining seed varieties held by Native Americans in the Southwest. Kimmey suggests that one can make a middle-class income by growing out selected varieties held in the seed bank. The seeds in this bank are some of the few places in the world that the old, hardy, pest-resistant and drought resistant seed can be found. Some of the varieties are dry-land adapted seed strains. Although the varieties exist in the seed bank, they are only samples. Someone must "grow them out" so there will be quantities for international aid organizations. Third World development groups have realized that the green revolution as it is practiced in some parts of the world is not going to help the people. In desertified areas or where they cannot afford to buy all of the factors of industrial agricultural production from the First World industrialists, the people need this seed. Growing out this seed and selling it to international aid organizations can provide available income.

Time To Move

This type of consideration can be applied to many watersheds. What we want is to return to the earth. We want congenial community with real friends and family who have no motive to be in conflict with us. We want all of us to be able to sit in the hot springs pools in peace. We want to be able to sit in our comfortable hand-made homes in the winter on the lower part of the watershed, doing our crafts or other creative work. In spring we want to go with our new health and strength, out onto the watershed to gather the first greens and other foods. In summer we want to be in the beautiful high mountain meadows grazing our bees or gathering. In the fall we want to be able to come down into the chaparral, each person of the community, including the older children, holding a deer tag, an elk tag, a turkey tag, a pronghorn tag, for our winter larder. The public lands as we know, are there for the exploitation of the welfare ranchers and the timber elite, but just the same the public land agencies are eager for other citizens to find ways to generate income from the land and from beneficial use. The agencies would encourage gathering for cottage industries.

We know that the Greenhouse Effect is progressing. We can measure the carbon dioxide increase. We know the ozone layer depletion is progressing, we can measure it. Even the industrial elite does not deny this. We simply cannot predict what the effects will be (even with dozens of computers to model what little information we have). Our work on our watersheds with seeds, permaculture and natural plants could enable us to be of some assistance to the human family and to the earth, as the ecosystems are impacted. This is wisdom, this is being responsible to life and the unborn. Now, those who act in a positive way to realistically help life, may be looked upon as fools for not grabbing what they can while it lasts, but as all of the exponential curves come together, some of those who have acted in a mature way will be there to point the remaining children toward a future of positive life.

Creating the Future

The crisis of our era offers us paradise. It offers us the opportunity to shed the tensions and dangers of civilization so that we may create a new world. Creating new culture is not an activity of gratification deferred in pursuit of a distant goal but of immediate increase in the satisfaction of life. Rather than watching helplessly as victims of historical trends, trapped in a boring and dangerous mass culture, people who step out and begin to create answers are living "real life." There are hundreds of thousands involved in wholistic health. There are tens of thousands of people already in the United States who are living in intentional communities and permaculture projects and bioregional groups are wide-spread.

Our task is to recreate paradise. There is no other way. We must restore the life of the earth and in order to do that we must have a benign, creative and potentiative culture. When we create nurturing culture, our children will have more opportunity than the lock-step of civilization, in which to further the human potential. We will become more creative, more conscious and more nurturing of life.

Gary Nabhan relates a Papago story about Coyote stealing some corn and deciding to grow his own. He ate most of the seed then threw the remainders along an arroyo. He slept all through the growing season and when it was harvest the corn turned out to be coyote tobacco, a wild plant. The problem according to the Papagos was that Coyote did not know the proper songs to sing to the corn, so it could not grow properly.

The story points up a neglected fact of the Pleistocene Native American culture and most other Pleistocene cultures -that they were cultures of song and dance. These groups had rich cultural content. There were songs for everything, for all of the natural acts. The people were given life and then gave that beauty back to the cosmos in song. They began with the real life-and extrapolated the song from there, out into the universe and into the immaterial. The song was grounded in the beauty of the earth and its forms of life.

We are forced to choose a life of beauty and a life that aids the whole.

We are embarking upon a transformative course, the inversion of the values of empire. When communities exist at the top of watersheds and the water running from them, downhill, is pure, then we know that a cosmically resonant human social pattern exists.

No studies are necessary, no protracted discussions are needed, human society is out of balance with the life of the earth and human society needs to regain balance. If our daily efforts are substantially directed toward regaining that balance then we are on the path to paradise.

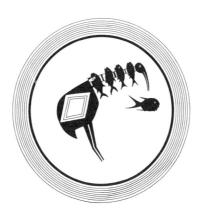

NOTES

1   Arid-Land Permaculture: (Special reference to central Australian Aboriginal Outstations). Bill Mollison. self pub. Tagari, Stanley, Australia. 1978.

2   ibid. p. 18.

3   Permaculture: A Designers' Manual. Bill Mollison. Reny Mia Slay, ed. Tagari Pub. Tyalgum, Australia. 1988.

4   ibid. p. 327.

5   Water For Every Farm/Using the Keyline Plan. P.A. Yeomans. Second Back Row Press Pty. Limited, 50 Govett Street, Katoomba, 2780 Australia. 1978. p. 29.

6   PERMACULTURE II: Practical Design and Further Theory in Permanent Agriculture. Bill Mollison. Tagari Pub. P.O.Box 96, Stanley, Tasmania 7331, Australia. p. 29.

7   ibid. p. 32.

8   Mollison. Permaculture: A Designers' Manual. op. cit. p. 393.

9   American Indian Food and Lore. Carolyn Niethammer. Collier Books. New York. 1974. op. cit. p. 47.

10   Forest Farming: Towards A Solution To Problems Of World Hunger And Conservation. J. Sholto Douglas & Robert A de J. Hart. Westview Press. Boulder Colorado. 1984. p. 39.

11   Niethammer. American Indian Food and Lore. op. cit. p. 55.

12   Permaculture One: A Perennial Agriculture for Human Settlements. Bill Mollison. Transworld Pub. Australia. Pty. Ltd. 1978. p. 122.

13   The International Permaculture Species Yearbook. Dan Hemenway, Editor. 7781 Lenox Ave., Jacksonville, FL 32221.
     International Green Front Report. Micheal Pilarski, Editor. P.O.Box 1064, Tonasket, Wa. 98855. ($7.00 + postage).

14   Hart & Douglas, Forest Farming. op cit. pp 161
     Mollison, Permaculture One. op cit. pp111.

15   Mollison, Designer's Manual, op. cit. pp. ix,x.

16   Niethammer. American Indian Food and Lore. op. cit. p. 52.

17   ibid. p. 94.

18   Farmland Or Wasteland: A Time To Choose. R. Neil Sampson. Rodale Press. Emmaus, Pa. 1981. p. 212.

19   Gathering the Desert. Gary Paul Nabhan. U. of Arizona Press. Tucson. 1987. p. 138.

20   ibid p. 170.
     Niethammer. American Indian Food and Lore. op. cit. p. 86.

21 Niethammer. <u>American Indian Food and Lore</u>. op. cit. p. 11.
22 ibid. pp. 88,89.
23 Mollison. <u>Permaculture One</u>. op. cit. pp. 10,11.
24 <u>Earth Sheltered Housing Design: Guidelines, Examples, and References</u>. prepared by: The Underground Space Center. U. of Minn. Von Nostrand Reinhold Co. pub. New York. 1979. pp. 51-94.
25 Information can be obtained from: Mattole Restoration Council, 3848 Wilder Ridge Road, Garberville, Ca. 95440.

Index

A

B

THE BOOKSEEDS BOOKSHELF

:███:

The Research Journals of Dr. Alan Kapuler

A true philosopher of the new culture, Dr. Kapuler recognizes coevolution as a fact of Life. He states, that as biological form manifest on earth, first there were bacteria, then the protocists such as amoebas and algae. Then came the animals, fungi and plants. The first form, bacteria, live also in all other cells of the more complex orders, (such that mitochrondria live in our cells). As the plants manifest, almost all have fungi (mycorrhizal association) with them at their root hairs. The animals eat plants, fungi, each other and engage in cooperative ecological associations with all forms. In this coevolutionary pattern, the central fact of all five forms is the common DNA code. Our bodies take in protein to make amino acids that the DNA then uses to make protein. Kapuler goes direct to design coevolutionary gardens to optimize the twenty amino acids for our diet. His other major contribution is the mapping of plant tribes and families three-dimentionally, so that we can actually see the growth of biological form on earth and its relationships. This layout then, aids us in the design of gardens where each area represents a tribe or family, thus allowing us to plant so that conservation of diversity becomes a major result.

"The gene pool is the collected set of biological experience stored in organisms inside the cellular chromosomes. It is the source of organisms. It is our past and future."

Journal 3 & 4 $10.00

Contains: Cross reference index of families, alphabetical to orders and super orders of flowering plants (angiosperms). Database for a coevolutionary garden of the coniferaphyta, asparagales and the solanaceae--also contains other useful articles.

8.5 X 11 inches, 58 pages, spiral bound.

"Our cellular protein synthesis and hence bodily health can be augmented by improving cultivars specific for individual amino acids and then mixing the juices, both raw and cooked."

Journal 5 $10.00
Contains: Tribal, subtribal and generic database for the asteraceae and an alphabetical index of genera in asteraceae (daisy group). This coevolutionary layout contains such examples as coneflowers, marigolds, lettuce, burdock, thistles, sunflowers and dandelions. This issue also contains articles such as "Gardening the Gene Pool," by Gabriel Howearth and "The Twenty Amino Acids As Primary Food," by Kapuler and Gurusiddah.
8.5 x 11 inches, 58 pages.

"In order to preserve diversity we must first know its structure."

Journal 6 $15.00
Contains: Database on the grass family poaceae (graminae) and an alphabetical index of genera. A kinship garden for the carrot-ginseng alliance (araliales) with database. "The World Peace Garden Project for Ecuador," by James Lawson gives a world database of arecaceae (palm family) and Ecuadorean palms in this rainforest-refuge area. Contains other useful articles including Dr. Kapuler's account of curing his lymphatic cancer by nutrition.
8.5 x 11 inches, 77 pages.

● ● ● ● ● ● ● ● ● ● ●

ENDURING SEEDS: NATIVE AMERICAN AGRICULTURE AND WILD PLANT CONSERVATION By Gary Paul Nabhan, Foreword by Wendell Berry. ISBN 0-86547-344-7, 225 pages, paperback, index, entensive notes and bibliography. $11.95

"In a handful of wild seeds taken from any one natural community, there is hidden the distillation of millions of years of coevolution of plants and animals, of their coming together, coexisting, partitioning various resources, competing or becoming dependent upon one another. In a gourdful of crop seeds taken from the fields of Native American farmers, we have the living reverberations of how past cultures selected plant characters that reflected their human sense of taste, color, proportion, and fitness in a particular environment."

-from the Prologue-

Nabhan begins with the question, "How have certain cultures managed to persevere in their locally-adapted farming traditions when so many others have-abandon traditional agriculture altogether?" In this engrossing essay we travel with seed collector/distributor and botanist extraordinare, Gary Paul Nabhan visiting tribes as far north as the Hidatsa, Arikara and Mandan in North Dakota. We also travel as far south as southern Mexico. On the way we visit many native peoples, present and past, to examine their unique agricultural systems. As we go, Nabhan keeps the central issue of our times before us-the protection of the dwindling biodiversity of our earth. In this volume Nabhan illuminates the previously obscure native plant varieties, both ancient and contemporary. Gary Paul Nabhan is the Director of Native Seed/Search in Tucson, Arizona.

SHATTERING: FOOD, POLITICS AND THE LOSS OF GENTETIC DIVERSITY By Gary Fowler and Pat Mooney. ISBN 0-8165-1181-0, 278 pages, paperback, extensive notes and index. $15.00

"With the discovery of modern genetics a few decades ago, the food system began to experience rapid change. With the arrival of the green revolution, the world's food supply has been faced with a new wave of genetic erosion. And with the coming of plant and gene patenting and the opportunity of monopolization, international companies have attempted to corner the market for the vanishing genes. The result may be the shattering of agriculture itself.

"What is at stake is the integrity, future and control of the first link in the food chain. How these issues are decided will determine to whom we pray for our daily bread."

-from the Introduction-

This book is simply the best examination of the world agricultural seed situation in print. Fowler and Mooney have a solid background of many years in the field but they stand exthically outside the system, not being on the payroll of the monopolies. In researching this book they visited more than forty-three countries. Their lively anecdotes gathered world-wide, combined with careful scholarship makes this volume a must, not only for hands-on planters but for anyone attempting to discern the social/environmental future.

In the first part the authors delve into the origins of agriculture. They then go on to examine the wide diversity in agricultural plant varieties and the dangers in the swift decline of that diversity that is now occurring. In the second section, Fowler and Mooney lead us into the power-politics of the life stream of the planet. The gentics supply industry, biotechnology, intellectual property rights, plant and seed patenting and biopolitics are exposed to the light of day. As the transnational corporate elite swing into the last phase of their stranglehold of the planetary food and indeed, life system, the authors point to what each of us can do to preserve the remaining agricultural genetic diversity.

• • • • • • • • • • • •

CORNUCOPIA: A SOURCE BOOK OF EDIBLE PLANTS By Stephan Facciola 8.5 x 11 inches, 677 pages, full table of contents, 13 page bibliography, various indexes, and appendixes. ISBN 0-9628087-0-9. $35.00

"Cornucopia is intended to be an authoritative reference book as well as a useful tool. It has been written for gardeners, small scale and alternative farmers, researchers dealing with new crops, cooks, economic botanists, genetic preservationists, natural food enthusiasts, nutritionists, those in the specialty and gormet foods business, and colleges and universities. References have been selected to provide a balance between technical and popular works."

-from the Introduction-

This source book is not an essay. It is indeed a source book. Over three thousand edible species in one-volume, it lists the plants and where to get them. The first section is the botanical listing of naturally occurring plants, fungi, algae and bacteria along with any cultivars of those plants. (One can find sources here for spirulina algae, and bacterias for fermentation of such things as Kefir, yogurt, pickle, sausage, and cheese). The botanical listing is extensive and includes thousands of plants and their varities. The second section is the most popular and important crop plants and their cultivars. This section is indexed by popular name. For example, the first listing, Almond has 23 cultivars listed. Thousands of cultivars are listed in this section. The next section of 53 large pages lists the sources for all of these botanicals and cultivars. These are not only small seed companies and nurserys, but wildcrafters and on up to botanical gardens and arboretums, both U.S. and international. The 13 page bibliography is a library of plant knowledge. The various indices cross reference the work by indexing the common names to latin, common names to page number in the text, plants' edible usage and edible parts to plant names, plants that are native or naturalized to North America and finally there is an index of family and genera listed by page number. This is a five pound handbook designed to be <u>used</u> and then handed down to the grandchildren.

• • • • • • • • • • •

THE PERMACULTURE RESOURCES

PERMACULTURE: A PRACTICAL GUIDE FOR A SUSTAINABLE FUTURE by Bill Mollison. ISBN 1-55963-048-5, 579 Pages, Hardbound. 400 Illustrations, forty 4-color plates. $39.95

This text outlines a method for designing environmentally sensitive and ecologically stable systems-from rural homesteads to urban neighborhoods. This manual teaches designers, students, farmers, gardeners, small and large property owners, agroforesters, ranchers, landscape designers, architects, engineers and planners about concepts, strategies and methods of designing and constructing sustainable systems. Based upon the ethical use of our natural resources, Permaculture (permanent agriculture) is the conscious design and maintenance of agriculturally productive ecosystems which have the diversity, stability and resilience of natural ecosystems. It is the harmonious integration of landscape and people, providing food, shelter and other material and non-material needs in a sustainable way. Permaculture is a philosophy and an approach to land use which weaves together microclimate, annual and perennial plants, animals, soils, water management, and human needs into intricately connected and productive communities. This is a manual of solutions, tried and tested, and presented in useable form. This is the "must have" major work in the field of Permaculture.

INTRODUCTION TO PERMACULTURE by Bill Mollison with Remy Mia Slay. ISBN 0-908228-05-8, 200 pages, 140 Illustrations, Paperback. $22.95

Topics in this book include: energy-efficient site analysis, planning and design methods; house placement and design for temporate, dry land and tropical regions; urban permaculture-garden layouts, land access and community funding systems; using fences, trellis, greenhouse and shadehouse to best effect; chicken and pig forage systems; tree crops and pasture integration for stock; orchards and house woodlots for temperate, arid and tropical climates; permaculture gardens-energy saving designs and techniques; how to influence microclimate around the house and garden; large section on selected plant species lists with climatic tolerances, heights and uses. Excellent introductory text. This book gives many practical, Hands-on examples, while the big *Permaculture* book deals in design concepts.

• • • • • • • • • • • • • •

THE NEW CULTURE NETWORK

Because ARROW POINT PRESS is focussing on information to create the new culture, this gives us opportunity to also network people who are interested in ecologically sustainable communities.

ARROW POINT PRESS does not propose to organize these communities but will assist the networked people to organize themselves in whatever way possible.

People that apply to be in the networking will be listed according to zip codes which roughly approximate your bioregion. When we receive a sufficient number of names in your bioregion, we will mail a computer printout of all names to each of you. Following your self organization, you will continue to receive names as they arrive. ARROW POINT PRESS will continue to function as a clearing house for information, such as methods of generating capital for land purchases, creating land based businesses, alternative economic systems and other useful information for the network.

To allow us to do the listing, collating, printing and mailing, we ask you to include $4.00 for each listing with your book order.

ORDER FORM

Support your Local Bookstore but if you cannot find these books, order them directly from ARROW POINT PRESS. At a time when all major print and electronic media are owned by fewer than 25 large corporations, we must develop our own institutions so that vital information can continue to be desseminated.

We guarantee our books. If you are not satisfied for any reason, please return books within 30 days for a full refund.

QTY.	TITLE	PRICE	
____	THE FINAL EMPIRE	$19.95 =	_____
____	KAPULER RESEARCH JOURNAL 3 & 4	$10.00 =	_____
____	KAPULER RESEARCH JOURNAL 5	$10.00 =	_____
____	KAPULER RESEARCH JOURNAL 6	$15.00 =	_____
____	ENDURING SEEDS	$11.95 =	_____
____	SHATTERING	$15.00 =	_____
____	PERMACULTURE, PRACTICAL GUIDE	$39.95 =	_____
____	INTRO TO PERMACULTURE	$22.95 =	_____
____	CORNUCOPIA	$35.00 =	_____

LISTING IN NEW CULTURE NETWORK $ 4.00 = _____

Shipping is $2.00 for the first book and .50 for each additional book.

SHIPPING = _____

TOTAL = _____

SHIPPING ADDRESS:

Name _____

Address _____

City/State/Zip _____

Phone Number (   ) _____

Please write to ARROW POINT PRESS for a catalog of new Books and Information being offered.

SEND ORDERS AND INQUIRIES TO:

ARROW POINT PRESS
PO BOX 14754-A
PORTLAND, OR 97214
(503) 236-7359